MUSIC IN THE MEDIEVAL ENGLISH LITURGY

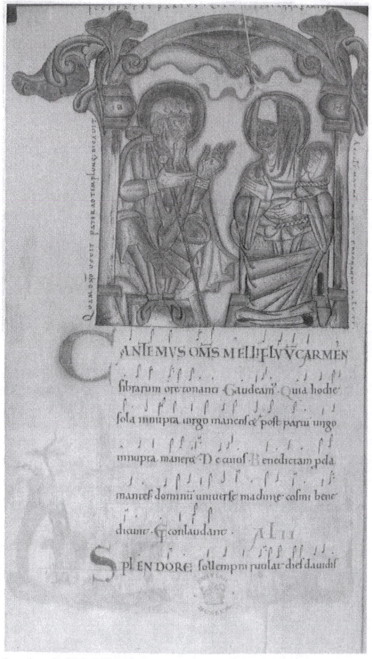

London, British Library Cotton Caligula A. xiv, fol. 26ᵛ.

Music in the Medieval English Liturgy

PLAINSONG & MEDIÆVAL MUSIC SOCIETY

CENTENNIAL ESSAYS

Edited by
Susan Rankin and David Hiley

CLARENDON PRESS · OXFORD

Oxford University Press, Walton Street, Oxford OX2 6DP
Oxford New York
Athens Auckland Bangkok Bombay
Calcutta Cape Town Dar es Salaam Delhi
Florence Hong Kong Istanbul Karachi
Kuala Lumpur Madras Madrid Melbourne
Mexico City Nairobi Paris Singapore
Taipei Tokyo Toronto
and associated companies in
Berlin Ibadan

Oxford is a trade mark of Oxford University Press

Published in the United States by
Oxford University Press Inc., New York

British Library Cataloguing in Publication Data
Data available

Library of Congress Cataloging in Publication Data
Music in the medieval English liturgy : Plainsong & Mediæval Music
Society centennial essays / edited by Susan Rankin and David Hiley.
Includes bibliographical references and index.
1. Church music—England—500–1400. 2. Church music—Catholic
Church—500–1400. 3. Catholic Church—England—Liturgy.
I. Rankin, Susan. II. Hiley, David. III. Plainsong and Mediæval
Music Society (Great Britain).
ML3031.2.M88 1993
782.32'22'009420902—dc20
ISBN 0–19–316125–7 (cloth)

3 5 7 9 10 8 6 4 2

Printed in Great Britain by
Biddles Ltd, Guildford and King's Lynn

Foreword

OF the two sides of the Plainsong and Mediæval Music Society's traditional activities, the scholarly and the practical, this collection of essays represents the former. It complements the more public and practical manifestations of the Society's activity which recently marked its centennial year.

The essays reflect the founders' interest in medieval music, both monophonic and polyphonic, and, particularly, their concern with chant. From its inception, the PMMS has directed much of its attention to the British sources of medieval music, the music which might contribute to a renewal of the liturgy of the Anglican church. The scholarly edifice erected through the Society's publications—erected, it may fairly be stated, almost single-handedly by Walter Howard Frere, whose editions of the Sarum Gradual and Antiphonal were printed by the Society in 1891–4 and 1901–12—still serves as a starting-point for the present-day generation of chant scholars.

It is a matter of deep regret that Frank Harrison, Chairman of the PMMS from early 1986 to 29 December 1987, did not live to see the publication of these essays. It was a project near to his heart and a manifestation of the new spirit of scholarly enterprise with which he infused the Society during his time as Chairman. The Society acknowledges the debt it owes to Frank Harrison by dedicating the volume to his memory.

The editors wish to thank all the contributors who responded so generously to the invitation to honour the Society. They also wish to thank, not least for their patience, Jeffery Dean, who prepared the music examples, and both David Blackwell and Bruce Phillips of Oxford University Press.

David Hiley

Susan Rankin
O sapientia, 1991

Contents

1. The Plainsong & Mediæval Music Society, 1888–1988   I
   David Hiley

I LITURGY AND LITURGICAL MUSIC IN THE ELEVENTH CENTURY

2. Unica in the Cotton Caligula Troper   11
   Ritva Jacobsson

3. Remarks on the Alleluia and Responsory Series in the
   Winchester Troper   47
   Michel Huglo

4. Winchester Polyphony: The Early Theory and Practice of
   Organum   59
   Susan Rankin

5. Stylistic Layers in Eleventh-Century Polyphony: How can
   the Continental Sources contribute to our Understanding of
   the Winchester Organa?   101
   Wulf Arlt

II LITURGICAL USES AND GENRES IN MEDIEVAL ENGLAND

6. Post-Pentecost Alleluias in Medieval British Liturgies   145
   David Hiley

7. Marian Antiphons at Cluny and Lewes   175
   Ruth Steiner

8. An English Noted Breviary of *circa* 1200   205
   David Chadd

9. British Rhymed Offices: A Catalogue and Commentary   239
   Andrew Hughes

10. Relations between Liturgical and Vernacular Music in
    Medieval England   285
    John Caldwell

III LITURGICAL POLYPHONY IN LATER MEDIEVAL ENGLAND

11. Plainsong into Polyphony: Repertories and Structures
    circa 1270–*circa* 1420   303
       Frank Ll. Harrison (d. 1988)

12. The Manuscript London, British Library Harley 1709   355
       Nick Sandon

Indexes

  Sources   381

  Incipits and Titles   386

  Names   404

I

The Plainsong & Mediæval Music Society, 1888–1988

DAVID HILEY

(University of Regensburg)

A volume of centennial essays calls for a historical introduction, an outline of the history and aims of the Plainsong & Mediæval Music Society. Unfortunately, any attempt to write such an account runs into a more or less insuperable obstacle: the lack of early records of the Society's activities. Some early publications list members of the Society, and one can be found in the first volume of *Paléographie musicale* (1889). Various editions of *Grove's Dictionary* state the original aims of the Society—'to be a centre of information in England for students of plainsong and medieval music, to publish facsimiles of important manuscripts, translations of foreign works, etc.; to form a catalogue of all plainsong and measured music in England dating from before the mid-16th century; and to found a choir' (*The New Grove Dictionary*, article by H. C. Colles revised by the present author). But as far as the management of the Society is concerned, there are now only two main sources of information: the Attendance Book for meetings of the Council of the Society, which contains signatures of all those Council members who attended meetings from 11 February 1889 to the present day; and the Minute Book, containing minutes of Ordinary Meetings, Annual General Meetings, and Council Meetings. The Attendance Book is a valuable record of those involved in the running of the Society, but contains no more than names. The Minute Book tells what was discussed and resolved at meetings, and, despite the usually laconic and businesslike tone in which transactions are recorded, reveals as much as will ever now be generally known about the affairs of the Society.

If the Minute Book were as aged as the Attendance Book, historians would have no cause to complain. But the first entries it contains are for a Council Meeting held on 19 June 1954, and no earlier Minute Books have survived. Did they perish on the sad occasion reported on 19 January 1957, when 'a bag containing most of the Society's books' was lost? In their absence, the most valuable source of information is Dom Anselm Hughes's *Septuagesima* (London: PMMS, 1959), which contains the reminiscences of the former Secretary and Chairman up until the late 1950s.

A proper history of the Society would therefore entail painstaking research into the affairs of those whose names are recorded in the Attendance Book. That is not the purpose of the present remarks. They are intended rather to point out a few recurrent themes discernible among the Society's activities. An effort has been made to carry on with the story from the time when Dom Anselm's account breaks off, through the last three decades or so. It is not, of course, conceived as an exact continuation of Dom Anselm's gloriously outspoken and invigorating book, which contains much autobiographical material not directly connected with the Society, retailed moreover at far greater length than is here possible.

The honorary head of the Plainsong & Mediæval Music Society is its President. The President is a figure-head, asked by Council to honour the Society by lending prestige to the Society's work. Distinguished churchmen, scholars, musicians, and peers of the realm, have been willing to do this. John Wordsworth, Bishop of Salisbury (related by marriage to W. H. Frere) and Sir John Stainer were the first two Presidents, and the Earl of Dysart, Niall Campbell Duke of Argyll, Ralph Vaughan Williams, and Herbert Howells have numbered among their successors.

Almost as distinguished is the list of Vice-Presidents of the Society, who likewise play no active part in its affairs but add lustre to its name. To mention only two recently deceased figures, Dom Eugène Cardine and Henry Washington were both for many years Vice-Presidents. (Vice-Presidents were not an original feature of the Society and were perhaps adopted after the example of the Henry Bradshaw Society, founded in 1890, whose first President was also the Bishop of Salisbury.) The day-to-day affairs of the Society are in the hands of its Council, led by the Chairman, Secretary, and Treasurer. From time to time the Council has also had an 'inner core' in the shape of an Executive Committee. This often included a Publications Secretary; and until its library was disposed of, the Society also had a Librarian.

The names of all early officers of the Society are not recoverable from the surviving books, for the Chairman, Secretary, and Treasurer did not usually sign themselves as such, though Anselm Hughes did sign himself as Chairman from 1949 to 1960. Since it has been the Secretary's custom to give the Attendance Book first to the Chairman to sign, the Chairman's name usually heads the list. Thus the name of Walter Howard Frere appears first among those present at meetings from 1903 until 1929 (from 1925 Walterus Truron). But the elected official was not always present and a variety of figures occupied the chair temporarily over the years. After Hughes, Alec Robertson was elected, on 26 November 1960. He was succeeded by Derek H. Turner, elected on 9 December 1964, and by Professor Frank Ll. Harrison on 8 January 1986. (It is especially regrettable that this great scholar should not have lived to lead the Society into its centennial celebrations, which he would have enjoyed so much and to which he had devoted much thought and time.)

The Secretary usually signed last, when the Attendance Book came back round. Although it is not clear who acted as Secretary at the first meetings of the Society, it is known that H. B. Briggs occupied the post for some years prior to his death. His name does not appear in the Attendance Book, which, however, has no entries between January 1895 and March 1903. J. A. Fuller-Maitland, in a notice on the Society published in the second edition of *Grove's Dictionary of Music and Musicians* (1913), reported that Briggs was among the seven founder members. (This notice, repeated in subsequent editions of *Grove*, is the only record of the date of the first meeting, November 1888.) Hughes usually referred to Briggs as *the* founder of the Society. Thereafter the list of Secretaries runs as follows:

Percy E. Sankey: 1901–26
Dom Anselm Hughes: 1926–35
K. Pearce Hosken: 1935–51
Ernest H. Warrell: 1951–57
Denis Stevens: 1957–62
H. Llewellyn Jones: Acting S. 1962–63, S. 1963–65
Charles K. Colhoun: 1965–67
Janet M. Backhouse: 1967–74
Sidney G. A. Kiddell: 1974–82
David Hiley: 1982–86
Catherine M. Harbor: 1986–.

It is well known that the Plainsong & Mediæval Music Society was called into being by musicians who were interested in bringing the riches of the plainchant of the Roman Church into the worship of the Church of England. Their aim was as much spiritual as musical, for it coincided with the leanings of the High Church Anglican party. It is important to realize that it was not until the revival of medieval plainchant on the Continent—by the monks of Solesmes and others—was well under way that the English movement became formally organized, half a century after the Oxford Movement had given new life to High Church ideals. From the beginning Briggs, Frere, and their colleagues saw the music of the Sarum rite as a vehicle for their aims. Here was a body of sacred music at once undeniably English and yet a member of the great Roman family of plainchant traditions. It was music of great beauty, and also completely recoverable from manuscript and printed sources. Independent of and yet one with Roman tradition, it was an ideal repertory to revive in the Anglo-Catholic cause.

The mixture of musical, scholarly, and theological aims—and I state them merely in alphabetical order—has always characterized the work of the Plainsong & Mediæval Music Society. Hughes reckoned that by the 1920s 'the PMMS had gathered the reputation of being no more than just another group within the Anglo-Catholic revival' (*Septuagesima*, 34). Yet Frere's work stands on an equal musicological footing with that of Peter Wagner, remarkably so when one considers how much Frere had to do in other fields. In recent years it may justly be said that musicologists, more than any other group, have taken the lead in the Society's activities. The record since the 1950s certainly bears this out. The Minute Book testifies to a colourful succession of musicological projects. Dom Anselm Hughes himself was a prime mover, but the names of those who pass in and out of the record reads like a roll-call of British medieval musicologists of the 1950s and 1960s.

Alas, the Society was rarely in a position to bring to fulfilment the wealth of noble projects mooted at its Council meetings: facsimiles of plainchant books (including an Old-Roman antiphoner, the famous Winchester Tropers in Oxford and Cambridge, and the York Antiphoner in the Bodleian Library, of which specimen plates were actually circulated in an advertising brochure), scholarly editions, the completion of Frere's *Bibliotheca Musico-Liturgica*, a catalogue of early polyphonic sources in Cambridge to match Hughes's Bodleian catalogue, a 'Dictionary of Mediaeval Musicians'—these are some of the projects suggested up to 1968, to say nothing of plans of the last twenty years.

Even when projects reached the stage of printing, difficulties were sometimes experienced. A minute of 1956 reads: 'Piae Cantiones. The Secretary said that he had taken five bales to the *** Press . . . Upon examination it was discovered that some of the sheets had been deliberately disfigured. [He] called at *** to arrange for the despatch of the remaining bales only to discover that they had been accidentally sent away with some salvage.' Nor was the Society always adept at distributing what it had produced. '100 Old Hall Vol. II had been discovered by the Secretary at a warehouse in Chatham' says a minute of 1955.

A list of what was actually published up until 1958 may be inspected in an Appendix to *Septuagesima*, a catalogue of all the Society's publications prepared by Hughes and Jeremy Noble. Among these, it is undoubtedly the small, practical plainchant editions which have sold most copies over the years. The best seller must be *An Order for Compline*, which long ago passed the 10,000 mark.

Little along these lines has been added in recent years. *Septuagesima* (1959) is of course the first addition to the Hughes/Noble list. W. L.

Smoldon's edition of 'The Play of Daniel' appeared in 1960; a revised edition by David Wulstan was published in 1976. In 1962 a second edition of Charles van den Borren's *Polyphonia Sacra* was published, and in 1968 an edition by Brian Trowell of *Four Motets by John Plummer*. Reprints of the practical plainsong editions continued through these years. Yet it is clear that with the rise of other scholarly projects the Plainsong & Mediaeval Music Society's contribution was proportionately falling off. The Répertoire Internationale des Sources Musicales, for example, eventually took care of cataloguing polyphonic music in Cambridge manuscripts and those of other British libraries (though new discoveries are continually being made). From its first publication in 1963 the new series Early English Church Music quickly gained a momentum which the PMMS lacked. Only in the matter of facsimiles was action not visible elsewhere, but such ventures seemed in any case to be beyond the Society's capabilities. Plans for a volume of essays to celebrate the 80th anniversary of the Society advanced far, but were eventually shelved; likewise a plan to revive the material in the form of a memorial volume to Dom Anselm Hughes, who died in 1974. Many prospective contributions were published elsewhere, but out of what remained the *Journal of the Plainsong & Mediaeval Music Society* was born. Ten issues of the *Journal* marked the Society's passage from its 90th year, 1978, through to the centennial. The 1500th anniversary of the birth of St Benedict in 1980 was taken as an opportunity to publish *Eight Sequences for St Benedict and St Scholastica*, edited from medieval manuscripts by the author of these lines. On 7 December, St Ambrose's Day, 1983, Terence Bailey's *The Ambrosian Alleluias* was published, the Society's first substantial (hardback) book (as opposed to musical editions) since the *Anglo-French Sequelae* in 1934. A happy combination of scholarly edition and practical reconstruction was the edition of *Matins at Cluny for the Feast of St. Peter's Chains* by Donat Lamothe and Cyprian Constantine in 1986, which showed that the many members of the Society whose interest is primarily that of practising church musicians had not been forgotten. Finally the centennial itself has seen the appearance of Mark Everist's *French 13th-Century Polyphony in the British Library*, where facsimiles step to the forefront again, sixty years after Hughes's *Worcester Mediaeval Harmony* of 1928 and sixty-five after the last full facsimile of a medieval source, Frere's *Pars Antiphonarii* of 1923.

Reading the Minute Book, one becomes increasingly aware of Hughes's importance to the Society. After the war, the Society might well have disappeared but for his reviving activity. His final fling as editor/author came with *Pre-Conquest Antiphons* (1958) and *Septuagesima* (1959). After his retirement from the Chairmanship he still attended Council meetings, until 1969, when a somewhat shaky signature appears in the Attendance

Book for the last time. His practical sense is striking, displayed both in his willingness, by actually taking over the Treasurer's work himself, to rescue the financial affairs of the Society from the chaos into which they had apparently descended at one period, and in his concern that scholarly editions should be accompanied by concerts and recordings in the programme of the Society's activities. Hughes himself attributed the regular singing of medieval music under the Society's auspices to the initiative of Pearce Hosken before the Second World War (*Septuagesima*, 61). From the Minute Book can be reconstructed a lively programme of lectures and recitals in the late 1950s and 1960s. Since that time standards in the performance of medieval music have improved dramatically, as more and more professional performers have been able to concentrate on the repertory and avail themselves of the results of scholarly research. But up to twenty years ago scholars themselves had to take the lead. Luckily the Council itself included experienced performers, and the Annual Concert, once a regular fixture, could safely be entrusted to Henry Washington and the Schola Polyphonica, or Bruno Turner and Musica Sacra, among others. In recent years, until the centennial celebrations, only one concert was attempted: on 23 February 1978 a concert of 'non-Gregorian' plainchant and early polyphony was given in St Margaret's Church, Westminster. Numerous lectures were given during the earlier period. Thus in 1960 we find that the PMMS held four Ordinary Meetings. On 30 January John Harvey FSA read a paper on 'Documentary Research in Mediaeval Music'. On 27 February the Revd Dr Peter Peacock talked about 'Instrumental Music of the Middle Ages', and on 30 April Jeremy Noble read a paper 'The term "Square" and its meaning'. While the last two speakers used tape recordings to illustrate their papers, the lecture on 28 May had live examples: Minute 1 of the Meeting reads 'Mr Brian Trowell gave an illustrated lecture on "English song abroad in the 15th century", the musical examples being provided by Miss Rhiannon James (soprano), Mr Paul Doe (viola) and Mr Stanley Sadie (bassoon).'

The educational aims of the Society have been furthered in several ways. For many years it had a library of books and music. Yet the logistical problems of making these available for consultation by the membership may have proved awkward (not least during the time when a former officer of the Society had some of them in his Scottish home for safe keeping). After a period when they resided in the Library of the Royal College of Organists, they were removed in 1957 to the Library of the University of London in Senate House. After two years of heated debate, and a postal ballot of members, the books were sold to the University in 1967, with the exception of a manuscript Dominican psalter and the Sarum Processional printed in 1554, disposed of by public auction.

The gramophone recordings which were Dom Anselm Hughes's special enthusiasm (since the greatly successful History of Music in Sound series) never became part of the Society's output, though a 'pump-priming' sum was devoted to help bring to fruition the record *Anglo-Saxon Easter*, recorded by the Schola Gregoriana of Cambridge under Mary Berry for Archiv in 1984.

Between 1970 and 1974 there was a complete cessation of activity. The pattern since then has been rather different, reflecting to some extent changes in the general perception of plainsong and medieval music in modern times. Anglican church musicians, for example, have had to grapple with new liturgies, deflecting attention from the revival of ancient practices. It is not clear how well attended were the lectures of thirty years ago, but they have not been revived (though each Annual General Meeting concludes with a lecture). Perhaps their absence is mitigated by the periodic disquisitions on medieval topics at meetings of the Royal Music Association, or the annual summer conferences on medieval and renaissance music. Yet the intelligent amateur, the church musician with an antiquarian bent, or the learned ecclesiastic who between them constituted the 'typical' PMMS member of yore would not find themselves so much at home with the newer, 'harder', and infinitely more technical papers heard at musicological meetings nowadays. As one Council member remarked in a letter of resignation (due to emigration), at the time he was first elected it had been felt that a 'non-learned' person should be a member of Council. The publishing activities of the Society have recently been paramount— though these are not designed to maximize profit, for according to its constitution the Society is a non-profit-making body—whereas the occasions when members could come together to listen to lectures or concerts, attend religious services with plainsong, even sing it themselves, have become fewer.

This is not necessarily to be regretted. The Society is no more than what its members make of it, and it can only respond to the initiatives of its membership and the Council elected by it; and these, as the Minute Book makes clear, are but human, each with his or her own ambitions and enthusiasms. If the members of the Society so decree, there is no reason why it should not continue to flourish, inspired by a common desire to know more of the creations of our medieval forefathers.

I

Liturgy and Liturgical Music
in the
Eleventh Century

2

Unica in the Cotton Caligula Troper

RITVA JACOBSSON
(University of Stockholm)

From Frere's text edition of 1894 until the fundamental examination of the repertory of Oxford, Bodleian Library Bodley 775 and Cambridge, Corpus Christi College 473 made by Planchart in 1977, the two Winchester Tropers have attracted much attention.[1] In these studies, both Frere and Planchart also discussed the third English troper, London, British Library Cotton Caligula A. xiv (henceforth London 14); set aside from the main focus of their studies, however, this source was treated more as an appendix to the two 'important' sources. As far as I know, the Cotton Caligula Troper has never been studied thoroughly for its own interest, except that its remarkable illuminations have drawn the attention of art historians.[2]

As it stands now London 14 is not a single, coherent manuscript but consists of three unrelated fragments. The first of these—now fols. 1–36— is a troper containing proper tropes with incipits of liturgical base chants. It seems to have been written in the second half of the eleventh century.[3]

[1] W. H. Frere, *The Winchester Troper*, Henry Bradshaw Society 8 (London, 1894); A. E. Planchart, *The Repertory of Tropes at Winchester*, 2 vols. (Princeton, NJ, 1977).

[2] The art historical literature includes: E. G. Millar, *English Illuminated Manuscripts from the Xth to the XIIIth Century* (Paris, 1926), 22–3; F. Wormald, 'Angleterre' in *Le Siècle de l'an mil* (Paris, 1973), 253; E. Temple, *Anglo-Saxon Manuscripts: 900–1066*, A Survey of Manuscripts illuminated in the British Isles 2 (London, 1976), 113–15. For detailed descriptions of the manuscript see H. Husmann, *Tropen- und Sequenzenhandschriften*, Répertoire Internationale des Sources Musicales B/v/1 (Munich, 1964), 154, and Planchart, *Winchester*, I, 43–50, and II, 21–9. See also H. Gneuss, 'Liturgical Books in Anglo-Saxon England and their Old English Terminology', in *Learning and Literature in Anglo-Saxon England: Studies presented to Peter Clemoes*, ed. M. Lapidge and H. Gneuss (Cambridge, 1985), 91–141.

[3] There is no firm evidence which has allowed a more precise dating of this fragment, and no consensus has yet been reached in scholarly discussions.

Only one scribe was responsible for the trope texts, and another for the musical notation;[4] the few marginal additions are made by more than one scribe. The second part of London 14 (fols. 37–92) is a fragment from a proser (fols. 43–92), also containing a few Ordinary tropes (fols. 37–42); this was copied in the late twelfth century (perhaps even the early thirteenth). Finally, the third part contains a fragmentary collection of lives of saints, including Ælfric's lives of St Martin and St Thomas the Apostle, and an anonymous life of St Mildred, written in Old English and copied in the eleventh century.[5] All three parts were bound together at least by 1696 (after 1622 and probably before 1638), when they formed a single volume in the library of Robert Cotton.[6]

This third English troper contains a substantial number of unique Proper tropes—sixty-three trope elements including two *versus ante officium* in all; it also has its own versions of several tropes known from other sources. London 14 contains virtually all the proper tropes found in the Winchester manuscripts—not only those which are apparently English (existing only in English sources or in English and northern French sources), but also those which are known in continental repertories. The only exceptions to this are, first, the large number of tropes missing in London 14 because of its incomplete state and, second, tropes in the Winchester sources for feasts that are not represented in London 14. In the case of the first group, we can presume with a high degree of probability that London 14 did offer the same repertory.

My aim here is to study the unique tropes in London 14 and to try to find out how they relate to the rest of the repertory in this source. Above all, it is interesting to see what character they have in terms of versification, style, metaphors, theology, and liturgical function. Do they show any coherent pattern? Why were they chosen? What do they represent? And what determined their order?

My method will consist of a close reading of the unica. Even if it were possible to separate these texts into stylistic or functional groups, I think that following the manuscript from feast to feast, folio to folio, will give a more legitimate picture of what is specific to the unique tropes in London 14. The final conclusions will sort out repertories and define the trope creativity that we can identify. The variants and errors in London 14 and its concordances with other manuscripts also demand consideration; but

---

[4.] Planchart, *Winchester*, I, 44.

[5.] See N. R. Ker, *Catalogue of Manuscripts containing Anglo-Saxon* (Oxford, 1957), 172.

[6.] See Planchart, *Winchester*, I, 43. The composite manuscript, as we know it, is listed in a catalogue of Cottonian manuscripts compiled before 1638; see A. G. Watson, 'Thomas Allen of Oxford and his Manuscripts', in *Medieval Scribes, Manuscripts and Libraries: Essays presented to N. R. Ker*, ed. M. B. Parkes and A. G. Watson (London, 1978), 279–313, and G. C. Tite, 'The Early Catalogues of the Cottonian Library', *British Library Journal* 6 (1980), 144–57.

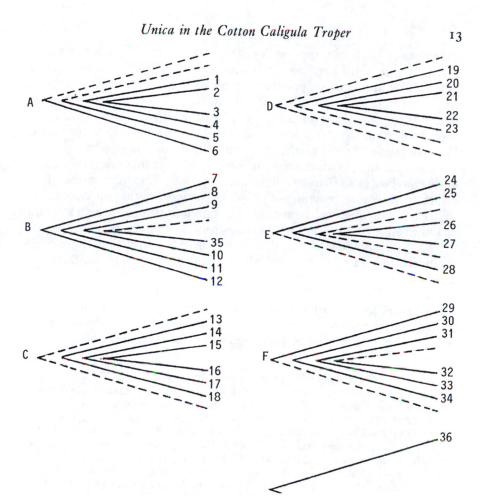

Figure 1. Collation and reconstruction of London, British Library Cotton Caligula A. XIV, fols. 1–36 (after Frere)

here these matters will be sketched only briefly, and subordinated to the main purpose of studying the content of the unica.

With its many illuminations in bright colours and gold, the Cotton Caligula Troper is an extremely beautiful book. The illuminations are surrounded by inscriptions in leonine hexameters, describing in words what is painted. The book is written with a particularly handsome text script, not without some mannerism, and the musical notation is stylish and professionally written.

At the same time, London 14 offers at least three major obstacles to those who wish to study it. First, it is seriously incomplete; Figure 1 shows the structure of the manuscript. A substantial number of folios is missing, perhaps because the precious illuminations invited thieves to steal whole folios.[7] This mutilated shape causes problems: we cannot know whether it would have been possible to solve some of the questions concerning repertories, place of origin, and so on, had the entire manuscript as first copied survived, but it is at least conceivable that a feast such as that of the Dedication of a church would have been helpful in this respect.

Second, in spite of all the missing folios, it is clear that this book had an unspecific liturgical character, including no tropes for local saints.[8] It is evidently insular, its repertory of proper tropes close to the two Winchester sources, but its liturgical content provides no hint through which it might be linked with a particular locality or institution, and this is probably why scholars have not felt attracted to work on it.[9] It has sometimes been attributed to Canterbury, principally because the other music fragment with which it is bound may have been written for the Cathedral of Canterbury.[10] Planchart has suggested that the book could have been written for King Edward the Confessor. This is an attractive hypothesis, in that it helps to explain the absence of corrections, as well as the unusually large number of tropes for St John the Evangelist (including unique tropes

[7] This drawing of Frere's reconstruction was kindly provided by Elizabeth Teviotdale, to whom I am indebted for many valuable discussions during the preparation of this study. The manuscript is now too tightly bound to allow a secure codicological analysis. The troper begins with the words: 'Clarisonas Christo prompsit his vocibus odas', introducing the Introit for the first Sunday of Advent, *Ad te levavi*. Whether the hexameter 'Almifico quondam perflatus flamine David', which precedes *Clarisonas* in both Winchester sources, was omitted here in error, or deliberately left out, or had, in fact, been inscribed on the verso of the now lost preceding folio, we cannot know. Although grammatically self-sufficient, the single hexameter in London 14 is less explanatory since the subject David (for the verb *prompsit*) is lacking. Other lost material includes tropes for part or all of the Christmas octave, Epiphany, Palm Sunday, Easter Day, Ascension, Pentecost, possibly St Paul and a local saint (see n. 8 below), St Benedict, St Laurence, Assumption of the BVM, Nativity of the BVM, St Michael, All Saints, Common of apostles, Common of martyrs, Common of a confessor and Common of virgins. The Troper ends with the rubric for the feast of the Dedication of a church.

[8] Through a comparison of incomplete or missing feasts with the gathering structure it might be conjectured that tropes for a local saint once appeared beween fols. 23 and 24 (Planchart, *Winchester*, I, 57).

[9] Since this article was written an important study has been published by Elizabeth Teviotdale, *The Cotton Caligula Troper (London, British Library, Cotton MS Caligula A. XIV, fols. 1–36): A Study of an Illustrated English Troper of the Eleventh Century*, Ph.D. diss. (Univ. of North Carolina, Chapel Hill, 1991).

[10] Frere, *Winchester Troper*, xxx, merely states 'which seems to have been written for use at Canterbury'. The arguments for the Canterbury origin of the second and third fragments are set out in Planchart, *Winchester*, I, 47 ff. Although the second fragment was associated with our Troper at an early date, we can be certain that there was no connection between these first two and the third fragment before they were bound together in the early 17th C.

for the vigil mass). The King was known to venerate this saint particularly.[11] However, since Edward died in 1066, this hypothesis would demand an earlier dating than that suggested by the script.

The third obstacle to the reader is the state of the Latin texts, which contain many errors. The London 14 errors are not of the same kind as those in southern French or Italian trope manuscripts, where the confused Latin often reflects language as spoken. The faults in London 14 range from mere slips of single letters and grammatical forms to incomprehensible mistakes of whole words, from errors that could be explained as palaeographic misreadings (or 'miscopyings') to some that could represent oral misunderstandings, and finally some that I find hard to explain at all. These imperfections are rendered all the more ironic by their presentation in the most wonderful calligraphic script.[12]

Christmas and St Stephen

The first unique trope copied in London 14 consists of two hexameters, introducing the Introit *Dominus dixit* of the first Christmas mass. Before this, London 14 presents the same four trope elements as the Winchester manuscripts, although in a reversed order (3, 4, 1, 2). These are in prose and have a theological rather than laudatory character; they seek to explain and contrast Christ's birth both in eternity and in historical time. Only afterwards, as a new introduction to *Dominus dixit*, do we find:

> Hymnidicis te, Christe, choris veneremur ovantes,
> qui patre progenitum propria te voce fateris:
> DOMINUS DIXIT AD ME: FILIUS MEUS ES TU.
>
> (fol. iv; AH 49. 6; P 41; CT I, 114)[13]

[11.] Planchart, *Winchester*, I, 49.

[12.] Errors in the texts of unica are discussed below (*passim*). I give here a few examples of errors in the London 14 texts for which concordances survive, making reference to the editions of Corpus Troporum (henceforth CT). CT I, *Tropes du propre de la messe 1: Cycle de Noël*, ed. R. Jonsson (Stockholm, 1975): 56, *Agmine credentium ex omni* (Lo. 14: *Agmine credendum*); 65, *Celse deus precibus Stephani plebibus adsis* (Lo. 14: *precibus Stephanum*); 162, *Principium reserans trinum deitatis et unum* (Lo. 14: *Principium reserans summus*); 208, *Ut decus est palmae sic iustus germine pulchro* (Lo. 14: *palmae: plane; iustus: iustis*). CT III: *Tropes du propre de la messe 2: Cycle de Pâques*, ed. G. Björkvall, G. Iversen, and R. Jonsson (Stockholm, 1982): 83, *Discipulis flammas infudit pectore blandas* (Lo. 14: *blandas: flammas*); 129, *Ipsi perspicuas dicamus vocibus odas* (Lo. 14: *perspicuas: perspicuos*); 143, *Ne valeant querulis lassari corda periclis* (Lo. 14: *lassari: quassari*); 154, *Ore coruscanti custodes . . . perculit exsangues* (Lo. 14: *perculit: pertulit*); 180, *Qui patris es virtus fidei dator* (Lo. 14: *dator: sator*).

[13.] AH: Analecta Hymnica Medii Aevi, ed. C. Blume, G. M. Dreves, and H. M. Bannister, 55 vols. (Leipzig, 1886–1922) (volume and item number). P: Planchart, *Winchester*, II (item number). The standard Corpus Troporum practice of differentiating between trope and chant texts, through the use of capital letters for the latter, is adopted here.

This not only provides a hexameter trope for the feast, but also contributes something that is otherwise lacking—direct praise in the first person subjunctive: 'let us venerate'. This praising is expressed in extravagant language: 'jubilating with hymn-singing choirs'. And the alliteration (a technique much loved by insular poets) in the second line—*patre progenitum propria*—also belongs to the rhetorical character, as does the use of expressions current in other trope hexameters.[14]

Another significant aspect of this trope—and one which it shares with many other continental tropes for *Dominus dixit*—is that the Introit is introduced in such a way that it becomes absolutely clear who is speaking. In other words, *Hymnidicis te* is one of those tropes which clarify the different roles suggested in the psalm text.[15] In the middle ages, the Psalms were often interpreted as being said to Christ or said by Christ to the Father, together with the faithful. The text *Dominus dixit* (from Psalm 2: *Quare fremuerunt*) belongs traditionally to the second category ('*Vox Christi*'). But this Introit text is not easily understood, since it contains both the *Vox Christi* ('Dominus dixit ad me') and a quoted utterance ('Filius meus es tu' . . .); thus the Introit text implies two roles. The text of the trope is directed to Christ ('te Christe, te fateris') and says literally 'you confess: THE LORD SAID TO ME . . .'. It has the deliberate function of making the traditional liturgical text perfectly comprehensible.[16]

For the Introit of St Stephen's feast (*Etenim sederunt*), London 14 offers six more trope elements than the Winchester Tropers, which give only the exact number of trope elements necessary for one celebration of a mass, with the Introit sung three times. London 14, however, has five sets of Introit tropes. These extra tropes are not unica, but belong to a repertory common to Mainz and northern France, as well as southern Italy.

The St Stephen Offertory (*Elegerunt apostoli*) shows the same pattern, London 14 having five more elements than Winchester. The Offertory verse has one unique element:

Exemplo domini patientis et in cruce fixi
  POSITIS AUTEM GENIBUS STEPHANUS ORABAT . . .

in cruce fixi: incrucifixi

[14.] Other examples of alliteration in insular sources include: *Qui mundum mundique minas* (P 69); *Quos mea perpetuo praescit providentia* (P 185); *Processisse paterno ex pectore* (P 192); *Quod mecum mansit manet . . . manebit* (P 244); *esuriem pellens populum per devia pascens* (P 265); *Pacifici psallant quos pax pia Christus* (P 283); *Christicolas cuneos mihi commendando* (P 300).

[15.] See R. Jonsson, 'The Liturgical Function of the Tropes', in *Research on Tropes*, ed. G. Iversen, Kungl. Vitterhets Historie och Antikvitets Akademien, Konferenser 8 (Stockholm, 1983), 99–123.

[16.] On the *Vox Christi* and *Vox Patris* and their relation to the tropes see P.-M. Gy, 'Les Tropes dans l'histoire de la liturgie et de la théologie', *Research on Tropes*, 7–16.

(Following the example of the suffering and crucified Lord,
STEPHEN WAS PRAYING ON HIS KNEES.)

(fol. 5r; AH 49. 592; P 239; CT 1, 89)

Compared to other trope texts for this feast, *Exemplo domini* is notable for
its way of linking Stephen's suffering with Christ's. The trope element
itself includes no direct reference to the saint, but only to his Lord. This is
a good example of the widespread custom in tropes for the feasts of saints
of focusing on God rather than on the saint directly. In this way, the saint
may be associated with the Lord's holiness.[17]

St John the Evangelist

For the feast of St John the Evangelist, London 14 contains not only two
introductory *versus ante officium* and six sets of tropes for the Introit *In
medio ecclesie* (two more sets than Winchester), but also tropes for the
Introit of the vigil mass (*Ego autem*). This is absolutely exceptional.[18]
Proper tropes always belong to the major feast day. The liturgy of the day
before—the vigil—prepares and anticipates the feast by introducing its
theme, but not in such an elaborate way as to be adorned with tropes.
Consequently, the vigil masses of even the most important feasts hardly
ever have tropes. We have no tropes at all for the vigil of Christmas. The
inclusion of the *Ego autem* tropes in London 14 is therefore unusual and
puzzling. One possible explanation of their presence is that St John the
Evangelist had a special significance for the institution or individual for
whom the book was prepared. And this would imply that this book was
created in its own way, apparently without the necessity to follow the usual
rules. When the contents of the book were planned, specific demands
rather than standard conventions could be fulfilled.

The trope set for the vigil mass has no introductory element. This is also
rather unusual (more often the situation is the reverse, with the trope
consisting of an introductory element only):[19]

EGO AUTEM SICUT OLIVA FRUCTIFICAVI IN DOMO DOMINI.
Hoc mihi donaverat, qui vera constat oliva.
SPERAVI IN MISERICORDIA DEI MEI,
Qui me preveniens lucidis inmiscuit astris,

---

[17] CT 1, 89, has a misreading of the text; cf. P 239, and my review in *Notes* 35 (1978),
63–7.

[18] But see the discussion of tropes for St Andrew below. Planchart, *Winchester*, II, 75,
notes one other example (from Benevento, for the vigil of the Assumption).

[19] The only other example of a trope set without an introductory element which I know
of is one for St Just copied in the two Winchester Tropers (AH 49. 272; P 69).

ET EXSPECTABO NOMEN TUUM;
Et prepotens spacium celi terreque gubernans,
QUONIAM BONUM EST ANTE CONSPECTUM SANCTORUM TUORUM.

(fol. 5v; AH 49. 264; P 53; CT 1, 105, 180, 90)

In this trope set, three trope elements paraphrase the Introit text, at the
same time having a rather loose syntactical relation to it. *Hoc mihi
donaverat* is an independent sentence. The element *Et prepotens spacium*
does not fit particularly well with the preceding part of the Introit.

This trope set makes no reference to St John the Evangelist at all. All
three elements focus on the Lord. It is interesting to see how the poet has
handled the olive metaphor. The Introit text (from Psalm 51. 10–11) is
clearly used symbolically for the saint, who is meant to be the *vera oliva*
(literally 'true olive tree'), hoping for the mercy of the Lord. In the trope
text the Lord is the 'true olive tree' who preceded the saint in heaven and
governs the universe.[20] The repetition of the prefix *pre-* (*preveniens,
prepotens*) might suggest some relation to the Christmas liturgy: the Lord
comes before John. There may also be echoes here of liturgical texts
associated with the other great saint who shares this name, John the
Baptist.[21]

The prosody of the hexameter verse is bad, with some syllables wrongly
measured. In the first line, there are two errors of prosody (*donăverat* for
donāverat, *verā* for *veră*), another in the second (*lŭcidis* for *lūcidis*), and a
further one in the third (*prĕpotens* for *prēpotens*).

To the long *versus ante officium, Hodie candidati sacerdotum*, for the main
feast-day, London 14 adds another introductory set, also consisting of four
parts:

ITEM MODUL < AMINA > ANTE INTR < OITUM >
   Tibi Christo regi plaudant omnes angeli,
   plaudant sacerdotes et cuncti ministri tui.
RESP < PONSUM >
   Qui inter natalis tui gaudia
   cari tui Iohannis nobis prestas suffragia,
ITEM PR < ESBYTERI >[22]
   Iohannis potatoris profundi pectoris tui
   et tutoris virginee genitricis tue,
RESP < ONSUM >

[20.] The word *sapientia* in the Old Testament has often been interpreted as denoting
Christ, and in Ecclesiasticus 24. 19 *sapientia* is described 'quasi oliva speciosa in campis'.
[21.] The tropes for St John the Baptist often contain expressions like *praeparare viam* (AH
49. 252), *praecursore, praenovit* (AH 49. 258), *praecurrit* (AH 49. 263).
[22.] Frere, *Winchester Troper*, 103, interprets RESP as 'Responsum' and PR as 'Praetitulati', but allows the alternative 'Presbyteri'. Planchart, *Winchester*, II, 43, interprets RESP
as 'respondeant' and PR as 'praetitulati'.

Ad cuius gloriam en tibi adstant
hymniste sacerdotes tui,
et tua in eo preconia efferunt ita modulantes:
< IN MEDIO ECCLESIE . . . > .

(fol. 6r–v; P 8; CT 1, 106)

Why was it considered appropriate to add a second *versus*? Stylistically, *Tibi Christo* has much in common with *Hodie candidati*, using structured prose, alliteration, repeated expressions, *traiectio*, rhymes, and words of praise and song. But there are also differences. First of all, *Tibi Christo* contains no less than nine instances of the second person singular pronoun (*tibi, tua,* etc.), while *Hodie candidati* has none. The London 14 text is thus repeatedly directed to a second person.

The second part, *Qui inter*, makes clear allusions to Christmas, and the third to two events in the life of St John the Evangelist: Christ's taking him to his breast at the Last Supper, and his giving over his mother Mary into John's care. The expressions 'Iohannis potatoris' and 'tutoris . . . genitricis' are both emotionally coloured. The first and the fourth parts, on the other hand, have the same character as *Hodie candidati*.

The word *sacerdotes* is important in both *versus*. In *Hodie candidati sacerdotum chori*, it clearly denotes priests in heaven, but the last line refers to the priests here and now: 'sacerdotes eia iubilemus'. Likewise, in *Tibi Christo regi*, we first have 'angeli' and 'sacerdotes', and at the end 'en tibi adstant hymniste sacerdotes', apparently referring to the singing in the church.

London 14 has two more tropes for the Introit *In medio ecclesie* than Winchester. The first of these, *Celica celestem*, is frequently found in Aquitainian sources. The other is unique to London 14:

Lux vera Christus
sui privilegio amoris
Iohannem honoravit apostolum atque
IN MEDIO ECCLESIE APERUIT OS EIUS,
Insignis ut esset
evangelice veritatis adsertor,
ET IMPLEVIT EUM DOMINUS SPIRITU SAPIENTIE ET INTELLECTUS,
Quo ceteris altius
verbi dei archana reseraret;
STOLAM GLORIE INDUIT EUM.

(fol. 7r; P 88; CT 1, 134, 122, 184)

In both syntax and content these prose elements are smoothly connected to the base text. Using powerful expressions, the first element evokes the specific relationship between Jesus and the apostle ('with the privilege of his love he honoured John as his apostle'). Through the opening epithet, 'the true light', this text calls attention to those liturgical texts for Christmas in which Christ is symbolically represented as the light. A significant number of Christmas tropes contain precisely this formula, 'Lux vera', for Christ.[23]

The second element is elegant; the first word, *insignis*, is linked to the last, *adsertor*, while the *ut* clause expands the Introit's words *aperuit os* ('HE OPENED HIS MOUTH IN THE MIDDLE OF THE CHURCH, that he might be a distinguished defender of the evangelical truth').[24]

The last element is clearly intended to refer to the opening of St John's Gospel, concerning the Word. Like the previous element it forms a final clause, explaining the meaning of the preceding phrase of the Introit: 'that he, in a deeper way than the others, should reveal the secrets of God's Word'. Another trope element, itself belonging to the *Celica celestem* set (and thus preceding *Lux vera Christus* in London 14) provides a parallel: 'Principium reserans trinum deitatis et unum' (CT I, 162). The interesting thing is, however, that in the London 14 version the word *trinum* is lost, leaving the meaning of the text confused: 'Principium reserans summus deitatis et unum'. At the very least, the scribe of London 14 had not understood the text.

In summary, the London 14 unica for the feast of John the Evangelist include three blocks of unique tropes. It is hard to interpret the whole pattern, but it is nevertheless evident that there are many links between the London 14 unica and the tropes in other repertories, particularly those in insular sources.

Holy Innocents

In the liturgy for the feast of the Holy Innocents, London 14 again offers unique tropes. Following a *versus ante officium* of six hexameters, *Laudibus alternis pueros* (also copied in Oxford 775), London 14 adds this text:

Eya, mater Sion,
gaude pro pueris tuo collocatis gremio,
quos impius rex puniens iniuste
transmisit ad aethera digne.
Gaudeat etiam mater ecclesia
in toto orbe iam diffusa,

[23.] See e.g. *quia hodie lux vera mundo rutilat* (CT I, 98); *Hodie lux vera effulserat* (CT I, 109); *quia lux vera fulget in caelis* (CT I, 113); *Iam venit lux vera* (CT I, 116, 133); *Lux vera emicat* (CT I, 134).

[24.] The word *adsertor* appears in Cyprianus (*Epist.* 44. 3) in the same sense: 'adsertor evangelii et Christi'. Also, the expression 'evangelice veritatis adsertor' has a parallel in another Christmas cycle trope: 'trinitatis assertor' (CT I, 73).

et quia dolet in passione,
gaudeat iam in remuneratione.
Dicantur igitur laudes
nostro redemptori summo,
cui est totum posse
totumque perficere,
et in illius laude verum proferimus,
quia ecce:
<EX ORE INFANTIUM, DEUS, ET LACTENTIUM PERFECISTI LAUDEM . . .>.

Eya: Eyia

(fol. 8r; P 2; CT I, 131)

In style and character, *Eya mater Sion* is rather similar to the preceding *versus ante officium*. However, it is written in prose, while that shared with Winchester is in hexameters. We can suspect that a number of different sources lie behind the London 14 text. Thus, for instance, there is at least one fragment of a hexameter in the line: '. . . injuste transmisit ad aethera digne'. There is also a clear parallel between the passage 'Gaudeat etiam mater ecclesia in toto orbe iam diffusa' and the pascal *Exultet*: 'Gaudeat et tellus . . . inlustrata, totius orbis se sentiat . . . Laetetur et mater ecclesia'.[25]

The contents and the range of metaphors in this unique text are of considerable interest. It is striking, first of all, that the mother metaphor plays such an important role. This is underlined visually by the expression 'pueris tuo collocatis gremio' (the children placed on your lap). 'Mater ecclesia' is, of course, a common expression in liturgical texts; here it is coupled with 'mater Sion', a symbol not found as such in the bible, but implied in the expression 'the children of Sion'. And the evocation of Sion (Jerusalem) as a mother immediately suggests Christ's utterance: 'Filiae Hierusalem, nolite flere super me: sed super vos ipsas flete et super filios vestros' (Daughters of Jerusalem, weep not for me, but weep for your-selves, and for your children; Luke 23. 28), thus accentuating the theme of the mothers' grief for their murdered children. At one and the same time, the Church is crying for her martyrs. The antithesis 'dolet in passione'— 'gaudeat iam in remuneratione' (she is suffering in pain—she must rejoice in her reward) exploits the mother metaphor in a refined way, the double expression referring to the Church, to the mothers of the innocent children, and to the mother Jerusalem who cries for her children.[26]

[25] *Missale Gallicanum vetus*, ed. L. C. Mohlberg, Rerum Ecclesiasticarum Documenta, Series Maior, Fontes III (Rome, 1958), 35.

[26] The expression 'mater ecclesia' is discussed by A. Blaise, *Le Vocabulaire latin des principaux thèmes liturgiques* (Turnhout, 1966), 496 ff. Although the expression 'mater Sion' is not biblical, Sion is described as a mother in several instances, e.g.: 'parturivit et peperit Sion filios suos' (Sion travailed and brought forth her children; Isa. 66. 8).

The closing lines sum up the twofold exhortation to the mother to rejoice (*gaude, gaudeat*) in a more general jubilation to the Lord. The substantivized verbs *posse* and *perficere* (power, perfection) seem to belong to a special insular style encountered elsewhere in the London 14 and Winchester repertories.[27] Again, it is tempting to believe that where, in Winchester, a strict choice from a stock of texts had been made, the London 14 scribe deliberately retained this text.

For the Holy Innocents' Offertory *Anima nostra*, London 14 fills out its trope set with another unique element, a slightly defective hexameter:

ET NOS LIBERATI SUMUS
Auxilio domini per tanta miracula fulti.
TORRENTEM PERTRANSIVIT ANIMA NOSTRA.

(fol. 9r; P 201; CT 1, 62)

This is a pale text, of the same kind as many others found in the insular tropers. It contains no references to a particular saint or category of saints, nor does it reflect any specific theological or biblical ideas. *Fulti* must refer to the last words of the Offertory ('et nos liberati sumus'), since the trope element comes before the Verse *Torrentem pertransivit anima* and the repetition of the Offertory. Together the base text and trope must then mean: 'and we were liberated, we who through such great miracles trusted in the help of the Lord'. The Verse *Torrentem pertransivit anima* is thus left hanging loosely, without any clear connection to the trope text.

Epiphany

The feast of Epiphany has concordances with both Winchester and French repertories, all tropes focusing on the traditional Epiphany themes, particularly that of Christ as King. The offertory tropes include a series of hexameter elements unique to Winchester, Cambrai, and Saint-Magloire; within this group, one element is unique to London 14:

REGES THARSIS ET INSULE MUNERA OFFERENT,
REGES ARABUM ET SABA DONA ADDUCENT;
Qui celum terramque simul per secla gubernat,
presepio parvus sed sydere, lumen habetur,
ET ADORABUNT EUM OMNES REGES TERRE;
OMNES GENTES SERVIENT EI.

sydere: sydera

(fol. 35v; AH 49. 552; P 273; CT 1, 177)

27. Cf. e.g. 'Per quem velle meum norunt pia corda meorum' (AH 49. 589; P 227); 'O dee virtutum, cui velle subest, cui posse' (AH 49. 593; P 250).

Grammatically, the two hexameters do not fit well with the base text. Their prosody is deficient, since *presepio* (*praesaepio*) contains two long syllables at the beginning. This element may be translated as: 'He who governs both heaven and earth through the centuries is a small child in the stable, but is regarded as a light in heaven, AND ALL THE KINGS OF THE WORLD SHALL ADORE HIM . . .'. The contrast made between the small child and the ruler of the universe is classic, encountered both in office texts and in other tropes. Certainly, it belongs especially to the Christmas liturgy.[28] In fact, the comparison of *Qui celum terramque* with the other offertory tropes for Epiphany in London 14 demonstrates how this single unique trope relates the Offertory directly to Christmas. For the rest, it is not very different from the surrounding tropes.

Easter

For the feasts of the Purification and Annunciation of the BVM as well as Palm Sunday and Easter Day, London 14 shares most of its tropes with Winchester, but has a few additions. This section contains a number of unica associated with the Offertory *Terra tremuit*. Following the old and extremely widespread series *Ab indignatione, Monumenta aperta, Christus surrexit* and preceding an insular series of three hexameter elements belonging to the Offertory Verses, we find this trope:

Iudicium magno metuens concussa pavore
TERRA TREMUIT ET QUIEVIT,
Actibus a pravis sectans monimenta salutis,
DUM RESURGERET IN IUDICIO DEUS,
Perderet ut reprobos, mites salvaret ut omnes:
ALLELUIA.

(Shaken by a great anxiety, fearing the judgment,
THE EARTH TREMBLED AND WAS STILL
from the wicked deeds, seeking the recommendations of salvation,
WHEN GOD ROSE IN JUDGMENT
to reject the false and to save all the good ones.
ALLELUIA.

(fol. 14v; AH 49. 554; P 281; CT III, 130, 55, 159)

This is a difficult text, using rather unusual words: *concussa pavore, pravis, sectans, monimenta*—this last in the sense of exhortation—*reprobos*. It involves two protagonists, the earth and God, and uses a pattern of

---

[28] AH 49. 552 describes this text as 'übrigens unverständlich'. If the manuscript version is kept, it would mean 'is regarded as stars (i.e. heaven) and light'. *Sydera* may be emended to *syderis*, 'the light of the star (heaven)', but this destroys the prosody.

contrasts: *pravis/salutis* and *reprobos/mites*. The whole trope set is closely tied to the base text, but its language is different from that of *Terra tremuit*, being rather more special and poetic, and gives to the psalm text a further dimension, that of the fight between good and evil.

For Easter Monday London 14 has one unique element, attached to the Introit psalm verse:

> Munere pro tali glomerantes munia nati
> CONFITEMINI . . .
>
> (fol. 15v; AH 49. 101; P 95; CT III, 141)

This appears after a well-known set of prose elements for the Introit *Introduxit*, and is followed by two exclusively insular trope elements—both elegiac distichs. Equally English elements, most with leonine rhymes, come immediately after as offertory and communion tropes. The unique trope *Munere pro tali* is thus placed as a transition between two groups of tropes for Easter Monday. In its sense, *Munere pro tali* belongs more to what follows. At the same time, *glomerantes* fits well with the previous elements, which have the rhyming words *memores*, *parentes*, *tripudiantes*. The unusual word *glomerantes* is typical of the insular style, as is the wordplay on *munere/munia*.[29] This element is also the only one for this Introit to mention the Son (*nati*). The rest focuses on the first person of the Trinity instead. These qualities make me believe that we have here a trope from a richer English repertory than that represented in the two Winchester collections.

Invention of the Holy Cross

One of the most interesting feasts in London 14 is the Invention of the Holy Cross, where most of the material is unique:

> Hierusalem solio primo peccante repulsi
> in mundo positi et sacro baptismate loti,
> NOS AUTEM GLORIARI OPORTET
> In ligno, per quod vite reparatur origo,
> IN CRUCE DOMINI NOSTRI IESU CHRISTI,
> Cuius principium nec finis cernitur umquam,
> IN QUO EST SALUS, VITA ET RESURRECTIO NOSTRA;

[29.] *Munus* is found in other tropes: see *Aeterno populos* (AH 49. 110), *Omnibus ecce piis* (AH 49. 115), *Cunctipotens domine* (AH 49. 161), *Germinis excelsi* (AH 49. 162), *Splendidus adventum* (AH 49. 163), *Laetetur cunctus quadro* (AH 49. 559). Concerning the English taste for unusual words, see M. Lapidge, 'Three Latin Poems from Æthelwold's School at Winchester', *Anglo-Saxon England* 1 (1972), 85–137. For *glomeratus* see: 'Christicola perpes sanctis glomeratus in aevum' (AH 49. 372).

Presens, preteritum cernit pariterque futurum,
PER QUEM SALVATI ET LIBERATI SUMUS.

(fols. 17r–v; AH 49. 83; P 110)

Perspicue crucis en magnum dicamus honorem!
NOS AUTEM GLORIARI OPORTET,
Qua mundum dominus pendens a morte redemit
IN CRUCE DOMINI NOSTRI IESU CHRISTI,
Sanguine qui fuso pro nobis victima cesa est,
IN QUO EST SALUS, VITA ET RESURRECTIO NOSTRA,
Quam nos auctore<m> surgendi credimus omnes,
PER QUEM SALVATI ET LIBERATI SUMUS.

(fol. 17v; AH 49. 81; P 112)

London 14 has three introit trope sets for this feast, while the two Winchester Tropers have only one (*Perspicuae crucis*). This comes second in London 14, where it has attracted a unique addition, *Quam nos auctorem*, for which musical notation was never added. London 14 thus offers one unique set, shares another with Winchester, and a third with three Aquitainian manuscripts (*Nos cruce regnantem*).

A striking feature of the first set (*Hierusalem solio*) is its highly theological character. From a grammatical point of view, the introductory trope element does not fit perfectly: the forms *repulsi, positi, loti*, normally refer to a masculine plural nominative, but here they refer to *nos*, which is in the accusative because of *oportet*. Nevertheless, the sense must be: 'Repelled from Jerusalem's throne because of the first man's sin, placed in the world and washed by the sacred baptism, WE SHOULD GLORY . . . IN THE CROSS'.

There is an interplay of different symbols in this first element. Adam and Eve driven out of paradise and original sin is one. Jerusalem's throne, the dominion of the sacred city where Jesus was crucified, is another. But the sacred city is also the heavenly Jerusalem where God sits on the throne, and from which mankind has been thrown out into the world. All this belongs to the first half of this element. The second means 'placed in the world and washed through the holy baptism'. As yet, nothing has been said about Christ's suffering and crucifixion, but there is an allusion to redemption through the baptism.[30]

The second element takes up the Introit's first phrase with *in ligno*: 'WE SHOULD GLORY in the tree through which the origin of life is restored, IN THE CROSS OF OUR LORD JESUS CHRIST'. The expression 'vite origo reparatur' is unusual; the origin of life, 'fons vitae', is normally an expression for God. And what is restored on the cross is fallen man. But since this trope text

---

[30.] The form of words 'vitiis baptismate lotis' appears as the second half of a Beneventan hexameter trope (see CT III, 117).

deals with fundamental theological ideas, we should perhaps interpret it as
'life's origin is brought back'. It should probably be understood together
with the other two elements: first 'whose beginning and end can never be
seen' (a classic expression of God's eternity), and second, 'he who beholds
the present and past as well as the future' (expressing God's omniscience).
Similar expressions figure in trinitarian tropes, such as those for the
Sanctus.[31] To conclude, the economy of salvation is here linked with God's
eternity.

This unique trope set for the Invention feast is, as far as I know, the only
one to bring such a pronounced theological dimension to the Introit *Nos
autem gloriari*, whose text is taken from a Pauline source (Galatians 6. 14).

Pentecost and Trinity

For the Ascension feast London 14 has no unique tropes. The Pentecost
repertory contains both widespread tropes and specifically insular pieces,
as well as two unique elements.[32] These occur in an arrangement where the
Introit *Spiritus domini* has been divided in an unusual way:

Cum pia per populos diffudit munera cunctos,
eia,
SPIRITUS DOMINI REPLEVIT ORBEM TERRARUM, ALLELUIA.
Gratias agamus alme trinitati semper.
ET HOC QUOD CONTINET OMNIA, SCIENTIAM—
Perfudit virtus credentium cordibus—
HABET VOCIS;
Replevit de celo dominus spiritu sancto
corda fidelium suorum.
ALLELUIA, ALLELUIA, ALLELUIA.

                    (fol. 19r; AH 49. 22; P 154; CT III, 90, 107, 159, 188)

The last two elements are unique to London 14.[33] It is strange that two of
these elements (*Gratias agamus*, *Replevit de celo*) are traditional in their
content and expression, while the two others are not. These have stylistic
similarities, although only the first (*Cum pia per*) is a hexameter. However,
Perfudit virtus might itself represent part of a destroyed hexameter.

The feast of Trinity is represented in London 14 but not in Winchester;
in fact, tropes for the Trinity feast appear in a much more restricted

---

[31] See G. Iversen, 'Sur la géographie des tropes du Sanctus', *La Tradizione dei Tropi
Liturgici*, ed. C. Leonardi and E. Menestò (Spoleto, 1990), 39–62. Cf. also *Sanctus ante
saecula deus* (P Sanctus 2).
[32] Most of the Ascension tropes and some of those for Pentecost are missing due to the
loss of at least two folios.
[33] See CT III, 244.

number of sources than those for Easter, Ascension, and Pentecost.[34] Like those for the Invention of the Holy Cross, the Trinity tropes consist of three sets. The first two are unique:

Effectrix rerum sanctarum, sancta, beatrix,
BENEDICTA SIT SANCTA TRINITAS ATQUE INDIVISA UNITAS,
Gignens et genitus, amborum spiritus unus;
CONFITEBIMUR EI
Mortis ab imperio Ihesu moriente redempti,
QUIA FECIT NOBISCUM MISERICORDIAM SUAM.

(fols. 19v–20r; AH 49. 137; P 22; CT III, 93, 105, 140)

Summe deus, sancta et indivisa,
tibi veneremur hodie sancta,
BENEDICTA
In excelsa sede maiestati < s > tue
SIT SANCTA TRINITAS,
Deitas, lux lucis et fons sanctitatis
ATQUE INDIVISA UNITAS.

benedicta: benedicamus

(fol. 20r; P 23; CT III, 81, 124, 199)

The first trope element is especially original, and does not follow any clear model. The word *effectrix* seems not to be used anywhere else. It is difficult to grasp the intended meaning: 'origin of all holy things'? The feminine form *trinitas* may have prompted the use of the two unusual adjectives *effectrix* and *beatrix* as well as the feminine form of the whole line. Christian Latin poetry usually focuses on masculine expressions for the Trinity of Father, Son, and Holy Spirit. Only the abstracted words *trinitas* and *deitas* are feminine.

This first element is, at the same time, a refined stylistic creation, with the -*trix* rhyme at the beginning and end of the line, and *annominatio* in between (*sanctarum*, *sancta*). The second element is a more normal trinitarian expression, not unlike a number of Sanctus tropes in using two forms of the verb *gignere*. It also contains a significant theological expression: 'amborum spiritus unus'.[35] In being christocentric, the last element is well adapted to the Introit phrase: 'Quia fecit nobiscum misericordiam' ('we were redeemed from the empire of death when Jesus died, SINCE HE SHOWED US HIS MERCY').

[34.] See CT III, 277; only one of the East Frankish manuscripts has Trinity tropes (Bamberg, Staatsbibliothek lit. 5, from Reichenau).

[35.] Cf. Ps. 2. 7 and Heb. 1. 5. See also expressions in other tropes: *Aeterno genitus genitore ex tempore Christus* (CT I, 56); *Gloria sit patri et genito cum pneumate sancto* (CT I, 99).

The second trope set in prose contains more well-known expressions. It is well adapted to the Introit text, both through the verb *veneremur*, which is parallel to *confitebimur*, and through feminine adjectives belonging to *Trinitas*. The trope introduces three other abstract words with *trinitas*: *maiestas*, *deitas*, and *sanctitas*. All three elements are completely focused on the solemn and the sacred (*summe deus*, *excelsa sede*, *lux lucis*, *fons sanctitatis*). The three persons of the Trinity are not mentioned, nor is the word *misericordia* from the Introit text developed.

It seems to me that the unique tropes in London 14 for the Cross and for the Trinity have a rather similar character. Neither of these feasts is often furnished with tropes. They are thus an important feature in London 14.

St John the Baptist

For the feasts of John the Baptist, Peter, Laurence, Andrew, as well as the Common of saints, London 14 includes unique tropes; the other saints' feasts in the book—Benedict, Michael, All Saints, and Martin—have no unica.

The feast of St John the Baptist contains three very widespread trope sets, each in prose and mostly paraphrasing the biblical text. They were copied in London 14 in the same order as in the Winchester Tropers. Following these London 14 gives a unique set of hexameter tropes and one more set (also in the Winchester Tropers) as well as two introit introductions. This is the unique set:

> Vatum firma fides, regis baptista Iohannes,
> ex utero sterili narrant preconia Christi:
> DE VENTRE MATRIS MEE
> Post longum senium inspirato germine foete
> VOCAVIT ME DOMINUS NOMINE MEO,
> Qui quondam Moysi dixit: 'te ex nomine vidi',
> ET POSUIT OS MEUM UT GLADIUM ACUTUM,
> Ut resecem valide perversi dogmatis acta.
> SUB TEGUMENTO MANUS SUE PROTEXIT ME,
> Ne feritas sevi valeat me sternere mundi,
> POSUIT ME QUASI SAGITTAM ELECTAM.
>
> (fols. 21r–v; AH 49. 261; P 35)

This text presents some difficulties. The first two hexameters use leonine rhymes, and seem to consist of four entities hardly connected syntactically: 'The firm belief of the prophets, the King's Baptist John, from the sterile womb, tell the proclaimings of Christ: FROM THE WOMB OF MY MOTHER'. If *fides* and *Iohannes* are read as the two subjects of *narrant*, and *preconia* as the accusative object, then we can translate: 'The firm belief of the prophets <and>, from the sterile womb, the King's Baptist John, proclaim the praise of Christ: FROM THE WOMB OF MY MOTHER, who after a long old age <became> pregnant through an inspired seed, THE LORD CALLED ME'. Another solution would be to treat 'regis baptista Iohannes' as a vocative. Then *fides* and *preconia* would probably both be subjects of *narrant*: 'The firm belief of the prophets, O John, the King's Baptist, <and> the proclaimings of Christ tell that from the sterile womb'. A further possibility would be to change *narrant* to *narrat* and to take *Christi* and *regis* together, thus: 'John the Baptist tells from the sterile womb the praisings of Christ the King'. This would accord well with traditional writings on John the Baptist.[36]

The third element, *Qui quondam*, develops the words *nomine meo* of the base text, words which, in the context of John the Baptist, evoke a fundamental symbol referring to Exodus 33. 17: 'He who once said to Moses: I know thee by name'. In this chapter the Lord tells Moses that he shall, with God's help, bring his people to the promised land, and that the Lord shall give his grace to his servant Moses. The possession of a name is an important symbol of election. In Isaiah 49. 1, the name has exactly the same symbolic function: 'De ventre matris meae recordatus est nominis mei'. And in the New Testament—especially the first chapter of St Luke's Gospel, where the birth of John is recorded—the name is again important. The angel Gabriel mentions the name *Johannes* already when the birth of the child is foretold to Zachariah (Luke 1. 13). When the child is born, his parents insist on this name in spite of the protests of others. Even Zachariah, who cannot speak, writes: 'Iohannes est nomen eius' (Luke 1. 63). The trope element *Qui quondam* effectively juxtaposes the text from Isaiah 49. 1–2 (the source of the Introit text) and that from Exodus.

The last two elements and their base text could be translated as follows:

HE MADE MY MOUTH LIKE A SHARP SWORD
that I should violently cut off the acts of a wicked doctrine,
IN THE SHADOW OF HIS HAND HE PROTECTED ME,
that the brutality of a cruel world should not crush me,
HE MADE ME LIKE A CHOSEN ARROW.

Again, we can observe how the symbolic language of the Old Testament Introit text has inspired similar expressions in the trope. *Valide resecare*, 'to cut off violently', takes up the metaphor of *gladium acutum*. *Perversi dogmatis* alludes both to what John preached and to threats against the learning of the Church.[37]

[36.] In AH, *inspirato* is emended to *insperato*, 'unexpected'.

[37.] The use of the expressions *perversus* and *perversio* for heretic dogma is frequent in the writings of the Church Fathers, especially St Augustine.

The whole trope set has regular leonine rhymes, except in two cases (trope lines 3 and 5). Its themes of the prophet's vocation and birth from an old mother, the severe preaching, and the Lord's protection, do not differ from the other insular tropes. But the choice of vocabulary is different: it uses poetic words like *vates, preconia, germine, sternere*. The reference to Moses is, as far as I can see, unique in the whole European repertory of tropes for John the Baptist.

St Peter

The feast of St Peter has one unique trope element in London 14. This is a communion trope in hexameter form and follows another communion trope, *Cui pater excelsus*, which is also known in Winchester:

Rex regum, dominus, sic nos olim pius infit:
SIMON IOHANNIS, DILIGIS ME PLUS HIS?
DOMINE, TU OMNIA NOSTI. TU SCIS, DOMINE, QUIA AMO TE.
PASCE OVES MEAS.

(fol. 23v; P 318)

There are many examples in tropes of the prophet 'having once said': *olim propheta, olim vates*, and so on.[38] In all cases the expression *olim* refers to the Old Testament. Here, however, the Communion text is taken from the New Testament (John 21. 15, 17), presenting Christ's question to Peter and Peter's reply. By calling Christ 'King of kings', the trope text gives a much more solemn dimension to the biblical words. *Olim* seems in this connection somewhat awkward—as is the case with a number of the unique texts or versions in London 14. While the reading *Olimpius* would add even greater dimensions to the sphere in which Christ dwells, I am reluctant to urge such a word without clear parallels elsewhere in this kind of liturgical poetry; besides, it would not fit the prosody.

St Laurence

The tropes for the feast of St Laurence contain two unique sets. The first is added in the margin:[39]

Adest alma dies, sancto decorata triumpho,
Laurentii sancti; ideo modulemur ovantes:

[38.] See, e.g. CT I, 111, 'de quibus olim propheta praedixerat'; CT I, 148, 'Olim propheta almo spiritu repletus'; 'Olim quem vates antiqui praecinebant'.

[39.] The only such example in the source (although there are a number of much briefer marginal additions and corrections).

CONFESSIO ET PULCHRITUDO IN CONSPECTU EIUS
Est, ubi pro meritis Laurentius hic coronatus,
SANCTITAS ET MAGNIFICENTIA,
Qui levita sacer flammas superavit atroces
IN SANCTIFICATIONE EIUS.

(fol. 25v; AH 49. 278; P 24)

The second unique trope follows one also found in Winchester (*Laudemus dominum*):

Laudibus organicis psallamus verba
quod clamant prophetica:
CONFESSIO ET PULCHRITUDO IN CONSPECTU EIUS,
Sacra cuius hodie celebremus sollempnia,
SANCTITAS ET MAGNIFICENTIA.
Premia pro meritis illum magnificasti
IN SANCTIFICATIONE EIUS.

(fol. 25v; P 26)

There are a number of metrical problems in these two trope sets. In the first, *Adest* is measured with two long syllables, and *coronatus* with a short second syllable. In the second half of the first element, there is a hiatus at the caesura (*sancti ideo*); this is a relatively rare procedure.

The introductory element in the second set is only partly a hexameter, the first part (*Laudibus . . . verba*) forming the first five feet. The rest not only upsets the metrical pattern, but also obscures the meaning. It could, nevertheless, be translated: 'Let us sing in melodious jubilations what the prophetic words proclaim: PRAISE AND BEAUTY ARE BEFORE HIM'.[40] Again, the third element seems to be created from a broken hexameter.

The content of the first two elements of the first set is completely conventional, without any mention of the particular category of saint occupied by Laurence (martyr). 'Adest alma dies' and 'ideo modulemur ovantes' are expressions that occur in several tropes.[41] *Coronatus* could be an allusion to the name of Laurence, but it is a frequent expression in texts on saints. Only the last element refers directly to the sufferings of this martyr by fire.

From the syntactical point of view, the elements fit badly with the base liturgical text. One gets the impression that they were just assembled

[40.] By changing *quod* to *quae*, the meaning (but not the metre) may be clarified: 'Let us sing in melodious praises the prophetical words that proclaim'.

[41.] There is, for example, a trope for the Purification beginning (London 14, fol. 10r; AH 49. 27): 'Adest alma virgo parens/adest verbum caro factum'. Cf. also: 'Ecce dies venerandus adest dicamus ovantes' (AH 49. 272); 'laetantur ovanter' (AH 49. 230); 'Patris adest votiva dies cantemus ovantes' (AH 49. 209); 'veneremur ovantes' (AH 49. 6); 'repetamus ovantes' (AH 49. 242); 'Adest enim festa Martini' (AH 49. 306); 'dicamus ovanter' (AH 49. 308); 'decantet ovanter' (AH 49. 359); 'reboemus ovantes' (AH 49. 382).

casually from stock phrases. The name of the saint, Laurence, is mentioned twice in the first trope set, the feast-day and the moment are evoked (*adest alma dies, hodie*), and words praising the saint (*sanctus, coronatus, merita*) and exhorting those present to sing (*modulemur, psallamus, celebremus*) are the material from which both trope sets are assembled. A number of expressions are more or less repeated: *Est ubi pro meritis* (from the first set), *praemia pro meritis* (from the second). There is only one trope element which gives specific information about the category (*levita*) and specific nature of the martyrdom of St Laurence (*atroces flammas*).[42]

The Blessed Virgin Mary

Tropes for the Purification and Annunciation feasts were copied in London 14 before those for Easter, and have already been mentioned in that context. The tropes for the Assumption and Nativity feasts in London 14 cause a certain amount of confusion. The beginning of the Assumption feast is lost, but most of what remains (fol. 26r) concords with Winchester. After this there follow on folios 26r and 26v two pictures representing the Annunciation to Joachim and Joachim and Anna with the infant Mary. There is no rubric to indicate the feast of the Nativity of the Virgin. Folios 26r–27v contain four sets of tropes for the Introit *Gaudeamus*. Three of these sets (*Cantemus omnes, Splendore sollempni,* and *Aurea post Christum*) are also found in continental sources, but not in Winchester. The fourth set, *Angelorum chori* (copied third in the sequence of four) is unique to London 14. Immediately following the tropes for *Gaudeamus* on fol. 27v are tropes for a different Introit, *Vultum tuum*; these tropes concord with Winchester. This second group of tropes clearly belongs to the Nativity feast. Planchart, reading the illumination of the Nativity as a rubric, believes that the tropes for both the Introits *Gaudeamus* and *Vultum tuum* belong to the feast of Nativity. However, the contents of the unique *Gaudeamus* trope indicate rather the feast of the Assumption:[43]

> Angelorum chori exultent,
> quod virgo sacra celi principem iam conspicatur;

[42] Expressions similar to those in the London 14 unica include: 'Haec tibi Laurenti flammas superare dederunt: SANCTITAS ET MAGNIFICENTIA. Unde coronatus lauro sine fine triumphat' (AH 49. 275); 'Pro meritis meritam' (CT III, 164); 'Mystica pro meritis' (AH 49. 329); 'Praemia pro meritis' (AH 49. 580).

[43] Planchart, *Winchester*, I, 127. See also the unpublished dissertation by A.-K. Johansson, 'Tropes for the Proper of the Mass (The Feasts of the Blessed Virgin)' (Institutionen för Klassiska språk, Stockholms Universitet, 1988). Johansson argues in favour of the assignment of the *Gaudeamus* tropes to the Assumption feast, pointing out that the *Cantemus omnes* and *Aurea post Christum* sets are thus assigned in continental manuscripts.

exultemus omnes dicentes:

GAUDEAMUS OMNES IN DOMINO DIEM FESTUM CELEBRANTES
SUB HONORE MARIAE VIRGINIS,

Que sui corporis celi domino hospitium prebuit,

DE CUIUS ASSUMPTIONE GAUDENT ANGELI.

In arce poli semper voce consona canunt

ET CONLAUDANT FILIUM DEI.

que sui: qui sui

(fol. 27r; P 66)

This prose text is mainly concerned with paraphrasing the theme of angels' and men's praise in the Introit antiphon. The subjunctive *Gaudeamus* is echoed in *exultent* and *exultemus* in the first trope element, and the indicative verb form *canunt* in the last element takes up the indicatives *gaudent* and *conlaudant*.

Several groups of words are quite common in tropes and sequences, for example, *Angelorum chori, exultemus omnes dicentes, in arce poli, voce consona*. However, among these expressions are enclosed two distinct theological conceptions: 'The holy virgin is now beholding the Prince of Heaven,' and 'She has offered the hospice of her body to the Lord of Heaven'. *Celi principem* and *celi domino* thus become the key expressions upon which both the general offering of praise and the words defining the role of the Virgin are focused.

The order of words in the second trope element is refined: the subject *que* and predicate *prebuit* begin and end the sentence, and the accusative object *sui corporis hospitium* encloses in the centre the dative object *celi domino*. This ordering makes a contrast between the small and the great— the Virgin's body and heaven, the hospice and the Lord—even more marked.

There is nothing in this trope set that refers to the Nativity of the Virgin. On the contrary, the expression 'celi principem iam conspicatur' fits perfectly the feast of the Assumption. Moreover, each trope element uses an expression for heaven: *celi principem, celi domino, in arce poli*. In this way, the aspect of heaven is strongly underlined, as would be appropriate for the feast of the Assumption. This unique trope set is extremely well built and well adapted to the base text.

St Andrew

The feast of St Andrew has two unique trope sets connected with the Introit *Dominus secus mare*. This is a New Testament text, from the Gospel according to St Matthew (4. 18–19). The more usual introit for St Andrew and other apostles is *Mihi autem nimis* from Psalm 138. 17; *Dominus secus mare* is most often sung at the vigil mass,[44] but in some manuscripts it seems to have been used for the feast-day itself, with tropes.[45]

It is possible that, as in the case of the St John the Evangelist tropes, we have here a troped vigil mass. Immediately after the St Andrew tropes in London 14 follow those for the Common of apostles, with the Introit *Mihi autem*. There is no rubric, only a picture of the twelve apostles. The tropes to *Mihi autem* may have been intended both for the feast-day of St Andrew and for those of other apostles. The London 14 offertory and communion antiphons for St Andrew confuse rather than clarify this picture. The Offertory *In omnem terram* is more usual for the feast of SS Simon and Jude; Oxford 775 follows this practice, while Cambridge 473 assigns it to the Common of apostles. For the communion, London 14 presents two possibilities; first, the Communion *Ego vos elegi* (Cambridge 473, Common of apostles; Oxford 775, Common of confessors), second, the Communion *Dicit Andreas* (not in Cambridge 473; Oxford 775 also for Andrew). The unique tropes (see Figure 2) are the following:

Intuitu placido qui cernit cuncta regendo,
DOMINUS SECUS MARE GALILEE VIDIT DUOS FRATRES,
Aecclesie proceres sese nuntiante futuros
PETRUM ET ANDREAM, ET VOCAVIT EOS
Ore benigniloquo germanis talia dicens:
VENITE POST ME.
FACIAM VOS FIERI PISCATORES HOMINUM.

Cum populis pietate sui medicamina ferret,
ad rectum revocans tramitem moribunda sequentes,
DOMINUS SECUS MARE GALILEE VIDIT DUOS FRATRES
Undosi studio peragrantes marmora ponti,
PETRUM ET ANDREAM, ET VOCAVIT EOS,
Cum mali illorum perflans dulcedine corda:
VENITE POST ME.
FACIAM VOS FIERI PISCATORES HOMINUM.

medicamina: medicamine

(fols. 30v–31r; AH 49. 201, 202; P 44, 43)

Neither the language nor the prosody is impeccable. *Nuntiante* must be scanned as three syllables, the vowel 'i' being taken as a consonant.

In a simple unrhetorical way, the Introit describes how Jesus, walking by the sea of Galilee, saw two brothers. But the introductory trope element

---

[44.] *Antiphonale Missarum Sextuplex*, ed. R.-J. Hesbert (Brussels, 1935), nos. 168–9.

[45.] Bamberg, Staatsbibliothek Msc. ad. Bibl. 30, fols. 7a–6b (from northern France, possibly Reims), and Paris, Bibliothèque nationale lat. 13252, fol. 16r (St-Magloire, Paris).

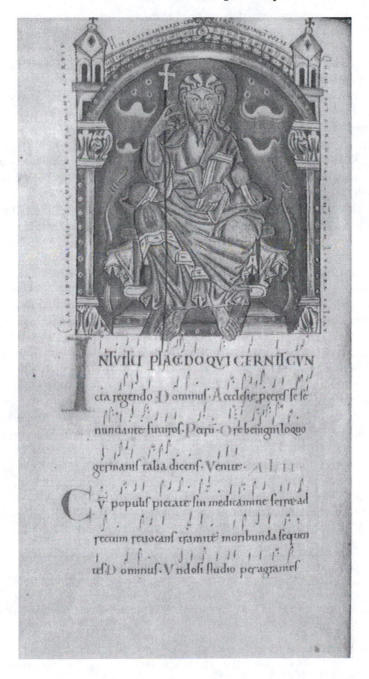

Figure 2. London, British Library Cotton Caligula A. xiv, fol. 30v

gives to this a totally new perspective: the Lord sees everything, 'cernit cuncta'. To this omniscience is added omnipotence: 'cuncta regendo'. Then there is even a third aspect, that of love, in this short hexameter line: *Intuitu placido*, 'with his kind regard'. The verb *vidit* in the Introit text has been expanded through two expressions, *intuitu placido* and *cernit cuncta regendo*. But more than this, the combination of this trope element with a straightforward narrative base text has been the means to express the divine qualities of Christ.

The next part of the Introit is again simple: '[he saw] Peter and Andrew, and he called to them'. The trope hints at their greatness through the word *proceres*, as well as a future perspective (*futuros*), and the first word in the trope, *aecclesie*, states their exact importance.[46]

Only the last part of the Introit, 'Follow me. I will make you fishers of men', has a spiritual perspective. To this the trope text just adds a kind of ornamental paraphrase. What gives character to this line is the opening word, *benigniloquo*, 'with the mildly-talking voice'. This way of composing a long word from two others is typical of English trope texts.[47]

The second trope is more rhetorical, using rather unusual words such as *tramitem* (path), and *undosi marmora ponti*, 'the wavy surface of the sea'. This hexameter is copied from Aldhelm or Alcuin, who use it in slightly different versions.[48] The introductory element is a short description of Jesus' activities when he walked in Galilee and met his future apostles. He was the healer and preacher, who called back to the right path those who followed things that bring death. The second trope element introduces the names of Peter and Andrew only by stating their occupation as fishermen with an almost Virgilian expression. This is a good example of how many tropes, particularly those in hexameters, infuse the Latin mass and its biblical world with a rhetorical style, using words characteristic of Latin classical poetry. The last hexameter contains a highly rhetorical expression that hardly could have been understood by many of the faithful worshippers: 'Blowing on their hearts with the sweetness of an apple'. The prosody makes it clear that *mali* does not have its usual meaning, 'evil', but instead 'apple'.[49] The whole trope element has apparently no other function than

[46.] The word *proceres* also appears in the hexameter inscription around the illumination of the 12 apostles, fol. 31r: *Bis seni proceres Christi sub pace valentes.*

[47.] Examples of composed Latin words in English tropes include: *almifico, clarisonas* (P 9); *almificus, veriloquum* (P 94); *vatidicis* (P 135); *altithroni* (P 147); *multiplico* (P 149); *veridica, celsithroni* (P 150); *stelligero, fluctivagi* (P 156); *pacificus* (P 160); *dulcisona* (P 164); *quadrafidi* (P 220). The hexameter inscriptions include *florigera* (fol. 3v) and *benefando* (fol. 20v).

[48.] *Venerat undosi vectus trans aequora ponti* (Alcuin, *Carm.* 1. 62, *MGH Poetae*, I, 171); *marmora ponti* (Aldhelm, *Aenigm.* 100. 75, *MGH Auc. Ant.* 15, 149; ibid. 71. 6, 129; Aldhelm, *Virg.* 825, *MGH Auc. Ant.* 388).

[49.] AH 49. 202.

to ornament beautifully the very simple statement of the Introit 'Follow me . . .'. The style of these tropes is far from that of the biblical tropes so often encountered.

The Common of Saints

The last part of London 14 contains a large repertory of Common tropes, with several unique items. Two of the eleven extant illuminations in the manuscript—the pictures of the twelve apostles (fol. 31r) and of virgins (fol. 36r)—belong within this section. By including an unusually expansive Common trope repertory, the manuscript makes direct compensation for its small number of saints' feasts; the Common tropes may be used for various saints not explicitly named in the book. The *commune martyrum* has this unicum:

> Contritis placidas prebes qui cordibus aures,
> INTRET IN CONSPECTU TUO, DOMINE, GEMITUS COMPEDITORUM,
> Quorum tu solita nexus pietate resolvis.
> REDDE VICINIS NOSTRIS SEPTUPLUM IN SINU EORUM,
> Quo semper dominum agnoscant te fore iustum.
> VINDICA SANGUINEM SANCTORUM TUORUM, QUI EFFUSUS EST.

(fol. 32r; AH 49. 375; P 92)

There is no allusion to martyrs. The text is not very clear but becomes quite comprehensible when considered mainly as an expansion and paraphrase of the Introit text:

> You who offer gentle ears to crushed hearts,
> LET THE SIGHING OF THE PRISONERS COME BEFORE YOU, LORD,
> whose bonds you resolve with your usual charity.
> RENDER TO OUR NEIGHBOURS SEVENFOLD, TO THE HEART,
> so that they always acknowledge you to be the righteous Lord.
> EXACT YOUR VENGEANCE FOR YOUR SAINTS' BLOOD THAT IS SHED.

The text is well organized, with two relative clauses expressing the Lord's gifts to his faithful, and a final exhortation to confess him as the righteous Lord. The function of this trope is clearly not only to embellish and expand, but, above all, to explain a difficult antiphon text.

The Introit text is itself a mosaic of three verses from Psalm 78 (11, 12, 10). Both the Psalm and the Introit contrast cruel enemies (the neighbouring peoples of Israel) with innocent victims (those who inherit). The expression 'sanguinem sanctorum tuorum' was apparently the reason for choosing this text as the Introit for martyrs. The trope text does not underline this. On the contrary, the three trope elements refer to Christians in general.

The word order in the first hexameter is entangled, the two main words (*prebes qui*) placed in the middle, surrounded by the two objècts with their attributes (*contritis cordibus, placidas aures*). In the second element the attribute *solita* and main word *pietate* enclose the accusative object *nexus*. Only the third element has a straightforward word order; but the hiatus *dominum | agnoscant*, where the last syllable in *dominum* is lengthened before the penthemimeral caesura, creates a striking pause. This trope set is rather refined; it belongs to the category of tropes which focus all the interest not on the saints but on the Lord.

The same feast has a set of unique offertory tropes, also in hexameter:

Firmati, vero vegetati flamine sancto
CONFITEBUNTUR CELI MIRABILIA TUA, DOMINE,
Qui satis ostendunt, quod sis mirabilis ipse,
ET VERITATEM TUAM IN ECCLESIA SANCTORUM,
Hanc tibi quo pulchram recinant per secula laudem.
ALLELUIA, ALLELUIA.
Mirificas et laudandas nimiumque stupendas
MISERICORDIAS TUAS DOMINE IN ETERNUM CANTABO . . .
Hoc resonent omnes, iubilent psallantque fideles,
QUONIAM QUIS IN NUBIBUS EQUABITUR DOMINO . . .

laudem: laudum   iubilent: iubilant

(Strengthened, truly inspired by the holy spirit,
THE HEAVENS WILL CONFESS YOUR WONDERS, LORD,
[the heavens] which show enough that you yourself are wonderful,
AND YOUR TRUTH IN THE SAINTS' CHURCH,
so that they will sing to you for ever this beautiful praise:
ALLELUIA, ALLELUIA.
Of the wonderful, praiseworthy and very amazing
COMPASSIONS OF THE LORD I WILL SING . . .
All the faithful will echo this and jubilate and sing,
SINCE WHO IN HEAVEN CAN BE EQUAL TO THE LORD.)

(fols. 32r–v; AH 49. 595; P 221–3)

This whole trope set is exclusively focused on the Lord. It expands the Offertory text using words of praise: *mirabilis, pulchram, laudem*. The three praising adjectives (*mirificas, laudandas, stupendas*) adorn *Misericordias* and fill up the hexameter, thus having the clear function of embellishment. The same could be said of the last hexameter, parallel in style, with its three verbs *resonent—iubilent—psallant*. Nothing is said about martyrs.

Alliteration on 'f' and 'v' is prominent in the first line. *Mirabilia* in the first part of the Introit is taken up in *mirabilis* in the second element, and perhaps also in *mirificas* in the fourth. *Laudem* in the third element is echoed in *laudandas* of the fourth. Certain unusual words like *vegetati* and *flamine* create a rhetorical effect.[50]

For the Introit *Ecce oculi*, London 14 offers three unique elements:[51]

Qui pariter cernunt moderamine cuncta, eia,
ECCE, OCULI DOMINI SUPER TIMENTES EUM,
SPERANTES IN MISERICORDIA EIUS, ALLELUIA,
Est que sola suis fiducia maxima servis,
UT ERIPIAT A MORTE ANIMAS EORUM,
Sponte sua qui dant pro domino corpora leto,
QUONIAM ADIUTOR ET PROTECTOR NOSTER EST.
ALLELUIA, ALLELUIA, ALLELUIA.

leto: loeto

(BEHOLD THE EYES OF THE LORD,
which equally, with government, see everything, eia,
ARE UPON THEM THAT FEAR HIM, HOPING IN HIS MERCY, ALLELUIA.
which only is the strongest security for his servants,
TO DELIVER THEIR SOULS FROM DEATH,
who willingly give their bodies to death for the Lord,
SINCE HE IS OUR HELPER AND PROTECTOR.)

(fol. 32v; AH 49. 750; P 298)

This is a coherent, though complicated, trope text; it expands and explains the text of the Introit. The *oculi domini* are taken up with the verb *cernunt*, and the aspect of omnipotence and omniscience is added through *moderamine cuncta*. The second trope element develops the word *misericordia*— the compassion of God is the only security. Only the last element, with its relative clause to *animas eorum*, refers to the martyrs: 'those who give their bodies'.

The hexameter verse has at least two problems. *Eia* has to be scanned as a three-syllable word with the 'i' as a long syllable. Further, there is a hiatus between *cuncta* and *eia*. The word *eia* is seldom contained within the hexameter in trope texts. *Domino* must be scanned as if the first syllable

---

[50] The word *vegeto* is also used, in a somewhat unclear sense, in the inscription for the first of the 11 illuminations (fol. 3v): 'Palmam victricem vegetans seseque felicem'.

[51] On fol. 32r, a trope for the Communion *Multitudo languentium* is followed by the rubric 'ALII', and this trope set with incipits from the Introit *Ecce oculi*. AH and Planchart, *Winchester*, II, mistakenly classify *Ecce oculi* as a Communion. For this correction I thank Dom Jean Claire of Solesmes.

were long and the last short. There is one rare poetical word, *leto*, instead
of *morti* (which would have fitted the verse perfectly); *cernunt moderamine*
and *fiducia* belong to a poetical repertory of words.

The majority of tropes assigned to the Common of martyrs in London
14 are unique, and the unique tropes are all in hexameter. The other
tropes, all in prose except one element, are biblical or more general in style
than those examined here.

The *commune unius martyris* has two widely known trope sets for the
Introits *In virtute* and *Laetabitur*. There are also two different antiphons
for the Communion, and the first of these has a unique trope:

Quem verum genui natum verax pater ipse,
SEMEL IURAVI IN SANCTO MEO:
SEMEN EIUS IN AETERNUM PERMANEBIT,
ET SEDES EIUS SICUT SOL IN CONSPECTU MEO . . .

(I HAVE ONCE SWORN IN MY SAINT,
whom I myself, the true father, have begotten as my true son:
HIS SEED WILL REMAIN FOREVER . . .).

                                  (fol. 33v; AH 49. 751; P 315)

This is strange. The Communion text is taken from Psalm 88. 36–8, and
used for different saints. However, using words that we often encounter in
the Christmas liturgy, the trope interprets the Communion text in a
christological way. Nothing gives the slightest hint of a martyr's feast. As
in the tropes for the Common of martyrs, we have here an example of a
trope element that is a relative clause preceding its correlate.

The last unique London 14 element belongs to the Offertory of the
Common of virgins, *Filie regum*. It is difficult to interpret. The base
liturgical text is that of Psalm 44 (the *Epithalamium Christi*). The trope
elements for the Offertory—known also in Winchester—praise chastity.
They do not give any difficulties. However, the Offertory verses and their
tropes are enigmatic. Only the second is unique to London 14:

Quod mecum mansit, manet, et per secla manebit,
ERUCTAVIT COR MEUM VERBUM BONUM.
DICO EGO OPERA MEA REGI.
Sustentans humiles concidens iure superbos.
LINGUA MEA CALAMUS SCRIBE VELOCITER SCRIBENTIS.

                              (fol. 36v; AH 49. 596; P 244, 245)

It is extremely difficult to find any good connection between these trope
elements and the base liturgical text. Where does *Sustentans* belong? The
best solution would be to understand it as referring to *regi*: 'God, the King,

who is supporting the humble but crushing the proud'. This is grammatically bad, but it is not exceptional and certainly not impossible.[52] Both trope elements are conventional in content. The first expresses God's everlasting existence. The second is a paraphrase of Virgil's famous description of Rome's power: 'Parcere subiectis et debellare suberbos' (*Aen.* 6. 853). Similar paraphrases can be found in other tropes.[53]

It does not seem unlikely that the two elements always belonged together; equally, they could easily be used in different contexts. They represent a way of troping liturgical texts where the reference to the subject of the feast, in this case Holy Virgins, is very weak. The base text belongs to the so-called '*Epithalamium Christi*', associated with the Song of Songs. The first element might refer to God's word, that will last forever—*verbum* has hardly any christological sense here. The second element alludes vaguely to God's upholding the humble.

Repertorial Aspects of the Unica Tropes

The London 14 trope repertory is closely related to that represented in the two Winchester Tropers, all three sources sharing a substantial number of tropes not known in continental books. The unique English repertory includes a particularly high proportion of offertory and communion tropes. Of the 560 trope elements preserved in London 14, sixty-three are, however, unique to this manuscript. These fall into two categories: first, either single, or, in some cases, pairs of elements added to an existing series, and second, complete trope sets for a particular chant.

To the first of these groups belong the unique elements for the first Christmas mass Introit, the Innocents Offertory, the Epiphany Offertory, the Easter Monday Introit, a Holy Cross Introit, the Pentecost Introit (two), the St Peter Communion, the Communion of a martyr, and the Offertory of a confessor. This makes ten in all. To the second group belong two full sets of trope elements for a St John the Evangelist Introit, one for the Easter Offertory, one for a Holy Cross Introit, two for the Trinity Introit, one for the St John the Baptist Introit, two for the St Laurence Introit, one for the BVM Assumption Introit, two for the St Andrew Introit, two for Martyrs' Introits and another for the Offertory.

---

[52] In Latin literature, particularly in vulgar or late texts, an apposition to a word in an inflected case may appear in the nominative. Dag Norberg explains that it can have 'den Character eines Nominalsatzes'. See his *Syntaktische Forschungen auf dem Gebiet des Spätlateins und des frühen Mittellateins*, Uppsala Universitets Årsskrift 9 (Uppsala, 1943), 64–74. Cf. also J. B. Hofmann and A. Szantyr, *Lateinische Syntax und Stilistik* (Munich, 1965), 27–8.

[53] Cf. *Parcens conversis qui pravis debita reddis* (CT 1, 154); *Parcere pacificis et debellare superbos* (*Iohannes Baptista*) (AH 49. 254).

With the exception of the offertory series for Easter, all the unique full trope sets in London 14 belong to saints' feasts or to the two less common feasts of Trinity and the Holy Cross. In fact, in the majority of tropers, the Trinity feast is not celebrated with tropes. But it is significant that a manuscript like Apt 17, which contains so much reworking and reorganization, as well as unica, should have a large number of Trinity tropes. The Beneventan tropers also contain Trinity tropes, while they are completely absent from Eastern Frankish sources.

The feasts of St John the Evangelist and St Andrew were apparently of some importance for the compiler of London 14. It seems likely that the rather clumsy unique trope for the vigil mass of St John, *Hoc mihi donaverat*, was created in England.

The St Laurence and St Peter tropes are all of a rather banal kind, using familiar stock phrases. And the texts of the tropes for Commons of saints could hardly be paler. It would not be astonishing if other collectors of tropes had preferred other items (which might at the very least focus on the category of saint). But the compiler of London 14 collected a range of tropes for different Commons of saints—more than we now possess, judging from the incomplete state of the book—and the lack of tropes for specific saints could thus be compensated for.

Among the unique tropes there are some of a more interesting and sophisticated character. These include the other two St John pieces, especially the *Lux vera Christus* set, which is reminiscent of East Frankish tropes. Likewise, the St Andrew hexameter tropes provide examples of a highly rhetorical style. In the tropes for the feasts of the Holy Cross and Trinity, theological ideas prevail over mere praising, and the choice of words is rather special.

Style

The vast majority of the unica are in hexameter verse. Those in prose include the two *versus ante officium* (John the Evangelist, Holy Innocents), the set for the feast-day of St John the Evangelist, the second St Laurence Introit set and that for the Assumption Introit. Even here, the structured prose (*Kunstprosa*) sometimes contains hexameter fragments. As one might expect at this time, all the hexameters except four have a penthemimeral caesura. There are very few cases of hiatus and elision, and only sixteen of the forty-eight hexameters with penthemimeral caesura are leonine. In most of these cases it is difficult to argue that the leonine rhymes were actually intended.

In such a limited amount of material it is impossible to make valid statistical investigations of the prosody. Various irregularities appear in more or less the same number of cases as in the Winchester repertory. However, London 14 contains a few instances of remarkably weak versification. The trope *Hoc mihi donaverat* for the vigil of St John has prosodic errors in every one of its three hexameters. The trope added in the margin for the Introit of St Laurence contains one error, as does the second trope set for St Andrew (*Cum populis pietate*), and the Introit trope set for martyrs (*Qui pariter cernunt*) has two clear anomalies. Further, in the unique elements inserted in the sets for the Innocents and Epiphany Offertories, we find irregularities. At the same time, some trope sets such as *Iudicium magno* (Easter Offertory), *Hierusalem solio* for the Holy Cross, *Effectrix rerum* for the Trinity, *Vatum firma* for St John the Baptist, the first set for St Andrew, and the Offertory set *Firmati vero* for martyrs, are almost perfectly correct. Thus, the style, versification, and linguistic character of the unique tropes apparently point to a variety of origins.

Content and Function

Equally, the metaphors used and the relation of the unique tropes to their liturgical base chants show a diversity of techniques and approaches. As already suggested, some of the trope sets are rather colourless in their theological content, and tend to employ standard metaphors and phrases. Some tropes, such as *Hoc mihi donaverat* (St John the Evangelist), *Vatum firma* (St John the Baptist), and the two Introit trope sets for St Andrew (*Intuitu placido, Cum populis pietate*) choose simply to paraphrase the base text. But this can be done with different degrees of originality. The choice of metaphors and words in the St Andrew tropes, for example, is specific and certainly not banal. The two *versus ante officium*, the Easter Offertory trope *Iudicium magno*, the Holy Cross tropes, and the first Trinity trope set have a fairly elaborate character. The Offertory trope for martyrs, *Firmati vero vegetati*, combines simple ideas with rhetorical language. A few of the unique tropes have the function of introducing the liturgical base text in an explanatory way; both *Hymnidicis te Christe* (Advent), and *Rex regum dominus* (St Peter Communion) are of this kind.

Relation to the Winchester and Continental Repertories

Out of a vast material from which the arrangers of the Winchester trope repertory must have made a selection, London 14 kept a great number of tropes. We can easily see this by comparing the concordance patterns of the Winchester and London 14 repertories with North Frankish, East Frankish, Aquitainian, and other groups. London 14 tropes with continental concordances (but absent from the Winchester books) are often of a similar character to those found in both Winchester and London 14 (and in continental books). One London 14 trope, *Hodie quemadmodum* (Purification), appears otherwise in Regensburg and Saint-Gall only, and another, *Promissam dudum gaudentes* (also Purification), only in southern Italy. All this suggests that behind the extant insular trope manuscripts lies access to a vast continental repertory.

The reasons why the Winchester repertory appears more selective than that in London 14 may be twofold. Whether composed in England or on the Continent, many of the tropes in London 14 are defective; the Winchester arrangers may simply have rejected these. Secondly, some of the London 14 material may not have been required at Winchester. The feasts of the Holy Cross and St Andrew, for example, are given much greater importance in London 14 than in either of the Winchester sources. And the Trinity feast is entirely unrepresented in the Winchester tropes.

Before the Winchester books were copied, at least one, perhaps two or three English tropers must have existed. We could imagine that these were of the 'anthology' type, collecting continental as well as insular tropes. Some of this material might also have circulated in *libelli* or on small sheets containing single tropes or groups of tropes. The two existing Winchester sources, Oxford 775 and Cambridge 473, represent another type of book. These include well-organized repertories, containing only what is needed for each celebration. Further, fragmentary trope sets were deliberately completed, using material either from continental books, or, if necessary, new compositions.

It is very clear that all the material copied in the Winchester books was also available to the compiler of London 14. What London 14 lacks from the Winchester repertory is precisely what we would expect to find on those folios now lost from the codex. It is not unthinkable that the compiler of London 14 had the two Winchester books in his own hands.

But I believe that the compiler of London 14 had access to much larger English trope collections, older than the existing Winchester books. Where the Winchester trope arrangers were reluctant to keep certain single trope elements, for the offertory verse or for a communion for example, these were copied into London 14. The later source probably includes, therefore, fragments of repertories older than that of Winchester. London 14 includes much French material as well as East Frankish and even Italian tropes. It has the only extant Alleluia *prosula* in an eleventh-century insular source, the famous *Iam redeunt gaudia*, in an absolutely unique version. All this might have been assembled in the first English trope books and later rejected by the Winchester monks but copied into London 14. Where the Winchester arrangers were selective and, perhaps for good reason, cut out material with bad verse or incomprehensible Latin, the compiler of

London 14 did not understand better than to keep it. When the liturgists in Winchester judged that the *versus ante officium* had to be of reasonable length in order to be used in the celebration, the original long creations were kept in London 14.

Preparation of London 14

Now, in the middle of the eleventh century, a new trope book was to be written, this time for a special purpose. It was to be extremely luxurious, perhaps intended for a private individual, or for a royal or archbishop's chapel. The following steps had to be taken: the tropes should be collected, chosen, and arranged in order; they should be copied out and supplied with musical notation, and the rubrics, initials, and illuminations added. Some details of the order in which this work was undertaken are unclear. But in one instance, an illumination destroyed the trope texts it accompanies. And some rubrics were never added.

The beautiful calligraphy of London 14 offers a juxtaposition of the most contrasting and varied material. Only the extensive errors reveal how little the text scribe really understood. Was he only copying a book placed before him, or was he executing the orders of someone who had collected tropes from various places and put several books in front of him? Given the fact that the book's presentation is so special, I am inclined to believe in the second alternative. London 14 has preserved for posterity not only less good tropes, but also some interesting and highly original tropes from otherwise lost repertories. It is not only the accomplished and interesting illuminations, but the literary content also, which together make this book an important witness to English medieval culture.

3

Remarks on the Alleluia and Responsory Series in the Winchester Troper

MICHEL HUGLO

(Centre National de la Recherche Scientifique, Paris)

The two surviving witnesses to the Winchester Troper, Oxford, Bodleian Library Bodley 775 (Oxford 775) and Cambridge, Corpus Christi College 473 (Cambridge 473), derive from an earlier model of the beginning of the tenth century.[1] Thanks to the critical edition of tropes published by the Corpus Troporum team and to Planchart's study of the Winchester repertory, it has been possible—on the basis of an examination of Christmas and Easter trope elements—to understand the relations of this Winchester trope repertory to that in the other extant English Troper (London, British Library Cotton Caligula A. xiv)[2] and to continental repertories, notably those of Prüm, Echternach, and Saint-Germain-des-Prés.[3]

[1.] Both manuscripts have been described several times, most recently by A. E. Planchart, *The Repertory of Tropes at Winchester*, 2 vols. (Princeton, NJ, 1977), I, 14–20, 34–43; for Cambridge 473 see also the entry by D. Leech-Wilkinson in *Cambridge Music Manuscripts 900–1700*, ed. I. Fenlon (Cambridge, 1982), 13–17. According to Planchart, the redaction of Cambridge 473 dates from the years 996–1006, at the time when Wulfstan, disciple of Æthelwold, took up the position of cantor at Winchester.

[2.] For a study of this repertory, with further bibliography on the manuscript, see R. Jacobsson, 'Unica in the Cotton Caligula Troper', *supra*.

[3.] *Tropes du propre de la messe 1: Cycle de Noël*, ed. R. Jonsson, Corpus Troporum I (Stockholm, 1975); *Tropes du propre de la messe 2: Cycle de Pâques*, ed. G. Björkvall, G. Iversen, and R. Jonsson, Corpus Troporum III (Stockholm, 1982). See also Planchart, *Winchester*, I, 392, and Michel Huglo, 'Centres de production, cercles de diffusion', paper read at the fourth European Science Foundation conference on tropes, Sept. 1987. The manuscript Paris, Bibliothèque nationale lat. 13252 is one of only three remaining fragments from the library of St-Magloire; however, it was probably written and notated at St-Germain-des-Prés.

To know more of the 'base repertory', that is, the proper chants of the mass and the office to which these tropes belong, however, we must return to the work begun by Walter Howard Frere in the introduction to his *Winchester Troper*.[4] The present study deals with two parts of this proper repertory:

1. the series of alleluias for summer Sundays;
2. the selection of responsories for the office, intended for 'organization', that is, to be sung in two-voice organum.

The Winchester Alleluia Series

The Winchester alleluia series for the Sundays after Pentecost is contained in full in Oxford 775 but only in reduced form in Cambridge 473.[5] It begins with the verse *In te domine speravi* drawn from Psalm 30, and contains twenty-three verses from the psalms which are not arranged in numerical order, as shown in the left-hand column of Table 1. Alleluia series which do not follow the numerical order of the psalms are transmitted by manuscripts older than those containing the numerically ordered series *Deux judex* (N. and W. Europe), *Domine deus meus* (Germanic-speaking countries), *Verba mea* (Aquitaine, Italy, etc.); these latter prevailed in the middle ages up to the age of printing.[6]

The lists of the series *In te domine speravi* in English and continental sources should now be compared. For Table 1 only those series which are related up to a maximum of four points of difference have been retained; the Metz–Verdun series was left out since it contains twenty verses in common with the series studied here but in a totally different order.

We note first that the Bury and New Minster (of Winchester) groups are precisely identical;[7] after the Norman Conquest, Winchester and Bury St Edmunds retained their old alleluia series rather than adopt Norman

---

[4.] W. H. Frere, *The Winchester Troper*, Henry Bradshaw Society 8 (London, 1894).

[5.] Cambridge 473 has organal settings of the verses for the 1st, 4th, 15th, 16th, 17th, and 19th Sundays after Pentecost only. A. Machabey ('Remarques sur le Winchester Troper', *Festschrift für Heinrich Besseler* (Leipzig, 1961), 67–90) omitted to point out that the manuscript also includes the plainsong melodies for alleluia verses, often corresponding to the organal voices copied in another part of the book.

[6.] For non-numerically ordered alleluia lists see M. Huglo, *Les Livres de chant liturgique*, Typologie des sources historiques 52 (Turnhout, 1988), table XI/1. On the later lists see M. Huglo, 'Les Listes alléluiatiques dans les témoins du graduel grégorien', *Speculum Musicae Artis: Festgabe für Heinrich Husmann zum 60. Geburtstag*, ed. H. Becker and R. Gerlach (Munich, 1970), 219–27.

[7.] The Bury list is from Laon, Bibliothèque municipale 238, and the New Minster list from Le Havre, Bibliothèque municipale 330 (ed. D. H. Turner, Henry Bradshaw Society 93 (London, 1962)).

series. This group is almost identical with Corbie,[8] which itself has two differences from the Saint-Denis series.[9] The Winchester (Old Minster) series has four differences from Corbie and three from the Saint-Denis series.[10] We should not be tempted to conclude too hastily, however, that the Winchester model depends on Corbie rather than on Saint-Denis; the differences are minimal. It is to the 'archaic Corbie–Saint-Denis group' that both the Old and New Minster series are related. This is unsurprising since Æthelwold, Bishop of Winchester (d. 984) had had trained cantors brought to Winchester from Corbie, who must be assumed to have brought with them an antiphoner and a gradual.

The Winchester Responsories with Organum

The repertory of office responsories deserves special study since it may help to orientate research on the sources of Winchester polyphony. Following a usage which dates back to the tenth century at least, responsories at the end of each nocturn were ornamented.[11] This ornamentation often consisted in the addition of a *neuma*; and, subsequently, the *neuma* was spread out over an assonanced text—which came to be known as a *prosa, prosula, prosella, prosellus*. This is the standard type of 'trope melogène' for the office. The function of the *neuma* and of the corresponding *prosula* is purely ornamental, not liturgical. Responsories which have been musically and textually elaborated in this way typically end one of the nocturns on feast-days—whence their place in the canonical office (R. III, VI, or IX) and in the monastic office (R. IV, VIII, or XII)—or are sometimes found in first vespers on high feast-days.

In the churches of the Loire valley and at Saint-Maur-des-Fossés, this kind of ornamentation was systematically introduced into every high feast in the liturgical cycle. But elsewhere responsories were provided with a vertical type of ornamentation by being sung in two voices.

[8.] The Corbie alleluia list is found in the well-known Antiphoner of Mont-Renaud (10th C.; facs. edn.: *Le Manuscrit du Mont-Renaud*, Paléographie musicale 16 (Solesmes, 1955)); Amiens, Bibliothèque municipale 155 (11th C.); Paris, Bibliothèque nationale lat. 18010 (11th C.); Paris, Bibliothèque nationale lat. 11522 (early 12th C.).

[9.] The St-Denis list appears in Paris, Bibliothèque Mazarine 384 (11th C.); Paris, Bibliothèque nationale lat. 1107 (mid-13th C.); Paris, Bibliothèque nationale lat. 10505 (14th C.); Rome, Biblioteca Casanatense 603 (13th C.); and a notated missal from St-Denis in the Victoria and Albert Museum, London. Two 9th-C. Parisian manuscripts (Paris, Bibliothèque Ste-Geneviève 111 and Rome, Vatican Ottoboni 313) diverge from St-Denis at several points after the 17th Sunday. On the St-Denis lists, see A. E. Walters, *Music and Ritual at the Royal Abbey of Saint-Denis 567–1567*, Ph.D. diss. (University of Yale, 1984).

[10.] The Tours series has four differences from Winchester (New Minster).

[11.] See M. Huglo, 'Le Principe d'organisation des répons nocturnes à Notre Dame de Paris', a paper given at the Wolfenbüttel Symposium *Das 'Ereignis' Notre-Dame*, Apr. 1985.

TABLE I. *Alleluia list* In te domine speravi *(the numbers in brackets refer to the psalm from which the verse is drawn)*

Saint-Denis	Corbie	Bury	New Minster	Winchester
1 In te domine speravi (30)	=	=	=	=
2 Diligam te (17)	=	=	=	Jubilate (99)
3 Venite exultemus (94)	=	=	=	=
4 Confitemini domino (104)	=	=	=	=
5 Qui timent (113)	=	=	=	=
6 Domine refugium (89)	=	=	=	=
7 Omnes gentes (46)	=	=	=	=
8 Quoniam deus (94)	=	=	=	=
9 Qui sanat (146)	=	=	=	=
10 Letatus sum (121)	=	=	=	=
11 Paratum cor (107)	=	=	=	=
12 Exultate deo (80)	=	=	=	=

13 Dominus regnavit (92)		=	=		
14 Jubilate (99)		=	=	=	
15 Domine deus salutis (87)		=	=		Lauda Jerusalem (147)
16 Laudate dominum omnes gentes (116)		=	=	=	
17 Deus judex (7)		=	=	=	
18 Qui posuit (147)		=	=	=	
19	Qui confidunt (124)	=	=	=	
— Adorabo (137) [Paris M. 384]	=(Paris 11522)	=	=		
— Eripe me (58)					
20	Redempt. (110)	=	=		
— Attendite (77)		=	=		Diligam te (17)
21 Te decet (64)		=	=		
22 De profundis (129)		=	=		+ V. Replebimur
23 Dextera dei (117)	Dextera domini	=	=		

One might ask oneself, therefore, whether these 'diaphonic' responsories for the end of the nocturn, of which so few traces remain in liturgical books or in historical sources, might not have been much more widespread than we can today assert in the light of the few extant written examples.[12] We might even go so far as to suggest that, where neither tropes nor *prosulae* were sung (as, for example, at Cluny, Corbie, and Saint-Denis), the responsories at the end of the nocturns on high feast-days would have been polyphonically elaborated. This is pure conjecture and without any documentary basis other than the example of Fleury (according to the Customary of Thierry of Amorbach).[13]

The Winchester sources have a wide repertory of tropes for both the proper and ordinary of the mass, but not a single *prosula* for responsories of the office. The Cambridge manuscript gives only a repertory of organa for the responsories of the office, with indications of when they are to be performed, usually at the end of the nocturn and most often in twelfth place—before the Te Deum, which may itself have been performed polyphonically.[14]

Cambridge 473 gives a list of around sixty organa for the office, some of them invitatories but for the most part responsories allotted to Sundays or to feasts of the Temporale and Sanctorale.[15] Within this repertory three special series, each for a particular feast, can be distinguished: one for the Trinity (nos. 127–36, listed in Table 2), the second for apostles and evangelists (nos. 137–48, listed in Table 3), and the last for St Swithun (nos. 153–64). This multiplicity of organa for single feasts runs contrary to the principle which has just been expounded and merits further discussion.

The responsories for feasts of the apostles and evangelists, twelve in number, borrow their text from the sublime vision of the prophet Ezekiel (Ezekiel 1). These twelve responsories, whose diffusion in manuscript form was extremely limited, were not all polyphonically performed on the feast of each apostle. Just one of the series sufficed for the twelfth matins responsory on an individual feast, the others being sung in plainsong.

[12.] On the extant early examples of French polyphony, see W. Arlt, 'Stylistic Layers in Eleventh-Century Polyphony', *infra*.

[13.] See A. Davril, 'Un moine de Fleury aux environs de l'an mil: Thierry dit d'Amorbach', *Études ligériennes d'histoire et d'archéologie médiévales*, ed. R. Louis (Paris, 1975), 97–104; the Customary is edited in Corpus Consuetudinum Monasticarum 9 (Siegburg, 1976), 296 ff.

[14.] As implied in the *Musica Enchiriadis* treatises; see H. Schmid, *Musica et scolica enchiriadis, una cum aliquibus tractatulis adiunctis* (Munich, 1981), and the commentaries in N. C. Phillips, *Musica et Scolica Enchiriadis. The Literary, Theoretical and Musical Sources*, Ph.D. diss. (New York University, 1984).

[15.] The organa are listed in A. Holschneider, *Die Organa von Winchester* (Hildesheim, 1968), 40–60; I have adopted here the numbering system used by Holschneider.

For the polyphonic settings of the Trinity responsories we can suggest two modes of use: first, on Trinity Sunday all the responsories could be sung in organum, except the tenth and eleventh, following the order indicated in Cambridge 473 with roman numerals; second, it is quite possible that on each Sunday during the summer only one of these responsories was sung at the end of the third nocturn, following a usage which was still practised in Paris in the twelfth century.[16]

Finally, in building up a group of organa for feasts of St Swithun, responsories of the Common were used. Swithun had died in 862 and, under Æthelwold's regime, a solemn translation of his relics took place on 15 July 971.[17]

It now remains to examine the origin of these three series and, if possible, discover a way of comparing these fragments of English office liturgy with continental liturgical books. While a comparison with books from Saint-Denis and Saint-Maur-des-Fossés can be made, the same cannot be said of Corbie, the liturgy of the office in the Picard abbey having had to cede to Cluniac practices in the twelfth century under the regime of Abbot Robert (d. 1142). Our only evidence of the office liturgy at Corbie in the earlier period comes from the tenth-century Antiphoner of Mont-Renaud, given that this book is certainly of Corbie origin. The base repertory of the Cambridge 473 responsory organa can usefully be compared with that of the monastic antiphoners edited in the second volume of *Corpus Antiphonalium Officii* (*CAO*)[18] and the Worcester Antiphoner, whose relations with both Winchester and Corbie–Saint-Denis have been demonstrated elsewhere.[19]

D = St-Denis   (Paris, Bibliothèque nationale lat. 17296)
F = St-Maur-des-Fossés (Paris, Bibliothèque nationale lat. 12584)[20]
S = Silos   (London, British Library add. 30850)[21]
W = Worcester   (Worcester, Chapter Library F. 160)[22]

[16.] 'In dominicis diebus estivalibus nonum responsorium de Trinitate cantamus': from Iohannis Beleth, *Summa de ecclesiasticis officiis*, ed. H. Douteil, Corpus Christianorum, Continuatio medievalis 41A (Turnhout, 1976), chs. 26b, 121t.

[17.] On the Swithun organa see S. Rankin, 'Winchester Polyphony', *infra*.

[18.] *Corpus Antiphonalium Officii*, ed. R.-J. Hesbert, 6 vols. (Rome, 1963–79), II, *Manuscripti 'cursus monasticus'* (Rome, 1965).

[19.] R.-J. Hesbert, 'Les antiphonaires monastiques insulaires', *Revue bénédictine* 92 (1982), 358–75, esp. 362–3.

[20.] This source also includes some polyphonic fragments; see M. Huglo 'Les débuts de la polyphonie à Paris: les premiers *organa* parisiens', *Aktuelle Fragen der musikbezogenen Mittelalterforschung*, Forum Musicologicum 3 (Winterthur, 1982), 93–164, at 98–107 and pl. 1, and Arlt, 'Stylistic Layers', *infra*.

[21.] This source uses Visigothic notation, but transmits a southern French repertory: facs. ed. I. Fernández de la Cuesta, *Antiphonale Silense* (Madrid, 1985).

[22.] Facs. ed. *Antiphonaire monastique (XIIIᵉ siècle)*, Paléographie musicale 12 (Tournai, 1922).

In the commentary below, each responsory is preceded by one, and sometimes two, numbers; the first refers to Holschneider's catalogue, the second—in roman numerals—to rubrics in the source, which may indicate the place of individual pieces within the matins series of twelve responsories.

INCIPIUNT MELLIFLUA ORGANORUM MODULAMINA (Cambridge 473, fol. 135r)

ORGANA SUPER RESPONSORIA (fol. 175v)

No. 110, *O Juda et Hierusalem*
The textual variant from the more usual *Judaea et Jerusalem* agrees with D (*CAO* IV, 7040). This responsory was intended for first vespers of the Nativity.[23]

No. 112, VIII, *Te laudent angeli*
The Mont-Renaud Antiphoner gives this responsory in twelfth place. It appears also in D and S (*CAO* IV, 7756).

No. 113, XII, *Descendit de caelis*
This responsory was universally known, but used in varied positions; most often it appeared in the first nocturn.

No. 115, IV, *Sancte dei pretiose*
Despite the explicit rubric, Holschneider thought that this was a hymn,[24] since the text does not contain a verse. In fact, the verse of this responsory, *Ut tuo propitiatus* (drawn from the same text as the main part of the responsory) appears in a polyphonic setting in another English source.[25] The responsory is found in D as R. VIII and in F as R. IV with a *prosula* (*CAO* I, 7575).

No. 119, XII, *Hodie martirum flores*
In the Mont-Renaud Antiphoner, this responsory is again in twelfth place, its melody added in Lotharingian neumes (rather than the central-French type more usual in this source). In W as R. XII, and D as R. VII (*CAO* IV, 6853).

No. 121, XII, *Gaude Maria virgo*
This also appears in twelfth place in D, F (*CAO* IV, 6759), and W. In a manuscript of Saint-Maur-des-Fossés its incipit is notated in organum.[26]

---

[23] The rubric can be read on fol. 175v of Cambridge 473, rep. in Holschneider, *Organa*, pl. 12a.

[24] Cf. Analecta Hymnica 48. 83.

[25] See the reproductions from Oxford, Bodleian Library Bodley 572 in H. E. Woolridge, *Early English Harmony* (London, 1897), pl. 1; E. W. B. Nicholson, *Early Bodleian Music* (Oxford, 1913), pl. 16; H. Besseler and P. Gülke, *Schriftbild der mehrstimmigen Musik*, Musikgeschichte in Bildern III/5 (Leipzig, 1973), pl. 2.

[26] See Huglo, 'Débuts', 112–15 and pl. 4, and Arlt, *infra*.

No. 123, XII, *O pastor apostolice*
For St Gregory (12 March), apostle of England, and found in very diverse sources.[27]

Nos. 127–36
Series of responsories for the office of the Holy Trinity. Stephen of Liège composed nine responsories in honour of the Holy Trinity, following for the melodies the order of the eight modes, the first responsory assigned to the first mode, the second to the second, and so on.[28] This special order is faithfully reproduced in three secular Antiphoners, all of which have connections with Liège: Durham, Chapter Library B III 11, originating from Liège (G), Bamberg, Staatsbibliothek lit. 23, originating from Bamberg Cathedral, whose school had as its first master Durant de Liège (B), and Verona, Biblioteca capitolare 98, from Verona Cathedral (V). Rathier, monk of Lobbes (d. 974), was Bishop of Verona from 932 to 940 and 962 to 968; for two years (954–6) he held the episcopate of Liège. With these three manuscripts can be associated the Hartker Antiphoner, Saint-Gall Stiftsbibliothek 390–1 which, here as in other places, only offers a series of nine rather than twelve responsories.

The order of the responsories set by Stephen of Liège is altered in other secular antiphoners but above all in monastic antiphoners, which required three extra responsories to achieve the twelve required by the rule of St Benedict. Table 2 shows the order of presentation in various sources; it is not clear from this comparison that the order of responsories in Cambridge 473 has any relation to French sources. The *de Trinitate* series was copied by a second hand in Cambridge 473.[29]

Nos. 137–48
Series of responsories for feasts of the apostles and evangelists. For a comparison with D, S, W, and F, see Table 3.

No. 150 *Advenit ignis*
This responsory occupies ninth place in the Parisian sources D and F (*CAO* IV, 6053), following the model of the Cathedral of St Stephen in Paris, before the Pentecost office was reduced from three nocturns to just one.

Nos. 153–64
The office for the patronal celebration of St Swithun consists of ten responsories drawn from the Common of confessors; these chants are found more or less anywhere, adapting the melody only for the name of the

[27]. Cf. M. Bernard, 'Un recueil inédit du xiie siècle et la copie aquitaine de l'office versifié de Saint Grégoire', *Études grégoriennes* 16 (1977), 145–59.
[28]. A. Auda, *L'École musicale liègeoise au xe siècle: Étienne de Liège*, Académie royale de Belgique, Classe des Beaux-arts, Mémoires II. 1 (Brussels, 1923), 58, 113, and 187; R. Jonsson, *Historia* (Stockholm, 1968), 115–83; M. Huglo, *Les Tonaires* (Paris, 1971), 126.
[29]. Cf. Planchart, *Winchester*, I, 22.

TABLE 2. Historia de Sanctissima Trinitate: *The Responsories of Stephen of Liège*

		In secular antiphoners	In monastic antiphoners				
G B V	Mode	E	D	F S	W	Winch.	
R. 1 Benedicat nos deus	I	1	1	1	1	1	
2 Benedictus dominus	II	2	2	2	2	2	
3 Quis deus magnus	III	3	3	3	3	3	
R. 4 Magnus dominus	IV	4	4	4	4	4	
5 Gloria patri, geniteque	V	5	5	5	5		
6 Honor virtus	VI	6	6	6	7	5	
		(7) Deum time	7	12			
R. 7 Summae Trinitati	VII	8	8	9	12	6	
8 Benedicamus patrem	VIII	9	9	7	8	8	
9 Te deum patrem	III		10	10	11	9	
Extra responsories						[10–11]	
Tibi laus, tibi gloria			11	8	9	7	
O beata Trinitas			12	11			
Benedictio et claritas					6	12	
Unus est dominus					10		

G =   French antiphoner (Durham, Chapter Library B III 11).
B =   Bamberg (Bamberg, Staatsbibliothek lit. 23).
V =   Verona (Verona, Biblioteca capitolare 98).
E =   Ivrea (Ivrea, Biblioteca capitolare 106).
D =   St-Denis (Paris, Bibliothèque nationale lat. 17296).
F =   St-Maur-des-Fossés (Paris, Bibliothèque nationale lat. 12584).
S =   Silos (London, British Library add. 30850).
W =   Worcester (Worcester, Chapter Library F.160).
Winch. = Winchester (Cambridge, Corpus Christi College 473).

saint celebrated. *Sint lumbi vestri* (no. 155) is of French origin.[30] *Pater insignis* (no. 156) is found only in D, adapted to the name of St Benedict. And finally, *Agmina sacra* (no. 157) could be adapted to several names (Martin, Vaast, Oswald, Eugene, etc.).

No. 166 *Inter natos*

This responsory occupies twelfth place in the office for 24 June (St John the Baptist) in D and F (*CAO* IV, 6979). In Cambridge 473 its position is not indicated.

[30.] Cf. Huglo, 'Débuts', 123, n. 119.

TABLE 3. *Responsories of the Common of apostles and evangelists*

D S W		Mode	F	Winchester
R.	1 In visione dei	I	1	1 (no. 137)
	2 Quattuor facies uni	II	2	2 (no. 138)
	3 Similitudo vultus	III	3	4 (no. 140)
	4 Facies et pennas	IV	4	3 (no. 139)
R.	5 Similitudo aspectus	V	5	5 (no. 141)
	6 Quattuor animalia	VI	6	6 (no. 142)
	7 Cum aspicerem anim.	VII	9	12 (no. 148)
	8 Statura erat	<u>VIII</u>	7	7 (no. 136)
R.	9 Cum ambularent	I	8	8 (no. 144)
	10 Euntibus animalibus	III	10	9 (no. 145)
	11 Species firmamenti	VIII	11	11 (no. 147)
	12 Audiebam sonus	I	12	10 (no. 146)

No. 167 *Petre amas me*
F has this responsory set in organum as the last for the third nocturn.[31] In D it is assigned to the end of the third nocturn (*CAO* IV, 7382) and in Parisian usage from the end of the twelfth century, it was performed polyphonically at the end of the second nocturn (i.e. in sixth place).[32]

No. 168 *Vir inclitus Dionisius*
Naturally, this responsory appears in D and F, in eighth place (*CAO* IV, 7897). In Cambridge 473 its position is not specified.

In 1913 E. W. B. Nicholson suggested for Cambridge 473 the name 'Tours–Winchester Troper'. More recent researches on this remarkable manuscript, notably those of Alejandro Planchart, have forced the abandonment of the Tours hypothesis, as the north of France and the Rhineland have emerged as appropriate fields of enquiry. If this conclusion is valid for the trope repertory, may it also be applied to the 'base repertory' of the Winchester gradual and antiphoner? The analyses presented above invite the conclusion that it is in the 'archaic Corbie–Saint-Denis group'[33] that the sources of the 'base repertory' of Winchester and its satellites should be sought.

It would be unwise, however, to attribute priority of influence to one or other of these two French monasteries since the number, nature, and date of the liturgical books used for the comparison are unequal for the two

---

[31.] Cf. Huglo, 'Débuts', 104.
[32.] See the table in Huglo, 'Débuts', 102.
[33.] This definition is Dom J. Hourlier's: often in the course of my research I have confirmed its correctness, but I am still searching for its ultimate reason.

sides. According to Planchart, one of the two Winchester neumatic notations is closely related to that of Saint-Denis;[34] at the same time we must recognize that certain insular notations are so close to the Corbie/ Beauvais type that a more rigorous examination is necessary in order to distinguish them.[35] Thus, at the end of this enquiry into the repertory of alleluias and office responsories, it seems more or less impossible to decide definitively whether the influence of Saint-Denis was more pervasive than that of Saint-Pierre-de-Corbie in the elaboration of the Winchester repertory.

None the less, it remains the case that the repertory on to which the organa were grafted was borrowed from two abbeys known for their abstention in the use of tropes, but which might well have practised vocal organum in offices, as at Saint-Maur-des-Fossés. To consolidate this conjecture it would be necessary to pursue in depth the enquiry which has scarcely been started in the preceding pages and consult the sources from other important centres such as Chartres, Cluny, and especially Fleury, on the question of the choice of responsories for the end of each nocturn.

History has conserved a precise reminder of the relations between Saint-Denis and Bury, one of the English abbeys in contact with the French royal abbey, at least in the eleventh century. After Edward the Confessor (d. 1066) had given to Saint-Denis the priory of Deerhurst, the monk Baudouin de Chartres, physician to the English king in 1059, became abbot of Bury in 1065.[36] According to Jean Vezin, Baudouin had probably brought with him a copy of Bede's commentary on the Gospel of St Luke, prepared at Saint-Denis at the beginning of the ninth century and recorded in the catalogue of books at Bury between 1150 and 1175.[37] Edward the Confessor's donation to Saint-Denis and Æthelwold's call to Winchester of cantors from Corbie were hardly chance occurrences: both episodes allow us to perceive a wide network of relations between the north of France and the south of England during the period preceding the Conquest of 1066.

Seen from this perspective, Winchester aligns itself beside Saint-Maur-des-Fossés in the category of indirect sources which reflect some light on the history of Parisian organum before the establishment of the school of Notre-Dame.

[34] Planchart, *Winchester*, I, 61.

[35] S. Rankin, 'Neumatic Notations in Anglo-Saxon England', *Musicologie médiévale: Notation et séquences*, Actes de la Table Ronde du CNRS à l'Institut de Recherche et d'Histoire des Textes, 6–7 Septembre 1982, ed. M. Huglo (Paris, 1987), 129–44, esp. 141, no. 3 (Cambridge 473) and 142, no. 12 (Oxford 775).

[36] A. Gransden, 'Baldwin, Abbot of Bury St Edmunds, 1065–1097', *Proceedings of the Battle Conference on Anglo-Norman Studies* 4, ed. R. A. Brown (Woodbridge, 1982), 65–76.

[37] J. Vezin, 'Les Relations entre St Denis et d'autres scriptoria pendant le haut moyen âge', *The Role of the Book in Medieval Culture*, ed. P. Ganz, Bibliologia 3 (Turnhout, 1986), 17–40.

4

Winchester Polyphony

The Early Theory and Practice of Organum

SUSAN RANKIN
(University of Cambridge)

vox principalis
vox organalis

Tu pa-tris sem-pi-ter-nus es fi- li-us

Sic enim duobus aut pluribus in unum canendo modesta dumtaxat et concordi morositate, quod suum est huius meli, videbis suavem nasci ex hac sonorum commixtione concentum.[1]

When the author of the *Musica Enchiriadis* refers to 'two or more singing together', his words could be interpreted as indicating extempore performance of a second melodic line (to accompany one already known) by more than one singer—with the corollary that any two trained singers could be expected to formulate a second voice in the same way. Described by Fritz Reckow as 'characterised by the search for a thoroughly "automatic" process in polyphonic performance',[2] the *Musica Enchiriadis* teaching presumes an unusually close relationship between the theory and practice of organum singing: the practice based on theoretical rules, the theory—in providing a thorough basic network of rules—sufficient to establish the realizations. This restrictive attitude finds an explanation in the nature of the whole *Musica Enchiriadis* treatise, and in the place accorded to parallel organum technique within a grander conception. For the treatise's primary

---

[1]. 'Thus, by the simultaneous singing of two or more voices with restrained and agreeable slowness, because it is proper to this music, you will see that out of this mixture of sounds, a smooth harmony is born': *Musica Enchiriadis*, 'De proprietate symphoniarum'. The chapters dealing with organum are edited in E. L. Waeltner, *Die Lehre vom Organum bis zur Mitte des 11. Jahrhunderts*, Münchner Veröffentlichungen zur Musikgeschichte 13 (Tutzing, 1975), 2.

[2]. F. Reckow, 'Organum', *The New Grove Dictionary of Music and Musicians*, ed. S. Sadie, 20 vols. (London, 1980), XIII, 799.

concern is 'a theory of the tetrachord as an organizing principle for song in general';[3] at the time when *Musica Enchiriadis* was written (before 900), the 'sensuous impact' of parallel organum 'validated the concept of the tetrachord' on which the theory of tonal order was based.[4] It is in the context of a lateral rather than direct interest in polyphonic singing that the six chapters on organum should be read, the procedures they describe recognized as the projection of a forceful didactic spirit.

The highly prescriptive approach of the *Musica Enchiriadis* represents an extreme; other theorists dealing with this type of organum (as opposed to the 'new' type discussed by twelfth-century theorists) allow the practitioner more freedom. In the *Micrologus* (written *circa* 1030),[5] Guido of Arezzo expresses himself principally in terms of definitive rules, but allows for exceptions, thus according some place to 'the singers' experience and judgement'.[6] Guido's less constrained attitude is unlikely to represent the outcome of an evolutionary process: against the testimony of *Musica Enchiriadis* can be set that of other early examples of organum theory. A short passage on organum written no later than the first half of the tenth century—the so-called 'Cologne treatise'—advises that the performance of organum demands care and reflection, implicitly rejecting a mechanical approach: 'Poscit autem semper organum diligenti et modesta morositate fieri'.[7] Yet even in these more liberal treatises the concept that the singing of polyphony depended largely on a thorough knowledge of the chant and facility in the application of rules for the improvisation of a second voice— in other words, that theory formed the basis of and controlled practice— remained fundamental.

This theory-dominated view of practice remains influential 1000 years on.[8] Modern accounts of early organum have tended to rely heavily on theoretical descriptions and examples as evidence of musical practice, leaving extant practical examples in the background and neglecting all

---

[3.] L. Gushee, 'Musica Enchiriadis', *The New Grove*, XII, 801.

[4.] Ibid.

[5.] Dated by Smits van Waesberghe between 1028 and 1032: see Guidonis Aretini, *Micrologus*, ed. Smits van Waesberghe, Corpus Scriptorum de Musica 4 (American Institute of Musicology, 1955); an earlier date of 1025–6 was proposed by H. Oesch, *Guido von Arezzo* (Berne, 1954). For a translation of the *Micrologus*, see *Hucbald, Guido, and John on Music*, ed. W. Babb, with introductions by C. V. Palisca, index of chants by A. E. Planchart (New Haven, Conn., and London, 1978).

[6.] Reckow, 'Organum', 799.

[7.] 'However, organum always requires to be made with care and measured thought.' Edited in Waeltner, *Die Lehre*, 54, with details of manuscript sources, 52–3; in two of its four sources, this short tract is associated with the *Musica* and *Scolica Enchiriadis* treatises.

[8.] With the exception of an excellent account, published too late to be extensively used in this study: S. Fuller, 'Early Polyphony', in R. Crocker and D. Hiley (eds.), *The Early Middle Ages to 1300*, *The New Oxford History of Music* 2 (2nd edn., Oxford, 1990), 485–556.

considerations of their musical character. More seriously, it has simply been assumed—rather than proven—that the aesthetic ethos of the theory applies equally to the practice. A recently published study of pre-twelfth-century organum theory is a case in point. In 'Die Mehrstimmigkeitslehre von ihren Anfängen bis zum 12. Jahrhundert', Hans Heinrich Eggebrecht raises no objection to the potential historical inaccuracy of the theorists' view of practice;[9] rather, he denies the existence of examples which might show practice to have gone beyond the limitations of theory:

In der Lehre des alten Organums, in der *Musica Enchiriadis* und in Guidos *Micrologus*, waren Lehre und Praxis gewissermassen noch ungeschieden beieinander: Eine artifizielle Praxis jenseits der Lehre ist hier nicht nur nicht greifbar, sondern auch vorstellungsmässig wohl noch kaum gegeben.[10]

Eggebrecht's belief that no creativity or originality was brought to bear in a practical situation is based on the observation that theory, even in the less dogmatic provisions of Guido's *Micrologus*, simply does not envisage such a dimension:

Doch schon bei den 'exempla' der Organumlehre Guidos handelt es sich um Beispiele für ein Organizieren mit 'wahlweisen Möglichkeiten'. Gleichwohl gab es auch hier zwischen den Regeln und deren musikalischer Ausführung noch kein Drittes, d.h. noch nicht das poietische Moment, das über die Regeln verfügte und die Praxis im artifiziellen Sinne als eigenständige, kreative Instanz begründete.[11]

But is there really no evidence of 'creativity' in examples of early organum? What was actually going on in practice? In what way do the surviving treatises help us to understand examples of practice?

Winchester Polyphony: 100 Years of Scholarship

In 1894—six years after the founding of the Plainsong & Medieval Music Society—a volume published by the Henry Bradshaw Society contained in its preface these words: 'the closing section of MS CC is a collection of organa: the term is used here and in many other places at this date as the equivalent of diaphony, that is early part-music . . . This collection is the most considerable practical document which has yet come to light on the subject of early harmony, and deserves to be closely studied in connection

---

[9] In H. H. Eggebrecht, F. A. Gallo, M. Haas, and K.-J. Sachs, *Die Mittelalterliche Lehre von der Mehrstimmigkeit*, Geschichte der Musiktheorie 5 (Darmstadt, 1984), 9–87.

[10] Eggebrecht, 'Mehrstimmigkeitslehre', 86.

[11] Ibid.

with the theoretical works of the time.'[12] The source referred to was manuscript 473 in the library of Corpus Christi College, Cambridge, the writer Walter Howard Frere.[13] Now famous as a source of tropes and sequences, as well as organa, this early eleventh-century manuscript had received but one mention in a publication dealing with sequences (*Analecta Liturgica* 2/ix–x, pub. March 1892), and had appeared neither among the manuscripts used for the edition of sequences in Analecta Hymnica,[14] nor in Léon Gautier's seminal study: *Histoire de la poésie liturgique au moyen âge: les tropes* (Paris, 1886). But a reproduction of fols. 16v–17r was included among the plates issued to accompany the second and third volumes of *Paléographie musicale* (in 1891–2), and Frere's description, study, and edition, *The Winchester Troper*, followed shortly after. Whether Frere's knowledge of the manuscript's existence came from the Solesmes monks, or theirs from him, is not known; Frere had been born in Cambridge, retained many family connections there, and had read Classics at Trinity College (1882–5). Even after his departure in 1886 to train and serve as an Anglican priest, he must have returned frequently to the university town.[15] What is clear is that there was direct contact between Frere and Solesmes: his name appears among the subscribers to Volume 1 of *Paléographie musicale*, published in 1889 (interestingly *not* in the list of members of the Plainsong & Mediæval Music Society appended at the end of this impressive list of subscribers).[16] And

[12.] The Henry Bradshaw Society had been founded in 1890 in memory of Henry Bradshaw (d. 1886), Librarian of the Cambridge University Library, 'for the editing of rare liturgical texts'. Although both this and the Plainsong & Mediæval Music Society owe their inception to a renewed historical interest in liturgy, and both elected John Wordsworth, Bishop of Salisbury, as their first President, the two societies had quite different aims and memberships.

[13.] W. H. Frere, *The Winchester Troper*, Henry Bradshaw Society 8 (London, 1894). Frere's work on the volume must have taken the best part of a year: the minutes of a meeting of the Master and Fellows of Corpus Christi College on 27 Oct. 1893 include the note 'also that Mr Frere have permission to transcribe for the purpose of publication by the Bradshaw Society, the Winchester Tropary MS 473 of Archp. Parker's Collection, and to photograph certain pages of the same'. Frere then completed his Introduction on 25 Aug. of the following year, 1894. It is characteristic of Frere's approach to the 'plainsong revival'— and informative about the very differing objectives of the PMMS and the HBS—that the Sarum Gradual should have been reproduced in facsimile by the PMMS (during 1892–4), and the Tropers edited, as text with accompanying plates, by the HBS. While the Troper was recognized as a document of historical interest, the Gradual was intended to provide a direct basis for liturgical practice.

[14.] Analecta Hymnica Medii Aevi; the early volumes dealing with sequences are 7–10, ed. G. M. Dreves (Leipzig, 1889–91). The publication of *Analecta Liturgica*, ed. E. Misset and W. H. I. Weale, was begun in 1888.

[15.] An engaging account of Frere's life and interests is given in C. S. Phillips *et al.*, *Walter Howard Frere, Bishop of Truro: A Memoir* (London, 1947).

[16.] The full title of the series is: Paléographie musicale: Facsimilés phototypiques des principaux manuscrits de chant Grégorien, Ambrosien, Mozarabe, Gallican publié par les

the Solesmes designation 'Tropaire de Winchester' became Frere's 'Winchester Troper' (or vice versa)—a term more suited to Cambridge 473 than to the sister manuscript in the Bodleian Library, Oxford (Bodley 775), also used by Frere for his Henry Bradshaw Society edition.

Frere had brought to light a major musical document, the significance of which has been rehearsed many times since. But appreciation of the musical qualities of these 174 organa has lagged far behind that of liturgical aspects of the collection (largely established by Handschin in 1936).[17] As late as 1954, Anselm Hughes was to write 'The most substantial example of early polyphony outside the theoretical treatises is the collection of 164 [*sic*] two-part organa known as the Winchester Troper, which dates from the early part of the eleventh century. Its music is more or less concealed from us . . .'.[18] As Hughes went on to explain, the major problem facing musical scholars was the notation: this is a detailed but only partially heighted neumatic notation *in campo aperto*, intended as a memory support rather than a self-sufficient record in itself. A further problem lay in the identification of appropriate melodic versions of chants for which second voices were notated in the manuscript. Hughes's own comments ended on a pessimistic note: 'It has been said more than once that the deciphering of the Winchester organa is the most pressing need in the investigation of early harmony; but until we can unearth a document in pitch-notation which contains a number of pieces identical with those in the Winchester Troper, the task appears hopeless.'[19]

Happily, without the aid of such a document (which probably never existed), much more in the way of transcription has since been achieved. In fact, the nature of the problems suggested their own solution. For—as Frere with characteristic insight had already realized—the Winchester organa employ a small number of simple 'contrapuntal' procedures, easily identifiable through the notation. (This must be how the notation was originally intended to be read: remembering the relevant chant melody, an eleventh-century musician could then recognize the 'procedural' relationship of the *vox organalis* to the chant, and thereby read the notation.) Through awareness of these procedures, study of their discussion in theoretical writing, and the perception that the added voices notated in Cambridge 473 represent 'accompanimental voices, whose contour results

Bénédictins de l'Abbaye de Solesmes. The circumstances that led to its creation by Dom A. Mocquereau and details of all published volumes are set out in E. Cardine and R. Sherr, 'Solesmes', *The New Grove*, XVII, 452–4.

[17.] J. Handschin, 'The Two Winchester Tropers', *Journal of Theological Studies* 37 (1936), 34–49, 156–72.
[18.] Dom Anselm Hughes, 'The Birth of Polyphony', ch. 8 in Dom Anselm Hughes (ed.), *Early Medieval Music up to 1300*, The New Oxford History of Music 2 (1st edn., Oxford, 1954), 280.
[19.] Ibid.

from that of the chant', first Jammers (1955) and later Holschneider (1968) made significant progress in transcribing the Winchester organa.[20] In this first monograph on the Winchester organa, Holschneider also recognized the usefulness of the thirteenth-century Worcester Antiphonal as a source of English Benedictine origin offering many 'concordant' chant versions.[21] The conclusions reached by Jammers and Holschneider confirm and deepen rather than alter Frere's early observations on the stylistic attributes of the Winchester organa. In summary, the interval relationship between *vox principalis* and *vox organalis* is based on the fourth, and the movement of the added voice is governed by three procedures or, in Frere's words, 'types of harmonic motion': parallel (Frere: similar motion), the holding of one pitch by the *vox organalis* against a moving *vox principalis* (Frere: oblique motion), and, occasionally, contrary motion.[22] Holschneider's transcriptions highlighted one further technique of especial significance in the Winchester organa: the *occursus* (coming together of both voices on a unison or 'cadential convergence'), often with an extra tone in the *vox organalis*.

Frere's hope that more such sources might be discovered has never been realized: the Winchester manuscript stands on its own as a large practical collection of polyphonic pieces copied in the first quarter of the eleventh century. Only with the various Saint-Martial codices—none copied before the early twelfth century—do we next find polyphonic pieces assembled together in a relatively systematic way. From the intervening period a few scattered sources, often fragmentary, contain small groups of polyphonic pieces copied as additions to monophonic repertories or scribbled on empty flyleaves. Mainly identified with Chartres, Fleury or Tours, and Saint-Maur-des-Fossés, these continental sources present a corpus of twenty or so pieces. Despite their stylistic diversity, an underlying trend of change towards a freer style, analogous to that described in the Montpellier and Milan treatises, is clear.[23] But it is the 'old' organum that is represented in the Winchester manuscript. And, precisely because of its evident use of procedures of the type described in *Musica Enchiriadis* and its associated treatises and in Guido's *Micrologus*, this collection offers a specific

---

[20] E. Jammers, *Anfänge der Abendländischen Musik* (Strasbourg, 1955), 11–21; A. Holschneider, *Die Organa von Winchester* (Hildesheim, 1968). For a discussion of previous attempts at transcription see Holschneider, ibid. 12–13.

[21] *Antiphonaire monastique XIIIᵉ siècle: Codex F. 160 de la Bibliothèque de la Cathédrale de Worcester*, Paléographie musicale 12 (Solesmes, 1922).

[22] See Frere, *Winchester Troper*, pp. xxxvii–xli, and Holschneider, *Winchester*, passim, esp. 94–5, 109, and 119–121.

[23] A comprehensive study of these pieces is presented in W. Arlt, 'Stylistic Layers in Eleventh-Century Polyphony', *infra*.

opportunity for study of the relation between theory and practice in the early period.

The conceptual picture presented by Eggebrecht allows no historical position for practice independent of that occupied by theory, and at no point does he even mention the existence of the Winchester collection. But it is only through direct and precise knowledge of the Winchester pieces and the musical techniques by which they were formulated that an open assessment can be made of the extent to which theoretical rules actually reflected practice—as exemplified in this one surviving repertory—and of the degree of freedom exercised by the Winchester musicians. While study of practical examples cannot afford to abandon theory (in that the latter provides much of the basic information necessary for transcription), theoretical rules and concepts may only be regarded as a starting-point for interpretation of the practical examples, rather than as controlling and limiting factors.

The following discussion concerns itself first with the transcription and analytical examination of two Winchester organa in different modes, second with an investigation of the treatment of similar chant phrases in different organa, and third with a new evaluation of the Winchester organa as witnesses of musical practice. Finally, the puzzle of Cambridge 473—a written source of organa, copied at a time when polyphony was not normally notated—is reconsidered.

Sint Lumbi Vestri Precincti

Sint lumbi vestri precincti is the third of thirteen organa for office responsories copied under the rubric ISTORIA DE SANCTO SWITHUNO (fols. 186v–189r). Its text combines two New Testament evocations of the Second Coming:

> Sint lumbi vestri precincti et lucerne ardentes in manibus vestris et vos similes hominibus expectantibus dominum suum quando revertatur a nuptiis [Luke 12. 35–6]
> V. Vigilate ergo quia nescitis qua hora dominus noster venturus sit
> [Mark 13. 35]
> Repetendum: Et vos similes . . .

In both biblical passages Christ speaks to his disciples. In a liturgical context, these words may be understood as addressed to those entrusted with stewardship of the Church; they, especially, must watch and wait, ready for Christ's return. And in singing these words, the worshippers appeal for the vigilance of their stewards, so that they may be prepared to act as intercessors on the Day of Judgement.

Although *Sint lumbi vestri* may represent a late addition to the Gregorian repertory of office responsories,[24] it enjoyed considerable popularity, especially in monastic liturgies.[25] The responsory was variously employed: for All Saints, for the Common of martyrs and Common of confessors, and for local saints, as in the case of Winchester. The diversity of its use obviously stems from the appositeness of the text to the feast of any disciple, martyr, or confessor. In the antiphonal copied by Hartker at Saint-Gall, for example, *Sint lumbi vestri* was entered five times (although never in Hartker's own hand): for St Otmar, for the Common of martyrs and in another assortment of chants for the Common (all in hands of the first half of the eleventh century), and in the Common of a martyr or confessor and the vigil of All Saints (hand of the thirteenth century).[26] Moreover, the parallel between the use of *Sint lumbi vestri* for Otmar's feast at Saint-Gall and for Swithun's feast at Winchester highlights its special relevance in a local situation. For Otmar and Swithun were both identified not only as priests, but also as leaders within their own communities—Otmar as first abbot of Saint-Gall and Swithun as bishop of Winchester. Each was celebrated as a prominent (in Swithun's case the most prominent) local patron, their shrines acting as a focus for prayer and worship. Rather than lose relevance in being transferred from one local situation to another, the responsory text makes a direct appeal to tangible mediators.

Both the respond and verse elements of *Sint lumbi vestri* have 'unique' melodies (see Example 1): the respond opens with a common second-mode intonation formula, but does not follow any recognized model thereafter, nor does the verse adopt the second-mode responsorial tone. The principal characteristic of the respond melody is the way in which it is built up in short phrases, each corresponding to two, three, or four syllables of the text, almost all of which lead to D. This is not to say that the melody lacks momentum or sounds monotonous;[27] rather it builds its own special structure. Some returns to D are heard only fleetingly, e.g. at (*lucer*)*ne*; others are prepared in a more deliberate way, e.g. (*manibus ves*)*tris*), and some of these stronger returns are repeated formulaically. This process of

---

[24] As Frere considered it to be: see *Antiphonale Sarisburiense*, facs. edn. with a dissertation and analytical index by W. H. Frere (London, 1901–24), 13.

[25] *Corpus Antiphonalium Officii*, ed. R.-J. Hesbert, 6 vols. (Rome, 1963–79), no. 7675; *Sint lumbi* appears in all six monastic sources edited in *CAO*.

[26] *Antiphonaire de l'office monastique transcrit par Hartker: MSS. St Gall 390–391 (980–1011)*, Paléographie musicale 2nd ser. 1 (Solesmes, 1900); the entries are on pages 345, 366, 192, 208, and 332 respectively.

[27] Writing about a responsory melody which moves within a restricted tessitura—rather like that of *Sint lumbi*—Peter Wagner uses the description 'monotonous', continuing: 'Fast sieht es aus, als ob die Schwungkraft des Sängers versagte, der diesen langen Text zu komponieren hatte': *Gregorianische Formenlehre* (Leipzig, 1921), 335.

Example 1. Responsory *Sint lumbi vestri*

constant return to one pitch, approaching it in different manners, but with some repetition of forms of approach, creates a cadential hierarchy, i.e. the returns to D are heard as stronger or weaker forms of arrival at a tonally stable pitch. The musical phrase structure is clearly derived from that of the text, musical intonations, melismas, and cadences being used to articulate sense units in an extremely subtle way. In Figure 1 a schema of the text, showing its articulation by the melody, is laid out. Four main phrase divisions (or 'periods' in Wagner's terminology) are shown on successive horizontal lines, divisions within these by ¦ and | (the latter representing stronger cadences than the former). The repeat of the opening intonation is indicated by ⌐ , substantial melismas by ___ , and forms of cadence by capital letters. Following the centrally placed melisma and strong cadence on *dominum suum*, the last part of the melody (beginning at *quando*) explores a new sonority based on F and the three tones above it. The contrast to what had gone before has a clear rhetorical significance: the Lord's return is divided from and contrasted with the period of waiting which must precede it.

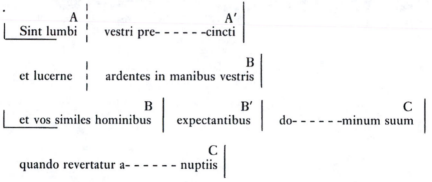

Figure 1. Responsory *Sint lumbi vestri*

In Example 2 the Winchester organum has been reconstructed using a Worcester model of the chant.[28] This Worcester version matches the number of notes in the Winchester notation (leaving aside the extra notes used to prolong *occursus*) in all but three places:

1. at *do(minum)*, the Winchester neumes imply a simple repeat of the Worcester melisma;

2. for *su(um)* the Winchester *vox organalis* has one more note than the chant, in a situation unlikely to involve *occursus*;

3. two versions of the melisma on *a* (nuptiis) were in circulation; later pitched versions, including that in the Worcester Antiphonal, often have a longer form than that implied by the Winchester neumes, which match the chant copied in Hartker's Antiphonal.

The *vox organalis* adopts three procedures of movement in relation to the chant—recognizable as the principal stylistic characteristics of the Winchester repertory of organa: parallel movement in fourths, the holding of one tone against changing tones in the chant, and frequent meeting

---

[28.] *Paléographie musicale* 12 (*Antiphonaire de Worcester*), 430.

Example 2. Responsory organum *Sint lumbi*

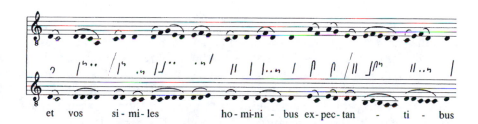

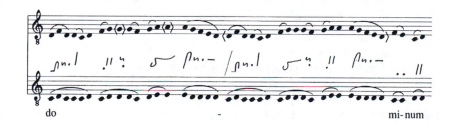

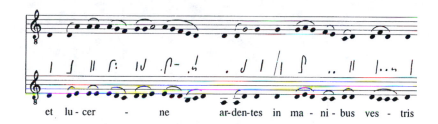

Example 2—*cont.*

quan-do   re-ver-ta - tur   a

nup - ti - is

with the chant on a unison (*occursus*). The whole organum can be divided
up into short groups based on one or other of these procedures. The
underlying principle of movement is basically parallel fourths, but these
are often abandoned in favour of oblique movement against a held pitch in
the organal voice, this in its turn leading to unison meetings of chant and
vox organalis. The three procedures follow each other in regular sequences
(although in some phrases the parallel component is abandoned):

> parallel movement : oblique movement (held tone) : unison

Described thus, *Sint lumbi vestri* conforms to the general principles of
diaphonia mollis laid out in Guido's *Micrologus*, but there are many
differences of procedure between Guido's teaching and this Winchester
piece. One major area of divergence is in the use of 'holding tones'
(*Haltetöne*). *Sint lumbi vestri* uses the pitch D, as well as C and F for
holding tones. Guido advised that the most apt (*aptissimi*) tones to be held
against the *vox principalis* were C, F, and G, because of the pattern of
intervals above them—a tone, ditone (major third), and perfect fourth.
The three intervals above D comprise the tone, semiditone (minor third),
and diatessaron. While he does not expressly forbid the use of the
semiditone (minor third), Guido nevertheless opposes it:

Troporum vero alii apti, alii aptiores, alii aptissimi existunt. Apti sunt, qui per
solam diatessaron quartis a se vocibus organum reddunt, ut deuterus in B et E.
Aptiores sunt, qui non solum quartis, sed etiam tertiis et secundis per tonum et

semiditonum licet raro respondent, ut protus in A et D. Aptissimi vero, qui sepissime suaviusque id faciunt, ut tetrardus et tritus in C et F et G. Hac enim tono et ditono et diatessaron obsequuntur.[29]

In using the available notes more freely than Guido wanted to allow, *Sint lumbi vestri* is typical of the Winchester corpus of organa. In his discussion of the Winchester organal style and its relation to theory, Holschneider explains the significance of holding tones as determinants of pitch boundaries in theoretical treatises up to and including that of Guido. He points out that, in the Winchester organa, holding tones—'a governing element of this style'—can be pitched on other notes besides the C, F, and G characterized as most suitable by Guido, and also that their function as boundary tones (*Grenztöne*) is lost, since the *vox principalis* frequently moves below a pitch held by the *vox organalis*.[30]

Example 3. Two interpretations of the neumes for the *pre(cincti)* melisma

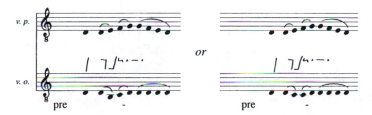

Nevertheless, although there are plenty of places where the notation for *Sint lumbi vestri* suggests stepping over a notional pitch boundary, nowhere is the notation prescriptive enough to specify this unquestionably; for example, when the *vox principalis* sings for the syllable '*pre(cincti)*' the notes DE FG, two interpretations of the *vox organalis* neumes are possible (Example 3). But in another passage the notation for the *vox organalis* necessitates an interpretation which breaks one or other of Guido's guidelines (Example 4). At the end of the '*pre(cincti)*' melisma the *vox principalis* sings CF FE; the *vox organalis* neumes either imply a first note below C, moving to C (thus breaking the boundary established by C), or C moving to D (creating a semiditone D/F). These two examples illustrate

[29.] Waeltner, *Die Lehre*, 92; 'Of the tropes, some are serviceable, others more serviceable, and still others most serviceable. Those are serviceable that provide organum only at the diatessaron, with the notes a fourth from each other, like the deuterus on B and E; more serviceable are those that harmonize not only with fourths but also with thirds and seconds, by a tone, and though only rarely, a semiditone, like the protus on A and D. Most serviceable are those that make organum most frequently and more smoothly, namely, the tetrardus and tritus on C and F and G; for these harmonize at the distance of a tone, a ditone and a diatessaron' (*Hucbald, Guido, and John*, 78).
[30.] Holschneider, *Winchester*, 124.

how the uncertainty as to whether or not a concept of boundary pitches is
in operation in *Sint lumbi vestri* actually constitutes the only remaining
obstacle to a completely secure interpretation of the notation.

Example 4. Two interpretations of the neumes for the *precincti* cadence

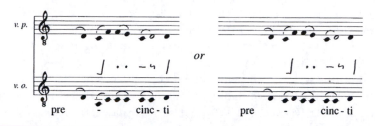

The whole question of the function and pitches of holding tones leads
into another sphere of procedural discrepancies between Guido's theory
and Winchester practice: the manner and frequency of arrivals at a unison.
Two short examples will illustrate how the choice of pitches for holding
tones and arrival at a unison are inextricably related: in Examples 5(*a*) and
5(*b*) two passages are reconstructed according to Guido's rules, and set
beside the Winchester versions. In both cases, the Winchester notation is
unequivocal in asking the *vox organalis* to hold D until the end of the
falling group GFED, resulting in a unison. But Guido's teaching suggests

Example 5. Reconstructions according to Guido's rules and the Winchester
neumes

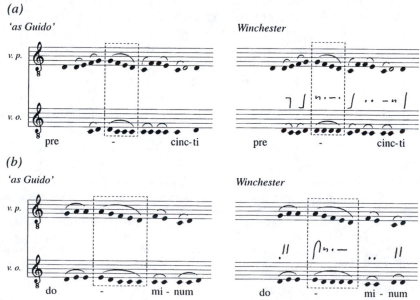

Example 6. *Micrologus*: passage from antiphon *O Sapientia*

quite different solutions to such situations; in the groups marked, the *vox organalis* would first keep moving down, parallel to the *vox principalis*, until it reached the lower pitch limit (C) and then hold this *until* the appropriate moment for *occursus*. Guido envisages *occursus* as wholly related to phrase structure in the chant: in the section entitled 'Dictae diaphoniae per exempla probatio', where through a series of examples he demonstrates ways to achieve *occursus*, the melodic unit referred to throughout is the *distinctio*. Earlier in the treatise he had defined this in two ways: as the sum of one or more 'parts' (*partes*: 'sounds' are grouped in 'syllables', and syllables in neumes or 'parts') and as 'a suitable place to breath';[31] in his terms, the *distinctio* represented the largest of the units into which a chant could be divided, thus a phrase of some substance. Guido's examples illustrate the extent to which he respected the integrity of the *distinctio* as a textual and musical phenomenon, for example in a passage from the Magnificat antiphon *O sapientia* (Example 6).[32] Here he does not allow *occursus* on the final of the mode (D) at '(*docen*) *dum*', but waits for the end of the sense unit '*Veni ad docendum nos*'. In contrast, *occursus* takes place in *Sint lumbi vestri* much more often than at the end of what might be considered to be a *distinctio*; in the two passages transcribed in Examples 7(*a*) and 7(*b*) the moments of *occursus* are indicated by vertical arrows.

Example 7. *Occursus* in passages from organum *Sint lumbi*

[31.] See *Hucbald, Guido, and John*, 70, and *Micrologus*, ed. Smits van Waesberghe, 162–3.
[32.] Waeltner, *Die Lehre*, 99.

Example 7—*cont.*

Rather than judging the Winchester treatment of *occursus* to be loose and unorganized, we may for the time being suppose it to represent musical practice in a different cultural situation, and, potentially, more deliberate than serendipitous. From this point of view, it can be argued that the freedom to use D as a holding tone in this organum has allowed the creation of a sonority quite different from anything which could be composed according to narrower rules, with a strong insistence on D, thus intensifying the original chant's own concentration on that tone.

More detailed study of *occursus* in *Sint lumbi vestri* reveals considerable variety in the way this procedure is set up, and deliberate order within this variety. Most significantly, through the inclusion of extra notes to prolong some moments of *occursus*, an organal technique is used to create a hierarchy of cadences—a dimension of structural organization not even hinted at by theorists. That is not to say that the phenomenon of cadential prolongation goes unmentioned in theory. In speaking of *occursus* Guido writes: 'Item cum occursus fit tono, diutinus fit tenor finis, ut ei et partim subsequatur et partim concinatur'.[33] Guido did not clarify this statement enough to prevent ambiguity, with the result that the illustrative examples appear in almost as many variant versions as the total number of surviving

---

[33.] Waeltner, *Die Lehre*, 94; 'When the cadential convergence is made by a whole tone, there is a prolongation of the final tone, so that it is accompanied partly from below and partly at the unison' (*Hucbald, Guido, and John*, 79).

medieval copies of the *Micrologus* (77 or so).[34] The notations of Winchester organa often show more notes at the conclusion of phrases in the *vox organalis* than in the corresponding chant melody (Examples 8(*a*) and 8(*b*)).

Example 8. *Occursus* with prolongation

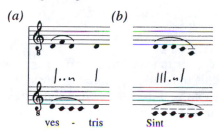

ves - tris   Sint

Literally interpreted, the notation sometimes shows these extra notes not only preceding the arrival on a unison but preceding the enunciation of the last text syllable by the *vox principalis* (8(*a*)). But is there really a difference between what Guido describes, the numerous variant examples in sources of the *Micrologus*, and these Winchester passages? Do they represent distinct performance practices or merely varying notations of the same phenomenon? For the present discussion, it is important to recognize that, although a phenomenon of cadential prolongation is found in both theory and practice, Guido does not speak of it as a structural tool but rather introduces the technique in the course of a discussion of how to deal with certain intervallic situations before an *occursus*.

In *Sint lumbi vestri* prolongation has become the means to emphasize certain moments of unison meeting more than others. Examples 9(*a*) and (*b*) show two occasions where, with identical note patterns in the chant, the *vox organalis* behaves differently; a unison D is arrived at at the end of both. In both cases the *vox organalis* has the same framework: it begins a fourth below the *vox principalis* (on E), falls parallel to the *vox principalis* (to D), and bases the rest of its phrase on D as a central tone. But where in Example 9(*b*) the *vox organalis* uses D as a holding tone, with the *vox principalis* moving obliquely towards it, in Example 9(*a*) the *vox organalis* first holds D (including against F, sounding a minor third), and then falls

[34.] Tables of variants are given in the edition by Smits van Waesberghe; philological study of the sources would certainly help to sort out many uncertainties about Guido's musical examples.

Example 9. *Occursus* with and without prolongation

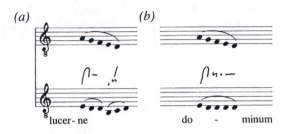

below (to B or C) in order to make an *occursus* using *both* contrary motion and prolongation. This tonal and rhythmic emphasis can be interpreted in terms of the relationship of music and text. While the passage in Example 9(*b*) is heard twice in the melisma on the first syllable of *do(minum)*, the passage in Example 9(*a*) belongs to the last syllable of (*lucer*)*ne*. In the latter case, the end of a sense unit is marked by an emphasized musical close, but the inappropriateness of mechanically repeating such a procedure in the middle of '*do(minum)*' has been recognized. Only at the end of the whole phrase formed by '*dominum suum*' is a similarly emphasized cadence heard.

Example 10. Intonation phrases

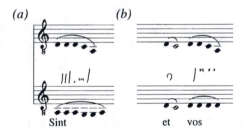

Another pair of examples illustrates an entirely different kind of relation between prolongation, tonal arrangement, and structure. Examples 10(*a*) and 10(*b*) show similar situations in the *vox principalis*, both phrase beginnings, and two different behaviours in the *vox organalis*. In Example 10(*a*) the *vox organalis* adopts the lower tessitura around A, towards which the *vox principalis* descends; for the *occursus* the *vox organalis* includes an extra note, drawing attention to this meeting on the low A. (This is a familiar Winchester formula: the pattern can be recognized in many other second-mode pieces with the same intonation phrase, and is discussed further below.) But when, later in the responsory, the *vox principalis* again falls DDCA at the beginning of a phrase, the *vox organalis* holds the D above—'*organum suspensum*' in Guido's terminology. Because the *vox organalis* remains a fourth above the *vox principalis*, there can be no *occursus* on the low A. Thus at this intermediate point in the responsory there is less emphasis of the melodic intonation gesture than at the beginning of the organum. This suggests that the behaviour of the *vox organalis* has been governed by a sense of the overall structure of the piece, the opening of the respond treated with rhetorical emphasis.[35] As a result, the structure of the organum has developed into something more complex than the bipartite structure given to the chant by its two similar intonations.

In other senses, however, the structure of the original chant has been strictly preserved by the organum. The two voices often move apart from or meet together in unisons. But use of the prolonged *occursus* is relatively restricted; Figure 2 shows the position of nine examples in the responsory.[36] A comparison of Figures 1 and 2 quickly reveals the close association between the structure of the chant and prolonged *occursus* in the organum: apart from the opening, the cadential pattern of the chant and the occasions of prolonged *occursus* exactly match. Had all the points of *occursus* been prolonged, the structure of the chant could have been lost in a confusion of detail; instead it is clearly articulated.

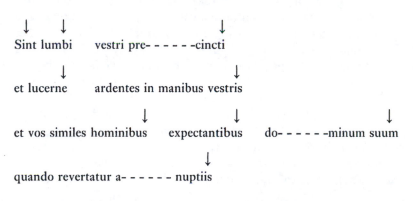

Figure 2. Points of prolonged *occursus* in organum *Sint lumbi*

[35] The prolonged *occursus* occurs so often at the beginning and end of individual organa in the Winchester repertory that it may be considered a standard procedure in these positions.

[36] At the end of the melisma on *a (nuptiis)*, the *vox organalis* has a prolongation, but there is no unison meeting.

In terms of sonorities too, the pattern of the original chant has been maintained. A long first section of the chant melody oscillates around D, never moving far away, and always returning quickly to it. In the organum, the emphasis on D has been intensified through the constant return of both voices to this tone. And when the *vox principalis* shifts to a recitation on F for the last phrase (*quando revertatur a nuptiis*), so also does the *vox organalis*, using F as a holding tone, and only moving back to the lower tessitura for the final cadence.

Both the emphasis on D and the shift to an F sonority for the last phrase would have resulted from the application of simple rules for the formulation of a second voice. Other qualities of *Sint lumbi vestri*, however, reflect considerably more complexity of organization than anything produced according to simple rules such as Guido's or those in the *Musica Enchiriadis* is likely to have possessed.

Gloriosus Vir Sanctus Swithunus

The use of the title 'ISTORIA' for the thirteen Swithun responsories reveals an intention to create a cycle for the whole Swithun office, in emulation of other famous offices such as that for Trinity (for which the Winchester manuscript also includes a group of organa).[37] However, the creator of this 'History' did not go as far as to compose a completely new set of texts and melodies, but drew largely on existing liturgy, especially that for other saints of the same grade as Swithun (confessor). Not only *Sint lumbi vestri* but most of the Swithun responsories can be shown to have been imported to the Winchester liturgy.[38] That the series of thirteen does not follow a narrative thread or refer in any recognizably unique way to Swithun's deeds as man or saint is thus hardly surprising, if somewhat disappointing.

In contrast to the general picture, one or two of the responsories may well have been composed at Winchester, or at least somewhere on English soil. *Gloriosus vir* is one of these. It appears in the Worcester Antiphonal for the office of St Oswald (as does much of the Winchester Swithun office)

[37] Cambridge 473, fols. 181r–182v.
[38] See M. Huglo, 'Remarks on the Alleluia and Responsory Series in the Winchester Troper', *supra*, and S. Rankin, 'Music for St Swithun', in *The Cult of St Swithun*, ed. M. Lapidge, Winchester Studies 4: ii (Oxford, forthcoming).

and in several books in an office for St Cuthbert.[39] The only continental concordances of which I am aware appear in books from the abbey of Saint-Benoît-sur-Loire at Fleury. In a ninth-century copy of Bede's *Historia Ecclesiastica Gentis Anglorum* (Bern, Burgerbibliothek 49), *Gloriosus vir* was written on to a flyleaf (in honour of St Gregory). The text hand is of the second half of the tenth century, the semi-diastematic neumes central French, and easily attributable to Fleury; in its nuances, this chant version matches the Winchester organa precisely. And, like the Worcester book, the thirteenth-century Fleury *Consuetudines* prescribe this responsory for several saints' feasts.[40] It is highly likely that *Gloriosus vir* came to Fleury through some direct line of communication with Winchester, or vice versa.

The responsory text is both short and straightforward, using a common apposition, *terrena–celestia*:

Gloriosus vir sanctus swithunus
relinquens terrena mercatus est celestia

Glorious man holy Swithun
who in relinquishing earthly things has exchanged them for heavenly things.

The rich language and imagery of this albeit brief text is matched by considerable melismatic development in the melody (Example 11).[41]

Example 11. Responsory *Gloriosus vir*

[39.] *Antiphonaire de Worcester*, 390 (Oswald) and 295 (Cuthbert); the other Cuthbert sources are listed in C. Hohler, 'The Durham Services in Honour of St Cuthbert', in *The Relics of St Cuthbert*, ed. C. F. Battiscombe (Oxford, 1956), 190.

[40.] Dom A. Davril (ed.), *Consuetudines Floriacenses Saeculi Tertii Decimi*, Corpus Consuetudinum Monasticarum 9 (Siegburg, 1976), and 'Fragments liturgiques dans des manuscrits du fonds de Fleury', *Questions liturgiques* 71 (1990/2), 116.

[41.] Reconstructed here following the Worcester version for Oswald (*Antiphonaire de Worcester*, 390).

Successive portions of this melody occupy different tessituras: from a recitation on G, the melody jumps in one movement to d, then moves within the fourth between c and f towards c. The next phrase starts from d and moves quickly to the high g; through a series of patterns based on a falling fourth it returns again to d; the next phrase descends via an elaborate melisma from d to G. Up to this point the melody has described an arch shape, its highest point sung to the words *relinquens terrena*. The last part, for *celestia*, develops a new sonority, based not on the G-c-d-g framework set up before, but on the contrasting chain F-a-c-f. And this new sonority is only abandoned at the very end, where the final G is approached through the one tone common to both tonal systems, c.

The pattern set up by melody and text together is one of short phrases, each only one or two words long, set off from each other by melismas, and closing on a series of different pitches, as set out in Figure 3.

```
G         G  G                        c
Gloriosus vir    sanctus Swithunus- - - - - -

d                    d  d              G  F              G
relinquens terre- - - - - -na    mercatus est- - - - - -    ce- - - - - -les- - -tia
```

Figure 3. Phrase divisions in *Gloriosus vir*, with opening and closing pitches

Unlike *Sint lumbi vestri* the shape and many details of the melodic formulation of *Gloriosus vir* are traceable to a family of 7th-mode responsories.[42] The melody usually appears in a longer form, associated with a longer text; rather than summarize the whole melodic pattern, the composer of *Gloriosus vir* chose to include some phrases integrally and omit others.[43] The group of melodies to which *Gloriosus vir* belongs was one of the more extensive 7th-mode groups, and the basic framework (the order of phrases, the shapes of melismas, and the closing pitches of phrases) must have been extremely familiar to the Winchester musicians.

A realization of the Winchester organa is shown in Example 12. As in *Sint lumbi vestri* the typical pattern followed by each phrase of the organum

---

[42] The melodic elements of this family are tabulated in Frere (ed.), *Antiphonale Sarisburiense*, 44–5.

[43] e.g. this melody corresponds to the 1st, 4th, 5th, beginning of the 6th, and the 7th phrases of the Responsory *Missus est Gabriel*.

Example 12. Responsory organum *Gloriosus vir*

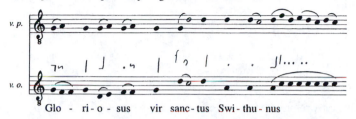

Glo - ri - o - sus vir sanc - tus Swi - thu - nus

re - lin - quens ter - re - na

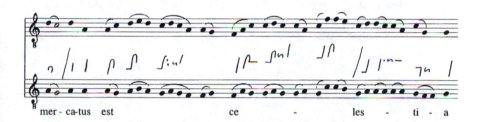

mer - ca - tus est ce - les - ti - a

is parallel movement, held tone, unison. Again, the organal voice reinforces important characteristics of the basic chant, while at the same time bringing new dimensions to the structure of the whole. The prolonged *occursus* is used much less than in *Sint lumbi vestri*; here it appears only three times, at the beginning, once in the middle, and at the end. As remarked above, the use of prolonged *occursus* at the beginning and end of a piece belongs to the standard rules of 'how to make an organum' at Winchester. But the use of a prolongation on the last syllable of '(*terre*)*na*' demonstrates neatly how the technique could be exploited to underline the rhetoric of a specific text; here it highlights the rhymed and contrasting words which frame and articulate the whole, *terrena–celestia*.

This kind of cadential emphasis represents one of the new compositional dimensions offered by a two-part texture. But simple arrivals at a unison (both contrary and oblique) and movements of both voices in unison can

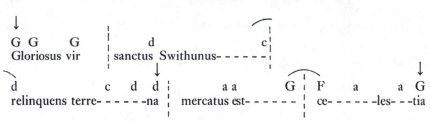

Figure 4. Unisons and prolonged *occursus* cadences in organum *Gloriosus vir*

also underline patterns already present in the basic melody. In *Gloriosus vir* unisons are made on a variety of pitches: F, G, a, c, d, each occurring in a part of the organum where that pitch is crucial to the overall structure. On two occasions, '(*sanc*)*tus*' and '(*merca*)*tus*', the unisons are arrived at by leaps rather than by stepwise convergence. At the beginnings of two phrases both voices move away from the same note (*relinquens* . . ., *celestia* . . .); since the voices had already come together at the end of each previous phrase, this sets up a unison movement—the simplest means by which to emphasize the contour of the *vox principalis*. In both cases the sonority to which the two voices move together turns out to be crucial to the tonal structure of the phrase which follows. Figure 4 shows how these various unisons and three prolonged cadences are placed in relation to the text.

Example 13. Winchester setting of *terrena*

A striking example of the manipulation of holding tones and unisons is provided by the setting of the word 'terrena'. The notation for this passage is unequivocal in its pitch indications (Example 13). Following a long held c, the first unison comes on c at the end of the third group. In the fourth group the organal voice moves up to a held tone on d, and again the two parts meet in unison; in the fifth group the organal voice falls to c again, so that an *occursus* can be made at the end of the sixth group. The choice of holding tones and pitch of unison meetings means that:

1. unison meetings occur, successively, on the pitches c d d; only the last is arrived at through contrary movement, and involves prolongation;

2. excepting the first group ('*ter*–'), the *vox organalis* sings only two pitches throughout the whole phrase: d/c/d/c/d;

3. the first two unisons, heard at the end of the third and fourth groups, coincide with the repetition of a melodic pattern in the *vox principalis* (a fall of a tone and then a third); these unisons underline the contrast already inherent between the two *vox principalis* groups (falling to c and then d);

4. the fact that d was *not* chosen as a holding tone for the second group is worthy of note, the more so since in *Sint lumbi vestri* and other Winchester pieces a scalic descent to the lower D is often accompanied by a held D; within the stylistic norms of this repertory the c constitutes an unusual and deliberate choice. By holding the c for a longer period the move upwards to d is set in starker relief. The combined effect of these various musical patterns is thus to strongly emphasize the upwards progress from c to d.

The most interesting point, however, is not the reinforcement by the organum of the chant's tonal structure, but the level of detail and the artful manner in which this has been accomplished. If we turn again to Guido's rules and examples, we do not find holding tones 'exchanged' with the same degree of frequency, least of all on the pitches c and d. A Guidonian treatment might have been more dominated by repeated cs, as shown in a hypothetical reconstruction (Example 14). In this Example, the bracket outlines a series of three notes sung as d in the Winchester organum, and crucial to that setting's parallel treatment of similar shapes in the chant, as well as the emphasis of the tone d at this point in the phrase. The comparison of this with the Winchester version shows the degree to which the Winchester organum is sensitive to this individual musical context, taking into account both the place of the phrase in a larger tonal structure and small details of melodic patterning.

Example 14. Reconstruction of *terrena* passage according to Guido's rules

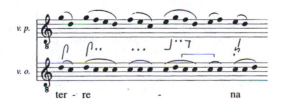

Example 15. Closing passage of *Gloriosus vir*

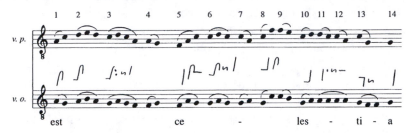

One last example deals with a similar set of variables: the pitches and placing of holding tones and unisons at the end of the organum (Example 15). Again the context is melismatic, and some of the arrivals at a unison create a purely musical effect. The procedures of movement in this last part of the organum are summarized in Figure 5. The four arrivals at a unison break the passage into four parts; the proportion of parallel movement to holding tones is much higher than usual. The two arrivals at a unison on a are tonally significant, in that they reinforce the new sonority F-a-c-f of the chant melody for *celestia* (groups 5–14). That another organal solution, *without* the unisons on a, was possible within the Winchester system becomes clear from a comparison of the beginning and end of the passage (groups 1–4, 10–14); for the pattern cdca followed by a fall to G is integral to the chant melody at both ends. But in groups 10–12 the *vox organalis* holds resolutely to a, only falling to G for the penultimate group, whereas in groups 3–4 there is no hint of any emphasis of a (other than that created by the chant melody on its own). As in the setting of *terrena*, the procedures chosen for each of these short passages depend on the large-scale tonal structure of the basic chant.

groups	unison beginning :	type of movement :	unison end
1–4	a	parallel + *occursus*	G
5–7	F	parallel + *occursus*	a
8–12		parallel + held tone	a
13–14		parallel + *occursus*	G

Figure 5. Procedures in the closing passage of organum *Gloriosus vir*

At the same time, a significant characteristic of this passage is variety for its own sake. While the different treatments of the cdca pattern in groups 3 and 10–12 may have been dictated by their different musical contexts, no such argument could be advanced about another pair of chant phrases, 6–7 and 10–12. In both cases the organum ends on a unison a, but this is arrived at through parallel movement and an *occursus* on the first occasion, and through a held a in the organal voice on the second occasion. Two different solutions were available; both were used.

Patterns and Conventions

Three procedures form the basis of the 'Winchester style', following each other in simple patterns. The close analysis of the responsories *Sint lumbi vestri* and *Gloriosus vir* has revealed how the frequency with which each of these is used, and the points at which one gives way to another, are governed by the musical and textual structure of both the chant itself and that of the composite organum. It has also produced examples of repetition and variation of organal configurations for similar melodic phrases in the chant. This raises questions about the extent to which particular melodic patterns in chant melodies invoked standard responses in the behaviour of the *vox organalis*. When Holschneider observed that several pairs of alleluias based on the same melodic model received similar organal treatment, he came to the conclusion that the Winchester 'contrapuntal style' was 'subject to fixed rules', allowing little room for variation.[44] At a certain level of abstraction this seems to present a correct assessment of the organa; but it confuses common procedures and specific examples. Whereas it would indeed be surprising if the Winchester organa did not generally repeat similar procedures in similar situations, the detailed examination of two organa has intimated that the Winchester singers had a great deal more room for manœuvre, and critical sense of musical results, than Holschneider's comments suggest.

Besides, the extensive marginalia (the vast majority of which are clearly contemporary, some even by the main organa scribe) indicate that the formulation of short phrases, even down to two-note groups, mattered to Winchester musicians.[45] Whether verifying the notation of the first version or presenting an alternative reading, these marginalia document, page by page, a concern with even the tiniest nuance. The actual function of each marginal addition may vary; yet, whether the annotation ♩ for ‖ in the main text was made because the chant itself was to be sung in a different

---

[44.] *Winchester*, 118: 'Die gleiche Vertonung gleicher Grundmelodien im Hauptcorpus sowie die Konkordanzen der Nachträge erlauben vielmehr den verallgemeinernden Schluss, dass jeder Cantus-Abschnitt nur in ganz bestimmter, melodisch kaum abwandelbarer Weise kontrapunktiert werden konnte, der kontrapunktische Stil also überaus festen Regeln unterworfen war.'

[45.] See Reckow, 'Organum', 800.

version,[46] or in order to alter the contour of the *vox organalis*, the fact remains that the annotator believed it worth while to record a different notation.

An evaluation of the degree of variation available in Winchester practice requires a wide-ranging and meticulous investigation of the conventions, possibilities, and limitations of the organa copied into Cambridge 473. For the present study, discussion will be confined to the exploration of organal 'solutions' to two short chant phrases. Since it is already understood that the Winchester organa are in some measure governed by conventions, an obvious place to look for repeated organal solutions is in association with commonly recurring chant formulations.

The next part of this discussion deals with two such cases. The first—a cadence formula—is frequently used in responsories of the 1st and 2nd modes. Its formulation is fixed, as is its function; unlike others which may be used as intonation or cadence, this figure always closes phrases, and is cadentially strong enough to be used at the end of a chant. Among the chants in the Worcester Antiphonal corresponding to Winchester responsory organa, this cadence appears fourteen times. The sixteen matching organa notations (including one marginal annotation, and one instance notated twice) are shown in Example 16. The order of listing in the Example does not follow the order of appearance in the Winchester

Example 16. Organal solutions to a D-mode cadence

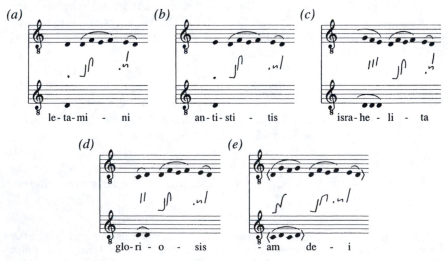

---

[46] The example is from the Responsory organum *Descendit de celis*, Cambridge 473, fol. 176v.

Example 16—*cont.*

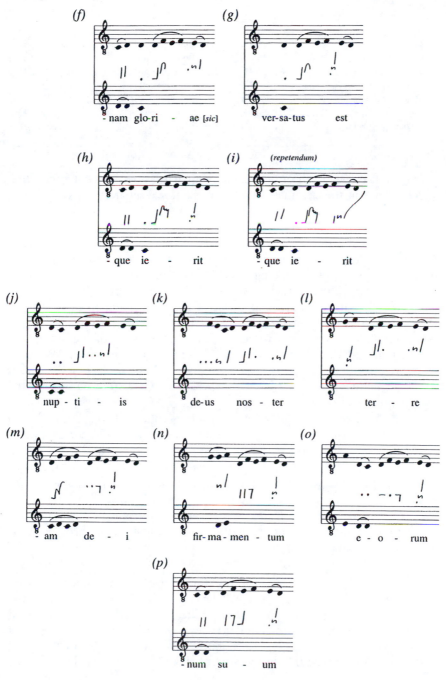

KEY

Responsory	fol.		
a	Agmina sacra................... 187v	i	O quam gloriosum 186r
b	Laudemus Dominum 188r	j	Sint lumbi...................... 187r
c	Ecce vere 188v	k	Benedicat nos 181r
d	Laudemus Dominum 188r	l	Benedicat nos 181r
e	Celi enarrant *(marginal annotation)* . 177r	m	Celi enarrant.................... 177r
f	Magnificavit eum 189r	n	Celi enarrant.................... 177r
g	Iste sanctus 189r	o	Celi enarrant.................... 177r
h	O quam gloriosum 186r	p	Sint lumbi...................... 187r

manuscript, but is based on notational similarity: notations corresponding to repetitions of the cadence within one chant are separated if they differ, e.g. two versions from *Sint lumbi vestri* are shown as 16(*j*) and 16(*p*), while 16(*m*), 16(*n*), 16(*o*), and 16(*e*) all come from *Celi enarrant*. Throughout the discussion, 'first group' refers to the notes for the penultimate syllable (not the ante-penultimate, although this is shown in the transcriptions). These sixteen versions present among them a total of five different notational patterns. In two of these (16(*h*)/(*i*) and 16(*p*)) the first group includes more notes than the chant's four. In the case of 16(*h*)/(*i*) the neumes ♪⌐ instead of ♪ʃ imply the same pitch series as in 16(*a*)–(*g*); the significance of the extension within the *clivis* shape is unclear. The neumes of the first group of 16(*p*), on the other hand, indicate a different melodic pattern. Without more precise knowledge of the corresponding melodic pattern in the chant, i.e. confirmation of its exact identity, these versions cannot be interpreted in any more detail.

In the three remaining notational patterns (16(*a*)–(*g*), 16(*j*)–(*l*), and 16 (*m*)–(*o*)), the four notes in the first group of the *vox organalis* correspond to four notes in the *vox principalis*, and the three notes of the second group allow for a prolonged *occursus* with the two-note close of the *vox principalis* on the final D. The marginal possibility that the three patterns do not all correspond to the same chant figure is somewhat diminished by the fact that 16(*e*) appears as a marginal substitution for 16(*m*). The notational implications and possible interpretations of each of these three patterns will now be separately pursued.

16(*a*)–(*g*)

When preceded by a *punctum*, the horizontal stroke of the opening *pes* is usually written on the same vertical level (16(*a*), (*b*), (*f*), (*g*)). But the *punctum* may have denoted any of the pitches A, C, or D. When preceded by a *virga*, however, the horizontal stroke of the *pes* is always written at a lower vertical level (16(*c*), (*d*)). Taking into account the transcribed pitches of the preceding notes, the implication of this placing is that the first note of the *pes* sounds lower than D, thus A or C. This leads to two possible interpretations, depending on whether the first three notes of ♪♪ are understood to mean ⌒⌒ or ⌒⌒. While the series of three rising notes might seem a suitable literal interpretation of ♪♪, it is by no means clear that it does. Winchester scribes often used ╎ for three rising notes, and ♩ for ⌒⌒. Leaving this question open, however, there are two ways of realizing these notations (Examples 17(a) and 17(b)). It cannot be excluded that the *same* notation denoted both organal solutions, and that the choice between them depended on the nature of the preceding passage. However, the notation provides no evidence to support this: no significative letters or other typical ways of rendering the notation more precise ever appear in these situations.

Example 17. Realizations of organal solutions to a D-mode cadence

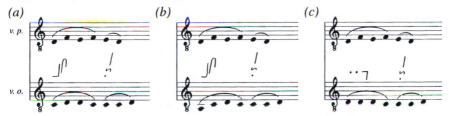

16(*j*)–(*l*)
The difference between this and 16(*a*)–(*g*) consists of the use of two separate notational signs, a *virga* and *punctum* ╎. instead of a *clivis* ♪. In the former notation the relation of the last note of the first group to the first of the second is unambiguous, the two *puncti* being written beside each other without division: ♩╎⁚. This notation leads to exactly the same realizations as 16(*a*)–(*g*), shown in Examples 17(a) and 17(b) above. If the 16(*a*)–(*g*) and 16(*j*)–(*l*) versions had ever been mixed within one piece, the odds against their indicating the same series of organal pitches (leaving aside details of expression and phrasing, of which we know so little) would have been higher. As it is, the two notations may have been interchangeable, indicating the same melodic outline.

16(*m*)–(*o*)
Although in each of these three instances, the first two signs in the first group differ, the pitches involved would not alter, since each notation indicates a held tone pattern. All three can only be realized in one way (Example 17(c)).

The juxtaposition of these realizations indicates that the same chant figure is matched by at least two different and possibly three organal solutions. One of these (17(a)/(b)) is used in a minimum of five separate organa, the other (17(*c*)) in only one. Finding what was evidently an unusual version in *Celi enarrant* (16(*m*)–(*o*) = (17(*c*)), a Winchester scribe was prompted to add the more usual version in the margin (16(*g*) = 17(*a*)/(*b*)). Despite the many unresolved questions, the general picture is clear: this chant cadence formula usually inspired the same response in the *vox organalis*, but not always; another solution was possible.

The principal difference between these solutions lies in the pitch of the first note of the first group, and the concord or discord thereby effected. Allowing that 17(*a*) and (*b*) may individually or together represent correct realizations of the neumes in 16(*a*)–(*g*), the interval sounded at the beginning of the first group is either a tone or a fourth; whereas the other version (17(*c*)) begins with a unison D. A comparison of 16(*j*) and 16(*o*) underlines the difference of effect sought in the organum *Celi enarrant*. In 16(*o*), rather than accompany the two-note group DC with a held tone CC, the organal voice holds on D, above the chant, thus avoiding a unison C, and allowing the unison D to be heard on its own without conflict.

Example 18. Responsory *O quam admirabilis*: intonation

      O   quam ad - mi   —   ra - bi - lis

For a second set of organal conventions associated with a common chant formula, I have chosen an intonation sung in responsories classified in the 2nd mode; this provides an equally large number of examples in the Winchester repertory (including two in *Sint lumbi vestri*). Beginning on D, the melody falls through C to low A, rising quickly to D again, usually through C (Example 18). The formula is often extended with a series of repeated Ds at the beginning; in individual instances other variations occur, without upsetting the basic outline. At least as significant for a study of organal treatment as the variants is the fact that the figure may either form a closed statement in itself, or the beginning of a longer figure. This flexibility inevitably complicates the comparison of different examples past a certain point. Example 19 shows fifteen instances drawn from the Winchester responsories; multiple instances from the same chant are shown in sequence. Immediately, the contrast of an *occursus* with prolongation on the low A to a held tone solution is evident: 19(*a*), (*d*), (*e*), (*f*), (*g*), (*i*), (*k*), and (*m*) have the *occursus*, while in 19(*b*), (*c*), (*h*), (*j*), (*l*), (*n*), and (*o*) one pitch is held. The two procedures are equally popular. The prolonged *occursus* is a more usual choice at the beginning of an organum (19(*a*), (*d*), (*g*), (*i*), (*k*)), but a held tone may also be used (19(*c*)). Nor must the same version be retained throughout one organum; whereas *O quam admirabilis*

Example 19. Organal solutions to a 2nd–mode intonation formula

(a)

fol. 187r

Sint lum - bi ves - tri pre - cincti ...

(b)

fol. 187r

et vos si - mi - les ho - mi - ni - bus

(c)

fol. 188v

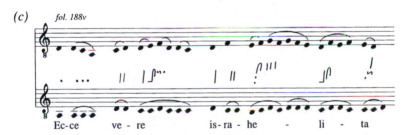

Ec- ce ve - re is- ra - he - li - ta

(d)

fol. 186v

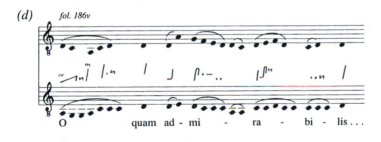

O quam ad - mi - ra - bi - lis ...

(e)

fol. 186v

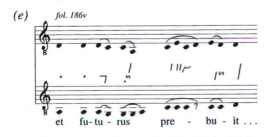

et fu- tu - rus pre - bu - it ...

Example 19—cont.

(f) fol. 186v

un - de   fe - li - ci - ter

(g) fol. 187r

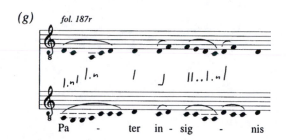

Pa - ter in - sig - nis

(h) fol. 177v

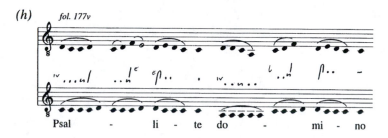

Psal - li - te do - mi - no

(i) fol. 178v

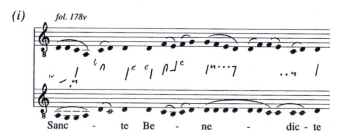

Sanc - te Be - ne - dic - te

(j) fol. 178v

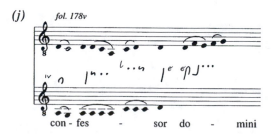

con - fes - sor do - mini

Example 19—*cont.*

(k) fol. 181r

Be-ne-dic-tus   do - mi-nus ...

(l) fol. 181r

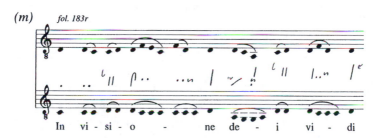

so - lus   et   be - ne - dic - tum

(m) fol. 183r

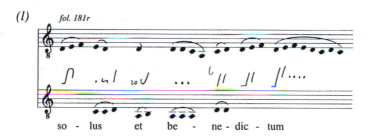

In vi - si - o - ne de - i vi - di

(n) fol. 186r

Sanc-tis - si - mi martyris IUSTI ...

(o) fol. 186r

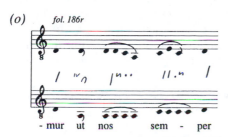

- mur ut nos sem - per

$((d)-(f))$ and *Sanctissimi martyris* $((n), (o))$ repeat the same procedures (prolonged *occursus* and held tone respectively), *Sint lumbi vestri* $((a), (b))$, *Sancte Benedicte* $((i), (j))$, and *Benedictus dominus* $((k), (l))$ each use two alternatives. In these cases the two alternatives *always* appear in the order: prolonged *occursus* followed by a held tone.

The pitch held to accompany the chant fall to A is clearly indicated in some instances, but not in others. In $19(b)$ it could be A, C, or D; in $19(c)$, A or C. In $19(h)$, (j), (l), (n), and (o) the significative letters iv or io (*iusum/iosum valde*)[47] at the beginning of a series of held tones ask the *vox organalis* to move to a pitch below the *vox principalis*; this rules out D, leaving A and C. And in two of these cases the subsequent progress of the *vox organalis* indicates explicitly that the held tone was A. However, while A is used in the only two instances of held tone procedure about which we have some certainty, we do not know enough about Winchester techniques in general to appreciate whether or not this implies that *all* such instances of held tones associated with this intonation formula used A. Again the arguments supporting a multiplicity of solutions against one solution and vice versa cannot be resolved here.

After the fall to A the chant usually returns quickly to D, either with a two-note group CD, or with the repetition CD D. The organal versions corresponding to these continuations exhibit an interesting pattern of repetition *and* variation. In response to the *vox principalis* group CD, the *vox organalis* always sings two repeated notes, probably DD rather than CC ($19(c)$, (k), (l), (m)). In response to the *vox principalis* continuation CD D, the *vox organalis* reacts in various ways; it may sing D right through ($19(a)$, with a possible variation in 19 (i)), set up a prolonged *occursus* on D ($19(d)$, (g), (j)), or move to a unison and away again ($19(b)$). This variety cannot always be explained as resulting from different *vox principalis* continuations (beyond the intonation formula): within at least one organum where the intonation formula is heard twice, both times with a similar continuation, the *vox organalis* acts in two different ways (*Sancte Benedicte*: $19(i)$, (j)). Finally, when the first and second parts of the chant formula are joined up, an even greater diversity of *vox organalis* behaviour emerges. Organa which agree in the first part may differ in the second (compare 19 (d) and (g) with $19(i)$); equally, organa which differ in the first part may agree in the second (compare $19(d)$ and (g) with $19(j)$).

The results of this examination of organal treatment of two chant formulas suggest that the Winchester singers of organa did have standard ways of responding to both figures, using in one case not just one but two set patterns. On the other hand, standard patterns could be rejected in favour of more unusual melodic solutions. Even in dealing with common

[47.] These letters are among the commonest used by the Winchester organa scribe to clarify ambiguities: see Holschneider, *Winchester*, 84.

chant patterns whose function in a phrase never alters (although their place in the large-scale structure may change), the Winchester organa provide evidence of some degree of flexibility. And, as the earlier analytical studies of two responsories revealed, diversity in small matters was often crucial to large-scale design, providing an effective means of articulation.

Theory versus Practice

A wide gap between contemporary theory, as represented in Guido's *Micrologus,* and the practice represented in the Winchester book has been exposed. It is not just that the Winchester musicians, in according to the interval of a minor third as much musical status as the tone and major third, permitted the use of a larger number of pitches as holding tones (C, D, F, G, A). While working with similar techniques, the Winchester organa show the musical options to be many more than Guido's short presentation suggests. And, as a corollary, the range of necessary decisions stretches well outside Guido's brief. Much of the ground not covered by Guido's theory can be defined under the general heading 'structure'. In the subtle and artful control of set contrapuntal procedures, the Winchester singers were able to underline and develop structural patterns in the words and melody of the chants they set in organum. Guido's two chapters on *Diaphonia* reveal some awareness of structural aspects, yet he never makes these the specific object of his exposition, preferring to deal with vertical intervals as static musical formulations, and with various ways of closing phrases, again determined by intervallic relationships. In this, Guido's treatment of the rules of organum is typical of almost all early theory; the usual place for consideration of phrase length and contour, the relation of music and text, and tonal qualities was within those sections of a treatise which dealt with monophony. The only example in early organum theory to deal seriously with structural matters in connection with organa is a short passage in the 'Schlettstädter Traktat', some pages of music theory dealing mainly with organ pipes (*Mensuratio fistularum ad organum*), copied in the late tenth century.[48] Here unison meetings of the two voices

---

[48.] Sélestat, Bibliothèque et Archives de la Ville 17 (1153); the passage referred to is brief and is reproduced here in full: 'Dyaphonia vel organo dupliciter uti possumus, id est vel per dyapente vel per dyatessaron. Quod vero organum invenitur in secunda et tertia similiter sicut in quarta et quinta, non naturale hoc dicitur. Sed propter fines erit, qui dividuntur in cola et commata. Cola et commata sunt incisiones et membra in cantu. Membrum in cantu dicitur, quando finis cantus in illum sonum cadit, quo incipit. Sic in praesenti Antiphona: *O sapientia.* Notandum autem, quod membrum cantus simul cum sensu verborum est. Incisio vero in medio melodiae et verborum erit. Propter ista duo, quae finalem locum custodiunt, erit organum in secundo et tertio loco. In aliis vero locis per dyatessaron et dyapente quaeritur.' (Waeltner, *Die Lehre*, 68). In the late 10th C. the manuscript probably belonged to the abbey of St-Gall.

are explicitly associated with phrase endings in both the melody and text of the *vox principalis*, described in the same terms as one would expect to find in a discussion of chant.[49]

In reality, however, even in dealing with the apparently simple texture of note-against-note organum, theory could never provide enough rules to satisfy musical requirements in a sensitive way; there would always be a gap between the abstracted performance procedures proposed by theorists and musical sounds explored and worked through in practice. In performance, a thinking (and listening) musician must have been faced by situations which stimulated more than one appropriate response, and had to make decisions in favour of one 'procedure' instead of another, or between a 'rule of behaviour' and a musical response naturally suggested by a unique melodic contour.

A final Winchester example illustrates this. In an organum for the responsory *Ecce vir* (in honour of Swithun), a long melismatic passage just before the end can be divided into five phrases (X, X, Y^1, Z, Y^2), cadencing on the unisons D, D, a, D, D.[50] In the *vox principalis*, Y^1 concludes with a three-note figure placed in a high tessitura, leading to a. Y^2 begins in exactly the same way as Y^1, but does not repeat the high movement; eventually it falls to D. In Example 20 brackets above the *vox principalis* indicate these phrases. The Winchester organum incorporates a prolonged *occursus* at the end of each phrase. According to Guido's teaching and the Schlettstadt guidelines, phrase divisions of this degree of significance should determine the behaviour of the *vox organalis*, i.e. from the beginning of each phrase, the *vox organalis* should envisage its goal. However, at the beginning of the last phrase (Y^2), the *vox organalis* notated in the Winchester manuscript does not sing in parallel fourths, as attention to the shape of the whole phrase, in particular its cadence on D, would have dictated. Instead, it repeats the opening outline of Y^1, holding F until it become inappropriate to continue to do so. The reason for this may lie in the domain of tonal boundaries, i.e. while the chant moves above F, the *vox organalis* should treat F as its lower boundary; but, if this were true, why should not the *vox organalis* hold F under the two following groups? Equally, the notated organum may represent a deliberate response to the repetition which linked the two chant phrases, Y^1 and Y^2. By emphasizing repetition in the second part of the melisma, the organum calls attention to

[49.] As, for example, in the *De musica* of Johannes; on this see R. Jonsson and L. Treitler, 'Medieval Music and Language: A Reconsideration of the Relationship', in *Music and Language*, Studies in the History of Music 1 (New York, 1983), 8 ff.

[50.] Cambridge 473, fols. 188r–v. Part of the melisma runs along the top of fol. 188v, where the page has been severely trimmed; the neumes are clearly legible in the manuscript, all except one, which has been cut off altogether. This, of course, helps in its reconstruction!

Example 20. Closing passage of Responsory *Ecce vir*

the organization of the whole melisma in two contrasting pairs of phrases: X, X, and A (= Y' + Z), A'.

The search for 'musical integrity' in a repertory such as this may seem misplaced; yet the *ad hoc* nature of this particular Winchester organum amply demonstrates the insufficiency of theory as a *basis* for practice. In reality, the early organum theorists could do no more than codify certain aspects of what they heard in practice; in musical terms, their achievements lagged far behind those of the practising musicians. The Winchester organa not only demonstrate how procedures such as those described by Guido could function in practice, but also how skill in the management of those (and other) procedures could lead to an interesting and sensitively nuanced result. However one evaluates their 'artistic' merit, the Winchester organa have a primary significance for modern understanding of this crucial phase in the history of Western music.

Cambridge 473: Notations of a Performance Practice

None of this explains precisely why the Winchester organa were written down. More complex musical forms do not of themselves presuppose written transmission.[51] Moreover, the organa fascicles of Cambridge 473 represent an isolated phenomenon considered in relation to other practical sources of polyphony copied in the eleventh century, which can at best be described as ephemeral. If, in French churches and monasteries, oral forms of transmission remained the normal support of polyphonic singing throughout the eleventh century, the Winchester organa fascicles may owe their existence to some special factor in the English situation. And the Benedictine reform may have provided just such an impetus.

[51.] See esp. L. Treitler, 'Transmission and the Study of Music History', in *International Musicological Society Report of the Twelfth Congress Berkeley 1977*, ed. D. Heartz and B. Wade (Kassel, 1981), 202–11.

For the English monasteries the last decades of the tenth century had brought new vigour, the reform instituted by a trio of Benedictine bishops, Dunstan, Oswald, and Æthelwold, having ensured the stability of the monasteries, and renewed their contacts with continental centres.[52] As a central element of liturgical expression music benefited enormously from this revitalization of monastic life. At Winchester especially, music in all its forms had reached a high point as the millennium passed.[53] The highly educated and poetically gifted cantor Wulfstan wrote about a great organ.[54] As well as the organa, the two 'Winchester Tropers' include a large repertory of new kinds of liturgical composition: tropes, sequences, and proses, of both continental and English origin. With this thriving musical culture can be associated the wide and progressively institutionalized introduction of musical notation.[55] At the time when the organa were written down, the notation of any music represented a relatively new departure in England.

But an explanation based on the impact of musical script on monastic culture is not sufficient—unless one were to argue that the organa notations supported a performance practice that had not yet formed indigenous roots. Even if more complex than extant examples from theory, the Winchester organa are not isolated in their nature or in the techniques they employ: they must be understood as representative of a much wider polyphonic practice, the larger part of which was never notated because it lay within the domain of performance art.

This is the context in which Cambridge 473 came into being. It is a book of tiny format (though very fat), its size and presentation contrasting with the other 'Troper', Bodley 775 (which is, in fact, a book collecting chants for the mass). One scribe was responsible for writing both text and musical notation throughout the main organa corpus; a large number of later additions indicate that this book continued to be used for collecting organa until at least the middle of the century. The organa fascicles contain a repertory not yet completely 'worked out': the aim of the first and main scribe appears to have been the compilation of a set of organa for the

---

[52] On various aspects of this revival see esp. *Tenth-Century Studies: Essays in Commemoration of the Millenium of the Council of Winchester and Regularis Concordia*, ed. with an introduction by D. Parsons (London and Chichester, 1975).

[53] On musical activities in Winchester during this period see A. E. Planchart, *The Repertory of Tropes at Winchester*, 2 vols. (Princeton, 1977), esp. chs. I and VII.

[54] On Wulfstan see Holschneider, *Winchester*, 76–81, and Wulfstan of Winchester, *The Life of St Æthelwold*, ed. M. Lapidge and M. Winterbottom, Oxford Medieval Texts (Oxford, 1991).

[55] See S. Rankin, 'From Memory to Record: Musical Notations in Manuscripts from Exeter', *Anglo-Saxon England* 13 (1984), 97–112.

celebration of mass and offices throughout the whole liturgical year, but this had not yet been achieved at the time when he planned and executed the collection.[56] And Cambridge 473 may represent the first written copy of these organa, for there are signs which could be read as indicating that they were not copied from an exemplar. In the responsory melismas, for example, the scribe first wrote out text syllables, placing the syllable for the end of a melisma some way away—for a long melisma at the end of the line, or at the end of the next, or at the end of the second following line. When he came to add notation, the space left was sometimes exactly right, but more often it proved to be either too much or too little.

From this book we can build up a much more differentiated picture of the interaction between oral and written practices, between performance techniques and 'composed' solutions. Both the rubrics, which describe the organa in terms such as '*melliflua*', '*pulcherrima*', '*iocunda*', and the extensive *marginalia* are evidence of the wish to fix *specific* versions of organa in script. These specific versions might represent ways of performing an organum arrived at through practice, and considered to be musically better than other possibilities. In other words, these written-down organa themselves provide evidence of a continuing *ad hoc* practice at Winchester. The enigma posed by this collection of organa may thus find an explanation in the initiative and creative energy of a small group of monks or even one individual monk, working out and writing down elements of a musical practice highly valued and much enjoyed in Winchester's Old Minster in the last years of the tenth century.

[56] See Handschin, 'Two Winchester Tropers', 170, and Rankin, 'Swithun'.

5

Stylistic Layers in Eleventh-Century Polyphony

How can the Continental Sources Contribute to our Understanding of the Winchester Organa?

WULF ARLT

(University of Basel)

Sources and Problems of Interpretation

The more we learn of the Winchester organa the more clearly does the special position of this earliest polyphonic collection emerge. The main corpus as well as most of the additions clearly belong to the first quarter of the eleventh century.[1] The collection is remarkable not only for its size—a total of 174 organa—but also for its systematic arrangement in fascicles, according to genre and the structure of the church year. In both respects it stands in sharp contrast to all of the other sources of polyphonic music copied before the middle of the twelfth century. From the ninth century on different kinds of organum had been dealt with in theoretical texts; however, polyphonic singing evidently belonged to a realm of *ad hoc* practice which required no written record. And the continental sources imply that, in every sense, the organized collection from Winchester constitutes an exception.

The earliest surviving sources of polyphonic music from the continent all come from France. None of them can be precisely dated. Nevertheless, the palaeographical evidence and musico-liturgical context of the seven

I would like to express my warm thanks to the editors of this volume, both for their invitation to write a study encompassing the results of long familiarity with early continental polyphony, and especially for the translation. In addition, I thank David Hiley for directing my attention to further chant sources, and Susan Rankin for numerous suggestions about the interpretation of individual examples.

[1.] On the dating and other aspects of the Winchester collection, see esp. A. Holschneider, *Die Organa von Winchester* (Hildesheim, 1968).

oldest continental sources indicate that they were copied in the second half of the eleventh century or, in the case of one or two, around the turn of the century.[2] These seven sources form the principal focus of this study, the first part dealing with palaeographical and codicological questions, the subsequent ones with an exploration of the musical nature and historical position of these organa.

A contrast to the Winchester organa is already apparent in what is probably the oldest French source with polyphonic notation: Chartres, Bibliothèque de la Ville 4. The polyphonic notation appears, characteristically, as an addition on the first folio (1r) of a ninth- or tenth-century patristic manuscript (see Figure 1). Along with the two other polyphonic sources belonging to this library, manuscript 4 is now preserved only in the form of photographic reproductions.[3] It can still be seen in these photographs that the polyphonic notation was itself written as a palimpsest over other musical notation erased from at least the first six lines of the left column. On the upper half of the page (whose lower part is missing from the photographic reproductions), three organal voices are written right across both columns, on every second horizontal ruled line. A partially texted alleluia melisma (*Alleluia . . . Iam nunc intonant preconia*) occupies the left column of the lower half, written on every successive horizontal line. This melisma and its text were evidently copied by a later hand. Even within the organal portion, several layers can be discerned. The text-hand of the first organum (Responsory *Circumdederunt V. Quoniam tribulatio*) is characterized by its straight d, a curved closing stroke for n and m, the st ligature, and a long s which regularly descends below the line. The two Graduals which follow (*Timete dominum V. Inquirentes* and *Posuisti domine V. Desiderium anime*) were entered by a different, but probably contemporary, hand. More detailed examination reveals further levels of inconsistency among these notations: not all of each chant text was written out in full, nor was all of the written-out text provided with polyphonic notation. The Responsory verse text was copied leaving spaces between words and syllables, indicating an unrealized intention to provide notation. For the two Graduals, two different practices were adopted. The first was written out and notated in full; of the second, only the beginning of the Gradual

[2] For a first placing of these sources in the context of early organum see J. Handschin, 'L'Organum à l'église et les exploits de l'abbé Turstin', *Revue du chant grégorien* 40 (1936), 179–83; 41 (1937), 14–19 and 41–8. A basic study of the early continental sources, involving detailed work on transmission and repertory, is M. S. Gushee, *Romanesque Polyphony: A Study of the Fragmentary Sources*, Ph.D. diss. (Yale, 1965). See also S. Fuller, 'Early Polyphony', in R. Crocker and D. Hiley (eds.), *The Early Middle Ages to 1300*, New Oxford History of Music 2 (2nd edn., Oxford, 1990), 485–556.

[3] Reproduced in *Fragments des manuscrits de Chartres*, ed. Y. Delaporte, Paléographie musicale 17 (Solesmes, 1958). On this source see also Gushee, *Polyphony*, 29–48, and Holschneider, *Winchester*, 37–40.

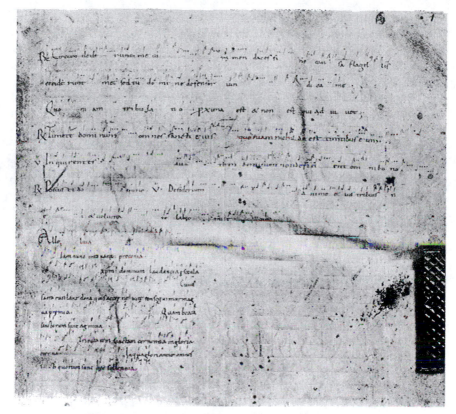

Figure 1. Chartres, Bibliothèque de la Ville 4, fol. 1r

and part of its verse were written out, implying a performance involving exchange between solo polyphony and choral monophony. The Responsory *Circumdederunt* was sung during the Palm Sunday procession in many places;[4] the two Graduals were used for saints' feasts.

The four organa of Chartres, Bibliothèque de la Ville 130 present a quite different picture. These appear on folio 50 recto and verso, with the *vox organalis* written out above notation for the corresponding chant. This organal notation uses neumes *in campo aperto* with partial clarification of the melodic line through spatial arrangement of neumes (see Plates 1 and

---

4. For details see Gushee, *Polyphony*, 35–40.

2).[5] Once again the organa constitute additions made on an outer leaf of a ninth/tenth-century manuscript; in this case the parent manuscript consisted of a collection of music theory texts, including the *Musica Enchiriadis* (fols. 1r–9v) and *Scolica Enchiriadis* (fols. 9v–28r). The three organa on fol. 50r are based on alleluias associated with major feasts of the Christmas period: *Alleluia V. Dies sanctificatus* for the third mass of Christmas, *Alleluia V. Multifarie olim* for the octave of Christmas, and *Alleluia V. Video celos apertos* for St Stephen's Day. These are followed on folio 50v by *Alleluia V. Pascha nostrum V. Epulemur in azimis* for Easter. All four Alleluias are fully notated up to a point close to the end of the verse; the last part of each was presumably chorally sung. The fact that the organal voices were notated by a different hand from that which wrote the chant suggests the involvement of a 'specialist' in polyphony. The somewhat rougher ductus of the *vox organalis* notation of folio 50v may indicate a second phase of work. A break in the notational process is further suggested by the last entry on folio 50r; here, on the last ruled line of the page, the cantus for an alleluia has been left abandoned, the space above (intended for the *vox organalis*) remaining empty. Since this alleluia melisma is usually connected with the verse *Non vos me elegistis* for the Common of an apostle, it can be seen that the alleluia series following the liturgical year has not been continued.[6] Likewise, the entry on folio 50v breaks off in the middle of an alleluia; the second verse of the Easter Sunday Alleluia is followed by the Alleluia melisma for Easter Monday, without the verse (*Nonne cor nostrum*) and again without organal notation.

Yet another use for and way of recording polyphony can be seen in Rome, Biblioteca Apostolica Vaticana Reg. lat. 592.[7] The material in the main codex is connected with Fleury, including amongst other texts a *vita* of Abbot Gauzelin (1004–30), probably copied during the lifetime of its

---

[5] These plates are reproduced from photographs in the collection of Jacques Handschin at the Musikwissenschaftliches Institut, Basel. Fol. 50r was first reproduced as Plate xxiii in *Paléographie musicale* 1 (Solesmes, 1889). The reproduction in *Paléographie musicale* 17 is less clear, although that of fol. 50v is good. On this source see Gushee, *Polyphony*, 68–86; Holschneider, *Winchester*, 64, and J. Smits van Waesberghe, P. Fischer, and C. Maas, *The Theory of Music* 1, Répertoire Internationale des Sources Musicales B/III/1 (Munich and Duisburg, 1961), 84–5.

[6] Later manuscripts from Chartres that confirm the usual function of the *Alleluia V. Non vos me elegistis* are Troyes, Bibliothèque de la Ville 894, fol. 186v (for the apostle Matthew), Provins, Bibliothèque municipale 12, opening ccxxxv left (for the Common of apostles), and Paris, Bibliothèque nationale lat. 17310, xiii.xiiij left (again for the Common of apostles.

[7] On this source see Gushee, *Polyphony*, 187–200; Holschneider, *Winchester*, 66–7, and H. M. Bannister, *Monumenti Vaticani di Paleografia Musicale Latina* (Leipzig, 1913), pl. 44 (= fol. 78v, *not* fol. 76v) and accompanying notes.

author, André of Fleury (d. 1056).[8] Immediately after this, a matins office for St Peter, composed in hexameters and known only from this source, fills the pages once left empty (fols. 78r–79r); the office is secular, having nine antiphons and responsories.[9] Evidently, the act of writing down a special office provided an opportunity to record in written form its polyphonic elaboration also. Thus, following the adiastematically notated office, the texts for all nine responsory verses, and for the intonation of the second, third, and ninth responsory, have been copied a second time. However, only the first verse and intonation of the second responsory (fol. 78v) and the intonation and verse of the ninth (fol. 79r) subsequently received notation. Marion Gushee has identified a concordance for the simple chant version of this ninth responsory in a manuscript from Saint-Maur-des-Fossés (Paris, Bibliothèque nationale lat. 12584, fol. 161r); but it is not known where the Peter office was added to the Fleury manuscript.[10]

Each of these three sources follows a different pattern, but all demonstrate that the notation of polyphony represented an exceptional circumstance. And the same holds true for the further polyphonic notations of the late eleventh century. In three sources from Saint-Maur-des-Fossés the 'pseudo-score' format of Chartres 130 reappears. Here, again, we are dealing with additions made to three manuscripts of quite different natures, all now collected in the *fonds latin* of the Bibliothèque nationale, Paris. The main codex of Paris 11631 contains a collection of Jerome's letters, copied in the ninth century. The organa are notated on leaves added before and after the main corpus: on the recto side of the front flyleaf, an entry of which only fragments can be deciphered, and on the verso side of a single leaf at the end (after fol. 71), following the text incipit for the Responsory *Gaude Maria* and its fully notated verse *Gabrihelem archangelem*.[11]

In only one of these sources has polyphony been added to complement the contents of a liturgical book.[12] In the combined Gradual and Antiphonal Paris, Bibliothèque nationale lat. 12584, a single folio (now fol.

[8.] See André de Fleury, *Vie de Gauzlin, abbé de Fleury*, ed. R.-H. Bautier and G. Labory, Sources d'histoire médiévale 2 (Paris, 1969), 23–5.

[9.] The texts are edited in Analecta Hymnica 45a, ed. C. Blume and G. M. Dreves (Leipzig, 1904), 168–9, and in Gushee, *Polyphony*, 233–6, with information on the provenance of individual texts, and including the Invitatory *Cum esses iunior*, omitted in Analecta Hymnica.

[10.] Michel Huglo stressed the secular arrangement of this matins office and suggested St-Pierre, Angers, as a possible place of origin: see his 'Les Débuts de la polyphonie à Paris: Les premiers *organa* parisiens', *Aktuelle Fragen der musikbezogenen Mittelalterforschung*, Forum Musicologicum 3 (Winterthur, 1982), 98 n. 25.

[11.] See Gushee, *Polyphony*, 131–40, and Huglo, 'Débuts', 112–17, with a reproduction on p. 114.

[12.] See Gushee, *Polyphony*, 141–51, and esp. Huglo, 'Débuts', 98–107, 117–22, with a reproduction of fol. 306r on p. 99.

306) containing more material for the patronal feast of St Peter was inserted. This was worked on by several hands. One copied a processional antiphon (*Sancte Petre apostolorum*), and then, allowing room for the notation of two voices, the incipit and verse of the Responsory *Petre amas me* (*V. Symon Iohannis diligis me*), then two settings of *Benedicamus domino*, and finally, a monophonic *Benedicamus* with *Deo gratias*. According to Michel Huglo, the text and chant notations were written by one hand, while the thinner neume ductus and lighter ink of the organa notation may indicate the work of a specialist in polyphony.[13]

In the third (and youngest) source of the group, Paris, Bibliothèque nationale lat. 12596, polyphonic material for the offices of Clement and Babolenus has been added—at the close of the eleventh century—to the beginning and end of a codex containing hagiographical texts.[14] The musical entries were made by several different hands. Only the left-hand side of the back leaf (fol. 166 *bis*) has survived; here the polyphonically notated beginning of the Responsory *Martir Clemens* and its verse, *Impetra gaudia*, can still be read. Once again, the hand which entered the organa notation differs from that which wrote the text and cantus notation.[15]

The organal notation in the manuscript Rome, Biblioteca Apostolica Vaticana Reg. lat. 586 offers much more direct information to the transcriber than any other continental source of the eleventh century, for here the arrangement of central-French neumes indicates the direction of melodic movement with considerable clarity.[16] In this source, three organal voices were written down on their own. However, all are for Graduals whose melodies are transmitted with great uniformity: *Viderunt omnes V. Notum fecit* for the third mass of Christmas, *Omnes de Saba V. Surge inluminare* for Epiphany, and *Gloriosus deus V. Dextera tua* from the Common of saints. The codex is made up of nine parts, written at various times and in various places (including Fleury and Tours); where these were brought together is not known. The organa were added on an empty page (fol. 87r) in the fourth part (fols. 83r–96v), which otherwise contains the

---

[13.] See Huglo, 'Débuts', 103.

[14.] See Gushee, *Polyphony*, 153–66, and Huglo, 'Débuts', 107–12, with a reproduction of fol. 166 *bis* on p. 110. Babolenus was the founder of the abbey of St-Maur-des-Fossés.

[15.] The main corpus of both Paris 12584 and Paris 12596 must have been copied before the end of the 11th C. Holschneider dates the polyphonic additions in all three sources at the beginning of the 12th C., without any explanation (*Winchester*, 120). However, even if the polyphony in these manuscripts was added *c.* 1100 or even in the early 12th C., it belongs in every sense to the 11th-C. context.

[16.] See Gushee, *Polyphony*, 167–84; Holschneider, *Winchester*, 65–6 and Pl. 9; Bannister, *Monumenti*, no. 177 (Pl. 29 = fols. 70v–71r), no. 228 (Pl. 43a = fol. 87v; best published reproduction of the polyphonic notations), no. 229 (Pl. 43b = fol. 66v), no. 304 and no. 534; also E. Pellegrin, 'Notes sur quelques recueils de vies de saints utilisés pour la liturgie à Fleury-sur-Loire au xiᵉ siècle', *Bulletin d'information de l'Institut de Recherche et d'Histoire des Textes* 12 (1963), 19–20.

sermons of St Augustine; no provenance has been established for this part of the codex. The neume forms resemble those of Chartres 4, another source containing Graduals with notation for the organal voices only.[17] And, as in the case of the last Gradual in Chartres 4, only the sections sung by soloists are notated.

Throughout the first half of the twelfth century, notated polyphony remains an ephemeral phenomenon. The dominant type of polyphonic source continues to be entries made subsequent to the main phase of preparation of a manuscript.[18] And even the group of organa of the 'new style' in Chartres, Bibliothèque de la Ville 109—the earliest to be copied in precisely pitched notation—constitutes an unfinished collection.[19] One surviving single folio (of unknown provenance) contains a series of alleluias and processional songs for the period from Easter to Pentecost, copied in the order of the church year. According to Henry Marriot Bannister (who actually saw the manuscript), no notation was entered for the texts on the verso side. In the oldest of the polyphonic sources from Saint-Martial (Paris, Bibliothèque nationale lat. 1139), polyphony appears in the context of a large monophonic collection and, typically, mostly in successive notation. Paris, Bibliothèque nationale lat. 1120 also contains one polyphonic entry, again made as a later addition to a monophonic source.[20] It is only in the later source, Paris, Bibliothèque nationale lat. 3549, copied in the middle of the twelfth century, that polyphony occupies a whole fascicle, compiled and organized according to a clear plan. Not before the last third of the twelfth century do we have evidence for the existence of a collection comparable in terms of size and systematic arrangement to that of Winchester. The collection of two-voice organa for the liturgical year reported on by the later theorist Anonymous 4—Leonin's '*Magnus Liber Organi*'—must have been compiled at that time.

The appearance of ordered collections of polyphony in the mid-twelfth century leads us to question the role of writing in polyphonic practice; in fact, the polyphony notated in twelfth-century sources such as Chartres 109, the Aquitainian manuscripts, and those associated with Notre-Dame

[17] Marion Gushee suggested a Chartres provenance (*Polyphony*, 173–7). However, the neumatic notation in Vatican 586 differs in style from that of the younger notations in Chartres 130, whose Chartres origin is much more secure (on the grounds of both notation and content).

[18] For details of the sources see Gushee, *Polyphony*, passim.

[19] On this source see H. M. Bannister, 'Un fragment inédit de "Discantus" ', *Revue grégorienne* I (1911), 29–33; Gushee, *Polyphony*, 68–86; Holschneider, *Winchester*, 64–5.

[20] On fol. 105r. This *Benedicamus* is transcribed in S. A. Fuller, *Aquitanian Polyphony of the Eleventh and Twelfth Centuries*, Ph.D. diss. (University of California, Berkeley, 1969), III, 131; see also II, 461. Fuller returns to the discussion of layers in, and additions made to, the main Aquitainian sources in 'The Myth of "Saint Martial" Polyphony: A Study of the Sources', *Musica disciplina* 33 (1979), 5–26.

of Paris, embodies a new compositional level, utilizing the potential of
script. This by no means signalled the end of the *ad hoc* type of
performance, regardless of whether this followed traditional rules or new
techniques.[21] But the Aquitainian and Parisian repertories show how
writing could be used to record special solutions and thereby provoke a
process of reworking. Of course, until much later, we find sources
containing polyphony of a kind which could otherwise be realized by a
qualified singer according to simple conventions, *without* the aid of written
records. For example, in the late medieval 'peripheral' sources from
German-speaking countries, extensive collections of such material were
copied.[22] Moreover, for many centuries to come, the artful combination of
voices in musical composition did not, of itself, presuppose the use of
notation. In the end, what matters most is our assessment of how any given
notated piece relates to the whole realm of unwritten and written practices,
for this forms a crucial part of our approach to an understanding of
sources, their functions and their historical significance. And this task
imposes itself all the more when we are dealing with early sources, copied
in a period dominated by unwritten musical practices.

The difference between the very large and systematic Winchester organa
collection and the scattered continental examples emphasizes the isolated
position of the former. One could, taking into account the observations of
Andreas Holschneider, suggest that the Winchester collection represents,
in large part, a way of saving in written form a performance practice based
on simple rules and clearly defined conventions. Holschneider demonstrated that the organa accompanying different texts with identical melodies were, in several cases, concordant, up to the level of minor variants.[23]
Even in examples where organa were copied twice (once in the main phase
of copying and once among the later additions to the manuscript), the
organal solutions are largely identical. And in their smallest details, similar

[21.] The rubrics and polyphonic pieces in London, British Library Egerton 2615 provide
an interesting example of the juxtaposition of traditional unwritten polyphonic performance
with a new kind of composition in the early 13th C. See W. Arlt, *Ein Festoffizium des
Mittelalters aus Beauvais in seiner liturgischen und musikalischen Bedeutung*, 2 vols. (Cologne,
1970).

[22.] See e.g. the facsimile with transcriptions, *Die Handschrift London, British Museum,
Add. 27630 (LoD)*, ed. W. Dömling, Das Erbe deutscher Musik 52/3 (Kassel, 1972), and
on this, T. Göllner, *Formen früher Mehrstimmigkeit in deutschen Handschriften des späten
Mittelalters*, Münchner Veröffentlichungen zur Musikgeschichte 6 (Tutzing, 1961). The
procedure of collecting can be observed in *Engelberg Stiftsbibliothek Codex 314*, ed. W. Arlt
and M. Stauffacher, Schweizerische Musikdenkmäler 11 (Winterthur, 1986); on this see
also W. Arlt, 'Repertoirefragen "peripherer" Mehrstimmigkeit: Das Beispiel des Codex
Engelberg 314', *Transmission and Reception of Musical Culture, Report of the 14th Congress
of the International Musicological Society, Bologna 1987* (Turin, 1991), 97–123.

[23.] For this and the following discussion, see Holschneider, *Winchester*, 117–18, transcriptions (*passim*), and the discussion of marginalia, 106.

problems tend to find similar solutions. Those of the fifty 'alternative' marginalia so far studied confirm the comparative narrowness of available formulations (in so far as the marginalia present more than notational clarifications). Finally, the extremely careful notation, using letters and heightening of neumes for greater precision, also points to a process of 'saving in written form' a practice which conformed to specific rules.

It is in the context of a major ecclesiastical reform in England in the later tenth century that the large Winchester trope repertory and the new English style of notation may be explained, and this may hold true for the polyphonic collection also. As in the case of parts of the *Regularis Concordia*, the import of a practice can be associated with the reform.[24] Thus, it could be argued that the extensive notation of a repertory was intended to preserve something which was not itself indigenous, and that the situation pertaining on the continent was the reverse, i.e. that the sporadic nature of written sources of polyphony reflects either its wider and more usual practice than in England, or attempts to fix special polyphonic solutions.

In any case, up till now very few plausible transcriptions of the Winchester organa and those in continental sources have been published, with the consequence that little effort has been dedicated to understanding their musical qualities. Andreas Holschneider was the first to demonstrate that the Winchester organa *could* be transcribed in a serious and credible way, but, understandably, he concentrated more on general aspects of the whole collection than on individual stylistic questions. No definitive answers for the questions raised here will be found without a full and detailed reconstruction of the rules and conventions which form the basis of the musical formulation.[25] In this context, we should note that even a superficial comparison of this early polyphonic material with theoretical writing shows that the latter deals only with basic aspects, using simple, unproblematic examples for clarification. And the ways in which the rules and conventions of the practical sources differ from those of theory are, of course, of much greater interest than the (very evident) common ground, which has so far received more attention.

[24.] On the general background to the reform and its consequences see *Tenth-Century Studies: Essays in Commemoration of the Millenium of the Council of Winchester and Regularis Concordia*, ed. D. Parsons (London and Chichester, 1975); on the tropes, see A. Planchart, *The Repertory of Tropes at Winchester*, 2 vols. (Princeton, NJ, 1977); on insular notation see S. Rankin, 'Neumatic Notations in Anglo-Saxon England', *Musicologie médiévale: Notations et séquences*, Actes de la Table Ronde du CNRS à l'Institut de Recherche et d'Histoire des Textes, 6–7 Septembre 1982, ed. M. Huglo (Paris, 1987), 129–40, and 'From Memory to Record: Musical Notations in Manuscripts from Exeter', *Anglo-Saxon England* 13 (1984), 97–112.

[25.] For an exploration in this direction, see S. Rankin, 'Winchester Polyphony: The Early Theory and Practice of Organum', *supra*.

With these questions in mind, the second, third, and fourth parts of this study present observations on the eleventh-century continental sources, dealing first with the relation between Chartres 4 and Winchester, then with the Chartres 130 organa, and third, with the juxtaposition of new tendencies and traditional procedures from the middle of the eleventh to the early twelfth century.

Organa from Chartres (1): Chartres 4

The examples of organum in Chartres 4 offer far fewer clues to the transcriber than those in the other early sources. While the disposition of the neumes on the page often indicates higher and lower pitches, there is no specific signal for the coming together of two voices in a unison comparable to the *punctum-oriscus-virga* group which so clearly denotes a cadential *occursus* in the Winchester organa notation. Letters are used to clarify the notation on four occasions only—not one of these at the beginning of a section. Thus it is not surprising that the musical qualities of the Chartres 4 organa have until now eluded serious discussion. Yet we are dealing not only with one of the earliest, possibly the oldest of the continental sources, but also with one of those rare cases which, because of its separate notation of the organal voices without the corresponding chants, invites comparison with the Winchester manuscript (and with Vatican 592 and Vatican 586). And closer examination of Chartres 4 contributes much to our understanding of the important English collection.

As with all eleventh-century notations of organum, the first question posed by Chartres 4 concerns the melodic version of the chant for which the organum was conceived. The identification or reconstruction of appropriate chant versions has until now constituted the greatest hindrance to an analysis of such pieces, especially where organa based on office chants are concerned (since here the degree of melodic variation is far greater than in chants for the mass). Thus, for example, the co-ordination of Winchester organa with chants in the Antiphoner published as Volume 12 of Paléographie musicale (Worcester, Chapter Library F. 160)[26] presents many problems; in the end, these can only be solved through a systematic exploration of the melodic transmission of responsories in French and English antiphoners of the eleventh and twelfth centuries. For alleluias the situation is rendered somewhat less difficult by the survival of a greater number of sources and the fact that a significant part of the transmission

---

[26.] *Antiphonaire monastique (XIIIᵉ siècle)* (Tournai, 1922).

pattern of alleluia melodies has been reconstructed.[27] Yet, even in the relatively stable repertory of Graduals, melodic variants are occasionally so significant that a convincing transcription only becomes possible once the exactly corresponding melodic version has been identified.

The two earliest manuscripts from Chartres which provide melodies for mass chants are Troyes, Bibliothèque municipale 894, a missal of the first half of the twelfth century with neumes *in campo aperto*, and Provins, Bibliothèque municipale 12, a gradual of the early thirteenth century, notated in square notes on a dry-point staff, with coloured F and C lines. It is striking that these two sources differ from each other both in melodic details as well as in the contour of whole melodies. Troyes 894 probably belonged to the monastery of Saint-Père-en-Vallée, Provins 12 to the cathedral.[28] And since the melodies notated in Provins 12 and later liturgical manuscripts from this cathedral for a particular Alleluia differ from all other transmitted versions *but* agree with the corresponding organum in Chartres 130, it can be established beyond doubt that Chartres 130 originated at the cathedral.[29]

The placing of Chartres 4 is less simple. At several points it appears to relate more closely to Troyes 894 than to Provins 12; but all such cases involve common formulas which turn up in many sources. The beginning of the Gradual *Posuisti* provides a typical example. Here Chartres 4 has the same number of notes and grouping as Troyes 894, while Provins 12 and the slightly later missal from the cathedral, Chartres, Bibliothèque de la Ville 520, have three notes less and a different grouping. However, the version in Troyes 894 may also be found in numerous other French manuscripts of the tenth and eleventh centuries, including Chartres,

[27] By K. Schlager in two publications: *Thematischer Katalog der ältesten Alleluia-Melodien aus Handschriften des 10. und 11. Jahrhunderts, ausgenommen das ambrosianische, alt-römische und alt-spanische Repertoire*, Erlanger Arbeiten zur Musikwissenschaft 2 (Munich, 1965), and *Alleluia-Melodien I bis 1100*, Monumenta Monodica Medii Aevi 7 (Kassel, 1968).

[28] *Le Graduel Romain: Édition critique II: Les Sources* (Solesmes, 1957), 116–17 (Provins 12), 145 (Troyes 894).

[29] For a discussion of this manuscript, see D. Hiley, 'Provins, Bibliothèque Municipale 12 (24): A 13th-century Gradual with Tropes from Chartres Cathedral', to appear in a forthcoming volume of studies on tropes in the publications of the Corpus Troporum (Stockholm), dedicated to Michel Huglo. The use of Provins 12 is confirmed by a slightly later notated missal from the cathedral: Chartres, Bibliothèque de la Ville 520, also destroyed in 1944. For a study of this manuscript see the forthcoming facsimile edition by David Hiley, based on microfilms produced for Jacques Handschin and Bruno Stäblein, now in the collections at Basel and Erlangen: Monumenta Monodica Medii Aevi 4. A further source for the liturgy of this cathedral is the notated missal from the early 14th C.: Paris, Bibliothèque nationale lat. 17310.

Example 1. Opening of Gradual *Posuisti* (Chartres 4)

Bibliothèque municipale 47 (fol. 11r),[30] Paris, Bibliothèque nationale lat. 903 (fol. 22r),[31] Paris, Bibliothèque nationale lat. 1087 from Cluny (fol. 18v), and Paris, Bibliothèque Mazarine 384 (p. 40), a Gradual from Saint-Denis.[32] And by following the common version of the base chant, the Chartres 4 neumes, and the rules of the older type of organum, it is relatively easy to establish a sequence of pitches for the *vox organalis* (Example 1). The beginning of the second Gradual, *Timete Dominum*, can be reconstructed in the same manner. In this case Provins 12 has a longer version, while Chartres 520 corresponds to the neumes of Troyes 894 and (with the exception of one tone) to the version of the chant available in the *Graduale Romanum*. The organum matches this shorter version (Example 2). The fact that the Chartres 4 organa have hardly any additional tones and generally follow the melodic grouping of the base chant lends significance to those places where Chartres 4 disagrees with the two Chartres chant manuscripts, and may indicate that the scribe who notated these organa was not from Chartres. Indeed, allowing for the idiosyncrasies of 'organal notation', the character of the neumes on this page may be likened to the notational style of other churches and monasteries in the Île de France, for example Saint-Denis (Paris 384).[33] In all probability, further explorations could isolate a precisely matching chant melody, and thus provide a clue to the provenance of the singer who notated these organal voices. Since appropriate versions of the chant melodies have not yet been identified, certain details of their melodic contour can only be established by trial and error, taking all available information into account. This, of

---

[30] *Antiphonale Missarum Sancti Gregorii (Xᵉ siècle): Codex 47 de la Bibliothèque de Chartres*, Paléographie musicale 11 (Tournai, 1912).

[31] *Le Codex 903 de la Bibliothèque nationale de Paris: Graduel de Saint-Yrieix*, Paléographie musicale 13 (Tournai, 1925).

[32] Monumenta Musica Sacrae 5, ed. R.-J. Hesbert (Paris, 1981).

[33] Ibid.

course, leaves some aspects of the interpretation of these organa open to question; nevertheless, large parts of both Graduals can be transcribed and stylistically evaluated.

Example 2. Opening of Gradual *Timete dominum* (Chartres 4)

The transcription of the *vox organalis* in the two examples shown above is astonishingly easy and the results are stylistically consistent. In the melismas the register of the organal voice is indicated both by repeated notes and by the correlation between the placement of *puncti* on the page and the pitch of the last tone of each neume group in the *vox principalis*. In both Graduals the opening is marked by a typically Dorian interval of a second (C/D) between the two voices—a technique found in the organa of Winchester; at the end of each passage the organal voice moves in parallel fourths below the chant to a unison with it on the fifth above the final (in *Posuisti* with a dissonance against the first of two repeated tones in the chant). The *pes* on (*Posui*)*sti* constitutes one of those rare cases in Chartres 4 of the addition of an extra note by the *vox organalis*, underlining the arrival at the fifth (a) in unison with the chant at the end of the word, and giving the *vox organalis* a distinct melodic quality. Questions arise mainly in connection with boundary tones; in Winchester, however, these were already handled in a freer manner than theoretical writing allowed.[34] And this degree of freedom was probably generally exercised by singers of organum.

The comparison of the two Chartres 4 openings with Winchester organa gives a first impression of similarity in general aspects of the style. In both cases the two voices move within the same tessitura, the register of the organal voice depends on that of the chant, movement is predominantly parallel or related to a drone, one pitch being held by the organal voice against a moving *vox principalis*, sectionalization of pieces as they unfold is based on musical and textual criteria, and so on. On the other hand,

[34.] See Rankin, 'Winchester Polyphony', *supra*.

characteristic Winchester techniques such as the addition of extra notes at the *occursus*, movement in unison for three or more notes as well as extended passages of parallel movement, or tones held above the chant are all lacking. And the way in which the two Chartres openings are organized—in short groups and using varied procedures—produces a quite different sound from that of the rather extended and often formulaic phrase arrangement of the Winchester organa. Of course, the difference has something to do with the genres involved: alleluias and office responsories in Winchester, Graduals in the fragment from Chartres. None the less, the initial impression of an extremely careful and differentiated organization—with features of the kind outlined in the discussion above—is confirmed at every turn.

The first half of the Verse *Desiderium anime eius tribuisti ei* for the Gradual *Posuisti* further exemplifies this highly controlled organization. In Example 3 the grouping of neumes in the chant version from Troyes 894 is shown by slurs, and for convenience each group of notes in the long melisma is numbered. Available versions of the chant largely agree. This reconstruction follows Provins 12 and Chartres 520 with just two exceptions: at the end of the melisma on the third word (*eius*) a *torculus* aGa has been shortened (following Troyes 894) to Ga, and in the last group of the melisma on (*tribu*)*i*(*sti*) G is added between a and F, corresponding to the notation of the *vox organalis*. The fact that the scribe notated the first note of the organal voice as a *punctum* rather than a *virga* (as in Example 1) may be the direct result of the return to the final pitch (D) from the fifth (a) with which the intonation closed. Both the Gradual and its Verse begin in similar manners. An important difference between them—the addition in the Gradual of an extra note before the unison a—finds an explanation in the relationship of words and music of the chant; while in the Gradual a subdivision is created at the end of the first word, the Verse intonation opens into a melisma on the last syllable of the first word, with only a light caesura on the unison a and an immediate emphasis on G at the end of the melisma's first group. And it is precisely this G which is decisive for the sonority of this long and artful melisma, well-known from 4th-mode Graduals (including *Domine praevenisti* and *Benedicta et venerabilis*) by the musicians of Notre-Dame who, in *clausulae* and motets based on the tenor passages *TAM* and *GO*, searched for ever more interesting settings.

The special quality of this melisma lies, on the one hand, in the tension between the Dorian series of thirds, D-F-a, and the contrasting sonority, E-G-b, and, on the other hand, in the double function of the tone a as the upper tone of both the Dorian fifth and the Phrygian fourth. Immediately before and after the melisma, a is heard in the context of the Dorian fifth. In the melisma itself a series of contrasts develops: from the first G (against a), which leads to the falling Phrygian fourth a-G-E, and then, with the

Example 3. Opening of V. *Desiderium* of Gradual *Posuisti* (Chartres 4)

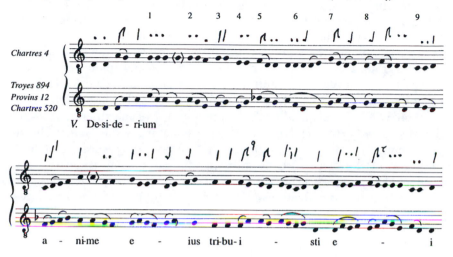

repetition of the third E–G, to the full chain E–G–b, and finally, the Dorian a–F–D before the half-cadence on E in the middle of the melisma. The four–note group at the beginning of the second half of the melisma 'summarizes' this set of relationships in the progression:

$$G\text{-}a\text{-}F\text{-}E$$

Its extended repetition Ga–F–F–FD leads back to the Dorian sonority. Organum composition of this period has a special ability to highlight the melodic structure of the chant through careful formulation of the second voice, although this latter has not yet taken on the melodic quality of a second chant voice in the manner of the organa in Chartres 109.

Given all this, I see the artistry of this organa in the way the *vox organalis* is made to repeat the tone G (rather than beginning a fourth below, and moving through E up to G), thus exposing the contrast of the melisma's first group (1) to the preceding a, in the way that the two following groups (2, 3) again emphasize this contrasting sonority, and in the stressing of the Dorian sonority through the held tone D in the linked groups 4–6, before the return to E, itself underlined by the inclusion of an extra note in the *occursus*. In this context the beginning of the second part of the melisma is of special interest: here two different organal settings for the same group of notes in the chant (G–a–F–) were chosen, underlining the varied ending of the two groups (7, 8) as the chant returns to D. Only in the last group (9) was the organal voice allowed to fall to C, setting up

a cadence on D which coincides with the end of the word (*Desiderium*);
then, for the beginning of the next word, the voices again return to the fifth
(a), moving in parallel fourths. And so it goes on: a new setting for the
group G-a-G-F in the melisma on *e*(*ius*) (G-E-E-F instead of G-F-F-F, as
at the beginning of the Gradual) provides a contrasting interpretation of
the note group a-G-F, heard in the *climacus* immediately preceding; and in
this passage the *vox organalis* follows a sequential pattern (a-F, G-E, F-D)
leading towards the end of the word, again underlined by the addition of an
extra note (F-G, corresponding to the previous use of an extra note, G-a, in
the *vox organalis* at the end of the Respond's opening word *Posuisti*, shown
in Example 1). This serves to link *eius* to the preceding word—matching
the sense of the text—and, by stressing the contrasting sonority of G
(against D-F-a), places a rhetorical caesura before the statement *tribuisti ei*.
These final words are themselves quite differently treated: the first has a
conspicuously long passage of parallel fourths, explicitly confirmed by the
letter q (*equaliter*), whereas for the second, motion is arrested by means of
(1) held tones, (2) emphasis of dissonances preceding their resolution,
indicated by the letter t (*tenere*) written before the series of intervals
a/E-G/E-E/E, and (3) the weight given to the E sonority before the
final D.

Compared to the Winchester organa, those in Chartres 4 are more
clearly divided into sections. This differentiation is clearly illustrated by
the first phrase of the Responsory *Circumdederunt me*, for which organal
notations appear in both manuscripts (see Example 4). The Winchester
version (Cambridge, Corpus Christi College 473, fol. 185r) begins at the
fourth below the *vox principalis* (indicated by the significative letters for
iusum) and uses this interval as its main mode of accompaniment throughout: first, up to the end of the second syllable, and then, after a new
beginning using the unison, and third, from the third up to the ninth note
of the melisma on *vi*(*ri*).[35] Melodic movement is broken often by *occursus*,
even within words and melismas: for example, at the end of the second
syllable, after the parallel movement for *vi*(*ri*), and then, immediately,
twice again, on the a at the end of the next four-note group and probably
again three notes later on b.

The version in Chartres 4 uses a strong *occursus* cadence first at the end
of the first sense unit (*Circumdederunt me*), and, second, at the end of the
whole phrase (as also Winchester), with an a held against the moving *vox*

[35.] For a transcription of the beginning of this organum, see Holschneider, *Winchester*,
100; in my reconstruction the chant has been provisionally extended following Worcester,
Cathedral Library F. 160, p. 113. This chant version, however, has for the 4th syllable one
note less than the versions for which the *voces organales* were notated. Thus, an a has been
added at the beginning of this melisma, following chant versions in numerous other sources
(e.g. Paris, Bibliothèque nationale lat. 17296 from St-Denis).

Example 4. Opening of Responsory *Circumdederunt me* (Chartres and Winchester)

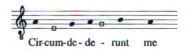

principalis line. In this version the *vox organalis* begins at the unison, then falls immediately to the e which will become the last tone of the *vox principalis* for the second syllable; for the third syllable, it moves away from the unison in contrary motion, and for the fourth, has a repeated a, then for three or four notes a contrary direction, and then a held G under the scalic-falling *vox principalis*. The sonorities brought into prominence by this variety of melodic techniques in the *vox organalis* themselves help to underline the melodic direction of the *vox principalis* (Example 5).

Example 5. Prominent sonorities in the Chartres 4 organum *Circumdederunt me*

Likewise, the rising movement at the beginning of *vi(ri)* is emphasized by the repeated b and d. From this point, it seems that, after a unison c, a short parallel passage begins, later closed with a triple repetition of one tone. In order to continue beyond this point, the correct version of the chant must be identified. Nevertheless, I find it typical that, through the use of held tones before the first and second *occursus* meetings, the *vox organalis* rejects its independent movement, thus allowing the cadential movement of the *vox principalis* to come to the fore; whereas, in the Winchester version, the falling phrases of the *vox principalis* are accompanied by repeated rising second to unison progressions. Differences of this kind can be observed in the rest of the piece.

Of course, it is possible that subtle analysis of the Winchester organa will lead to correspondingly differentiated examples. Our current understanding of the English organa may have been distorted by a concentration on simple, easily interpreted notations, and the difficulties of finding appropriate chant versions. At the same time, the remarkably careful 'working out' of the organal lines in Chartres 4 offers a plausible and sufficient indication of their having been notated at a time when musical composition first began to exploit the potential of writing.

The style of the Chartres 4 organa evidently encompassed a variety of procedures in the combination of the voices. The act of writing down allowed an especially successful organal formulation to be fixed. When one takes into account the appearance of musical notations in a literary manuscript, the variety of hands making the musical entries, the variants between the implicit *vox principalis* and that available in Chartres sources, and not least the specific and subtle qualities of the composition, it is but a short step to the explanation that we find here the traces of a foreign singer: one who, because of his impressive singing of organa, was requested to *write down* and thus securely record his art. For this no special book was available. Seen in this light, the inconsistencies of presentation of this material are of no significance.

Organa from Chartres (2): Chartres 130

Whereas the provenance of the notator of Chartres 4 remains open to question, the four pieces in the slightly more recent source Chartres 130 can be unequivocally connected with practice at the cathedral. The third organum on the recto, *Alleluia V. Video celos apertos*, provides decisive proof of this: exceptionally, the text *Video celos apertos* is associated here with the melody of the *Alleluia V. In conspectu angelorum*—as Karlheinz Schlager recognized.[36] This rare combination is typical for Chartres Cathedral and may even have originated there. Even the noted missal from the monastery of Saint-Père-en-Vallée in Chartres has *Alleluia V. Video celos apertos* for St Stephen's Day with the usual, widely disseminated melody of *Alleluia V. Dies sanctificatus* (Troyes 894, fol. 19v). In contrast, the Gradual Provins 12, copied at the beginning of the thirteenth century from an old exemplar belonging to the Cathedral, has on the left of opening xix (in this manuscript numbers appear on the left-hand side of each opening) the St Stephen Alleluia with the *In conspectu angelorum* melody. The same holds true for entries in the thirteenth-century missal Chartres 520 (fols. 35v–36r) and the early fourteenth-century missal Paris 17310 (on the right of opening xix). A systematic comparison reveals that, with minor exceptions only, Provins 12, Chartres 520, and Chartres 130 transmit precisely the same melody, notated with the same grouping of notes. All

---

[36.] Schlager, *Thematischer Katalog*, 144.

the other organa notated on this recto in Chartres 130 match the melodies in Provins 12 and Chartres 520 equally closely.

An essential prerequisite for the reconstruction of these organa was the isolation of the right chant versions. Following the work on Chartres 4 the transcription of the Chartres 130 organa posed no serious problems: stylistically they belong between Chartres 4 and the pieces contained in Chartres 109, which can be associated with the 'new organum' described in treatises of the early twelfth century. As the most cursory glance already shows (see Plates 1 and 2), the division into note groups and short phrases is carried still further than in Chartres 4. Even in melismas, two-note groups are occasionally set apart from each other; more often the groups consist of three, four, or five notes. The 'drone effect' based on a repetition of one pitch by the *vox organalis* disappears almost entirely. Most often these short phrases close on a unison, usually arrived at through contrary motion. Evidently, the only form of parallel movement occurring in these pieces uses the fourth below the chant. The voices sing within the same tessitura and only exceptionally arrive at intervals larger than a fourth. Thirds appear mainly in progressions from unison to fourth and vice versa.

In the interpretation of the neumes, it should be remembered that shapes are only rarely modified to reflect the size of the interval involved. Thus, the *porrectus* in this script almost always shows the third note higher than the first: √ . And even the extraordinarily long vertical strokes of the *pes* seem to represent nothing more than a scribal habit.

Those few places where it is unclear which of two intervals is intended involve the choice between a third and a fourth and consequently sometimes between thirds and seconds. On the basis of the large number of passages which, because of the melodic contour and the heightening of the neumes, can be securely transcribed, I have in doubtful cases preferred a more conservative, theoretically determined reading favouring the fourth; but here again we find ourselves dealing with a situation in which singers could make their own decisions.

Before transitions to monophonic sections, and occasionally also at divisions within melismas and other parts of an organum, a progression in unison appears. In some places, as already in Chartres 4, fifths occur— provoked by the modal structure of the chant melody. And on one occasion an octave may have been intended. The differing melodic patterns of the chants involved lead to quite different arrangements of the *vox organalis*. Thus the procedures, style, and problems of interpretation can be explored in greater detail through the confrontation of two pieces in different modes: (1) *Alleluia V. Video celos apertos*, which, at its beginning and for large parts of the verse, has the character and tonal hierarchy of a piece in a D mode, but ends on E, and is therefore classified as plagal E mode, and (2) *Alleluia V. Multifarie olim* in the authentic G mode.

Chartres 130: Alleluia V. Video celos apertos

The clear co-ordination of the note groups in the two voices and the degree to which the melodic contour of the *vox organalis* is clarified by its notation together allow an unequivocal transcription of the piece to be made (Example 6).[37] The four syllables of the word Alleluia are taken as one unit. Within the melisma the last note of each short phrase of three, four, or five notes is approached by contrary motion, as laid down in the simple rules of 'new organum' in the Montpellier Treatise.[38] A longer passage of parallel fourths is heard only at the very end of the melisma.

Example 6. Opening of *Alleluia V. Video celos apertos* (Chartres 130)

The balanced proportions and contrasting sonorities of different sections of this first phrase are remarkable. The first ten notes emphasize a plagal Dorian range. The following ascent to G (through a) in two phrases of five notes each insists on the interval of a third; the descent, first to E and then C, is made from two groups of three and four notes respectively, using parallel fourths before the contrary motion. The final E is underlined by the use of unison progressions: first, after the fifteenth note of the melisma, and second, after the twenty-seventh of forty-six notes; the first of these two cadences on to E divides the whole passage in a proportion of 1 : 2 (15 : 30 notes), the second in a proportion of 3 : 2 (27 : 18 notes). At the same time, another structural relationship results from the balancing of the initial Alleluia phrase against the closing phrase of the melisma, built from

[37] For the last groups of the Alleluia melisma the two Chartres 130 voices have a different number of notes (one more in the chant than in the *vox organalis*). This is the one place in this Alleluia where Provins 12 and Chartres 520 do not agree with Chartres 130 (which repeats the last a, but has no corresponding tone in the *vox organalis*). In the transcription presented here the *vox principalis* follows the two chant manuscripts from the cathedral (thus omitting the repeated a in Chartres 130).

[38] See H. H. Eggebrecht and F. Zaminer, *Ad organum faciendum. Lehrschriften des Mehrstimmigkeit in nachguidonischer Zeit* (Mainz, 1970), 185–206; on the 'new organum' see H. H. Eggebrecht, 'Die Mehrstimmigkeitslehre von ihren Anfängen bis zum 12. Jahrhundert', in *Die Mittelalterliche Lehre von der Mehrstimmigkeit*, ed. F. Zaminer, Geschichte der Musiktheorie 5 (Darmstadt, 1984), 40–58, and S. Fuller, 'Early Polyphony', 508–17.

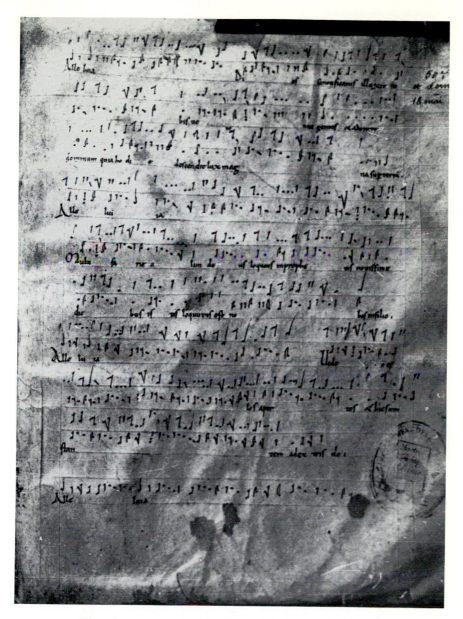

Plate 1. Chartres, Bibliothèque de la Ville 130, fol. 50r

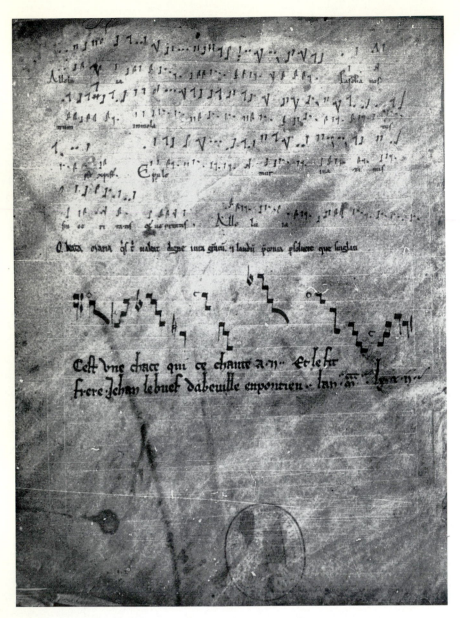

Plate 2. Chartres, Bibliothèque de la Ville 130, fol. 50v

ten successive parallel fourths. The resulting effect is one of a subtly worked out and well-proportioned structure, which even leads to a new shaping of the chant: where, in the single melody, the group E-E-D had formed a strong cadence, dividing the melisma into two parts, in the polyphonic composition these tones are set as the beginning of a second part. These aspects of the composition are, of course, derived from the balanced formulation of the chant; but they are developed in new ways by the sonorities of the organal melody, thus exploiting the possibilities of the new medium.

Example 7. Opening of Alleluia verse *Video celos apertos* (Chartres 130)

In the same way the word *Video* at the beginning of the Verse is divided into 6 + 11 notes, or two series of consonant progressions (4 and 7 respectively), preceding unison progressions which lead to cadences on E and D—that is, to half and full closes in the Dorian sonority, which dominates the Verse (Example 7). The articulation of the long melisma on *celos* corresponds to that of the Alleluia melisma. Once again forty-six notes are divided in the proportion 3 : 2. In the first twenty-seven the Dorian fifth D/a governs the sonority. It is heard at the beginning and end of the passage (first and twenty-seventh intervals). The first four groups end, respectively, on a/a and the fifth D/a (each after five notes) and then two unisons D/D and again a/a (each after six notes). These relatively long and differently shaped phrases (the third uses held tones, the fourth parallel fourths), are counterbalanced by the succeeding short note-groups of 2 + 2 + 1; with two progressions of a fourth moving to a unison followed by the fifth D/a, these closing phrases of the first part of the *celos*

melisma accentuate the melodic outline of the chant, G–F–a. In the second part of the melisma, the restricted movement of the *vox organalis* together with the predominance of repeated notes underlines the return to D with which this passage of 6 + 3 + 6 + 4 notes finishes.

The following word, *apertos*, expands the sonority to encompass the plagal Dorian range, while at the same time being connected to the previous word (corresponding to the sense of the text) through the continued use of held tones. The passage is divided into three (to D), six (to C), five (to D), and four (to D) notes, thus 9 + 9 in all. The last two groups are linked through the use of the same cadential progression C/F–C/E–D/D.

Example 8. Continuation of *Alleluia V. Video celos apertos* (Chartres 130)

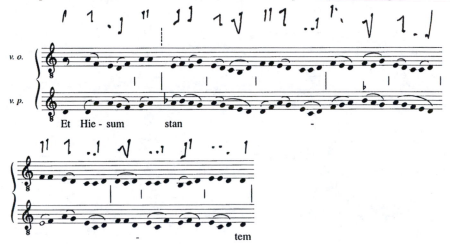

The last section of the piece reinforces these observations on the procedures and style. The statement '*Et Hiesum stantem*' (Example 8) is treated as a unit, and begins—as *celos*—with the Dorian fifth. In response to the extended melodic repetition in the chant, the melisma is built up in three phrases: the first two (comprising sixteen and eighteen notes respectively) with corresponding cadences on unison G, D, and D at the end of groups of 4/6, 5, and 2 + 5 notes. Each note group in the third phrase (3 + 6 + 3 + 1) closes on D.

Precisely because the shape of the chant limits the scope for individual invention in this type of organum considerably, those places where an '*organista*' has exercised discretion are of special interest, for example where similar contours of the chant are differently set (and vice versa). To this sphere of musical decisions belong accentuated unison progressions used to create subdivisions, as well as the insistence on the Dorian fifth. All of this puts the Chartres 130 organa into a time and situation in which simple rules may be abandoned in favour of particular sonorities within a subtly formulated structure.

Chartres 130: Alleluia V. Multifarie olim

This Mixolydian piece illustrates how, using the same techniques and working with similar sonorities on both horizontal and vertical levels, an even stronger emphasis on the interval of a fifth and with it an altogether different sonority has been created (Example 9). This different sonority is already revealed in the Alleluia invocation and the beginning of its Verse:

Example 9. Opening of *Alleluia V. Multifarie olim* (Chartres 130)

here the chant never rises above e, and is characterized by the two sets of fifths F-(a)-c, G-(b)-d. Already at the beginning, the same series of intervals appears twice (1–5 and 7–11, shown in the example by ⌐---), opening the first time to the fifth F/c, and the second time continuing through the fourth G/c to a unison on the recitation tone D. In the following phrases, which both lead to G (shown in the Example by ——┐), the

Example 10. Continuation of Alleluia verse *Multifarie* (Chartres 130)

interval of a fourth is taken up at the opening of the first (3 + 3 notes), and the unison at the beginning of the second (3 + 2 + 3 tones of the chant). The next two phrases, each four or five notes long, remain in the lower part of the tessitura and present cadences on the 'contrasting' and 'main' pitches, a and G. The last two phrases each consist of seven notes divided 3 + 4, the first opening with a fifth (and ending on b) and the second closing with the same cadence as that of the third-to-last phrase (or possibly with a slightly different end: E and F as antepenultimate and penultimate notes in the organal voice).

The second half of the Verse proceeds along similar lines; in Example 10 vertical lines show the phrase divisions. The chant versions in Provins 12 and Chartres 520 differ from each other and from Chartres 130 in minor details: both chant manuscripts have a *pes* FG over *lo(cutus)*, and the word *est* and the penultimate note above *diebus* are missing in Provins 12. The transcription of the neumes for *(prophe)tis* poses some problems. The first inclination would be to read these as d c-d b; then, just at the point when Old and New Testament are confronted in the text, the word *prophetis* would end on an 'open' sound (fourth). In view of the subject-matter and the subtle relationship between text and music—such as may be observed in both monophonic and polyphonic compositions of the twelfth century[39]—it seems quite conceivable that this unusual procedure might have been intended. For the moment I have decided in favour of a solution based on the normal rules, with a unison cadence on e.

Chartres 130: Alleluia V. Dies sanctificatus

The first organum notated in Chartres 130 exemplifies, on the one hand, the disparity between this highly differentiated polyphony and traditional singing based on simpler models and, on the other hand, the distance from this to the 'new organum' of the twelfth century. To illustrate the first the Chartres 130 *Alleluia* invocation and beginning of its Verse will be compared to the Winchester setting; for the second, after a brief glance at Aquitainian polyphony, the organa of Chartres 109 will serve as a point of comparison.

(a) Chartres 130 and Winchester

The parallel arrangement of the Alleluia and Verse is absolutely typical of the methodical approach to structure in the Chartres 130 organa (see Example 11). Both begin with a long phrase (of twelve and sixteen notes respectively); in the case of the Verse this corresponds to the word *Dies*. In the next part of both the Alleluia and Verse many sonorities are repeated (more often than suggested by the chant itself). In the Alleluia it is the fourth C/F which returns, always with new continuations: at first in five (2 + 3) notes moving from F to a unison G; then twice to unisons on D, where the counterpoint FD CD against the chant's CD FD produces a

Example 11. Opening of *Alleluia V. Dies sanctificatus* (Chartres 130)

[39] See my remarks in '*Nova Cantica*: Grundsätzliches und Spezielles zur Interpretation musikalischer Texte des Mittelalters', *Basler Jahrbuch für historische Musikpraxis* 10 (1986), 13–62, esp. 28–33 and 61.

Example 11—*cont.*

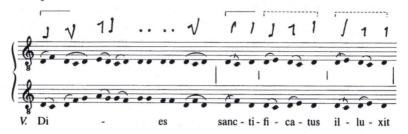

V. Di - es   sanc - ti- fi - ca - tus   il - lu - xit

repetition; and lastly, with the prolongation of the C/F fourth in two
phrases which end on a unison D, followed by a standard four-note
cadence on to D. In the Verse the phrase for *sanc(tificatus)* establishes a
correspondence with the opening (indicated in the example by ⌐——, and
then a melodic repetition in the chant is mirrored by another in the *vox
organalis*.

The transcription of the Winchester organum can be confirmed through
comparison with several concordances within the collection (Example
12).[40] And here too the first phrase of the Alleluia stretches as far as the
twelfth note, with a setting which has cleverly recognized the possibility of
shaping the opening through the repetition of the first three notes by the
organal voice—first heard in unison with the chant and then as the
beginning of a passage in parallel fourths which leads to the first *occursus*.
In the second part, by contrast, each phrase is independently constructed,
the first with held tones leading to an *occursus*, the second beginning with
an interval of a second and continuing in unison, the third with a fall
through repeated Es and Cs, the fourth again in unison, with the resulting
occursus, and the last using held tones to lead to an *occursus* from the note
below the final. The first part of the Verse demonstrates how similar
structural arrangements in Chartres 130 and Winchester are achieved by
quite different means. In Winchester the word *Dies* is again set in one
phrase, using continuous parallel fourths which are brought to a close by
held tones and an *occursus*. The establishment of a connection between the
beginning of the Verse and the second word is dispensed with; however,
the two similar (chant) phrases on *sanctifi-* and *-catus* are set in the same
way, with a repeated *occursus* which underlines the repetition while at the

[40.] Cambridge, Corpus Christi College 473, fol. 165r; for a transcription and commentary
on this organum, see Holschneider, *Winchester*, 160–3, 117–18, and *passim*. My own
transcription adopts the main outlines of Holschneider's, as does that published by S.
Fuller, 'Early Polyphony', 506–7.

Example 12. Opening of *Alleluia V. Dies sanctificatus* (Winchester)

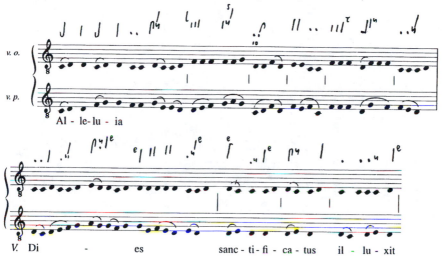

same time upsetting the unity of the word. What seems to be missing in this Winchester setting is a feeling for correspondence between the Alleluia and its Verse, as well as for that other type of parallelism between phrases through repetition of sonorities which in Chartres 130 takes its lead from aspects of the chant but also develops them further.

(b) Chartres 130, Paris 1139, and Chartres 109

The way in which these techniques of the late eleventh century were taken up in Aquitainian polyphony of the early twelfth is shown by the earliest version of the Benedicamus *Noster cetus* (Paris 1139, fol. 61r; Example 13).

Example 13. Opening of Benedicamus *Noster cetus* (Paris 1139)

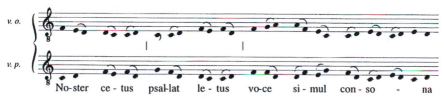

In its first verse a sonority based on the unison, and intervals of a third and a fourth is expanded to include the fifth, exploiting the Dorian sonority; melodic and harmonic correspondences between short phrases are explored and so on. But here, the context is that of a freely composed song with an original text.

Example 14. Continuation of *Alleluia V. Dies sanctificatus* (Chartres 130)

The comparison of the second half of the Chartres 130 Verse *Dies sanctificatus* with the organa in Chartres 109—notated on lines—shows the extent to which, building on the foundations of Chartres 130 and, of course, extending the realm of technical possibilities, the organa of Chartres 109 have achieved a new dimension: the organal voice taking on a melodic quality more akin to that of a second chant voice. In the section of the *Dies sanctificatus* Verse shown in Example 14 the consistency of notational practice, notably that of the relative disposition of neumes on

Example 15. Alternative interpretation of neumes in *Venite* melisma

the page, can be observed in the related passages *nobis* and *magna*. Beyond what has already been discussed only one other new trait needs to be pointed out: in the melisma for *ve(nite)*, the interval of an octave between the voices may be intended. But these neumes can be interpreted in other ways, as in Example 15.

Example 16. Extant portion of *Alleluia V. Christus resurgens* (Chartres 109)

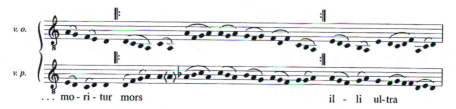

... mo - ri - tur mors   il - li ul-tra

Continuing the comparison of the Chartres 130 organa with those in the younger manuscript, I turn now to the extant part of *Alleluia V. Christus resurgens* preserved in Chartres 109.[41] The principal new aspect exemplified by the extract shown in Example 16 is the degree to which the melodic quality of the organal voice can be developed using the octave as a cadential interval. One of the consequences of this growing melodic independence — which consequently finds an echo in theoretical writings — is a certain freedom in the treatment of dissonances produced by the melodic shape of the *vox organalis*; this can be observed not only in these organa but also in the early Aquitainian repertory.[42] It is evident in the extant portion of the processional Verse *Crucifixum in carne* (Example 17). The progression above *se(pultum)*, where the voices move from a third to a second and again to a third, may be compared to the third–second–unison progressions typical of holding-tone passages. Yet in this example the interval of a second results not from a cadential procedure but from the similar melodic

[41.] Since they were first published by Bannister (see n. 19 above), the organa of Chartres 109 have been reproduced several times. Here again I have made use of reproductions from Handschin's collection in the Musikwissenschaftliches Institut, Basel. The repetition of the melisma is indicated in my transcription by a repeat sign.

[42.] A detailed study of these aspects, involving discussion of several pieces (including *Alleluia V. Angelus Domini*), is in W. Arlt, 'Peripherie und Zentrum I: *Dulcis sapor novi mellis* in einem um 1200 aufgezeichneten mehrstimmigen Satz aus Apt und die ältesten Sätze des "Saint Martial"-Repertoires', *Forum Musicologicum* I (Bern, 1975), 169–222. For the corresponding theory see F. Reckow, 'Kompilation als Innovation: Eine Methode theoretischer Darstellung als Zugang zum Charakter hochmittelalterlicher Mehrstimmigkeit', *Festschrift Martin Ruhnke zum 65. Geburtstag* (Neuhausen and Stuttgart, 1986), 307–320.

Example 17. Extant portion of V. *Crucifixum in carne* (Chartres 109)

contour of the two voices in the scalic fall GF-ED; in the chant voice this is heard for *(se)pultum*, and in the *vox organalis* already for *sepul(tum)* (as well as for *laudate* at the beginning of the transcribed passage), both times preceded by the step D-E. Something similar happens with the progressions in seconds at *glo(rificate)*, where the *vox organalis* follows the characteristic plagal Dorian outline D-C-A, at *(resur)gen(temque)*, and once again at the end of a passage from the Verse of *Alleluia V. Surrexit Christus* (Example 18), on *(mi)ser(tus)*.

Example 18. Opening of the Alleluia verse *Surrexit Christus* (Chartres 109)

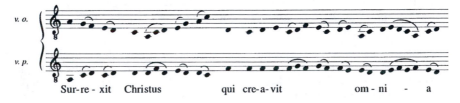

In these organa artful assimilation of the voices is guided not only by the chant melody and its latent sonorities but also by a careful division of the text into words and sense units. Their composition even involved the illustrative treatment of text content, a phenomenon already familiar in the Gregorian repertory. Thus, for example, the little melisma on (*Chris*)*tus* in Example 18 could, in this style, have been treated in less dramatic ways than the striking rise from the plagal Dorian range through a tenth from A to the high c. That this sharp ascent was indeed provoked by the announcement '*Surrexit Christus*' is confirmed by the fall of a seventh after the rise to c, an absolutely unique progression in this source (even if, because of the caesura, it may be understood as a 'dead interval').

In view of these observations on the compositional and historical position of the Chartres 130 organa, we may explain the fact of their having been notated as the natural outcome of a desire to fix in writing some examples of what could be achieved in the new style of organum singing — a style shortly to be codified and discussed in theoretical writings on 'new organum'.[43] So it may be no accident that precisely these organa are transmitted on an outer folio of a manuscript which contained music theory texts (on organum among other things), and that these four pieces encompass, in the appropriate order, four principal feasts of the church year (despite a break in the content).[44] With this in mind we might even speculate that Chartres 109 (itself an unfinished collection) represents but a fragment of a larger repertory.[45]

Continuance of Old and Development of New Practices

Having once reconstructed the organa in Chartres 4 and Chartres 130 it is tempting to overrate the evolutionary aspects of eleventh-century polyphony in its development from unwritten 'simple' practices of the 'old' to the artistic potential of the 'new' organum. The continued use of old practices and stylistic elements well beyond this period would in any case show this view to be one-sided.[46] Indeed, the question arises as to whether

---

[43] See the literature cited in n. 38 above.

[44] I shall discuss the fourth organum, *Alleluia V. Pascha nostrum V. Epulemur*, in a separate study.

[45] Gushee (*Polyphony*, 52–3) stressed the fact that this folio came from another, unidentified, manuscript (therefore of unknown provenance).

[46] The diversity and many-layered nature of this aspect of musical culture is already evident from the examples of the early 12th C. discussed by Gushee.

the meagre number of surviving pieces (even allowing for the loss of a large number of sources) is not itself an indication of the continuing unquestioned use of older, generally simpler, techniques.

Saint-Maur-des-Fossés: Paris 12584, 12596, and 11631

In this context a small group of pieces surviving in sources from Saint-Maur-des-Fossés is of particular interest. While they are transmitted in some of the latest sources which can be considered relevant to the discussion of eleventh-century polyphony and are notated in the 'newer' way (with one voice written above the other), these pieces present a comparatively simple accompaniment to the chant. A typical and easily transcribed example is provided by the Responsory *Petre amas me V. Symon Iohannis* (see Example 19); this was notated at Saint-Maur towards the end of the century on a leaf added to Paris 12584 (fol. 306r). Although some details of the chant melody cannot be precisely established, the main features of the style are extremely clear.[47] This piece shares some aspects with the organa in Chartres 4 as well as those in Chartres 130, although—assuming this reading to be correct not only in general stylistic aspects but also in details—it appears to have noticeably fewer dissonances (and a correspondingly high number of thirds). But whereas the Chartres organa reveal an especially subtle compositional approach, thereby suggesting the reason for their preservation in written form, we see in the Saint-Maur piece a careful but fairly standard formulation. Appearing as part of a varied group of pieces used to supplement the liturgy of the patronal feast, it is clear that the organum was notated not for its own sake but because it belonged to this larger context. Of several entries made by different scribes on this single leaf, that including the organum concerns processional pieces, beginning with the monophonic antiphon *Sancte Petre apostolorum summe*. The Responsory follows immediately after. Evidently it was customary to sing this Responsory polyphonically: it already appears in a polyphonic setting in Winchester (fol. 189v), although without the verse. And in the festal office from Beauvais copied in the early thirteenth century from an earlier (now lost) exemplar, a rubric calls for polyphonic performance of the Verse, again in a processional context, and after first vespers 'ante crucifixum'. The Responsory was then to be sung by the

---

[47.] Michel Huglo ('Débuts', 108) reconstructed the chant melody using two antiphoners: Paris, Bibliothèque nationale lat. 12044, fol. 153v (St-Maur-des-Fossés), and Paris, Bibliothèque nationale lat. 17296, fol. 178r (St-Denis). I have adopted his version, making some small modifications based on the neumatic notation. The as yet unidentified melisma inserted into the verse is not dealt with here. The '*Aliud*' melisma appears in London, British Library 2615 (fol. 9v), and is here taken from this Beauvais source, with two minor adjustments.

Example 19 (a) Responsory *Petre amas me* (Paris 12584)

Example 19 (b) Alternative version of the verse opening

choir 'redeundo in choro' followed by the Verse 'in choro *cum organo*' (my emphasis).[48] In fact the alternative verse melisma notated in Paris 12584 under the rubric 'Aliud' is known elsewhere only in this Beauvais Office (where it appears not as *aliud* but actually within the Verse), underlining the connection between the two sources.

Example 20 (*a*) Extant portions of Responsory *Martir Clemens* (Paris 12596), based on chant reconstruction by Huglo

Example 20 (*b*) Extant portions of Responsory *Martir Clemens* (Paris 12596), based on chant reconstruction by Gushee

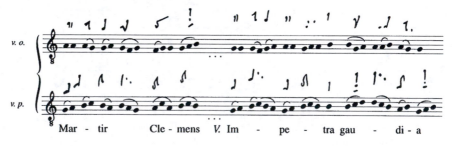

The surviving fragments of a polyphonic Responsory, *Martir Clemens V. Impetra gaudia*, notated on the last leaf of Paris 12596—again in a monophonic context—present the same picture, regardless of whether the reconstruction of the chant by Michel Huglo, with a typical Dorian intonation (Example 20(*a*)), or that by Marion Gushee, based on a concordance on fol. 213v of Paris, Bibliothèque nationale lat. 12044 (Example 20(*b*)), is followed.[49] The polyphonic setting of the Verse

---

[48.] This processional liturgy is edited in Arlt, *Festoffizium*, II, 15–23 (the Responsory on 21); on the lost 12th-C. exemplar see *Festoffizium* I, 30–1, and D. G. Hughes, 'Another Source for the Beauvais Feast of Fools', *Music and Context, Essays for John Ward*, ed. A. D. Shapiro (Cambridge, Mass., 1985), 14–31.

[49.] Huglo, 'Débuts', 111; Gushee, *Polyphony*, 162 and 166, using a chant version from Paris 12044.

Example 21. Opening of Responsory verse *Gabrihelem archangelem* (Paris 11631)

Gabrihelem archangelum for the Responsory *Gaude Maria* added to Paris 11631 (fol. 72v) is, if anything, simpler. It needs no more than the opening phrases to illustrate this (Example 21); once again some details of the chant melody remain unclear.

Vatican 586

The three organal voices notated at a much earlier date in Vatican 586 (fol. 87v) present an entirely different picture. Here the arrangement of neumes on the page, following the melodic contour with exceptional precision, provides unequivocal information for reading the notation. Because of this they have been transcribed several times, although with significant differences of detail.[50] In its articulation in short phrases and frequent use of holding notes, the basic elements of this style match those of the Chartres 4 organa. Individually they exhibit an extraordinarily wide spectrum of formal techniques, ranging from the simplest chant accompaniment, a *vox organalis* constructed mainly from holding tones (including passages with the organal voice above the chant), to a structure characterized by extreme differentiation of vertical sonorities—including

---

[50.] The first (*Viderunt omnes*) by Bannister, *Monumenti*, Testo, 79b; all three by Gushee, *Polyphony*, 179–84, and Holschneider, *Winchester*, 172–7, with whom I largely agree.

the use of fifths and sixths in exposed positions—which finds no counterpart among other extant examples of eleventh-century polyphony.

   The simple holding-tone accompaniment is found in the third Gradual,
Gloriosus deus V. Dextera tua, as shown in the reconstruction of the
Gradual's intonation and the beginning of the Verse (Example 22). The
chant version used in this example is taken from the *Graduale Romanum*;
but details of the *vox organalis* in each of these organa—in particular that
for the Gradual *Omnes de Saba*—indicate that they were based on different
chant versions. The identification of these versions would, of course,
provide a key to the provenance of these organa, or at least to that of the
singer-notator who was responsible for formulating them. The articulation
of these passages in short phrases is accentuated by the addition of extra
tones in the *vox organalis* (at least in so far as the differing number of notes
between chant and organal voice in the transcription is not due to chant
variants), and by the frequent use in the *vox organalis* of an interval of a
third to reach the cadence note. The resulting sound is dense and rich in
dissonance.

Example 22. Opening of Gradual *Gloriosus deus* (Vatican 586)

Example 23. Opening of Gradual *Viderunt omnes* (Vatican 586)

The most individual and stylistically diverse composition in this source is the setting of the Christmas Gradual *Viderunt omnes V. Notum fecit*. Its rich sonorous quality permeates the intonation (Example 23). Here techniques familiar from other eleventh-century organa are used to highlight the rising movement of the chant melody through a Lydian third-chain F-a-c to the high e (corresponding to the theological import of this Christmas text), most clearly by the repeated unison c above *om(nes)*, and to emphasize the fifth F/c, and its two thirds F/a and a/c. Thereby a sonority unique in the eleventh century has been created. The 'open' fourth at the end of the second word is repeated within the final melisma, binding the whole together. With this in mind, I do not agree with Andreas Holschneider's description of parts of the melisma on the third word of the Verse (see Example 24) as requiring a 'more satisfactory solution' (*befriedi-gendere Lösung*),[51] but see instead a free, deliberate, and exhaustive working out of the potential of this type of organum by an artistic singer-composer. Most certainly, it is astonishing to find in the second four-note group of this melisma a pair of parallel fifths leading via the third a/c to a unison b (marked ⌐——⌐), thus creating a tritone resonance with the beginning; no less astonishing is the continuation in parallel sixths before the return to a

Example 24. Opening of Gradual verse *Notum fecit* (Vatican 586)

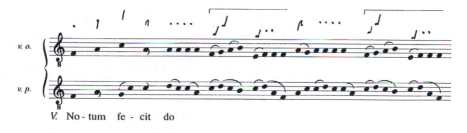

51. Holschneider, *Winchester*, 173.

Example 24—*cont.*

mi - nus

unison F. There can be no doubt about the scribe's intentions here, not only because of the notation of the phrase and its adjacent repetition, but also since the same melodic contour occurring in the subsequent entry (a Gradual for St Stephen's Day) receives the same treatment. And when actually heard, the tension created by the tritone and the entry on a sixth can immediately be recognized as exceedingly artful harmonic responses to the melodic structure of the chant. If—according to the procedures of this type of organum—each of the four-note groups marked in brackets is taken as a unit, then the first group is heard to end on a tone (b) which not only contrasts with the third-chain F-a-c but sets up an extreme tension; for this b (*mi*) leads in the chant to c (*fa*), and thus the chant melody is cut in two at a crucial moment. The E sung by the organal voice at the beginning of the second group is nothing other than the echo a fifth lower of a note heard prominently in both voices. In this way parts of the melodic contour treated as separate groups in the process of composition of this organum are actually brought together again by the resultant sonority.

The comparison of this setting with that of *Gloriosus deus* (Example 22) shows that there too, in the context of a radical limitation of the *vox organalis* to the simplest means of accompaniment (in drones), a specific dimension of organum composition has been consciously explored. And it is not just in these two examples but in all the organa of Vatican 586 that a level of formal organization not conceived of in the canon of textbook rules can be recognized.

A historical perception of polyphonic practice concentrated on the evolution from 'old' to 'new' organum and conceived in terms of the echo of musical practice in theoretical texts would leave out of consideration the compositional subtlety of organa such as those in Vatican 586, at the same time implying that a relatively simple organal accompaniment such as that for the verse of *Gaude Maria* in Paris 11631 was, at the time of its notation (*circa* 1100), old-fashioned. In view of the observations presented here, this traditional, rather simplistic, picture, must be revised. Indeed, the whole question of the way in which theory and practice interacted in the period from the tenth to the twelfth century needs to be re-examined, taking into special account the conditions which tend to determine the nature of the content of each.[52] And, as with other musical repertories in this time of new beginnings, it seems characteristic of polyphonic practice in the second half of the eleventh century that it should encompass a plurality of quite different procedures—a plurality which contributes much to our understanding of the new qualities in song and polyphony of the early twelfth century.[53]

Perspectives

The question 'how can the continental sources of the eleventh century contribute to our understanding of the Winchester organa?' has necessarily led far beyond that period at the beginning of the century when this first great, entirely unique, collection of polyphony was notated at an English cathedral. The exploration of the continental sources, including the reconstruction of the earliest Chartres notations of organa, has brought new perspectives to our understanding of early polyphony, unearthing an astonishing richness of artistic composition, and throwing much new light on the Winchester organa. At every turn, the comparisons have confirmed the nature of the English source as a collection motivated primarily by the wish to make a written record of a special performance practice.

Nevertheless, the fact that we are only just beginning to deal with matters of musical style in this field must not be overlooked; above all, further and more differentiated answers to our questions will not be found until various fundamental matters—such as a comprehensive examination of the transmission of chants used in organa—have been sorted out. Inevitably, such studies will lead to the modification of the reconstructions and interpretations offered here, and may indeed bring new insights into those specific aspects and artistic dimensions of the Winchester organa which have tended to be obscured rather than illuminated by their comparison with the later continental sources.

---

[52] For such an interpretation of the theoretical texts see M. Haas, 'Der Epilog des Mailänder Organum-Traktates: Zum Problem von Dialektik und Sachbezug in der Musiktheorie des ausgehenden elften Jahrhunderts', *Schweizer Beiträge zur Musikwissenschaft* 2 (Bern and Stuttgart, 1974), 7–19; S. Fuller, 'Theoretical Foundations of Early Organum Theory', *Acta musicologica* 53 (1981), 52–84, and F. Reckow, 'Kompilation als Innovation', *passim*.

[53] On the 'new song' see W. Arlt, 'Das eine Lied und die vielen Lieder: Zur historischen Stellung der neuen Liedkunst des frühen 12. Jahrhunderts', *Festschrift für Rudolf Bockholdt zum 60. Geburtstag*, ed. N. Dubowy and S. Meyer-Eller (Pfaffenhofen, 1990), 113–27.

II

Liturgical Uses and Genres
in
Medieval England

6

Post-Pentecost Alleluias in Medieval British Liturgies

DAVID HILEY

(University of Regensburg)

It may well have been Walter Howard Frere who first pointed out how useful post-Pentecost alleluias were in determining the derivation of a missal or gradual. At least, I am aware of no earlier reference. In the introduction to *Graduale Sarisburiense* he wrote: 'a synoptic table of Alleluias is by far the best test by which to discriminate between varying uses'.[1] Frere himself never followed through this recommendation with any systematic published survey of alleluia series. Nor did his colleague John Wickham Legg in the extensive commentary for his edition of the 'Lytlington Missal' of Westminster Abbey.[2] In fact, the alleluia series of that manuscript is one of the most important clues as to its derivation, since it is a highly characteristic one used at Fécamp, Jumièges, Saint-Evroult, and Mont-Saint-Michel. Since then the existence of the method has become widely known. Michel Huglo gave an account of its development in the hands of Dom Gabriel Beyssac, and its utilization in several recent studies.[3] Most of the latter have been concerned with small groups of sources—Michel Huglo's contribution to the present collection of essays is a case in point—although it is clear that knowledge of a large number of series lies behind many of them. Only Heinrich Husmann has so far published the results of what approaches a Europe-wide survey of alleluia

[1] W. H. Frere, *Graduale Sarisburiense* (London, 1894), 1.

[2] J. W. Legg, *Missale ad usum ecclesiae Westmonasteriensis*, Henry Bradshaw Society 1 (London, 1891), 5 (London, 1893), 12 (London, 1897).

[3] M. Huglo, 'Les Listes alléluiatiques dans les témoins du graduel grégorien', *Speculum Musicae Artis: Festgabe für Heinrich Husmann zum 60. Geburtstag*, ed. H. Becker and R. Gerlach (Munich, 1970), 219–27.

series,[4] and his articles are the most convenient starting-point for any such investigation.[5]

A brief account of the technique of comparison is in order here. While the alleluias used on a few of the most important feasts of the year, such as Christmas Day, St Stephen's (26 December), St John the Evangelist's (27 December), and Easter Day, are more or less constant through all sources from the late eighth century onward (see the sources edited by Hesbert,[6] or the list published by Apel[7]), the choice of alleluias for other occasions tends to vary from one source to another. In contrast to alleluias for most major feasts, those for Sundays (often referred to as 'dominical' alleluias—for the seasons of Advent and Epiphany and the summer Sundays after Pentecost) usually employ psalm verses for the texts of the alleluia verses. Frequently the first verse of the psalm is chosen. It is convenient to refer to these alleluias simply by the number of the psalm from which they are taken. So *Alleluia V. Omnes gentes plaudite manibus* may be referred to simply as 46, *Alleluia V. Attendite popule meus* as 77. Sometimes two or more different alleluias have verses from the same psalm, and in such cases I give the verse number as well. So *Alleluia V. Domine deus meus* is 7.2 and *Alleluia V. Deus iudex iustus* is 7.12. A list of alleluias referred to in this essay is included in the Appendix.

Sometimes an alleluia has more than one verse, as for example *Alleluia V. Venite exultemus V. Preoccupemus*. Not all manuscripts with *Alleluia V. Venite*, even from the same church, will employ the second verse; and if a source gives simply a text incipit one cannot tell whether a fully notated gradual of the same church would have contained a second verse. In such cases I therefore refer only to the first verse.[8]

For some time (varying from place to place but, generally speaking, from the ninth to the late eleventh century), full alleluias were usually copied in a separate fascicle of a gradual or cantatorium, although a text incipit in the correct liturgical place might indicate when an alleluia should be sung. This is the procedure adopted, for example, in Chartres, Bibliothèque

[4.] H. Husmann, 'Studien zur geschichtlichen Stellung der Liturgie Kopenhagens: Die Oster- u. Pfingstalleluia der Kopenhagener Liturgie u. ihre historischen Beziehungen', *Dansk Aarbog for Musikforskning* (1962), 3–58; and (1964–5), 3–62.

[5.] Several scholars have over the years accumulated what are reported to be vast collections of alleluia series, including notably Beyssac's papers, in Bouveret, Switzerland, those of Leroquais in the Bibliothèque nationale, Paris, and those of Cosmo Alexander Gordon in the Bodleian Library at Oxford. I have not been able to consult any of these in the preparation of this study. Jeremy Noble is now gathering the evidence of all surviving printed liturgical books of the 15th and 16th C. (See nn. 20 and 25 below.)

[6.] R.-J. Hesbert, *Antiphonale missarum sextuplex* (Brussels, 1935).

[7.] W. Apel, *Gregorian Chant* (Bloomington, Ind., 1958), 379.

[8.] For an account of the double verses see K. Schlager, 'Anmerkungen zu den zweiten Alleluia-Versen', *Archiv für Musikwissenschaft* 24 (1967), 199–219.

municipale 47. Missals with or without music (such books are not usual before the twelfth century) give the full alleluia, or full text, at the correct liturgical place. Some 'forerunners' of the missal, sacramentaries with chant incipits in the main text or in the margin, may also cite the alleluia to be sung (for example Rouen, Bibliothèque municipale 273, from Saint-Evroult).

Sunday alleluias are sometimes given separately as a continuous series. The use of a title such as *Alleluia dominicis diebus vel nataliciis sanctorum per circulum anni* (Saint-Gall, Stiftsbibliothek 339) or *incipiunt alleluia per circulum anni* (Saint-Gall, Stiftsbibliothek 359) at the beginning of such a series has given rise to the idea that many of these alleluias are older than the festal alleluias not using psalm verses, and may once have been used more widely throughout the church year.[9]

Among the groups of dominical alleluias, that for the Advent Sundays is relatively stable from source to source. That for the Sundays after Epiphany is slightly less so.[10] Variation is most visible (because of the longer period of the church year in question), and therefore most conveniently studied, among the Sundays after Pentecost: in the British and North French sources, which are the main focus of attention in this essay, over sixty different alleluias are to be found for the twenty-three or so Sundays. Most sources have from twenty-two to twenty-four alleluias (the number of weeks would vary from one year to another, depending upon the date of Easter), but some have thirty or more. A possible reason why sources differ so much from one another is that they may have selected their twenty-three alleluias from larger fascicles: different churches would select differently. And a certain number of new alleluias no doubt entered the repertory at different times and in different places.

The result of this process is that when one comes across sources with a similar or even identical series of alleluias in the post-Pentecost season, some sort of relationship between them may be surmised. Often the relationship is clear, such as that between mother and daughter monastery. Sometimes the connection is not so obvious, but seems to be the result of geographical proximity.

It should hardly be necessary to state that investigation of post-Pentecost alleluias is only one element in the systematic analysis of

[9] This was a favourite idea of Husmann's: see his remarks in *Revue Belge de musicologie* 10 (1956), 113, and in *Acta musicologica* 38 (1966), 128. Clear evidence of the process is not, however, easy to detect. Apel (*Gregorian Chant*, 379) points out that, whereas the sources edited by Hesbert agree in assigning *Alleluia V. Dominus regnavit decorem* (92) to the Monday of Easter week, it was shortly replaced by an alleluia with verse not drawn from the psalter.

[10] See Husmann, 'Studien'. Lack of space forbids my discussing these parts of the church year here, likewise the interesting deployment of (usually non-psalmic) alleluias in Easter week and the succeeding period.

liturgical books. Liturgies are composed of layers of material, each with its own history. Lessons, prayers, and chants were not deposited in medieval churches like blocks of granite, impervious to change. Each was subject to modification and renovation. Even within the chant repertory of a church—which would not necessarily have undergone the same evolution as the lessons and prayers—numerous layers of material can be discerned. Nevertheless, the post-Pentecost alleluias have proved to be a surprisingly useful indicator of relationships between uses. If one has not taken them into account in the investigation of a particular book, one can hardly be said to have explained its derivation adequately.

The question of the origin of these hypothetical fascicles, indeed of the very selection of psalm verses to be sung when the repertory was being formed (why is it usually just the first verse of a psalm?), is well beyond the scope of this essay. In a volume devoted to English liturgies and church music it will obviously be appropriate to concentrate on English alleluia series. Fortunately, previous research has served the English liturgies well in this respect. In his edition of the Missal of the New Minster, Winchester, and his contribution to Anselm Hughes's edition of the Missal of Bec in Normandy, Derek Turner gave an exposition of two of the most important English alleluia series.[11] To one of these Michel Huglo has just returned with further observations. I myself have added further material in two contributions.[12] In the present essay I shall recapitulate previous writings as little as possible, and seek instead to broaden the investigation both historically and geographically. I hope that this will provide a clearer context for understanding the British post-Pentecost alleluia series.[13]

Non-Numerical Series

The post-Pentecost series of alleluias is usually arranged in numerical order by psalm verse. But several important early series are not. Michel Huglo has just discussed one, found among other places at Winchester, to which I shall shortly return. Another such is the Old-Roman series, reproduced from Rome, Biblioteca Apostolica Vaticana Vat. lat. 5319, in

[11.] D. H. Turner, *The Missal of the New Minster, Winchester*, Henry Bradshaw Society 93 (Leighton Buzzard, 1971); A. Hughes, *The Bec Missal*, Henry Bradshaw Society 94 (Leighton Buzzard, 1963).

[12.] D. Hiley, 'The Norman Chant Traditions—Normandy, Britain, Sicily', *Proceedings of the Royal Musical Association* 107 (1980–1), 1–33; id., 'Thurstan of Caen and Plainchant at Glastonbury: Musicological Reflections on the Norman Conquest', *Proceedings of the British Academy* 72 (1986), 57–90.

[13.] Some of the material now presented is a condensed version of ch. 8 of my Ph.D. dissertation 'The Liturgical Music of Norman Sicily: A Study Centred on Manuscripts 288, 289, 19421 and Vitrina 20–4 of the Biblioteca Nacional, Madrid' (University of London, 1981).

Table 1. If we were to rearrange the series numerically, as in Table 2, we should notice that all alleluias but one are from Psalms 90–150 (92 appears twice).

TABLE 1

Rome 5319

| 146^3 | 147^{12} | 147^{14} | 99 | 94^1 | 146^1 | 145 | 92 | 64 | 94^2 | 137^1 | 137^2 | 107 |
| 95 | 97 | 112 | 121 | 124 | 116^2 | 116^1 | 94^3 | 92 | | | | |

TABLE 2

Rome 5319 in numerical order

| 64 | 92 | 94^1 | 94^2 | 94^3 | 95 | 97 | 99 | 107 | 112 | 116^1 | 116^2 | 121 |
| 124 | 137^1 | 137^2 | 145 | 146^1 | 146^3 | 147^{12} | 147^{14} | | | | | |

What is possibly the oldest Carolingian source, Brussels, Bibliothèque Royale lat. 10127–10144 (the famous 'Blandiniensis', edited by Hesbert), likewise concentrates on this part of the psalter (some non-dominical alleluias are interspersed in the list). Only two alleluias have texts from the first half of the psalter (see Table 3). Only slightly later than the above source is Zurich, Zentralbibliothek Rheinau 30, from Nivelles, of *circa* 800. Here the fifth to eleventh alleluias, and four near the end, are deployed in numerical order (see Table 4). One would like to know the reason for the concentration on the last part of the psalter. Were verses from the rest sung elsewhere in the year? If so, they have vanished almost without trace. The other alleluias in Rome 5319, for example (excepting the non-psalmodic alleluias for the Christmas season, Easter Day, and SS Peter and Paul), show no special interest in the first half of the psalter.[14] Curiously, in the post-Pentecost Sundays, the other proper chants of the mass have a

[14.] The two Advent texts come from Psalms 79 and 84, those for the first two masses of Christmas from 2 and 92, the three post-Epiphany ones from 64, 92, and 137. The alleluias of Easter week, including the special alleluias of vespers, touch on only 46, 64, and 89 out of the first 90 psalms. The pattern is repeated in the weeks after Easter (only 64), and Whitsun week (64 again). Ascension Day uses verses from Psalms 46 (again) and 67, the Sunday after Ascension reverts to Psalms 124 and 145. What is more, the selection in the Sanctorale is almost equally biased. The psalms used are as follows (in ascending order): 32—*Gaudete iusti*; 36—*Justus non conturbabitur*; 44—*Diffusa est gratia, Specie tua*; 88—*Disposui testamentum, Confitebuntur celi*; 97—*Cantate domino*; 111—*Beatus vir qui timet*; 131—*Memento domine David*; 138—*Nimis honorati*; 144—*Sancti tui domine*; 149—*Exultabunt sancti*. Feasts of the Holy Cross and St Michael have alleluias also found in the dominical series.

TABLE 3

Brussels 10127–10144

| 99 | 92 | 94[1] | 96 | 131 | 84 | 121 | 1 | 145 | 147[12] | 150 | 112 | Elegit te |
| 94[3] | 137[1] | 117 | 146[3] | 147[14] | 124 | 64 | 97 | 104 | Disposui, Mittat, Exultabunt | | | |

TABLE 4

Zurich 30

| 106 | 92 | 34 | 94[3] | 64 | 92 | 94[1] | 94[6] | 97 | 99 | 104[lac.] |
| 112? | 146[1]? | 137[1] | 137[2] | 145 | 146[3] | 131 | | | | |

complementary bias toward the first part of the psalter. Of the nineteen introits whose texts are drawn from the psalter, only two are from Psalms 90–150; seven of the twenty-one graduals; four out of sixteen offertories; and five out of fourteen communions.

However, the reasons for these peculiarities of selection can hardly be pursued further here. Suffice it to remark that the bias toward the latter part of the psalter distinguishes these ancient alleluia series from most later ones.

I have already alluded to the alleluia series which is common to liturgical books from Westminster in England and the Norman monasteries of Fécamp, Jumièges, Saint-Evroult, and Mont-Saint-Michel. This is also non-numerical in order. In England it is found in a missal from Abingdon as well.[15] The common factor in this grouping is of course the monastic reform instituted in Normandy by William of Dijon (or Volpiano) and his followers. And sure enough, the same alleluias are found in two chant books from William's monastery of Saint-Bénigne at Dijon. But in these codices the alleluias are arranged in numerical order. One would expect that to be a secondary development, for it seems unlikely that any cantor would deliberately 'scramble' a numerically ordered series. And some support for this explanation comes from the fact that in one of the Dijon codices the *Alleluia V. In te domine speravi* is counted as 30, in the other as 70 (both those psalms begin with the same verse). It is as if we are seeing two attempts to order the non-numerical series in a logical way. Yet the

[15]. See Hiley, 'Norman Chant Traditions', 14–16 (list of sources) and 19 (table 2a).

numerical arrangement must have been carried out at a relatively early point, for one of the Dijon sources is none other than the famous tonary Montpellier, Faculté de Médecine H. 159, usually dated in the eleventh century, and thus considerably earlier than most of the Norman monastic sources that have the non-numerical order. (The other Dijon source is the thirteenth-century gradual Brussels, Bibliothèque Royale II. 3824.) The series are given in Table 5.

TABLE 5

Norman and English monastic sources
5   116^1 117 145^2 30 or 70   104   64 94^1 17   20 146^3 113^{BII} 101^{16}
80   94^3 147^{14} 46   77   87 7^{12} 129   89 7^2

Montpellier, Faculté de Médecine H. 159
5   7^2 7^{12} 17   20   30   46   64   77   80   87   89 94^1
94^3 101^{16} 104   107 113^{BII} 116^1 117   129   145 146^3

Brussels, Bibliothèque Royale II. 3824
5   7^2 7^{12} 17   20   46   64   70   77   80   87   89 94^1
94^3 101^{16} 104   107 113^{BII} 116^1 117   129   145 146^3

The possibility of numerical reordering of non-numerical series should therefore be considered in other cases as well. If we reorder the series just discussed by Huglo, found at Winchester and Bury St Edmunds in England, and at Saint-Denis, Saint-Corneille of Compiègne, Corbie, Tours, Reims, and Angers in North France, there results a series which bears a strong resemblance to others in France. This raises a clear possibility that the liturgy of what one may call the 'Corbie–Saint-Denis' group was influential on other areas. The import of Table 6 is that the Limoges Cathedral manuscript has only one alleluia not found in the Corbie–Saint-Denis series, Nevers only two, Saint-Martial of Limoges, Sens, and Cluny only three.[16]

One further non-numerical series need not be discussed here, even though it is found in an area with historical, liturgical, and musical links with England. This is the one found in early Breton sources: Chartres, Bibliothèque municipale 47, Angers, Bibliothèque municipale 91 (from Angers) and Paris, Bibliothèque nationale lat. 9439 (from Rennes).[17] That

[16.] In my dissertation 'The Liturgical Music of Norman Sicily' I gave additional sources: the printed missal of Vienne of 1534 has four alleluias not in the Corbie–St-Denis set, and the following have five: Limoges, Bibliothèque municipale 2 (from Fontevrault), Paris, Bibliothèque nationale lat. 909 (St-Martial of Limoges), and Paris, Bibliothèque nationale lat. 1136 (St-Martial).

[17.] Discussed in G. Benoît-Castelli and M. Huglo, 'L'Origine bretonne du Graduel No 47 de la Bibliothèque de Chartres', *Études grégoriennes* i (1954), 173–8.

TABLE 6

	7[12]	17	20	30	46	64	70	77	80	87	89	92	94[1]	94[3]	96	99	104	107	110	112	113[1]	113[B11]	116[1]	117	121	124	129	137	145	146[3]	147[12]	147[14]
Corbie/St-Denis list numerically ordered	×	×	?	×	×	×	×	?	×	×	×	×	×	×	×	×	×	×	×	×	×	×	×	×	×	×	×	×	×	×	×	×
Paris, Bibliothèque nationale lat. 9438—St Stephen's Cathedral, Limoges	×	×	×	×	×	×	×	×	×	×	×	×	×	×	×	×	×	×	×	×	×	×	×	×	×	×	×	×	×	×	×	
Paris, Bibliothèque nationale nouv. acq. lat. 1235—Nevers	×	×	×	×	×	×	×	×	×	×	×	×	×	×	×	×	×		×	×	×	×	×	×	×	×	×	×	×	×		
Paris, Bibliothèque nationale lat. 1137—St-Martial, Limoges	×	×	×	×	×	×	×	×	×	×	×	×	×	×	×	×	×	×	×	×	×	×		×	×	×	×	×	×	×	×	×
Paris, Bibliothèque nationale lat. 864—Sens	×	×	×	×	×	×	×	×	×	×	×	×	×	×	×	×	×	×	×	×	×	×	×	×	×		×	×	×	×		
Cluny, printed missal of 1493	×	×	×	×	×	×	×	×	×	×	×	×	×	×	×	×	×	×	×	×	×	×	×	×	×		×	×	×	×		×

is the second non-numerical series known from Angers, for Angers 96 has the Corbie–Saint-Denis series. But unlike the latter, this Breton series is not found in Britain.

Large Alleluia Fascicles

The notion that a group of similar alleluia series, such as those of Nevers, Sens, and Limoges, might derive from an earlier and larger fascicle receives some support from two groups which I have previously discussed elsewhere. The post-Pentecost alleluia series of Rouen Cathedral, Evreux Cathedral, the monastery of Saint-Wandrille in Normandy, and most books from Sicily (conquered by the Normans in the eleventh century) are very similar to one another. And it turns out that all their alleluias are found in one and the same larger series in the earliest of the Norman-Sicilian tropers, Madrid, Biblioteca Nacional 288. If the hypothesis is correct, then Madrid 288 represents, at a point not very distant from the inception of the tradition, the larger fascicle from which the other series were selected.[18]

Just as striking is the resemblance between alleluia series in a large number of English and Norman sources where the connecting factor is the post-Conquest settlement in the English Church imposed by Lanfranc of Bec, succeeded by Anselm of Bec. The English sources with a series of this type come from Christ Church at Canterbury, St Augustine's at Canterbury, St Albans, Worcester, and Durham. In Normandy, not only sources from Bec itself have it, but also those from the monastery of Saint-Ouen at Rouen. Since Bec was a much more recent foundation than Saint-Ouen, it is possible that some elements of its liturgical use were borrowed from Saint-Ouen. But since the surviving Saint-Ouen sources which transmit the alleluia series are relatively late, it could also be argued that Saint-Ouen revised its own liturgy after the Bec model. It so happens that a late manuscript from Durham (London, British Library Harley 5289), includes all the alleluias found in the other series of this type. It might conceivably be a copy of some original collection from which the others derive, or, more likely, it simply records all the possibilities known to its editor by the late middle ages, including additions accumulated over the years.[19]

The differences between these groupings—the Norman-Sicilian and that of Bec—are not actually very great. The most characteristic difference is that Madrid 288 and its relatives count *Alleluia V. In te domine speravi* as Psalm 30, whereas the Bec group count it as 70. Otherwise the series in the true Bec sources, Paris, Bibliothèque nationale lat. 1105 and St Petersburg,

---

[18.] These series are given in Hiley, 'Norman Chant Traditions', 19, table 2b.

[19.] These series are given in Hiley, 'Norman Chant Traditions', 20, table 2c.

Public Library O. v. I. 6, would be contained in Madrid 288. One other Norman series hovers between the two, so to speak. The printed missal of Coutances of 1557 has twenty-five alleluias, which contain all the twenty-three of St Petersburg O. v. I. 6. and all twenty-four of Paris 1105. But it also has 101. 2, which belongs to the Madrid 288 fascicle (see Table 7). Let us suppose for a moment that the Bec series was composed (or borrowed from Saint-Ouen) in a form like that of St Petersburg O. v. I. 6. It would not be unreasonable to hypothesize that its origins were close to those of the Madrid 288 series, for we have seen the confusion of 30 and 70 even in books from the same monastery, in Dijon. Where then did the other alleluias found in English members of the Bec family come from? Perhaps some came from Winchester, for two of the alleluias in question, 110 and 116. 1, are in the New Minster Missal. 116. 1 is also in the Dijon series. The third supplementary alleluia found among English daughters of Bec is 147. 12. This is found, as we shall shortly see, in the Fleury series. But all three of these alleluias were also well known in North-East France. Further speculation therefore seems pointless.

TABLE 7

Madrid 288	5	7^2	7^{12}	17	20	30	46	47	58	64
	77	80	87	89	94^1	94^3	101^2	104	107	113^{BII}
	117	124	129	137^1	145	146^3	147^{14}			
Coutances	5	7^2	7^{12}	17	20	47	58	64	70	77
	80	87	89	94^1	94^3	101^2	104	107	113^{BII}	117
	124	129	145	146^3	147^{14}					
Paris 1105	5	7^2	7^{12}	17	20	47	58	64	70	77
	80	87	89	94^1	94^3	104	107	113^{BII}	117	124
	129	145	146^3	147^{14}						
Leningrad O. v. I. 6	5	7^2	7^{12}	17	20	47	58	64	70	77
	80	87	89	94^1	94^3	104	107	113^{BII}	117	124
	129	146^3	147^{14}							

These are not the only large fascicles which have come down to us, and it is worth dwelling a moment on some other examples in order to try to learn something about the transmission of the repertory.

The Normans brought two alleluia series to Sicily. One has just been mentioned. The other came from Chartres and was used in books of

Palermo Cathedral. Table 8 shows the alleluias in the following sources: Provins, Bibliothèque municipale 12 and Chartres, Bibliothèque municipale 520 (destroyed in 1944) are Chartres Cathedral Graduals of the thirteenth century, and Oxford, Bodleian Library Can. lit. 344, a missal without music of the fourteenth century. It is interesting that Chartres 520 has assigned the two verses from Psalms 64 and 94 to different days; normally *Te decet* and *Replebimur* (64. 2 and 64. 5) are sung consecutively on the same day, as also *Venite exultemus* and *Preoccupemus* (94. 1 and 94. 2). Palermo Cathedral is represented here by three manuscripts, all of the twelfth century. Madrid, Biblioteca Nacional Vitrina 20–4 is a gradual, Palermo, Archivio Storico e Diocesano 8 is a noted missal, and Palermo, Archivio Storico e Diocesano 11 is a missal without music.

The Palermo books add *Alleluia V. Verba mea auribus percipe* (5) at the start; in fact in Palermo 8 the first Chartres alleluia, 7. 2, is dropped altogether. It is interesting that a later hand attempted to alter the series in Madrid 20–4 in order to bring it into line with the other Sicilian series. Text incipits of other alleluias are written in beside the alleluias for Sundays 2–7 and 10–16, in all cases giving the alleluia of the 'rival' series. After that the alterations peter out. There was no need to alter the alleluias for Sundays 1, 8, and 9, for they were the same in both series.

I mentioned earlier that geographically proximate churches often have similar alleluia series. This means that the importation of a foreign use can result in the juxtaposition of strongly contrasting series. This is what is revealed when the Beneventan and Cassinese series are seen side by side with the Sicilian ones. (In Table 9, the first five sources are from Benevento, the last from Montecassino.) In this case Benevento 35 might represent the hypothetical original collection. Or one might consider the unica in the above lists (78, 110, 146. 3, 147. 12 and 147. 14) as belonging to a foreign tradition, the remaining twenty-six alleluias being an original series of some sort. At any rate, the contrast with Norman Sicily is clear. Eight of these twenty-six alleluias are not to be found in Madrid 288.

The problem of distinguishing between possible native and imported alleluias is particularly interesting in the case of the very large Aquitainian series, principally:

Paris, Bibliothèque nationale lat. 903	(Saint-Yrieix)	37 alleluias
Paris, Bibliothèque nationale lat. 776	(Gaillac)	35 alleluias
London, British Library Harley 4951	(Toulouse)	28 alleluias
(lacuna after the 22nd Sunday)		
Paris, Bibliothèque nationale lat. 875	(Arles)	30 alleluias
Paris, Bibliothèque nationale lat. 1135	(St-Martial?)	29 alleluias
Paris, Bibliothèque nationale lat. 1084	(Aurillac?)	29 alleluias

TABLE 8

	7^2	7^{12}	17	20	22	46	47	58	64	70	77	80	87	89	94^1	94^3	107	113^{B11}	116^1	124	129	137^1	146^3
Provins 12	7^2	7^{12}	17	20	22	46	47	58	64	70	77	80	87	89	94^1	94^3	107	113^{B11}	116^1	124	129	137^1	146^3
Chartres 520	"	"	"	"	"	"	"	58 + 64^2	64^5	"	"	"	"	89 + 94^1	94^2		"	"	"	"	"	"	"
Oxford 344	"	"	"	"	"	"	"	58	64	"	"	"	"	89	94^1	145 + 94^3	"	"	"	"	"	"	"
Palermo Cathedral	5 + 7^2	"	"	"	"	"	"	58	64	"	"	"	"	89	94^1	94^3	"	"	"	"	"	"	"

TABLE 9

	5	7^2	7^{12}	20	30	33	54	58	64	77	78	80	87	89	94^1	94^3	96	99	101^2	107	110	113^1	113^{Bii}	114	116^1	120	124	129	146^3	147^{12}	147^{14}
London, British Library, Egerton 3511 (*olim* Benevento, Archivio Capitolare VI. 29)	×	×	×	×	×	×	×	×	×	×	×	×	×	×	×	×	×	×	×	×	×	×	×	×							
Benevento, Archivio Capitolare VI. 33	×	×	×	[								*lacuna*						]	×	×	×	×	×	×	×						
Benevento 34	×	×			×		×									×	×	×	×	×	×	×		×	×	×		×			
Benevento 35	×	×	×	×	×		×		×	×	×	×	×	×	×	×	×	×	×	×	×	×		×	×	×		×	×		×
Benevento 38	×	×	×	×	×	×	×		×	×	×	×	×	×	×	×	×	×	×	×	×	×		×	×	×	×	×	×		
Rome, Biblioteca Apostolica Vaticana Vat. lat. 6082	×	×	×	×	×	×	×		×	×	×	×	×	×	×		×	×	×	×	×	×		×	×	×					

Can one find other series within these large fascicles? Could they represent ancient parent series from which others are descended? We may limit the enquiry for the present to Paris 903.[20]

Within Paris 903 numerous smaller series may be found. Several are from Aquitaine itself, which is what we should expect:

Paris, Bibliothèque nationale lat. 780 (Narbonne) and the printed missal of Narbonne of 1528
London, British Library Add. 17006 (Grasse)
Carcassonne, Bibliothèque municipale Mb 130 (Carcassonne)
Carcassonne, Bibliothèque de la Séminaire, missal (Montolieu?)
the printed missal of Nîmes of 1511
the printed missal of Auch of 1555
Langres, Bibliothèque municipale 312 (Bazas)
Paris, Bibliothèque nationale lat. 1234 (Uzès)
Paris, Bibliothèque nationale lat. 14447 (Maguelone).

To the north of this group lies:

Le Mans, Bibliothèque municipale 154 (Chezal-Benoît, near Château-roux).

But several others point much further afield:

Paris, Bibliothèque nationale lat. 10511 (?)
the printed missal of Amiens of 1487
London, British Library Add. 34662 (Saint-Valéry)
London, Victoria & Albert Museum L. 404 (Lesnes, Arrouaisian)
the printed missal of Rouen of 1497
Oxford, Bodleian Library Bodley 579.

The geographical centre of this group is difficult to determine, but the general area is undoubtedly that of North France. The provenance of Paris 10511 is unfortunately unclear, though Saint-Laurent de Longré, north of Nevers, has been suggested. Amiens and Saint-Valéry, at the mouth of the Somme, are close enough. If London L. 404 reflects the Use of the mother house, Arrouaise, then we have a third witness for the Amiens area (Arrouaise lay between Amiens and Cambrai). The origins of Oxford 579 are disputed, for it is not even clear if it was copied in North France or in England according to North French models. Perhaps the choice of alleluias

---

[20]. The series in Paris 903, Paris 776, and London 4951 were given in *Le Codex 903 de la Bibliothèque nationale de Paris (XIᵉ siècle), Graduel de Saint-Yrieix*, Paléographie musicale 13 (Tournai, 1925), 45. Numerous Aquitainian series, including some of those listed here, are given by J. Mas, 'La Tradition musicale en Septimanie. Répertoire et tradition musicale', in *Liturgie et musique (IXᵉ–XIVᵉ s.)*, Cahiers de Fanjeaux 17 (Fanjeaux, 1982), 269–86; see esp. 274. I am grateful to Professor Jeremy Noble for kindly supplying me with the Amiens series.

is a small indication of the area in which its examplars are to be sought (see Table 10).

It may be that this apparent bringing together of Aquitainian and North French elements in the Saint-Yrieix manuscript is an illusion. For one cannot actually point to an alleluia in Paris 903 that is specifically 'northern', that is, one found in the northern sources but not in other Aquitainian ones. It is true that in Table 10 147. 14 is not found in the Aquitainian sources; but these are only a few among many, and 147. 14 was certainly known elsewhere. The same is true of 110, seen here only at Chezal-Benoît and in Paris 10511. The fusion of the traditions, if that is what it is, is complete. One might, however, see it another way. Perhaps we have here an old northern layer of material used in Aquitaine as the basis for further expansion. At the time of compilation of Paris 903 the expansion was still going on: 31 and 32 are not found in the other sources in Table 10.

This reasoning would have to be substantiated by further historical and repertorial studies. It is sufficient for the moment to have pointed out the possibilities offered by the large post-Pentecost series for elucidating the formation of liturgical repertories. It is time to follow the direction northward just indicated and discuss the remaining alleluia series found in English sources, with their continental relatives.

Other English and North French Series

We have so far seen four series, or groups of closely related series, in English manuscripts: (i) the non-numerical Dijon series; (ii) the non-numerical Corbie–Saint-Denis series; (iii) the Bec series; (iv) series which resemble that of Amiens. This leaves a number of others not yet accounted for, in connection with which the continental background also needs to be filled out a little more. The series which now follow are presented according to their similarity to each other. I have not pursued connections between sources which display more than two differences from each other. (I have reckoned the differences on the basis of the 'shorter' of any two series being compared: thus in Table 11 both Montpellier H. 159 and Hereford have twenty-two alleluias, whereas Oxford C. 892 has twenty-four. Montpellier H. 159 has two alleluias not in Oxford C. 892 and Hereford has three. The differences are counted as 'two' and 'three' respectively. If we were to take the 'longer' series as basic, then we should have to reckon with four alleluias in Oxford C. 892 not in Montpellier H. 159, and five not in Hereford.)

TABLE 10

Saint-Yrieix	5	7¹²	17	18	20	30	31	32	46	47	54	58	64	77	80	87	88	89	94
Narbonne	×	×	×		×	×			×	×			×		×	×		×	×
Grasse	×	×	×		×	×			×	×	×	×	×	×	×	×		×	×
Carcassonne 130	×	×		×		×			×	×			×	×		×	×	×	×
Carcassonne Sém.	×	×	×	×	×	×			×	×			×	×	×	×	×	×	×
Nîmes		×	×		×	×			×	×			×	×	×	×	×	×	×
Auch	×	×	×	×	×	×			×	×			×	×	×	×	×	×	×
Bazas	×	×	×	×	×	×			×	×			×	×	×	×	×	×	×
Uzès	×	×	×		×				×	×	×	×	×	×	×	×			×
Maguelone	×		×	×	×	×			×	×	×	×	×	×	×	×			×
Chezal-Benoît		×	×		×				×			×	×	×	×	×		×	×
Paris 10511		×	×		×				×			×	×	×	×	×		×	×
Amiens		×	×		×				×			×	×	×	×	×		×	×
Saint-Valéry		×	×		×				×			×	×	×	×	×		×	×
Lesnes		×	×		×				×			×	×	×	×	×		×	×
Rouen	×	×	×		×	×			×			×	×	×	×	×		×	×
Oxford 579		×	×		×	×			×			×	×	×	×			×	×

No other English series shows a close resemblance to Dijon in its numerically ordered form. Only the Downpatrick Gradual, Oxford, Bodleian Library Rawl. C. 892, comes close, showing two differences. At the same time, Oxford C. 892 displays only two differences from the Hereford series. The three series are given in Table 11.[21] But Hereford itself is similar, again at two differences' remove, from several other sources: those from Lille, Saint-Valéry, Rouen, Saint-Wandrille, Chelles, and Fleury. We shall inspect this grouping more closely in a moment.

There is nothing else in England approximating to the Corbie–Saint-Denis series, but two more members can be attached to the Bec family. Only one alleluia (8) in the series of the missal of Whitby Abbey, Oxford, Bodleian Library Rawl. lit. b. 1, is not found in the Bec group. The missal of nearby Guisborough Priory, London, British Library Add. 35285, also has only one such (46) (see Table 12).

[21.] The Hereford series used here is that in the printed missal of 1502, ed. W. Henderson, *Missale Herefordense* (Leeds, 1874). The variants to be found in manuscript sources of the Hereford liturgy occasionally give other alleluias: e.g. London, British Library Add. 39675 also has 87, 145, and 147. 14. Consideration of such variants would lengthen the present essay uncomfortably; they are best dealt with in studies devoted to each individual liturgy. (For the record, the series in London 39675 contains all the alleluias in the Rouen and St-Valéry series.)

TABLE 10—*cont.*

³	97	101¹⁶	104	107	109	110	113¹	113^B11	116¹	116²	117	124	129	145	146³	147¹²	147¹⁴
×		×	×					×	×	×		×	×	×		×	
×	×	×	×						×				×				
×	×		×	×			×		×			×	×				
×	×	×		×			×	×				×	×				
×	×		×	×			×	×				×	×				
×	×	×	×	×			×						×				
×	×	×	×	×			×	×				×	×	×			
×		×	×	×				×			×	×	×	×	×		
×		×	×					×			×	×	×	×	×		
		×	×			×	×				×	×	×	×	×	×	
		×	×			×	×					×	×	×	×	×	×
		×	×						×	×	×	×	×	×	×	×	×
		×	×						×	×		×	×	×	×		×
		×	×						×	×		×	×	×	×	×	×
		×	×						×		×	×	×	×	×		×
		×	×						×	×	×	×	×	×	×	×	×

Apart from the three sources already mentioned, that is London L. 404, Oxford 579 (both with similarities to Amiens), and Hereford (similar to Chelles, but also to other series), all other English sources incline towards Norman secular uses, principally those of Rouen and Evreux. Since the interrelationships are somewhat complicated, a small diagram may help elucidate matters. Figure 1 shows two groups of closely related sources whose alleluia series have only one difference from each other. (Lines join the sources which are similar. Thus Rouen has only one difference from Evreux, but is not directly related to Angers.) One group contains the Sarum and Haughmond series, the other is composed only of continental sources. As soon as one looks for alleluia series which have two differences, the relationships multiply almost meaninglessly. As already noted, Hereford has two differences from six other sources. St Mary's York has two differences from Evreux and Angers, Fleury has two differences from Evreux and Sicily, the Dominican series has two differences from Sarum and Evreux. What is more, the Saint-Valéry Missal displays only one difference from a large number of North French sources. To include all these would complicate the diagram still further; but it would not bring us closer to any other English sources, and they are omitted from further

TABLE 11

	5	7²	7¹²	17	20	30	46	58	64	77	80	87	89	94¹	94³	101¹⁶	104	107	110	113^B11	114	116¹	117	124	129	137¹	145	146³
Montpellier H. 159	5	7²	7¹²	17	20	30	46		64	77	80	87	89	94¹	94³	101¹⁶	104	107				116¹	117		129		145	146³
Downpatrick	5	7²	7¹²	17	20	30	46	58	64	77	80	87	89	94¹	94³		104	107	110		114	116¹	117	124	129		145	
Hereford	5		7¹²	17	20	30	46	58	64	77	80		89	94¹	94³		104	107		113^B11		116¹	117	124	129	137¹		146³

TABLE 12

	5	7²	7¹²	8	17	20	46	47	58	64	70	77	80	87	89	94¹	94³	104	107	113^B11	116¹	117	124	129	146³	147¹²	147¹⁴
Whitby	5	7²	7¹²	8	17	20		47		64	70	77	80	87	89	94¹	94³	104	107	113^B11	116¹		124	129	146³	147¹²	147¹⁴
Guisborough	5	7²	7¹²		17	20	46		58	64	70	77	80	87	89	94¹	94³	104	107	113^B11	116¹	117		129	146³		147¹⁴

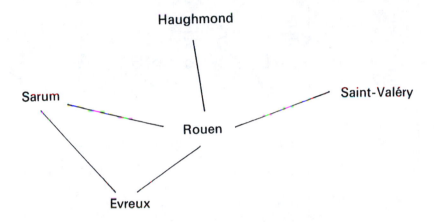

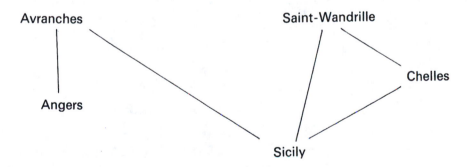

Figure 1. Two groups of alleluia sources

Lines connect sources with only one different alleluia in the post-Pentecost series.

TABLE 13

	5	7	8	17	20	30	46	47	58	64	77	78	80	87	89	94^1	94^3	95	96	101	104	107	112	113^1	113^3	113^{B11}	114	116^1	117	121	124	129	137^1	145	146^3	147^{12}	147^{14}	148
Haughmond	5	7^{12}		17	20	30	46		58	64	77		80	87	89	94^1	94^3				104	107	112			113^{B11}					124	129		145	146^3		147^{14}	
Rouen	5	7^{12}		17	20	30	46		58	64	77		80	87	89	94^1	94^3				104	107				113^{B11}			117		124	129		145	146^3		147^{14}	
Evreux	5	7^2		17	20	30	46		58	64	77		80	87	89	94^1	94^3				104	107				113^{B11}			117		124	129		145	146^3		147^{14}	
Sarum	5	7^{12}		17	20	30			58	64	77		80	87	89		94^3				104	107				113^{B11}			117	121	124	129		145	146^3		147^{14}	
St-Valéry		7^{12}		17	20	30	46		58	64	77		80	87	89		94^3				104	107						116^1	117		124	129		145	146^3		147^{14}	
Angers	5	7^2		17	20	30	46		58	64	77		80	87	89	94^1	94^3			101^2	104	107		113^1		113^{B11}						129			146^3		147^{14}	
Avranches	5	7^2		17	20	30	46		58	64	77		80	87	89	94^1	94^3			101^2	104	107		113^1		113^{B11}					124	129			146^3			
Sicily	5	7^2		17	20	30	46		58	64	77		80	87	89	94^1	94^3			101^2	104	107				113^{B11}					124	129		145	146^3			
St-Wandrille	5	7^2		17	20	30	46		58	64	77		80	87	89	94^1	94^3				104	107			113^3						124	129	137^1		146^3		147^{14}	
Chelles	5	7^2		17	20	30	46		58	64	77		80	87	89	94^1	94^3		96		104	107				113^{B11}					124	129	137^1	145	146^3			
Hereford	5	7^{12}		17	20	30	46		58	64	77		80		89		94^3				104	107				113^{B11}			117		124	129	137^1		146^3			
Sherborne	5	7^2		17	20	30	46		58	64	77		80	87	89	94^1					104	107				113^{B11}					124			145			147^{12}	147^{14}	148
St Mary's York	5	7^2	8	17	20	30		47	58	64	77	78	80	87	89	94^1	94^3			101^2	104	107				113^{B11}	114		117			129			146^3		147^{14}	
Fleury	5	7^2		17	20	30	46		58	64	77		80	87	89	94^1	94^3				104	107				113^{B11}			117			129		145	146^3	147^{12}		
Dominican	5	7^{12}		17	20	30			58	64	77		80	87	89	94^1	94^3			101^{16}	104	107				113^{B11}			117		124	129			146^3		147^{14}	
Lille		7^{12}		17	20	30	46		58	64	77		80	87	89		94^3	95			104	107				113^{B11}		116^1	117		124	129			146^3		147^{14}	

consideration.[22] (See Table 13.) The Fleury series nevertheless makes a curious appearance in Exeter Cathedral manuscript 3515, a gradual whose provenance is unknown, yet which seems to have been copied in England and used in the Exeter diocese.[23] Further investigation of the book will confirm or weaken this continental link.

Some English uses are not yet accounted for. York has three differences from its nearest 'relatives', which are St Mary's York, Rouen, and Saint-Valéry. The ordinal of the convent at Barking has a series which is separated by three differences from the Downpatrick Gradual (see Table 14).[24]

[22.] Figure 1 is based on the following sources: HAUGHMOND: Shrewsbury, Shrewsbury School xxx (12th-C. gradual from Haughmond itself); London, British Library Harley 622 (13th-C. gradual from the daughter house at Ronton or Ranton); Cambridge, University Library Kk. 2. 6 (noted missal with many Sarum elements from Hanley Castle near Malvern). ROUEN: printed missal of 1497. EVREUX: London, British Library Add. 26655 (13th-C. noted missal used at Vernon). SARUM: Salisbury missal in its 13th-C. state as edited by J. Wickham Legg, *The Sarum Missal Edited from Three Early Manuscripts* (Oxford, 1916). I give here the alleluias for the 1st to the 23rd Sunday after Trinity. After that two more alleluias appear, for the 24th and 25th Sundays if required. And these reach back in the numerical order, to 7. 2 and 101. 16. If we were to include these alleluias in the comparison with other sources, then the Sarum series would contain all the Evreux alleluias. ST-VALÉRY: London, British Library Add. 34662 (missal). ANGERS: Angers, Bibliothèque municipale 93 and 97. Angers 93 has as its last three alleluias 117, 129, 147. 14, another variant which cannot be considered further at present. AVRANCHES: printed missal of 1505. SICILY: Palermo, Biblioteca Nazionale XIV. F. 16 (12th-C. noted missal). ST-WANDRILLE: Rouen, Bibliothèque municipale 291 (missal). CHELLES: Paris, Bibliothèque nationale lat. 13254 (13th-C. gradual). The sources in Table 13, but not included in Figure 1, are as follows: HEREFORD: printed missal of 1502. SHERBORNE: missal in the possession of the Duke of Northumberland at Alnwick, now on loan to the British Library; I have rearranged its last eight alleluias numerically. ST MARY'S YORK: Cambridge, St John's College D. 27 (ordinal), ed. Abbess of Stanbrook [L. McLachlan], *Customary of the Abbey of Saint Mary, York*, Henry Bradshaw Society 73 (London, 1936); 75 (London, 1937); and 84 (Maidstone, 1951). FLEURY: Orléans, Bibliothèque municipale 129 (ordinal), ed. Dom A. Davril, *Consuetudines Floriacenses saeculi tertii decimi*, Corpus consuetudinum monasticarum 9 (Siegburg, 1976). DOMINICAN: London, British Library Add. 23935. ST-PIERRE, LILLE: Cambrai, Bibliothèque municipale 61 (62).

[23.] There is a summary description of the manuscript, which dates from the 13th–14th C., in N. R. Ker, *Medieval Manuscripts in British Libraries* II: *Abbotsford-Keele* (Oxford, 1977), 825–7.

[24.] For YORK I have had recourse to W. Henderson's edition, *The York Missal*, Surtees Society 59–60 (Durham, 1874). BARKING: Oxford, University College 169 (ordinal), ed. J. B. L. Tolhurst and L. McLachlan [the Abbess of Stanbrook]: *The Ordinale and Customary of the Benedictine Nuns of Barking Abbey*, Henry Bradshaw Society 65 (London, 1927) and 66 (London, 1928). The manuscript actually specifies the *prosula* text *Arva cuncta* instead of 5 *Verba mea*, something I have seen elsewhere only in a gradual from Jerusalem (Rome, Biblioteca Angelica 477). DOWNPATRICK: Oxford, Bodleian Library Rawl. C. 892 (12th-C. gradual).

TABLE 14

York	5	7^{12}	8	17	20	30	46	47	58	64	77	80	87	89	94^1	101^2	104	107	113^{B11}	116^1	117	129	145	146^3	147^{14}		
St Mary's York		7^2	7^{12}	8	17	20	30	47	58	64	77	80	87	89	94^1	94^3	104	107	113^{B11}	116^1	114	117	124	129	145	146^3	147^{14}
Rouen	5	7^{12}	17	20	30	46	58	64	77	80	87	89	94^1	104	107	113^{B11}	117	124	129	145	146^3	147^{14}					
St-Valéry	7^{12}	17	20	30	46	58	64	77	80	87	89	94^1	94^3	104	107	113^{B11}	116^1	117	124	129	145	146^3	147^{14}				
Barking	5	7^{12}	17	20	30	58	64	77	80	87	89	94^1	94^3	104	107	113^1	114	116^1	117	124	129						
Downpatrick	5	7^2	7^{12}	20	30	46	58	64	77	80	87	89	94^1	94^3	104	107	110	114	116^1	117	124	129	145				

TABLE 15

Troarn	5	7^2	17	20	30	46	58	64	77	80	87	89	94^1	107	113^{B11}	117	129	137^1	145	146^3			
St-Wandrille	5	7^2	7^{12}	20	30	46	58	64	77	80	87	89	94^1	94^3	104	107	113^{B11}	124	129	137^1	146^3	147^{14}	
Guisborough	5	7^2	7^{12}	17	20	46	58	64	70	77	80	87	89	94^1	94^3	104	107	113^{B11}	116^1	117	129	146^3	147^{14}

TABLE 16

Lisieux	7^{12}	17	20	30	46	58	64	77	80	87	89	92	94^1	94^3	96	99	104	107	110	113^{B11}	117	129	147^{14}
Bayeux	7^{12}	17	20	30	46	58	64	77	80	87	89	92	94^1	94^3	96	99	104	107	110	113^{B11}	129	146^3	147^{14}
Séez	5	7^{12}	17	30	46	58	64	77	80	87	89	94^1	94^3	96	99	104	107	113^{B11}	116^1	121	129	146^3	
Beauvais	7^{12}	17	20	30	46	58	64	77	80	87	89	94^1	94^3	96	104	107	113^{B11}	116^1	129	145	146^3	147^{14}	
St-Quentin	7^{12}	17	20	30	46	58	64	80	87	89	92	94^1	94^3	96	99	104	107	113^{B11}	116^1	129	146^3	147^{14}	
Palermo 131	7^2	7^{12}	17	20	30	46	58	77	80	87	89	92	94^1	99	[end of manuscript missing]								

In taking the next step, that of inferring lines of influence from the similarities reported above, one is inevitably plagued by the loss of information about many liturgical uses. The lacunae for England itself are plain enough, but how secure is the situation on the Continent? Despite gaps, it seems to me that no use that is likely to have been influential in England is missing. A final survey will make this clear.

Starting in the west, the alleluia series of Avranches and Angers are closely related to each other, as we have seen. But they do not appear closely similar to any English uses. The Coutances series sits, as already stated, between the Rouen–Evreux group and the Bec family. The manuscript missal thought to come from the monastery of Troarn, near Caen (Paris, Bibliothèque nationale lat. 14446) has two differences from both Guisborough (which we have related above to the Bec group of sources) and Saint-Wandrille. (See Table 15.)

Moving on through Normandy, the series of Lisieux, Bayeux, and Séez Cathedrals are quite distinct from those of other Norman cathedral churches. Lisieux and Bayeux have only one difference from each other, but Séez has three alleluias not in Bayeux, four not in Lisieux. Their closest relatives lie to the north-east. Thus Séez has only two alleluias not in the Beauvais series, Lisieux three; while Bayeux has three differences from the manuscript missal of Saint-Quentin.[25] The remnants of another series of this type are to be found in Sicily, in the manuscript Palermo, Biblioteca Comunale 2. Qq. G. 131. This paper manuscript of the seventeenth/eighteenth century presents a series in numerically disturbed order, incomplete at the end. (See Table 16.)

Chartres, with its unique inclusion of *Alleluia V. Dominus regit me* (22) has already been mentioned in connection with Sicilian uses. The next important use in a north-easterly direction is Paris. The Paris alleluia series is closely related to that found in the books of the Benedictine monastery of Saint-Maur-des-Fossés, which is in turn similar to the Cluny series. (See Table 17.)[26]

Books from Arras and Cambrai, though not especially close to each

[25]. BAYEUX: Bayeux, Bibliothèque municipale 121 (ordinal), ed. U. Chevalier, *Ordinaire et coutumier de l'église cathédrale de Bayeux*, Bibliothèque liturgique 8 (Paris, 1902). SÉEZ: printed missal of 1488. I am indebted to Professor Noble for supplying me with the series in the printed missal of BEAUVAIS of 1538, and the printed missals of LISIEUX of 1504 (?), 1517, and 1547. ST-QUENTIN: London, British Library Add. 15419 (missal).

[26]. PARIS: printed missal of 1501. ST-MAUR: series cited by A. Renaudin, 'Deux antiphonaires de Saint-Maur: BN Lat 12584 et 12044', *Études grégoriennes* 13 (1972), 53–150, see p. 78. The series of the printed CLUNY missal of 1493 is given by G. de Valous, *Le Monachisme Clunisien* (Macon, 1935), 410–11.

Table 17

Paris	7^{12}	17	20	30	58	64	77	80	87	89	94^1	94^3	96	104	107	110	113^{B11}	116^1	117	129	145	146^3	147^{14}	
St-Maur	5^2	7^{12}	17	20	30	58	64	77	80	87	89	94^1	94^3	104	107	110	113^{B11}	116^1	116^2	129	137^1	145	146^3	147^{12} 147^{14}
Cluny	7^{12}	17	20	30	46	64	77	80	87	89	94^1	94^3	104	107	110	113^{B11}	116^1	129	137^1	145	146^3	147^{12} 147^{14}		

Table 18

Arras	7^{12}	17	20	30	58	64	77	80	87	89	94^1	94^3	104	107	113^{B11}	116^1	116^2	121	129	145	146^3	147^{12} 147^{14}	
Cambrai	7^{12}	17	20	30	46	58	64	77	78	80	87	89	94^1	94^3	101^2	104	107	113^{B11}	116^1	107	113^{B11}	116^3	129 145 146^3
Amiens	7^{12}	17	20	30	46	58	64	77	80	87	89	94^1	94^3	104	107	113^{B11}	116^1	116^2	124	129	145	146^3	147^{12} 147^{14}
St-Omer	7^{12}	17	20	46	58	64	77	80	87	89	94^1	94^3	95	104	107	113^{B11}	116^1	116^2	124	129	145	146^3	147^{12} 147^{14}

other, find their closest relatives in Amiens use.[27] And the same is the case with the eleventh-century noted missal of Saint-Omer (Saint-Omer, Bibliothèque municiple 252), which deserves consideration because of the time spent by Dunstan in exile at Saint-Omer. Yet no similarity with an English alleluia series can be seen, another indication that the foundations of English pre-Conquest liturgical practice—at least those have come down to us in writing—were laid principally by Æthelwold at Winchester, following Corbie usages, rather than by Dunstan. (See Table 18.) Thus no other books from the areas geographically closest to England suggest a relationship with the English uses known to us.

Perhaps because of the secrecy with which some former scholars guarded their lists of alleluias (Leroquais, for example, might easily have published the list for each source he described), a certain mystique has sprung up around them. Yet there is nothing mysterious or magical about them. It is certainly gratifying to note down the post-Pentecost series in a manuscript not previously investigated, and then discover that its alleluias match some other source. But what one is really doing is taking a short cut, picking out this small portion of the repertory instead of checking every chant throughout the whole year. It is a first step, ideal for those, like Leroquais, who were concerned to provide basic information about a large number of sources. More detailed investigation of each source must then follow, for, as has repeatedly been shown, not all elements of the liturgy will necessarily tell the same tale as the alleluias.[28]

[27.] ARRAS: printed missal of 1508. This series can already be found in the 11th-C. St-Vaast manuscript, Cambrai, Bibliothèque municipale 75, but with 46 and 89 (thus twice altogether) as the 5th and 6th alleluias respectively. CAMBRAI: printed missal of 1507, and Cambrai, Bibliothèque municipale 60 (with 147. 14 at the end) and 78 (lacking 145 but having 147. 14 and 148 at the end). Professor Noble kindly supplied me with the series of the AMIENS missals of 1487 and 1529.

[28.] The best example of this is still the hiatus observed by K. D. Hartzell ('An unknown English Benedictine Gradual of the Eleventh Century', *Anglo-Saxon England* 4 (1975), 131–44) in Durham, University Library Cosin v. v. 6 (from Christ Church Canterbury). Here one finds the Bec alleluia series but pre-Conquest melodic variants in the proper chants of mass. The composition of these liturgies out of overlapping layers of material is the theme running through my two articles cited in n. 12. Something similar may sometimes be observed when monastic houses became affiliated to Cluny. The Cluny alleluia series is to be found in Douai, Bibliothèque municipale 114, from Marchiennes, and 90, from Anchin, and in Valenciennes, Bibliothèque municipale 121 and 117, and Paris, Bibliothèque nationale lat. 1101, all from St-Amand. The first three of these were included by the monks of Solesmes in their survey of variants in proper chants, *Le Graduel Romain* 4 (Solesmes, 1962), under the sigla RIC 2, KIN, and SAM 1, respectively. This revealed that they had no close relationship with Cluny sources in their melodic readings. The same is true of Paris, Bibliothèque nationale lat. 1132, from St-Martial of Limoges; this again has the Cluny alleluia series but different melodic readings.

By simply counting concordances, I have adopted a very straightforward approach to the assessment of these series. It will also have been noticed by those who have checked against my sources that I have ruthlessly straightened out occasional numerical inconsistencies. More sophisticated investigations are naturally possible. One might, for instance, take into account the Sunday to which each alleluia is assigned: in this case one would have to allow for the wholesale displacement caused by the arrival of Trinity Sunday in the liturgical calendar, and the disruption caused when just one different alleluia appears early in the series (compare Sarum and Evreux in Table 13 above). Or the 'méthode des couples' employed by Dom Hesbert for responsory series might be employed, whereby like pairs of alleluias are counted.

Yet the results obtained do not seem to warrant use of such complex procedures. The identity of the alleluia series in two manuscripts is conclusive enough, even if in some parts of Europe, where monastic reform movements caused substantial ironing out of differences, the information is not very valuable.[29] But even one difference has to be investigated with circumspection, as we have seen above. One immediately feels the need for support from other evidence, before using the alleluia series to establish a relationship between sources.

Nevertheless, a booklet with alleluia series, and a method for comparing them quickly, is an essential part of a chant scholar's equipment. If the present essay has filled a few lacunae in the reader's collection, it will have served a purpose. I hope too that the remarks on how this material may be used will also have suggested new possibilities and areas for investigation.

[29.] See Dom Jacques Froger's discussion in the introduction to *Le Manuscrit 807 de la Bibliothèque de l'Université de Graz (XIIᵉ siècle), Graduel de Klosterneuberg*, Paléographie musicale 19 (Berne, 1974), 23* ff.

APPENDIX

Post-Pentecost Alleluias

1. *Numerical Order of Psalms*

1	Beatus vir
5	Verba mea (or *prosula* Arva cuncta)
7. 2	Domine deus meus
7. 12	Deus iudex iustus
8	Domine deus noster
17	Diligam te domine
18	Celi enarrant
20	Domine in virtute tua
22	Dominus regit me
30	In te domine speravi (. . . accelera)*
31	Beati quorum remisse
32	Verbo domini celi firmati
33	Venite filii audiat
34	Iudica domine
46	Omnes gentes
47	Magnus dominus et laudabilis
54	Exaudi dominus orationem
58	Eripe me
64	(v. 2) Te decet, (v. 5) Replebimur
70	In te domine speravi (. . . et salva me)*
77	Attendite popule meus
78	Propitius esto
80	Exultate deo
84	Ostende nobis
87	Domine deus salutis mee
88	Misericordias domini
89	Domine refugium
92	Dominus regnavit decorem
94. 1	Venite exultemus
94. 2	Preoccupemus
94. 3	Quoniam deus magnus
94. 6	Venite adoremus
95	Cantate domino (. . . cantate domino)**
96	Dominus regnavit exultet
97	(v. 1) Cantate domino (. . . quia mirabilia), (v. 2) Notum fecit**

* and ** It is not always possible to distinguish between 30 and 70, or between 95 and 97.

99	Iubilate deo
101. 2	Domine exaudi orationem
101. 16	Timebunt gentes
104	Confitemini domino
106	Confiteantur
107	Paratum cor meum
109	Dixit dominus
110	Redemptionem misit
112	(v. 1) Laudate pueri, (v. 2) Sit nomen
113. 1	In exitu Israel, (v. 2) Facta est
113. BII	Qui timent dominum
114	Dilexi quoniam
116. 1	Laudate dominum omnes gentes
116. 2	Quoniam confirmata est
117	Dextera dei/domini fecit
120	Levavi oculos meos
121	(v. 1) Letatus sum, (v. 2) Stantes erant pedes
124	Qui confidunt in domino
129	De profundis clamavi
131	Memento domine David
137. 1	Confitebor tibi domine
137. 2	Adorabo
145	Lauda anima mea dominum
146. 1	Laudate dominum quoniam bonus
146. 3	Qui sanat contritos
147. 12	Lauda Ierusalem
147. 14	Qui posuit fines tuos
148	Laudate dominum omnes angeli
150	Laudate dominum in sanctis

2. *Alphabetical Order of Psalms*

137.2	Adorabo
5	Arva cuncta
77	Attendite popule meus
31	Beati quorum remisse
1	Beatus vir
95	Cantate domino (. . . cantate domino)**
97. 1	Cantate domino (. . . quia mirabilia)**
18	Celi enarrant
106	Confiteantur
137. 1	Confitebor tibi domine
104	Confitemini domino
129	De profundis clamavi
7. 12	Deus iudex iustus
117	Dextera dei/domini fecit

114	Dilexi quoniam
17	Diligam te domine
109	Dixit dominus
7. 2	Domine deus meus
8	Domine deus noster
87	Domine deus salutis mee
101. 2	Domine exaudi orationem
20	Domine in virtute tua
89	Domine refugium
22	Dominus regit me
92	Dominus regnavit decorem
96	Dominus regnavit exultet
58	Eripe me
54	Exaudi dominus orationem
80	Exultate deo
113. 2	Facta est
113. 1	In exitu Israel
30	In te domine speravi (. . . accelera)*
70	In te domine speravi (. . . et salva me)*
99	Iubilate deo
34	Iudica domine
145	Lauda anima mea dominum
147. 12	Lauda Ierusalem
150	Laudate dominum in sanctis
148	Laudate dominum omnes angeli
116. 1	Laudate dominum omnes gentes
146. 1	Laudate dominum quoniam bonus
112. 1	Laudate pueri
121. 1	Letatus sum
120	Levavi oculos meos
47	Magnus dominus et laudabilis
131	Memento domine David
88	Misericordias domini
97. 2	Notum fecit
46	Omnes gentes
84	Ostende nobis
107	Paratum cor meum
94. 2	Preoccupemus
78	Propitius esto
124	Qui confidunt in domino
147. 14	Qui posuit fines tuos
146. 3	Qui sanat contritos
113. BII	Qui timent dominum
116. 2	Quoniam confirmata est
94. 3	Quoniam deus magnus
110	Redemptionem misit

64. 5	Replebimur
112. 2	Sit nomen
121. 2	Stantes erant pedes
64.2	Te decet
101. 16	Timebunt gentes
94. 6	Venite adoremus
94. 1	Venite exultemus
33	Venite filii audiat
5	Verba mea
32	Verbo domini celi firmati

7

Marian Antiphons at Cluny and Lewes

RUTH STEINER
(Catholic University of America, Washington)

In 1076 William de Varenne, the count of Surrey, and his wife Gundreda began a pilgrimage to Rome.[1] A relative of William the Conqueror, William de Varenne was a Norman baron who had more than once fought in battle at the side of his kinsman. As William and Gundreda crossed France, they paused from time to time to visit abbeys and other holy places. When they arrived in Burgundy, news came to them of strife between the pope and the emperor that made a trip to Italy inadvisable. Forced to abandon their plan of a pilgrimage to the tomb of St Peter, William and Gundreda decided to extend their stay in the region in which they found themselves, and made their way to Cluny. Abbot Hugh was absent temporarily, but they were warmly received by the prior Odo de Lagery, the future Urban II.

In accounts of the period Cluny is spoken of with admiration and respect. Peter Damian wrote in praise of the spiritual life there: he observed that at Cluny even though the monks did not live as anchorites, yet their achievements were comparable to those of Paul and Anthony. The buildings and furnishings were renowned for their splendour. A full description is made of them in the *Liber Tramitis*: particular attention is given there to the abbey church, in which mass and the divine office were celebrated with unusual solemnity.[2]

[1.] In his study *Le Bréviaire-missel du prieuré clunisien de Lewes* (Paris, 1935), 13–18, V. Leroquais gives an account of the circumstances surrounding the founding of Lewes that is summarized here. See also S. Holder, 'The Noted Cluniac Breviary-Missal of Lewes: Fitzwilliam Museum Manuscript 369', *Journal of the Plainsong & Mediaeval Music Society* 8 (1985), 25–32.

[2.] The *Liber Tramitis* provides a description of monastic life at Cluny. The first draft was compiled around 1030 and revised in 1033. For the most recent scholarly edition see P. Dinter (ed.), *Liber Tramitis Aevi Odilonis Abbatis*, Corpus Consuetudinum Monasticarum 10 (Siegburg, 1980).

For William, who had for some time shared with Lanfranc of Canterbury a desire to found a priory in Britain, Cluny was an object of special interest. The warm welcome he had received there, along with what he had observed of the excellence of the place—'quia invenimus sanctitatem et religionem et caritatem tam magnam ibi'—led William, shortly after his return to Britain, to frame a request. Could the abbot of Cluny be persuaded to send a few monks—two, three, or four—to establish a community in William's castle at Lewes? Some delicate negotiating took place; Hugh was insistent that Cluny should maintain control over the new community. Eventually in 1077 Lanzo was sent from Cluny to become prior at Lewes, and with him came three other monks.

Tracing the early development of liturgical chant at Lewes is difficult, since the one notated liturgical manuscript that is unquestionably from there dates from the end of the thirteenth century (Cambridge, Fitzwilliam Museum 369). That some parts of its liturgical repertory follow Cluniac use and show melodic variants similar to other Cluniac manuscripts has already been demonstrated by Hesbert and Holder.[3] The present study examines another part of its repertory, its Marian antiphons. To what extent are the chants of the daughter house those of the parent?

The study has other, wider implications, however. A necessary first step is a consideration of Marian antiphons at Cluny itself, and it turns out that their employment underwent changes as time went on. The pattern is one of initial flexibility, later replaced by specific liturgical assignment. By following the career of the antiphons presented in the earliest known Cluniac breviary, it will be possible to review almost all the known Cluniac office chant books, culminating in the Lewes manuscript. In doing so, we shall also learn something about the course of liturgical and musical history through the medieval centuries, for the fate of these Marian antiphons is typical of many parts of the repertory. Untypically, however, we shall even be able to suggest a possible composer for the main group of antiphons.

Studies of the medieval divine office have repeatedly demonstrated the stability of the tradition of each particular institution.[4] Once a repertory of

[3] R.-J. Hesbert, *Corpus Antiphonalium Officii*, 6 vols. (hereinafter *CAO*; Rome, 1963–79), includes the Lewes manuscript as source 631 in his massive survey of Advent responsories. It has the same series of responsories as numerous other Cluniac sources. See also Hesbert's article 'Les Antiphonaires monastiques insulaires', *Revue bénédictine* 112 (1982), 358–75. Holder, 'Cluniac Breviary-Missal' 28–9, shows that the manuscript has the Cluniac series of post-Pentecost alleluias and that the variant readings in its mass proper chants are closer to those of the 11th-C. Cluny Gradual Paris, Bibliothèque nationale lat. 1087 than to any other source.

[4] In *CAO* v, viii, Hesbert speaks of 'la continuité remarquable de la tradition dans chaque église ou monastère', and uses that to justify taking into account in his comparative studies the testimony of sources dating from the 14th and even the 15th C. It should be remembered, however, that Hesbert was studying series of matins responsories and the office repertory overall, rather than musical readings.

office chants had been committed to writing, there were few places in the liturgy where new works could be added. Any change or growth in a repertory is thus significant; and this is what has come to light in an examination of Marian antiphons in manuscripts from Cluny.

The Seventeen Marian Antiphons of Paris 12601

The earliest of the notated sources from Cluny itself to be considered here is an eleventh-century breviary, Paris, Bibliothèque nationale lat. 12601.[5] On the feast of the Assumption, after the service of lauds (fol. 86r), there are seventeen 'extra' antiphons, which are divided by rubrics into two main groups (see Table 1).

The first group is made up of five antiphons on non-biblical texts. The rubric 'In matutinis laudibus' identifies this as an alternative series of lauds antiphons; this may indicate that they are intended for use on the Sunday within the octave. The first chant in the series reads like an invitatory antiphon: it is an exhortation to magnify Christ as King on the occasion of the exaltation of Mary. The others are prayers addressed to Mary.

1. *Exaltata est gloriosa*: The glorious ever-virgin Mary has been exalted above the choirs of angels. Come, all—let us magnify Christ the King, whose kingdom is eternal.

2. *Maria virgo semper laetare*: Virgin Mary, rejoice always, for you were deemed worthy to bear Christ, the Creator of heaven and earth; because from your womb you brought forth a Saviour for the world.

3. *Sub tuum praesidium*: Beneath your defence we take refuge, O Mother of God; despise not our supplications in need but deliver us from peril always, blessed Virgin.

4. *Sub tuam protectionem*: We take refuge under your protection, where the infirm have received strength: on this account we sing praise to you, Virgin Mother of God.

---

[5] Even in fairly recent studies concerning Cluny one catches an occasional lingering echo of the notion that very little of its office chant has survived. One reason for this is that the origin of Paris 12601 had not yet been identified when L. Delisle drew up his *Inventaire des manuscrits de la Bibliothèque nationale. Fonds de Cluni* (Paris, 1884). The list of office manuscripts from Cluny compiled by A. Wilmart for the *Dictionnaire d'archéologie chrétienne et de liturgie*, III, 2 (Paris, 1914), cols. 2084–5, consists primarily of lectionaries. It was V. Leroquais who established that Paris 12601 originated at Cluny; see *Les Bréviaires manuscrits des bibliothèques publiques de France*, 6 vols. (Paris, 1934), III, 226–8. The later history of the manuscript is detailed by J. Hourlier in 'Le Bréviaire de Saint-Taurin', *Etudes grégoriennes* 3 (1959), 163–73. For a complete matins service edited from this source, see D. Lamothe and C. Constantine, *Matins at Cluny for the Feast of Saint Peter's Chains* (London, 1986).

TABLE 1. *Text sources for antiphons in the series in Paris 12601 (fol. 86r)*

CAO number	Text incipit	Source
2763	Exaltata est gloriosa	non–biblical
3708	Maria virgo semper laetare	non–biblical
5041	Sub tuum praesidium	non–biblical
5040	Sub tuam protectionem	non–biblical
1570	Beata mater et innupta	non–biblical
2547	Ecce tu pulchra es	SSongs 1. 14
4937	Sicut lilium inter spinas	SSongs 2. 2
2855	Favus distillans	SSongs 4. 11a, 11c
2641	Emissiones tuae	SSongs 4. 13a
2887	Fons hortorum	SSongs 4. 15
5329	Veniat dilectus meus	SSongs 5. 1a
5325	Veni in hortum meum	SSongs 5. 1b
1856	Comedi favum cum melle	SSongs 5. 1c
2224	Dilecte mi apprehendam	SSongs 8. 2
1418	Anima mea liquefacta	SSongs 5. 6b–8
2155	Descendi in hortum	SSongs 6. 10, 12
5162	Tota pulchra es	SSongs 4. 7, 11a, 11b, 10b; 2. 11, 12a, 13b, 12c, 10b; 4. 8a, 8c

5. *Beata mater et innupta virgo*: Blessed Mother and Virgin unwed, glorious Queen of the world, intercede for us with the Lord.

The rubric for the second group is simply 'Infra ebd*omadam*'—'during the week [following the feast]'. First in this group come eight short antiphons on texts from the Song of Songs. The texts are all exact quotations, with no centonizing, although the third omits a phrase. The texts of the sixth, seventh, and eighth antiphons come in order from a single verse; texts of the previous five, though borrowed from separate verses or chapters, are arranged in the order in which they appear in the bible.

1. *Ecce tu pulchra*: Behold thou art fair, O my love, behold thou art fair, thine eyes are as those of doves.

2. *Sicut lilium*: As the lily among thorns, so is my love among the daughters.

3. *Favus distillans*: Thy lips, my bride, are as a dripping honeycomb; and the fragrance of thy garments, as the smell of frankincense.

4. *Emissiones tuae*: Thy plants are a paradise of pomegranates with the fruits of the orchard.

5. *Fons hortorum*: The fountain of gardens: the well of living waters, which run with a strong stream from Lebanon.

6. *Veniat dilectus*: My beloved comes into his garden in order to eat the fruit of his apple trees.[6]

7. *Veni in hortum*: I am come into the garden, o my sister, my spouse, I have gathered my myrrh, with my aromatical spices.

8. *Comedi favum*: I have eaten the honeycomb with my honey, I have drunk my wine with my milk.

This systematic arrangement of the texts has a counterpart in the plan for the melodies: the first chant is in mode 1, the second in mode 2, and so on through all eight.[7] (Since the manuscript does not indicate the modes of the chants, this plan is not immediately evident.)

The next three chants are different in character, although no rubric separates them from what has preceded. They are longer; and although they are once again on texts from the Song of Songs, there is occasional rewording of the biblical original. One omits a verse, one adds a few words. With one exception, the chants are given in the order in which their texts appear in the bible: *Dilecte mi*, which comes first, should be last. The modes of these chants seem not to follow any plan.

1. *Dilecte mi*: My beloved, I will take hold of thee, and bring thee into my father's house, and into my mother's chamber: there thou shalt teach me the precepts of the Lord.

2. *Anima mea*: My soul melted when he spoke: I sought him, and found him not: I called, and he did not answer me. The keepers that go about the city found me: they struck me: and wounded me: the keepers of the walls took away my veil. O daughters of Jerusalem, tell my beloved that I languish with love.

3. *Descendi in hortum*: I went down into the garden of nuts, to see the fruits of the valleys, and to look if the vineyard had flourished, and the pomegranates budded. Return, return, O Shulamite; return, return that we may behold thee.

[6] In Hesbert's reading of this antiphon (*CAO* III, 5329), the first word is 'veniat'. The Cluny sources give this verb in the indicative mood. In general, the readings of chant texts are given here in the normalized spellings adopted by Hesbert, and have the capitalization and punctuation that he supplies.

[7] For a study of other antiphon series of this type, with an overview of earlier work on the subject, see R. L. Crocker's comments on what he terms 'the numerical office', in 'Matins Antiphons at St. Denis', *Journal of the American Musicological Society* 39 (1986), 441–90.

The final chant in the series of seventeen is *Tota pulchra es*. Though based on the Song of Songs, it differs from all of the others in having a text that is centonized.

The First Five Antiphons

The chants of the first group are also named in a list of chants of the divine office from the abbey of Nonantola, where they come after the last of the chants for second vespers for the Assumption. This list of chants has all of the characteristic features of the divine office at Cluny; and it is included in a manuscript that contains a redaction of the *Consuetudines Cluniacensium antiquiores*—the older Cluny customary. The source—Rome, Biblioteca Casanatense 54—dates from the second half of the eleventh century. The model for this part of it is apparently a Cluny breviary or antiphonal of the first quarter of the century—a manuscript compiled at a point before the other series of Marian antiphons had come to join the first.[8]

The antiphons of this first series do not appear in a comparable position (that is, as a series) in later manuscripts from Cluny itself. But four of them are found in an eleventh-century manuscript of Saint-Maur-des-Fossés (Paris, Bibliothèque nationale lat. 12584) embedded in a series of extra chants for the feast of the Assumption.[9] This series recurs, with some changes, and with the fifth of the Cluny chants added at the end, in a manuscript of the same monastery, Paris, Bibliothèque nationale lat. 12044, copied in the first half of the twelfth century.[10] The two are

---

[8.] For the older Cluny customary, see K. Hallinger (ed.), *Consuetudinum saeculi X/XI/ XII Monumenta: Introductiones*, Corpus Consuetudinum Monasticarum 7, Pars prima (Siegburg, 1984), 93–100. Concerning the two tonaries of this manuscript, see M. Huglo, *Les Tonaires: Inventaire, Analyse, Comparaison* (Paris, 1971), 41–5, 170.

[9.] This is one of the manuscripts surveyed by Hesbert in *CAO* II. In the preface to this volume, he explains his reason for including a manuscript of the Cluniac tradition ('la tradition clunisienne'), and he continues, 'A défaut d'un manuscrit provenant de Cluny même, on s'est arrêté au plus ancien témoin du groupe' (p. vi). Because in this volume Hesbert's comparisons were to extend over the complete liturgical year, Paris 12601 (a summer breviary) would not have served his purpose; but there are numerous points at which Paris 12584 does not follow the tradition of Cluny itself.

[10.] In 'Deux antiphonaires de Saint-Maur', *Etudes grégoriennes* 13 (1972), 53–[150], A. Renaudin compares the chants for the winter cycle of offices in Paris 12584 and 12044. Paris 12044 is better known than most manuscript antiphonals (except, of course, for those available in facsimile editions) because of Peter Wagner's interest in it. In his *Einführung in die gregorianischen Melodien*, III. *Gregorianische Formenlehre* (Leipzig 1921), 188–216, transcriptions and analyses of the formulas for responsory verses are based in large part on material in Paris 12044. Wagner also draws his example of a responsory *prosula* from Paris 12044 (I [1911], 293), and refers to the manuscript frequently in connection with a variety of topics. Students of chant seeking versions in staff notation of melodies notated in neumes in Paris 12601 often find Paris 12044 the most convenient source to use, but see below.

TABLE 2. *Marian antiphons in series in manuscripts of Saint-Maur-des-Fossés*

Paris 12584, fols. 319v–320r	Paris 12044, fols. 178r–v
Exaltata est gloriosa	*Exaltata est gloriosa*
Ecce adest dies praeclara	Ecce adest dies praeclara
Assumpta est in altum	
Paradisi porta per Evam	Paradisi porta per Evam
Maria virgo semper laetare	*Maria virgo semper laetare*
Sub tuum praesidium	*Sub tuum praesidium*
Sub tuam protectionem	*Sub tuam protectionem*
Sancta Maria succurre	
Succurre sancta genitrix	
Haec est regina virginum	
O gloriosa genitrix virgo	O gloriosa genitrix virgo
Gaude Maria virgo . . . quae	
Virgo Christo amabilis	
Ave rosa paradisi frondens	Ave rosa paradisi frondens*
	Beata mater et innupta virgo

Antiphons for the Psalms in first vespers (fol. 174v):

Sancta Maria succurre
Succurre sancta genitrix
Haec est regina virginum
Beata dei genitrix

Antiphons in the little hours (fol. 177r–v):

Ibo mihi ad montem myrrhae
Virgo Christo amabilis
Alma redemptoris mater
Ave regina coelorum

* = incipit only.

Note: Antiphons in the bold face appear in Paris 12584 in the series on the feast of the Assumption and in Paris 12601 and Rome, Casanatense 54 as alternative chants after second vespers of the Nativity of the Blessed Virgin; antiphons shown in italics are included in the series in Paris 12601.

compared in Table 2, where the incipits of the five chants from Cluny are shown in italics.

The appearance of the four (and later, five) antiphons in a series that includes other material requires some explaining. Saint-Maur-des-Fossés was reformed by Cluny toward the end of the tenth century: the monastery was practically defunct, and it was repopulated by monks from Cluny. But it soon regained its independence.[11] There was a parallel series of events at

---

11. Renaudin, 'Deux antiphonaires', 68.

TABLE 3. *Marian antiphons in the Marmoutier Breviary, Rouen, Bibliothèque municipale 243 (A. 164)*

CAO number	Text incipit
Antiphons for the Psalms of first vespers on the feast of the Assumption (fol. 228v):	
1566	Beata es virgo Maria
3002	**Haec est regina virginum**
4703	**Sancta Maria succurre**
4699	Sancta dei genitrix
Antiphon for the Benedictus of lauds (of the Sunday within the octave?) (fol. 231v):	
3708	*Maria virgo semper laetare*
Antiphons for use per octavam *(fol. 231v):*	
1570	*Beata mater et innupta virgo*
5041	*Sub tuum praesidium*
4703	**Sancta Maria succurre***
1566	Beata es virgo Maria*
3002	**Haec est regina virginum***
4699	Sancta dei genitrix*
3137	Hortus conclusus*

* = incipit only.
Note: Antiphons in bold face appear in Paris 12584 in the series on the feast of the Assumption, and in Paris 12601 and Rome, Casanatense 54 as alternative chants after second vespers of the Nativity of the Blessed Virgin; antiphons shown in italics are included in the series in Paris 12601, Paris 12584, and Paris 12044 (except for *Beata mater et innupta virgo*, which does not appear in Paris 12584).

the monastery of Marmoutier, within the same decade (the 980s).[12] There are some similarities in the repertories of Marian antiphons at Marmoutier (preserved in the notated breviary Rouen, Bibliothèque municipale 243 (A. 164), of the late eleventh century) and at Saint-Maur-des-Fossés that seem to result from the two repertories having a common source—the Cluny repertory of the late tenth century, a repertory for which we have no direct witnesses. Developments at Cluny that took place after that time seem not to be reflected in sources from Marmoutier and Saint-Maur-des-Fossés, even if they date from much later.

[12.] C. Waddell, 'The Pre-Cistercian Background of Cîteaux and the Cistercian Liturgy', *Goad and Nail*, Studies in Medieval Cistercian History 10, ed. E. R. Elder (Kalamazoo, Mich., 1985), 119. It will be evident to anyone who reads Fr. Waddell's article that the present study was in many ways modelled on it: the method of enquiry is the one vividly set forth and demonstrated there, and even the individual manuscripts are in large part those to which Fr. Waddell draws attention.

The similarities are evident in a comparison of Tables 2 and 3. They include some common material, and—in particular—the presence in the series of two antiphons that in Paris 12601 and in Casanatense 54 are given as 'extras' on another day, the feast of the Nativity of the Blessed Virgin. The sources apparently based on the earlier model mix these two antiphons in with the others, suggesting that in the late tenth century this particular division of material between the Assumption and the Nativity had not yet been made.

Example 1 shows the five antiphons as they are given in staff notation in Paris 12044. *Exaltata est gloriosa* is evidently a late addition to the chant repertory overall: it is included in only two of the sources surveyed in Volumes I and II of *CAO*.

By contrast, *Maria virgo semper laetare* appears in all of them (except for the one that has a lacuna at the relevant point in the liturgical year).[13] It is most often found at the head of the series of extra antiphons on the feast of the Assumption,[14] though in one source it is the second antiphon in the series, in another source, the third. In still other manuscripts it is assigned to one of the psalms of vespers, matins, or lauds. The melody has the direct appeal of a folk-song, especially at the beginning, where two ten-syllable lines of rhymed accentual verse are set as antecedent and consequent musical phrases. In the third line, of eight syllables, the setting of the first three accented syllables stresses the dominant of the mode. Only in the last line does the music become discursive, and less popular in quality.

Sub tuum praesidium has been discussed in a recent article as 'The Oldest Marian Antiphon Text'.[15] This chant appears in various roles in the Ambrosian mass, the Byzantine office, and the Coptic rite, as well as in the 'Gregorian' divine office. The original Greek version is preserved in a

---

[13] This is the manuscript to which Hesbert assigned the siglum 'G'. It is an antiphonal from Liège notated in 11th-C. neumes—Durham, Chapter Library B. III. 11. (A facsimile of this manuscript was published by the Plainsong & Mediæval Music Society in 1923, ed. W. H. Frere, entitled *Pars Antiphonarii*.) In it the chants of the Temporale and of the Sanctorale are for the most part kept separate, and the Sanctorale is incomplete, ending in the cycle of chants for saints in paschal time. One can only guess what Marian antiphons it might have included: see S. Burstyn, 'Early 15th-Century Polyphonic Settings of Song of Songs Antiphons', *Acta Musicologica* 49 (1977), 206.

[14] It would thus appear that the compiler of the Cluny breviary has placed a more recent chant (*Exaltata est gloriosa*) before one belonging to an older tradition (*Maria virgo semper laetare*); this is not an unusual procedure in liturgical manuscripts. The latter chant is one of those discussed in a valuable article by H. Barré, 'Antiennes et répons de la Vierge', *Marianum* 29 (1967), 153–254, where it appears under the serial number 100. The others are *Sub tuum praesidium*, 89; *Sub tuam protectionem*, 90; *Beata mater et innupta virgo*, 55; and *Dilecte mi*, 125.

[15] This study, in *Liturgy* 20 (1986), 41–60, is by C. Waddell. It includes an account of earlier research concerning this chant.

papyrus that appears to date from the third century, though this has been disputed. Here is how Chrysogonus Waddell presents the matter.

If our papyrus had presented only the mutilated text of a bill of lading, no one would for a moment have disputed its third-century date; but that the papyrus offers instead a text redolent of Marian piety obviously argues [*to some*] for a demonstrably later date. . . . Whatever the date of the text, it is admittedly true

Example 1. Five Marian antiphons (from Paris, Bibliothèque nationale lat. 12044, fol. 178r)

Example 1—*cont.*

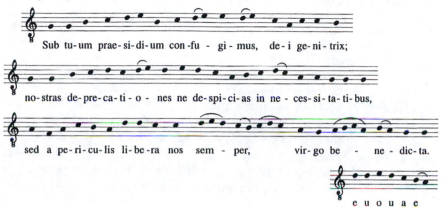

Sub tu-um prae-si-di-um con-fu - gi - mus, de-i ge-ni-trix;

no-stras de-pre-ca-ti - o - nes ne de-spi-ci-as in ne-ces-si-ta-ti-bus,

sed a pe-ri-cu-lis li-be-ra nos sem - per, vir-go be - ne-dic-ta.

e u o u a e

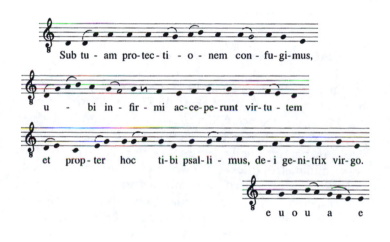

Sub tu - am pro-tec-ti - o - nem con - fu-gi-mus,

u - bi in - fir - mi ac-ce-pe-runt vir-tu - tem

et prop-ter hoc ti-bi psal-li - mus, de-i ge-ni-trix vir-go.

e u o u a e

Be-a-ta ma-ter et in-nup-ta vir - go,

glo-ri-o-sa re - gi-na mun-di,

in-ter-ce - de pro no-bis ad do-mi-num.

e u o u a e

that it is not quite correct to refer to it, in its earliest recoverable form, as a *liturgical* text. Devotional it is; but since prayers offered in church in the setting of the liturgy were traditionally directed to God the Father, less often to God the Son, it seems unlikely that the text had its immediate origin in the liturgy. But the liturgy no more exhausted all possibilities for praying in the third century than it does in the twentieth century.[16]

   Sub tuum praesidium is followed by *Sub tuam protectionem*. These two chants often come together in the sources. Their most usual positioning seems to be midway in a series of optional antiphons on the feast of the Assumption, although they are occasionally found incorporated into one or another of the services on that day, or (in the case of *Sub tuam protectionem*) on the feast of the Nativity of the Blessed Virgin. *Beata mater et innupta virgo* appears in the *CAO* sources on five different days—the four Marian feasts and Christmas—though it appears most often on the feast of the Assumption. It is variously assigned to matins, lauds, and vespers; it is also included in series of extra antiphons.

The Eight Antiphons of the Second Series

In similar fashion, the eight antiphons that begin the second series appear in numerous sources in varying roles; but these do appear in later sources from Cluny itself. One of these sources, the Breviary of Saint-Victor-sur-Rhins, dates from the end of the thirteenth century.[17] It is a big book; although the pages are not unusually large (they measure 340 by 240 millimetres), it is 150 millimetres thick. (One writer estimates at more than 160 the number of sheepskins required for its preparation.)[18] Even so, the beginning of the Temporale is lacking: the manuscript begins part-way through Friday of the ferial office and continues through the Sundays after Epiphany, and then through all the rest of the Temporale and the full

---

[16.] Waddell, *Liturgy* 20, 46.

[17.] For a detailed codicological description, see A. Davril, 'A propos d'un bréviaire manuscrit de Cluny conservé à Saint-Victor-sur-Rhins', *Revue bénédictine* 93 (1983), 108–22; and M. Huglo, 'Remarques sur la notation musicale du bréviaire de Saint-Victor-sur-Rhins', ibid. 132–6. I thank M. Huglo for writing the letter of introduction that caused me to be received with great courtesy at St-Victor-sur-Rhins in Aug. 1986.

[18.] R. Étaix, 'Le Prieuré de Saint-Victor-sur-Rhins au moyen-âge, et son bréviaire', *Revue du Lyonnais* 2 (1980), 6.

Sanctorale.[19] Here and there, pages have been removed, presumably because they contained illuminations.

The book was given to the monks and to the church of Saint-Victor in 1317 by the sacristan of Cluny. About ten years later, when the building needed repairs, the breviary passed into other hands: it was used as security for a loan. It was redeemed in 1338 and has remained at Saint-Victor since then. Both text and music are written large; and one can imagine it being set on a lectern, with two or three monks reading from it. (The community of monks at the priory was always quite small.)[20] When the priory was no longer active, responsibility for the manuscript became that of the parish priest alone. Now that there is no longer a resident parish priest, the manuscript is looked after by the mayor, who keeps it in a safe in the town hall.[21]

The breviary has been the subject of publications that date back as far as 1888. Even so, the paths of research that it opens to chant scholars are only just beginning to be explored: it is by far the most complete extant source containing chants of the divine office copied at Cluny in staff notation. Its testimony is of critical importance to the study of the development and dissemination of the chant repertory of Cluny.

A second source, which is slightly later (early fourteenth century), and which has many lacunae, is a notated breviary now at Solesmes (Rés. 334).[22] This is a book designed to be held in the hand: it measures 172 by 114 millimetres, and thus it appears to have been intended for use by an individual.

In these two later manuscripts, the series of eight antiphons is divided into two sets of four, for use in the little hours through the octave of the Assumption. They are treated similarly in two Cluny customaries of the

---

[19] Davril suggests that the copyist began his work with the ferial office and the Sundays after Epiphany, intending to place Advent, Christmas, and Epiphany at the end of the book, and then for some reason failed to follow through. It seems more likely that the plan for this manuscript was comparable to that of the 11th-C. antiphonal of St-Maur-des-Fossés, Paris 12584, and many other sources, in which the ferial office is incorporated into the week following the Sunday after Epiphany (often called the Sunday *Domine ne in ira*, after its first matins responsory; see *CAO* II, 26–33). If that is the case, then several fascicles have been lost from the beginning of the volume.

[20] Étaix, 'Saint-Victor-sur-Rhins', 4–5.

[21] Fortunately, the energetic young mayor of St-Victor-sur-Rhins, M. M. Chartier, is aware of the unique importance of the manuscript, not only to the place in which it has remained for more than six and a half centuries, but also to scholars. He and his secretary, M. A. Patay, have been exceptionally gracious in making it available for study.

[22] P. Blanchard, 'Un bréviaire de Cluny', *Revue bénédictine* 57 (1947), 201–9. Dom J. Claire, who made it possible for me to examine this manuscript, also called my attention to its unusually full series of Marian antiphons.

second half of the eleventh century—those of Bernard and Ulrich.[23] Bernard's formulation is as follows: 'As for the arrangement of the antiphons to be sung through the octave, I don't know what needs to be said other than that in nocturns [*matins*] of the individual nights, antiphons from among those [*in nocturns*] of the first night are sung, at lauds from [*the first*] lauds, and similarly for the Magnificat antiphon at vespers. In the remaining [*little*] hours these antiphons are sung: *Ecce tu pulchra, Sicut lilium, Favus distillans, Emissiones, Fons hortorum, Venit dilectus, Veni in hortum.*'[24] Ulrich, whose customary is thought to have been based on an earlier version of Bernard's, condenses the last part of this to 'In the remaining hours, these antiphons ought to be sung, of which the first is *Ecce tu pulchra es.*'[25] By contrast, the *Liber Tramitis* leaves open the choice of antiphons for the little hours through the octave: 'In the little hours may be chosen appropriate antiphons from nocturns, or from lauds, or from the Magnificat at vespers, or [*those based on texts*] from the Song of Songs.'[26]

The variety in the manuscript tradition for the first thirteen antiphons in Paris 12601 suggests the following chronology:

1. *The 980s*: The Cluny repertory of supplementary or optional Marian antiphons is still fluid. It includes *Exaltata est gloriosa, Maria virgo semper laetare, Sub tuum praesidium, Sub tuam protectionem, Beata mater et innupta virgo, Haec est regina virginum, Sancta Maria succurre*, and probably others. They are not formally arranged into a series; and individual chants may be sung either on the feast of the Assumption or on the Nativity of the Blessed Virgin. (For this there is only indirect evidence in the later repertories of Saint-Maur-des-Fossés and Marmoutier.)

2. *The first quarter of the eleventh century*: Cluny has five 'extra' antiphons on the feast of the Assumption that are set in a definite

---

[23.] For Bernard's customary, see M. Herrgott, *Vetus disciplina monastica* (Paris, 1726), 134–364. That of Ulrich is available in J. P. Migne, *Patrologia latina* 149 (Paris, 1882), cols. 635–778. In her study of change in the role of the cantor, M. E. Fassler identifies the relevant Cluny customaries and examines their evidence: see 'The Office of the cantor in early western monastic rules and customaries: a preliminary investigation', *Early Music History* 5 (1985), 29–51, esp. 43–51.

[24.] 'De ordine antiphonarum per Octavas dicendarum quid aliud dicam, nescio; nisi quod ad Noct. singularum noctium dicuntur de Nocturnis primae noctis, ad Mat. de Mat. & ipsae in Evang. Ad caeteras Horas hae cantantur Ant. *Ecce tu pulchra, Sicut lilium, Favus distillans, Emissiones, Fons hortorum, Venit dilectus, Veni in hortum.*' (Herrgott, *Vetus disciplina monastica*, 346.)

[25.] 'Ad caeteras horas hae cantari solent antiphonae, quarum prima est, *Ecce tu pulchra es.*' (*Patrologia latina* 149, col. 684.)

[26.] 'In horis assumantur antiphonae nocturnales quae conveniant, sive de Laudibus seu ex euangelio aut de *Canticis canticorum*.' (*Liber Tramitis*, 153.)

order, and two on the Nativity. (See the list of chants in Rome, Casanatense 54.)

3. *The period 1030–3*: At Cluny, the compiler of the *Liber Tramitis* is aware of the existence of the series of antiphons from the Song of Songs, but treats them as optional, suggesting that they are new to Cluny—either newly composed or newly introduced.

4. *The period around 1075*: The compiler of Paris 12601 presents the five older antiphons as an alternative series of lauds antiphons, but neither Ulrich nor Bernard mentions them. Since Bernard specifies different antiphons for lauds through the octave, perhaps Paris 12601 is in this instance adhering to a tradition that is no longer observed. The series of antiphons on the Song of Songs, for which Paris 12601 provides only the rubric 'Infra ebdomadam', is said by the writers of both customaries to be intended for the little hours.

In the Cluny breviaries that have staff notation, the sixth antiphon is written in transposition, so that it ends on G; and it is given a mode 8 differentia. A twelfth-century breviary representing the use of the monastery of Corbie after its reform by Cluny, Amiens, Bibliothèque municipale 115,[27] assigns it to the correct mode, giving it in transposition with an ending on c (and a b flat just before the end). But the Corbie breviary adds two antiphons to the series, once again disturbing the original plan. Example 2 shows the eight antiphons as they appear in the Saint-Victor breviary.

The antiphons appear in other monastic sources assigned to matins of the feast of the Nativity of the Blessed Virgin. In an eleventh-century antiphonal from Silos, six antiphons from the series—the first, second, third, fifth, sixth, and seventh—serve as the six antiphons of the first nocturn.[28] The first four of these are also employed as antiphons for the psalms of first vespers on this day. In a thirteenth-century antiphonal from Rheinau, antiphons one to six are in the first nocturn, with seven and eight at the beginning of the second nocturn.[29]

[27.] See V. Leroquais, *Les Bréviaires*, I, 17–20. The reform took place while one Robert was abbot, during the second quarter of the 12th C. Concerning the change in the divine office at Corbie, see also *CAO* v, 444.

[28.] London, British Library Add. 30850; it is also surveyed in *CAO* II. Even though its chants are essentially those of the 'Gregorian' divine office, its notation consists of Mozarabic neumes. Another distinctive feature is its practice of specifying procedures that are elsewhere assumed to be understood: Hesbert writes of 'une explicitation singulière des rubriques, une répétition incessante des formulaires' (p. xvii). (A facsimile of this manuscript has just been published by the Sociedad Española de Musicología, Madrid, 1985: *Antiphonale Silense*, ed. I. Fernández de la Cuesta.)

[29.] It is in the last section of Zurich, Zentralbibliothek Rheinau 28. Hesbert surveys its contents in *CAO* II.

Ruth Steiner

They are also found in sources of the Roman cursus. An eleventh-century antiphonal of the cathedral of Verona includes them in an alternative series of matins antiphons for the feast of the Assumption, adding one antiphon at the end to complete the series of nine—*Talis est*

Example 2. Eight Marian antiphons from the Breviary of Saint-Victor-sur-Rhins

Example 2—*cont.*

E - mis - si - o - nes tu - ae pa - ra - di - sus

ma - lo - rum pu - ni - co - rum cum po - mo - rum fruc - ti - bus.

e u o u a e

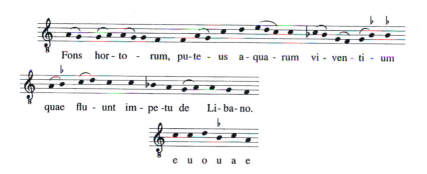

Fons hor - to - rum, pu - te - us a - qua - rum vi - ven - ti - um

quae flu - unt im - pe - tu de Li - ba - no.

e u o u a e

Ve - nit di - lec - tus me - us in hor - tum su - um,

ut co - me - dat fruc - tum po - mo - rum su - o - rum.

e u o u a e

Ve - ni in hor - tum me - um, so - ror me - a spon - sa,

mes - su - i myr - rham me - am cum a - ro - ma - ti - bus me - is.

e u o u a e

Example 2—*cont.*

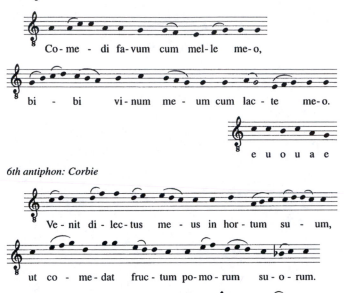

Co-me - di fa-vum cum mel-le   me-o,

bi - bi   vi-num me - um cum lac - te   me-o.

e u o u a e

6th antiphon: Corbie

Ve - nit di - lec-tus   me - us in hor - tum   su - um,

ut co - me - dat   fruc - tum po-mo-rum   su - o - rum.

e u o u   a e

dilectus (*CAO* III, 5098), in mode 6.[30] At Salisbury, the eight antiphons form the main series of matins antiphons for Assumption, with a different antiphon rounding out the series—*Surge aquilo et veni auster* (*CAO* III, 5070), in mode 7.[31] And at Bamberg, the first five antiphons are in first vespers of the Nativity of the Blessed Virgin, the three others in the little hours on this day. *Talis est dilectus* is assigned to the office of none to fill out the series.[32]

Thus in the office manuscripts, the eight antiphons tend to stay together and in order, even as they are shifted from one position to another in the liturgy. When for liturgical reasons the series needs to be extended, the antiphons added to it vary. It appears that the series came into being independent of any particular liturgical role: a composer set himself the task of providing music for a series of brief texts excerpted from the Song

[30.] Verona, Biblioteca capitolare xcviii (see *CAO* I).

[31.] Cambridge, University Library Mm. ii. 9: see W. H. Frere (ed.), *Antiphonale Sarisburiense* (2 vols., London 1901–24; repr. in 6 vols., Farnborough 1966), v, 493–7.

[32.] Bamberg, Staatsbibliothek lit. 23 (end of the 12th C.; see *CAO* I). The chants have the same role in a later antiphonal of Bamberg (Staatsbibliothek lit. 25), where they are written in staff notation (fols. 94r–96v). The melody of *Venit dilectus meus* has been partially erased, perhaps because of that confusion concerning its modal classification to which reference has already been made.

of Songs, leaving it to others to find places for them in the liturgy. In Paris 12601, the antiphons are incorporated more or less as 'raw material'—with a liturgical role only hinted at—and thus in something approaching their original state. It is significant that at Cluny even at the end of the thirteenth century they had not been allowed to replace traditional proper chants but only to assume roles previously played by ferial antiphons. This is true even on the feast of the Nativity of the Blessed Virgin, where the Cluny matins antiphons are nearly all borrowed from the Assumption.

None of the eight antiphons has been identified as an adaptation, although the melodies are all in the traditional style.[33] It is remarkable that four of the antiphons in the series are singled out and referred to by incipit in the Sarum Tonary, those of modes 1, 2, 5 and 6.[34] I can only guess that the modal organization of the series attracted the attention of the compiler of the tonary, and caused him to give it special attention.

The Three Antiphons of the Third Series

For the next three antiphons in the Cluny series, the usual order is that in which their texts come in the Song of Songs: *Anima mea, Descendi in hortum, Dilecte mi apprehendam*. In both the later Cluny breviaries they are put to service as antiphons for the psalms of vespers during the octave of Assumption. (Once again, these are roles that would otherwise have been filled by chants of the feria.) Since there are four psalms in monastic vespers, an additional antiphon must follow them. The Solesmes manuscript adds to the series the incipit of the antiphon *Hortus est conclusus*, which it has already given as the last antiphon of matins. The Saint-Victor breviary writes out *Hortus est conclusus*, and then supplies the incipit of *Tota pulchra es*, bringing the number of antiphons to five. In both sources, *Salve regina* is specified as the antiphon for the Magnificat.

Only one of the Cluny customaries refers to these three antiphons by incipit. Bernard writes that they are to be used through the octave with the

---

[33] Crocker reports similar findings in his study of 'numerical' antiphons at St-Denis, 'Matins antiphons', 464.

[34] W. H. Frere (ed.), *The Use of Sarum II: The Ordinal and Tonal* (Cambridge 1901), i–lxxxvi. *Fons hortorum* is the only antiphon assigned to the 12th *variacio* of the 1st *differencia* of mode 5, and *Venit dilectus* is one of only five antiphons assigned to the 6th of the transposed *variaciones* of mode 6. The other two antiphons are treated routinely. But several theorists single out *Ecce tu pulchra es* for comment. The John 'who probably wrote [his] treatise in the area between St Gall and Bamberg around 1100' observes that 'although the antiphon *Ecce tu pulchra es* descends into the range of the second tone, nevertheless, since it quite often iterates the fifth above the final, it is assigned to the first tone'. See C. V. Palisca (ed.), *Hucbald, Guido, and John on Music* (New Haven, Conn., 1978), 95, 122. My thanks to H. Powers for calling my attention to this and several other references.

psalms of vespers.[35] But he may be thinking of having them used in alternation, one each day, as the sole antiphon for all the vespers psalms. (He refers elsewhere to such a practice.)[36] At Corbie, each of the four psalms for vespers through the octave has its antiphon identified. They are *Felix namque es beata*, *Virgo prudentissima*, *Anima mea*, and *Descendi in hortum*.

Other examples could be added here, but they would not change the broad outlines of the picture: once again, it is a question of new chants for which a place is being found.

How stable is the musical tradition at Cluny for these longer antiphons? Less so than one might perhaps have hoped: the readings of *Anima mea liquefacta est* in five Cluny or Cluniac manuscripts differ significantly. The sources that have been compared include Paris 12601, the breviaries at Saint-Victor and Solesmes, the Corbie breviary (Amiens 115), and finally a manuscript from Montier-la-Celle, a monastery reformed by Marmoutier around 1038, Troyes, Bibliothèque municipale 109.[37] Example 3 shows the melody as it appears in the Corbie breviary and in Troyes 109, and Figure 1 the neumes of Paris 12601. Paris 12601 often gives a slightly more elaborate version of the melody than does the Corbie manuscript: there are eleven syllables for which it has a two- or three-note neume rather than a *punctum*; and it twice shows liquescence where Corbie has none. There are just three instances where Corbie is more elaborate, and two where Corbie has a double note rather than a single one. These are all indicated by numbers written over the transcription of the Corbie melody: a '3' over a single note means that at that point Paris 12601 has a neume indicating three notes, rather than a *virga* or a *punctum*.

If the Corbie manuscript presents the melody in a 'stripped-down' reading, the later manuscripts tend in general to present it in a form that is at least as ornamented as that of Paris 12601. The reading that is perhaps the most extreme in this respect is that of Troyes 109. Certain passages merit particular attention. One is the phrase 'invenerunt me', which Paris 12601 highlights by placing a *pes stratus* on the second word, and for which Troyes 109 furnishes a comparable figure. Another is the leap between the phrases 'custodes murorum' and 'Filiae Jerusalem': the size of this ranges

---

[35] 'Ad Vesp. super Psal. Ant. *Anima mea*, *Descendi*, *Dilecte mi*. Et hae eadem dicuntur usque ad Nativitatem ejusdem Dominae nostrae: super *Magnificat* ad Process. post Vesp. si fit ad sanctam Mariam, nisi festum sit de quo R. cantetur.' (Herrgott, *Vetus disciplina monastica*, 346)

[36] e.g. in first vespers of the Assumption, he directs that 'super Psal. una tantum Ant. *Tota pulchra* dicitur' (ibid. 345–6).

[37] Concerning the reform of Montier-la-Celle, see C. Waddell, 'Pre-Cistercian Background', 120–1. It is through Montier-la-Celle and Marmoutier that Molesme (and, later, Cîteaux) and Cluny are linked. The extent and nature of the correspondences between the divine office of the Cistercians and that of the Cluniac monks remain to be explored.

Example 3. *Anima mea* in Amiens 115 (Corbie) and Troyes 109 (Montier-la-Celle)

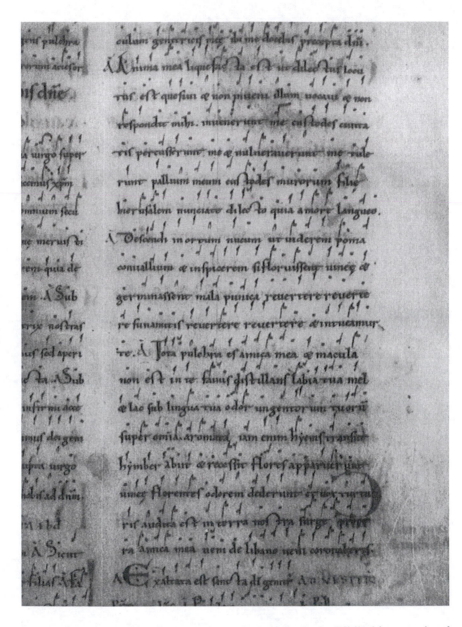

Figure 1. The antiphon *Anima mea liquefacta est* in Paris, Bibliothèque nationale lat. 12601, fol. 86r

in the various sources from a fourth to a sixth; and Troyes 109 makes it a seventh. Here and there through the melody one observes a tendency on the part of this manuscript to enlarge intervals. Some examples are '(non inveni il)lum, vo(cavi)', and 'in(venerunt)'. In general, Troyes 109 seems to be making use of musical resources to intensify the delivery of the text, a tendency that is already present in Paris 12601, and which the other sources (not shown here) seem not to attempt.

Do we have an adequate basis for the 'restoration' of the late eleventh-century melody? The divergences among the readings provide more than one occasion for a would-be restorer to wring his or her hands. They also raise important questions about how the melodies were transmitted (it was clearly not through mechanical copying from one manuscript to another).

Figure 2 presents in schematic form the relationships of the manuscripts to which reference has been made here. The names of monasteries with cycles of Marian antiphons descending from those of Cluny are given, along with the dates of their founding or reform by Cluny. Vertical lines lead to the actual manuscripts, which are designated by library and call number, and located according to their presumed time of compilation.

In some instances, the manuscript dates from long after the founding or reform—Montier-la-Celle, for example, which was reformed in the mid-eleventh century, and for which our source is nearly three centuries later. How much change, and what kind of change, took place at Montier-la-Celle during this long period? Is the change to be attributed to decay occasioned by less than perfect precision in the oral transmission of chant? Or is it the result of intentional reworking of the melodies? It may be that both are factors. Reference has already been made here to Renaudin's comparative study of the two antiphonals of Saint-Maur-des-Fossés, Paris 12584 and 12044, which highlights many differences between them. They are separated in time by perhaps fifty years, a critical period during which staff notation was introduced at this monastery.[38] During this interval, there was a major change in the system of invitatory tones and antiphons. Not only were new antiphons introduced at Saint-Maur, a new tone was added; and the whole pattern of relationships among tones and antiphons was revised.[39] In this type of development one senses the hand (and the mind) of a scholar-composer-theorist, an individual working to improve and refine, rather than the unintended result of long-term communal practice. And so, by analogy, it is difficult to know how exactly the Troyes manuscript transmits the observance of the divine office that

[38] See n. 10.

[39] R. Steiner, 'Reconstructing the Repertory of Invitatory Tones and their Uses at Cluny in the Late 11th Century', *Musicologie médiévale: Notations et séquences*, Actes de la Table Ronde du CNRS à l'Institut de Recherche et d'Histoire des Textes, 6–7 Septembre 1982, ed. M. Huglo (Paris 1987), 175–82.

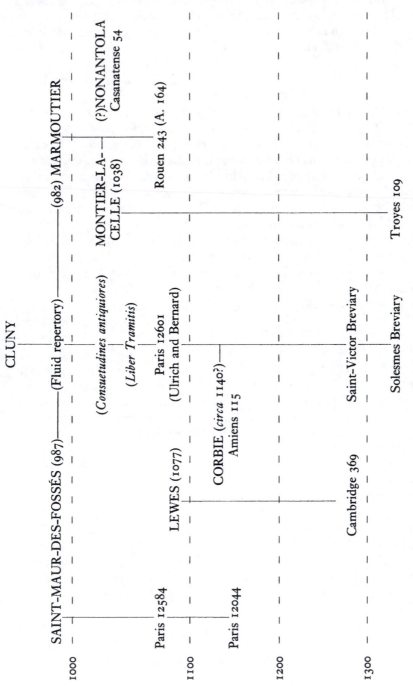

Figure 2. Manuscript sources for Marian antiphons of the Cluny tradition

Names of monasteries are given in capital letters; dates of Cluniac reforms are in parentheses, as are references to customaries. Vertical lines represent the [presumably] unbroken traditions of individual houses. Bands across the chart represent centuries; within them the positioning of particular manuscripts is intended to suggest their approximate dates.

was introduced at Montier-la-Celle in the decades around 1040.

Similarly, it should be remembered that monasteries were open to outside influences. The office of the Blessed Virgin in which Troyes 109 presents *Anima mea liquefacta est* is a liturgical innovation, and too recent to be contained in the Marmoutier breviary (Rouen A. 164) from which most of the divine office of Montier-la-Celle appears to descend. Nor is the chant itself present. It must have been borrowed from some other establishment; and perhaps that explains some of the distinctive features that we have observed in the melody.

The Final Antiphon Tota pulchra es

For the chants discussed thus far, the focus has been on the texts and their sources, on the roles they have in the liturgy, and on the music, and aspects of its style. For the final chant of the series, *Tota pulchra es*, another consideration enters—its ritual function. In the *Liber Tramitis*, *Tota pulchra es* is specified as the chant that accompanies a procession.[40]

On the feast of the Assumption, the early mass (the *missa matutinalis*) is followed by the service of terce; and then a procession forms. The *Liber Tramitis* outlines the order in which the various groups assemble, and it enumerates the objects that are carried—holy water, a reliquary, three crosses (one of which is a crucifix), two censers, four candelabra, two Gospel books, a picture of Christ and the Virgin Mary, two golden sceptres and a golden apple (gifts to Cluny from the Emperor Henry II after his coronation in 1014), the arm of St Maur, and a vial containing milk of the Blessed Virgin.[41] When everyone is in place, the paraphonista intones the antiphon *Tota pulchra es*.

Tota pulchra es: Thou art all fair, O my love, and there is not a spot in thee. Thy lips are as a dripping honeycomb, honey and milk are under thy tongue, the sweet smell of thy ointments is above all aromatical spices. For winter is now past, the rain is over and gone. The flowers have appeared, the vines in flower yield their sweet smell, and the voice of the turtledove is heard in our land. Arise, make haste, my love, come from Lebanon, come, thou shalt be crowned.[42]

[40] *Liber Tramitis*, 150–1.

[41] Concerning these, see the account of 'Liturgische Neuerungen, Reliquien und Kultgegenstände' in the introduction to the edition of the *Liber Tramitis*, pp. xlviii–lii.

[42] 'Tota pulchra es, amica mea, et macula non est in te; favus distillans labia tua, mel et lac sub lingua tua, odor unguentorum tuorum super omnia aromata; jam enim hiems transiit, imber abiit et recessit, flores apparuerunt, vineae florentes odorem dederunt, et vox turturis audita est in terra nostra: Surge, propera, amica mea; veni de Libano, veni, coronaberis.' (*CAO* III, 5162. Of 5161, also beginning 'Tota pulchra es', I find no trace at Cluny.)

As this is sung, the procession enters the oratory of St Mary, where a priest says a versicle and a collect; and then the altar is censed by two other priests with censers. The procession continues into the cloister, and goes from there to the atrium of the church, where it pauses. At length, it returns to the church. Four responsories are sung during this part of it.[43]

William of Dijon: Composer of Antiphons from the Song of Songs?

Of the seventeen antiphons that have been under consideration, twelve have texts from the Song of Songs.[44] These twelve chants are given (with one substitution) as the antiphons for the first and second nocturns of matins on the feast of the Assumption in a fourteenth-century breviary of Saint-Bénigne de Dijon (Paris, Bibliothèque de l'Arsenal 274, fol. 439v). Chrysogonus Waddell, who called my attention to this series, sees it as the prototype, and the Cluny series as derived from it.

There are two points that strongly support this interpretation. First is the fact that the arrangement of the antiphons in the Saint-Bénigne manuscript and the substitution of one antiphon for another restores to the chants the order in which their texts appear in the Song of Songs: *Talis est*

[43.] 'Cum perdicta ibi fuerit antiphona dicat sacerdos versum atque collectam ex eadem beata quam velit. Qua exacta incensetur altare a duobus sacerdotibus cum duobus turibulis. Tum cantor inchoet responsorium *Quae est ista* et postmodum aliud *Ista est speciosa*, quamdiu veniant ambo canendo in claustro. Et sic ordinate procedant absque mora in atrio aecclesie sicuti peragrarunt. Et cum ibi fuerint, stent ordinata processione in medio ut venerunt. Seniores assistant veluti in choro usus est standi, dicant ibi hoc responsorium *Super salutem*. Quo peracto intrent ecclesiam hoc responsorium decantando *Felix namque* sonantibus cunctis signis' (*Liber Tramitis*, 151). In his magisterial study, *Cluny: Les Églises et la maison du chef d'ordre* (Macon 1968), K. Conant provides a ground-plan for the Cluny of the mid-11th C. that enables the reader to follow the course of this procession (Plate 4). But how was the procession modified when Cluny III was completed? A. Walters [Robertson] has shown how the processions at St-Denis changed their course over time ('The Reconstruction of the abbey church at St-Denis [1231–81]: the interplay of music and ceremony with architecture and politics', *Early Music History* 5 (1985), 187–238). Surely there were comparable changes at Cluny.

[44.] The Song of Songs is also drawn on in the classic chants for the feast of the Assumption; several have texts from it. In non-Cluny sources there are many other antiphons on the same literary themes. And at Cluny the lessons for matins on the Nativity of the Blessed Virgin came from the Song of Songs until, in the 11th C., a sermon by Fulbert of Chartres was set in their place: See R. Étaix, 'Le Lectionnaire de l'office à Cluny', *Recherches augustiniennes* 11 (1976), 91–159, esp. 125. But later additions to the repertory of Marian antiphons tended as often as not to involve non-biblical texts. We find additional antiphons in both of the later Cluny breviaries: they follow the *Salve regina*, which is specified as the antiphon for the Magnificat in vespers through the octave. In the breviary at St-Victor there are five such antiphons: among them are *Alma redemptoris mater*, *Ave regina celorum*, and *Mater patris et filia*. These three are also among the 14 in the breviary at Solesmes.

dilectus (5. 16b) comes after *Anima mea*, and *Dilecte mi* (an antiphon borrowed by Cluny from the older repertory) is dropped.

Second, Fr. Waddell thinks it possible that these antiphons come from William of Dijon, 'whose liturgical compositions circulated widely thanks to his reforming activities which took in Saint-Germain, a large number of Norman abbeys, and, by way of the Norman abbeys, a whole group of English abbeys'.[45] This attribution seems likely in view of the fact that the twelve antiphons of Saint-Bénigne de Dijon are given precisely the same liturgical function in a twelfth-century manuscript from Fécamp, Rouen, Bibliothèque municipale 244 (A. 261). Dom Raymond Le Roux has identified the latter as 'le seul ms. noté qui ait le cursus de l'abbé Guillaume'.[46]

The case for attributing the first eight antiphons to William is further strengthened if one recalls the role assigned to him by Finn Hansen, that of head of the group of scribes who copied the celebrated mass Tonary, Montpellier, Bibliothèque de l'École de Médecine H 159.[47] It would be quite in character for the architect of a tonary to want to explore the possibilities of all of the modes in his work as a composer. The case for the four remaining antiphons is less clear. In the *Liber Tramitis*, the eight antiphons are optional, but *Tota pulchra es* has an important role assigned to it. And *Anima mea* and *Descendi in hortum* resemble each other, at least in length, more than they do either *Talis est dilectus* or *Dilecte mi* (which are significantly shorter).

To sum up: it seems quite possible that Cluny borrowed the series of twelve antiphons from Saint-Bénigne; one can even imagine the copyist of Paris 12601 using as his model (at this point) a manuscript leaf sent from Saint-Bénigne on which one antiphon had been crossed out and another entered. It also seems likely that William was the composer of at least the first eight of the twelve. For the remaining four, the evidence is less clear. To think of the twelve as having been composed for their use at Saint-Bénigne, as a series of matins antiphons, one would have to attribute to an eleventh-century composer the planning of a series in which antiphons nine and eleven are a good deal longer than any of the first eight, and in which the twelfth antiphon is quite long and, unlike the others, has a centonized text—a series that reaches a climax at the end of the second nocturn. At Cluny, on the other hand, the liturgical assignment of the antiphons (unspecified in Paris 12601, explicit in the later breviaries) takes their length into account, and in that respect is more along traditional lines.

[45.] Chrysogonus Waddell, letter to the author, 18 January 1987.

[46.] 'Guillaume de Volpiano: son cursus liturgique au Mont-Saint-Michel et dans les abbayes normandes', *Millénaire monastique du Mont-Saint-Michel* I (Paris 1966), 419.

[47.] *H 159 Montpellier: Tonary of St Bénigne of Dijon* (Copenhagen 1974), 21.

The Lewes Breviary-Missal

Clearly, at the end of the thirteenth century, when the Lewes manuscript was compiled, the repertory was still growing and changing. A few words need to be said about the book itself.[48] As a noted breviary-missal, it contains an enormous number of chants and texts; but it is in fact smaller than any of the other sources that have been commented upon in this study, the pages measuring 193 by 136 millimetres. Thus it is a book to be held in the hand although, with 516 folios, it is quite thick. Leroquais suggested that it might have been intended for a monk who was prevented by illness from being present in choir, or that it was used for travel.[49] Except in the mass prefaces, the music is written so small that the precise pitch of a note or neume is frequently difficult to determine. And yet, because of its completeness, the manuscript has enormous importance for those who wish to explore the musical tradition of Cluny.

Comparison with the two later Cluny breviaries reveals that the Lewes manuscript presents a faithful record of the liturgy of Cluny. Hence there is a potential benefit in both directions: one can go to the Cluny breviaries for musical notation that can be read with precision, and to the Lewes manuscript for the sections of the liturgical year that are missing from the other sources. If one works from all three, and also the other Cluniac manuscripts referred to above, one has the possibility of assembling the complete repertory of the Cluny divine office with its music, even though questions about the readings of individual chants may still inevitably remain. And one also can trace, through observing the occasional disagreements among the sources, how later developments at individual monasteries were permitted to follow their own courses.

For each of the cycles of Marian antiphons discussed above, Lewes provides counterparts. The eight antiphons in modal order appear in Lewes on fols. 342r–v with the same function assigned to them as in the later Cluny breviaries: they are antiphons for the little hours through the octave of the Assumption. They are followed, on fol. 342v, by *Anima mea liquefacta es*, *Descendi in hortum*, and *Dilecte mi*, intended for the psalms of second vespers (just as in the Saint-Victor manuscript); and after them comes the incipit of *Hortus conclusus*, which is identified as the antiphon for the Magnificat. (*Tota pulchra es* has been given earlier, on fol. 339r, as the antiphon for all of the psalms of first vespers, a role also assigned to it in the later Cluny breviaries.) Thus far what Lewes shows is as much in the Cluny tradition as any manuscript from Cluny. But two other cycles of chants need to be considered.

[48.] The work by Leroquais cited in n. 1 is still the standard reference; for a description of the musical notation see S. Holder, 'Cluniac Breviary-missal'.

[49.] Leroquais, 20.

In one of these, the two later Cluny breviaries agree, and Lewes does not; in the other, all three manuscripts differ. The latter is the series of alternative Magnificat antiphons for use through the octave of the Assumption. A few comments have been made above concerning the two Cluny series; that of Lewes is as follows. (Although the total number of chants is seven, it is nowhere said—though perhaps it is understood—that the chants must be used in this order through the week.)

Exaltata est gloriosa
Haec est regina virginum
Speciosa facta es
Salve regina
Alma redemptoris mater
Ave regina caelorum
Felix namque es (CAO 2861)

A comparison of this series with those of other neighbouring institutions might lead to valuable results, as might also a comparison of the readings in which Lewes gives these chants with those of other sources from Britain.

Lewes and the two Cluny breviaries also provide a series of antiphons for lauds of the vigil, and here Lewes departs from the Cluny tradition. The two series are shown in Table 4, with *CAO* numbers added for identification.

TABLE 4. *Lauds antiphons for the vigil of the Assumption*

CAO no.	Lewes (fol. 338v)	CAO no.	Cluny mss. (late 13th, early 14th C.)
3002	Haec est regina virginum	5041	Sub tuum praesidium
2924	Gaude Maria virgo cunctas	3002	Haec est regina virginum
3708	Maria virgo semper laetare	3708	Maria virgo semper laetare
1574	Beatam me dicent	5040	Sub tuam protectionem
4699	Sancta dei genitrix virgo	2861	Felix namque es
			Ad Benedictus
		4029	O gloriosa dei genitrix

Paris 12601 has nothing in lauds for the vigil, and one might have expected the compilers of the later sources simply to move the five antiphons that form the first group on fol. 86r into this position. That is not quite what happened: the Cluny series includes only three of those antiphons. *Haec est regina virginum* comes from the Nativity of the Blessed Virgin, and *Felix namque es* and *O gloriosa dei genitrix* are new additions. Lewes has retained only one chant from the old list, *Maria virgo semper laetare*. Along with *Haec est regina virginum* it has added *Sancta dei genitrix virgo* which comes from an old collection of Marian antiphons also drawn on in the series of Marmoutier (see Table 3). *Gaude Maria virgo* is borrowed from the feast of the Purification. *Beatam me dicent* is on a text from the Magnificat, and its usual function is that of Magnificat antiphon in vespers on the Monday following the third Sunday of Advent. Its use in Lewes as an antiphon for the Benedicite is striking. The independence of this series of lauds antiphons in Lewes from the Cluny series seems an indication that by this period—at the time in which it seemed appropriate to establish a series of lauds antiphons for the vigil of the Assumption— there was a certain freedom at Lewes in liturgical matters.

A fuller examination of these antiphon series would undoubtedly be valuable; but it seems likely that the conclusions would not be different in any significant way from those to which we have already been led. In the additions made to the basic repertories of office chants through the course of the middle ages there is abundant evidence of changing interests and tastes. At times the prevailing principle seems to be a yearning for order, a seeking for systems of organization, at other times an openness to the spirituality of each age comparable with that expressed in non-biblical prayers and their music. It is a sign of the flexibility of the divine office that places could continue to be found in it for new material.

The basic orientation of this study on chants for the feast of the Assumption has meant that devotion to the Blessed Virgin has been a recurring sub-theme. The antiphons discussed here need further study, perhaps as much from the literary and theological points of view as from the musical. Their presence in the sources is further evidence of that continuing impulse toward the glorification of Mary, and devotion to her, which shapes so much of the sacred art of the later middle ages. It is something we need to understand more fully.

8

An English Noted Breviary
of circa *1200*

DAVID CHADD
(University of East Anglia)

The manuscript Oxford, Bodleian Library Lat. liturg. c36 was acquired by purchase in December 1964. It is the Sanctorale of an insular breviary which I date *circa* 1200. The purpose of the present paper is to give an account of this manuscript and in particular of the antiphoner which is contained within it, to draw attention to some of the more interesting of its contents, and to suggest a hypothesis which could account for its idiosyncrasies. In the course of doing this, I wish implicitly to examine the methods of comparative analysis which seem to be available to us for assessing the significance and meaning of the contents of books of this kind.

The importance of this manuscript within a study of insular musico-liturgical survivals seems to me to rest primarily upon the coincidence of its secular origin, its independence from known liturgical uses, and its early date. Despite grave lacunae, we are not uninformed about English monastic offices in the middle ages. Few insular monastic sources may be as early as this, but there is good reason to infer that they often preserve their material in arrangements much older than they themselves are. To cite just one general observation in support of that premiss, the breviaries of the abbeys of Hyde and Peterborough (both normally dated to *circa* 1300) and that of the abbey of Evesham (1350s or 1360s) are witnesses to

An early version of this paper was read as the annual lecture of the Plainsong & Mediaeval Music Society in London on 26 June 1987. I am grateful to the Society for giving me that opportunity to focus my attention on this manuscript. I would also like to thank Mr Christopher Hohler for pursuing with me a spirited correspondence on these and related issues over many years. Many of the better ideas in this paper are the result of his suggestions and criticisms.

the early eleventh-century liturgical work of William of Volpiano.[1] With the secular uses we are bedevilled by the popularity of that liturgical portmanteau usually called 'Sarum', and to a lesser extent that of other standardized uses, whose widespread adoption led quite successfully to the obliteration of other and older evidence. Some hint of earlier practices may be discerned in the contents of 'aberrant' Sarum books, though never on any substantial scale. It is really only with the Austin Canons, whose surviving English office books are not numerous, that we find secular uses which may sometimes not conform to widespread standards such as Sarum. This, however, is not always the case. The antiphoner of the Barnwell Canons is (if one excepts the few additions which they made to it to comply with their own observances) an exemplar of 'standard' Sarum Use around the middle of the thirteenth century, and was most usefully published in facsimile as such by the Plainsong & Mediaeval Music Society during the early years of this century.[2] Any English secular office book from around 1200, when by definition it is going to be comparatively exempt from the pressures of conformity to national standards, is therefore something of a *rara avis*.

The manuscript we are concerned with here (and which I shall henceforth refer to as 'Oxford c36') is, as I have said, the Sanctorale of a breviary, and it is preceded by the last six months of a kalendar. This manuscript is not in good condition. It is unbound—that is, it is in sheets and gatherings from which the stitching has disappeared—though it is between boards which fit it. These are the remains of a medieval binding, and there is no obvious reason why they should not be close in date to the body of the book.[3] Leaves have been lost from several places, and the whole of the last part of the book is missing—it commences with Andrew (30 November), which was presumably the original start, but it ends with

[1] For the Hyde Breviary see J. B. L. Tolhurst (ed.), *The Monastic Breviary of Hyde Abbey, Winchester*, Henry Bradshaw Society 69–71, 76, 78, 80 (London, 1930–2, 1937, 1939, 1941–2). Peterborough is Cambridge, Magdalene College F. 4. 10. Evesham is Oxford, Bodleian Library Barlow 41. For the work of William, see Raymond Le Roux, 'Guillaume de Volpiano: Son *cursus* liturgique au Mont-Saint-Michel et dans les abbayes normandes', in *Millénaire monastique du Mont-Saint-Michel* I (*Histoire et Vie Monastique*, ed. J. Laporte) (Paris, 1966); and, in great detail, N. Bulst, *Untersuchungen zu den Klosterreformen Wilhelms von Dijon (962–1031)*, Pariser historische Studien 11 (Bonn, 1973).

[2] W. H. Frere (ed.), *Antiphonale Sarisburiense* (London, 1901–24). The manuscript is Cambridge, University Library Mm. ii. 9.

[3] The physical description of the manuscript, which I take from Bodley's current catalogue, is: 106 leaves, text in two columns of 38 lines = 19 music notation staves of four red crayon lines; pages 326 × 235 mm., margins often cut away; text space *c.* 220–3 × 138–45 mm., collation 1⁴ (1–2 missing), 10⁸, 11⁸ (1 missing), 12⁶ (leaves disordered: fols. 78–83), 13⁸ (1 and 4 missing), 14⁸ (3 missing), 15⁸ (4–5 missing), 16⁸ (1, 4, 5, 8 missing); quires missing at end.

Maurice (22 September), so that all feasts between 22 September and 30 November are absent. There is nothing to suggest that we are dealing with a much larger book from which Temporale and Common have been lost. Indeed, were that the case, it would be surprising that so much of the Sanctorale remained while those other portions had disappeared so completely. Sectionalized antiphoners of this sort are, of course, not uncommon in the middle ages. What we have in the book is either provided with Proper chant material, about which much of what I have to say will be concerned, or with a prayer, with or without lessons, implying either material for a Commemoration or else an office whose chants were to come from the Common. Rubrics are at a minimum. What we have is the basic sequence of chants, prayers, and lessons of the office. In the terminology of Stephen van Dijk, this book is therefore a 'noted portable breviary'.[4] This fact enables us to reconstruct the kalendar which lay behind it; a task that is in fact not as otiose as it would seem from the existence of a physical kalendar at the beginning of the manuscript.

The surviving part of the kalendar in Oxford c36 runs, as I have mentioned, from May to December. It includes the Birthday feast of Thomas of Canterbury (28 December), though his Translation (7 July) was not in the original and has been added by a later hand. Thomas's Birthday is graded in blue, a particularly high distinction, if one is to read it as such, shared here only by the Christmas feast. The fact that it is thereby accorded a higher grading than, for example, the feast of the Assumption (which is in red) must leave some doubt as to whether colour is being used here solely to reflect grading. If it does have a meaning, it is perhaps an indication of a date not far removed from the canonization in 1173.[5] In its distinctive features this kalendar is a close ally of that which prefaces the 'Queen Isabella' Psalter. Those features are the attention paid to both the Birthday and Translation feasts of Augustine in August and October,[6] and the inclusion of the feast of St Wulfhad on 24 July.[7] The observation of Augustine's two feasts in this manner can leave little doubt that we are dealing with a house of Canons. The inclusion of Wulfhad, especially with a red grading, must lead one to localize the kalendar at Stone in Staffordshire. Wulfhad was, according to legend, a Mercian prince

[4.] S. J. P. van Dijk and J. Hazelden Walker, *The Origins of the Modern Roman Liturgy* (London, 1960), 33.

[5.] The absence of Thomas's Translation will date the kalendar before c.1220.

[6.] The Queen Isabella Psalter is Munich, Bayerische Staatsbibliothek Cod. gall. 16. On this MS see D. D. Egbert, *The Tickhill Psalter and Related Manuscripts* (New York, 1940); and now L. F. Sandler, *Gothic Manuscripts 1285–1385*, A Survey of Manuscripts Illuminated in the British Isles 5 (London, 1986), I, 25–6. The two feasts are graded red in the kalendar of c36, with the Birthday octave in green. The Isabella Psalter has the Birthday in red, with its octave and the Translation feast in black.

[7.] Red in Oxford c36, black in the Isabella Psalter.

baptized by St Chad and murdered, together with his brother Rufinus, by his apostate father Wulfhere. Stone was the place of their martyrdom, and here, between 1138 and 1147, a house of Canons was founded from Kenilworth, the church being dedicated to Wulfhad and containing his relics.

If we turn from the kalendar to the body of the book, there are some notable discrepancies. Most obviously, in the antiphoner Augustine has his Birthday alone provided for, and that with no more than a prayer and six lessons. Such an office for him could hardly have come from an Augustinian house, which would have provided for at least his Birthday with the history R′1 *Invenit se Augustinus*, which was the order's proper history for him. Other discrepancies within the five months for which kalendar and antiphoner coexist are numerous kalendar feasts which have no material, not even a collect, in the antiphoner (these include Aldhelm, Botulph, Birthday of Swithun, Translation of Bertin, Wulfhad, Christine, Samson, Oswald) and material in the antiphoner for Leufred and Wulmar, who do not appear in the kalendar. In short, despite the fact that these two elements of the book go together physically, to the extent that the (possibly) original binding took them both, none the less they do not in some sense 'belong' together. Discrepance between kalendar and sanctorale is not an unusual feature in liturgical books, but it is worth noting that in this instance the two seem to come from institutions of different kinds, the one Augustinian, the other not.

The Office for Benedict

In considering the contents of the antiphoner proper, I shall concentrate on two of the proper histories which it contains, and append before summarizing some of the other interesting points which Oxford c36 raises. The first of these propers is that for St Benedict's Birthday on 21 March. Most secular breviaries, in England at least, celebrate both the Birthday and Translation feasts of Benedict with lessons from his legend and chants from the Common. Sarum, for example, has nine proper lessons for the Birthday and six for the Translation.[8] York has nine lessons for the Birthday from the same legend but differently arranged, and ignores the Translation.[9] Hereford has six lessons for the Birthday and like York

---

[8.] F. Procter & C. Wordsworth (eds.), *Breviarium ad usum . . . Sarum* (Cambridge, 1879–86), III, cols. 225 ff. and 467 ff.

[9.] S. Lawley (ed.), *Breviarium ad usum insignis ecclesie Eboracensis*, Publications of the Surtees Society 71 and 75 (London, 1880–3), II cols. 230 ff.

provides nothing for the Translation.[10] In all cases there are no proper chants provided, and this is the expected norm with secular books.

In contrast, monastics naturally put greater stress upon Benedict's feasts, and provide proper histories for them. In English books there are three main offices. Two are familially close prose histories derived from his legend, the first with R'1 *Fuit vir vite venerabilis*, the second with R'1 *Relicta domo rebusque patris*. The third is a rhyming history, R'1 *Florem mundi periturum | despexit tanquam aridum*. The sources given in the modern edition of this history,[11] numbering in excess of fifty, are monastic with the exception of a Freising breviary of 1479 and two breviaries from the Passau diocese.[12] Though there are houses such as Saint-Vaast which use this rhymed history exclusively,[13] there are many more which have it beside the prose histories. Saint-Benoît-sur-Loire at Fleury, for example, uses *Fuit vir vite venerabilis* for the March feast (called by them the 'Transitus') and the rhymed history for their own celebration of the Translation ('Illatio') on 4 December.[14] The Worcester Antiphoner takes the principal of mixture to an extreme for the Birthday, celebrated by what is in the main *Fuit vir vite*, by plundering the rhymed history and using four of its responds to make its third nocturn.[15]

The second of the prose histories, *Relicta domo*, is found almost exclusively in English monastic sources—the breviaries of Canterbury, Durham, Muchelney, and Battle, and in the antiphoner of Peterborough.[16] Its sole appearance abroad seems to be in secular form in the Nidaros breviary, a Use which relies heavily upon English precedent.[17]

[10] W. H. Frere and L. E. G. Brown (eds.), *The Hereford Breviary*, Henry Bradshaw Society 26, 40, 46 (London, 1903, 1910, 1913), II, 129–30.

[11] C. Blume, G. Dreves, H. M. Bannister (eds.), Analecta Hymnica Medii Aevi (Leipzig, 1886–1922), 25. 146 ff.

[12] I know no more than this about these three books, though it may be significant that Freising and Passau were both suffragans of Salzburg. However, on the basis of the 1519 print of the Passau Antiphoner, which provides only for Benedict's March feast, and that from the Common, I would have thought that the two books from Passau diocese were some sort of special case. For a facsimile of the 1519 Passau book, see K. Schlager (ed.), *Antiphonale Pataviense*, Das Erbe Deutscher Musik 87 (1985).

[13] L. Brou (ed.), *The Monastic Ordinale of St Vedast's Abbey, Arras*, Henry Bradshaw Society 86–7 (London, 1954–5).

[14] A. Davril (ed.), *Consuetudines Floriacenses saeculi tertii decimi*, Corpus Consuetudinum Monasticarum 9 (Siegburg, 1976).

[15] *Le Codex F 160 . . . de Worcester*, Paléographie musicale 12 (Tournai and Paris, 1922–5), 296 ff.

[16] Canterbury (the 'Burnt Breviary') is Canterbury, Cathedral Library Add. 6. Durham is London, British Library Harley 4664 (Breviary of Coldingham, a cell of Durham). Muchelney is the Breviary of the house, London, British Library Add. 43405–6. Battle is Cambridge, Trinity College o. 7. 31. For the Peterborough Antiphoner see n. 1 *supra*.

[17] L. Gjerløw, *Antiphonarium Nidrosiensis Ecclesie*, Libri liturgici provinciae Nidrosiensis medii aevi 3 (Oslo, 1979), 167.

The other prose history, *Fuit vir vite*, seems to appear first in the Compiègne Antiphoner of around 860, and its early popularity with monastics is attested by its appearance in some form or other in all the monastic sources used in the second volume of Hesbert's *Corpus Antiphonalium Officii*.[18] There seem to be only four surviving secular versions of this history, three of them English. One of this insular trio is Oxford c36. I have laid out in tabular form in Appendix 2, Section 2 the constituent elements of this history as it is found in the Compiègne Antiphoner and the six monastic sources of *CAO*, and have added (as source X) the arrangement found in a north German book of approximately the same date as c36. In Section 3 of Appendix 2, I give the same information for the six monastic and three secular books from England which use this history for the Birthday. The fourth of the quartet of secular books which have *Fuit vir vite* is the Breviary of Odense, which seems to be the only Danish or Swedish breviary to celebrate Benedict in this way. As Lilli Gjerløw has pointed out, the presence of this history can be seen as 'a relic of the Benedictine origins of the See of Odense, founded by Evesham monks in the late eleventh century'.[19]

Of the two English witnesses beside Oxford c36, Paris, Bibliothèque nationale lat. 16304 (MS F in Section 3 of Appendix 2) is a breviary datable to around 1200. Its placement is due to Lilli Gjerløw, who used it in her splendid study of the Nidaros Antiphoner.[20] Leroquais found that this book had too many lacunae to be localized securely,[21] but Lilli Gjerløw has demonstrated that its idiosyncrasies taken together can leave no doubt that it is English. Among these is the secular form of *Fuit vir vite*, which as we have seen has a preponderance of English witnesses, and the remains of a secular form of the history for St Cuthbert, that with R′1 *Cuthbertus puer bone*.

The last of the English secular sources is Paris, Bibliothèque nationale lat. 12036, an antiphoner/diurnal of the early years of the thirteenth century. At first sight it would seem to be of Sarum type, but its peculiarities are a welcome corrective to the temptation to simply categorize as 'Sarum' all those books which seem to fulfil some few standard criteria. The Sanctorale of this manuscript has a number of notable

---

[18.] R.-J. Hesbert, *Corpus Antiphonalium Officii*, 6 vols. (Rome, 1963–70), henceforth *CAO*.

[19.] Gjerløw, *Antiphonalium Nidrosiensis*, 167.

[20.] I am most grateful to Mrs Gjerløw for allowing me to see in advance her remarks on this MS.

[21.] V. Leroquais, *Les Bréviaires manuscrits des bibliothèques publiques de France*, 6 vols. (Paris, 1934), III, 264.

features besides the proper office for Benedict. In addition to transmitting some very unusual prayers, it is another secular witness to the history for Cuthbert,[22] it is the unique source of a metrical history for St Bridget of Kildare (R′1 *Celebremus concinentes | Brigide magnalia*),[23] quite unlike that for her found in Irish sources, and it transmits an unusual office for Thomas of Canterbury (R′1 *Sacrat Thomas primordia*), which does not seem to occur in any other insular source.[24] Leroquais considered the book to be from the Ely diocese,[25] on the grounds that another of its peculiarities is a secular version of the history R′1 *Sanctissimum presulem Wilfridum* for St Etheldreda, an Ely composition found otherwise only in monastic form in the breviary/missal of that house.[26] Patricia Stirnemann has now shown, however, that not only does the liturgical evidence point to Scotland, but that palaeographically the manuscript is a close relative of Paris, Bibliothèque nationale lat. 1218, the 'de Bernham' Pontifical, and that the likely home of lat. 12034 is St Andrews.[27]

Lilli Gjerløw's observation about the probable Benedictine pedigree of the Odense version of *Fuit vir vite* must lead to the consideration that the three other sources for this history are evidence for the secularizing of a monastic use. The problem I am outlining can be stated in a general way. It is well known that there is one aspect of the organization of many English cathedrals in the middle ages which distinguishes them from almost all other cathedrals in Europe—that is, the phenomenon of cathedrals which were also monastic churches, with chapters composed of monks. In liturgical terms, this poses one of the most taxing of the unresolved questions. When a cathedral was monastic, what breviary Use did the secular churches in its diocese observe? No doubt this was no less of a problem at the time than it is now. Standardized national secular Uses such as Sarum must have seemed like a heaven-sent solution to it when they became available, and it is little wonder that their adoption led so completely to the obliteration of their predecessors. But, in that there are

---

[22] C. Hohler, 'The Durham Services in Honour of St Cuthbert', in *The Relics of St Cuthbert* (Oxford, 1956), 155–91.

[23] Edited in Blume *et al.*, Analecta Hymnica, 13. 85.

[24] Edited in ibid., 13. 242, from Beauvais and Cambrai manuscripts which vary from Paris 12036 in their disposition of the items. This history is known from eight manuscripts (one of which hybridizes it with the more usual history for Thomas, R′ 1 *Studens livor*) which do not at first sight seem to cohere in any convincing way. I am grateful to Professor Andrew Hughes for making available to me his information about this history.

[25] Leroquais, *Les Bréviaires*, IV, 382–4.

[26] Cambridge, University Library Ii. 4. 20.

[27] F. Avril and P. D. Stirnemann, *Manuscrits enluminées d'origine insulaire, VIIe–XXe siècle* (Paris, 1987), 60.

one or two exceptions to the rule that this was an exclusively insular phenomenon, the problem was not confined to England. One of the exceptions is, of course, Odense, in which diocese—to give an instance which gives point to the issue—the Bridgettines of Maribo petitioned in 1431 to be allowed to follow the Use of the secular cathedral of Lund, since that of their own cathedral, being monastic, had been found to be unsuitable.[28] Might there then be the possibility of pursuing a hypothesis which saw in these three English books elements of secularized monastic Use? More particularly, could Oxford c36 be the book of a secular church whose cathedral was monastic?

One of the more obstructive of the many difficulties that are involved with the study of liturgical books is that we can hardly ever be sure of having examples of filial relationship. More often than not, existing books with similar features will stand in the relationship of distant cousins. Dom Deshusses's statement that each copy of a liturgical manuscript is 'une petite édition critique'[29] is as true for later medieval choirbooks as it is for ninth-century versions of the Gregorian sacramentary. Even with books which stand in the filial line, the interposing 'editions' will as often as not have introduced innumerable variants, some of them substantial. The problem does not stop with familial relations, for two or more families may interbreed, with characteristics of both, almost certainly in uneven quantities, being found in the otherwise disparate offspring. Some process of this sort must be behind the presence of distinctive East Anglian elements in an unquestionably Scottish book, as we have seen with Paris 12036. The version of the history for Etheldreda which this manuscript transmits could, when set beside that of the Ely breviary/missal, be seen as a model for one method of secularizing of a monastic history, at least in so far as the sequence of chant items for matins is concerned.[30] It does not, however, seem that it was to the books of Ely which Paris 12036 turned for the office for St Benedict, for the East Anglian house celebrated him with the rhymed history, rather than with the history *Fuit vir vite venerabilis* which Paris 12036 transmits. When it comes to the histories for Bridget and Thomas of Canterbury, the St Andrews provenance of the book might lead

---

[28.] P. King, 'The Cathedral Priory of Odense in the Middle Ages', *Kirkehistoriske Samlinger* VII/6 (Copenhagen, 1967).

[29.] J. Deshusses, *Le Sacramentaire Grégorien*, Spicilegium Friburgense 16, 24, 28 (Fribourg, 1979–82), Introduction.

[30.] The matins antiphons in Paris 12036 are nos. 1–9 of the Ely set. With the responds, the final item of each nocturn in the Ely sequence is, in Paris 12036, either anticipated or postponed so that it becomes the final respond of the secular nocturns—that is, Paris 12036 gives a respond order of 1, 2, 4; 3, 5, 8; 6, 7, 12 of the Ely set.

to the hypothesis that its compilers had looked for authoritative offices to Dunkeld and Arbroath respectively.[31]

Difficult as factors such as this may make the business of tracing the relationships between a distinct group of phenomena (such as one particular history), it is what we have to work with, and a recognition of it must underlie any attempt to make sense of the sort of information contained in the tabular appendices. There is a level of information which, taken at face value, has a self-evident meaning. The close correspondence, amounting virtually to identity, between the matins and lauds material of manuscripts H and R in Section 2 of Appendix 2, must mean the existence of a type sufficiently firmly established to be transmitted without essential change to these two sources. The question which has to be addressed here seems to me to hinge around the means by which that firm establishment has occurred. On the other hand, the matins antiphon series of manuscripts S and L may be seen to have a familial relationship set up by the sharing of the initial diad 36a–1 closely followed by the triad 56a–73–71, but the correspondences then break down completely and the remaining eight antiphons show not one single item shared between the two manuscripts. With the respond sequence the dichotomy is even more acute, only the first item (36b) being held in common. One might with some justice ask if these two can be considered as the same history. Between these two black-and-white extremes is an infinite array of grey shades. To take one instance, does the presence of R′ 17 in only manuscripts D, F, S, and X of Appendix 2, Section 2, speak simply about a point at which their lines of antecedence have crossed? Does its presence in the triad 20–64b–17 stress the relationship of manuscripts D and S, and how does this relate to its position in the chains 20–17–45b–64b of manuscript F and 17–45b–64b of manuscript X? In sum, what exactly is the significance of phenomena such as these? Does it relate to the means by which histories were transmitted between centres, and how are we to distinguish between the mechanics of transmission and the play of choice or 'taste'—always assuming that these things had a part? Certainly, no answers to questions such as these can be hazarded on a sample as small as that which I give. Only when all surviving sources of a particular history are tabulated can one hope to be in a position to essay such essential preliminaries as the establishment of families of

---

[31.] I hope to be able to deal with Paris 12036 in a future article. The background to its compilation seems to me to be remarkably complex. It may well have a St Andrews provenance, but the slight attention paid to St Augustine of Hippo will mean that it could not have been used in the cathedral there, which was staffed by canons. The Ely connection—if it is indeed an Ely and not a Cambridge one—suggests at first glance some association with the Scottish Earls of Huntingdon. The snag there is that the Honour of Huntingdon was in the diocese of Lincoln, not of Ely.

variants, each family having, for some purposes, the statistical value of one, whatever the number of its components.

If one collates the tables in sections 2 and 3 of Appendix 2, grouped families of antiphons and responds do indeed emerge. Manuscripts E, H and J of Section 3 show antiphon sequences for matins and lauds identical with those of the sources F and X of Section 2. This familial relationship carries over, though with less unanimity, into the arrangement of the responds. This ensemble, I would suppose, represents an 'authoritative' version of this history—one, no doubt, of many such. A hypothesis to explain it (though one which I have not tested) should certainly involve examining the significance in this group of a Cluniac book, for what Cluniacs did is likely to have had an impact beyond their own houses. Be that as it may, our manuscript Oxford c36 can also be seen to belong to a 'family' in the same way. Its own arrangement of the chant elements (column B of the Section 3 table) is identical to that transmitted in the St Andrews manuscript (column C). Further, the choice and arrangement of constituent elements in these two is obviously close to that of the monastic source in column A, to the extent that it would be not unreasonable to see this as one possible model for the adaptation of the monastic form of a history for secular use. There seems every probability that we have here three sources which witness another 'authoritative' version of the history *Fuit vir vite venerabilis*.

The monastic source in this group (column A of the Section 3 table) is not, strictly speaking, a liturgical book. London, British Library Harley 1117 is a compilation dating from the first half of the eleventh century, and containing Lives of Benedict, Cuthbert,[32] and Guthlac, each with an appended history. In his study of the proper office of Cuthbert[33] Christopher Hohler has designated the form transmitted by this manuscript as the 'southern version'. Purely on the grounds of its contents, Glastonbury or Sherborne would suggest themselves as the possible home of this book. On palaeographical grounds, however, it is clearly a product of the scriptorium of Christ Church, Canterbury,[34] a workshop which produced a substantial number of volumes clearly not intended to be used in that house, and

---

[32.] B. Colgrave, *Two Lives of St Cuthbert* (Cambridge, 1940), where it is MS H.

[33.] Hohler, 'The Durham Services', n. 22.

[34.] T. A. M. Bishop, 'Notes on Cambridge manuscripts, Part VII: the early minuscule of Christ Church, Canterbury', *Transactions of the Cambridge Bibliographical Society* 3 (1959–63), 412–23. The first part of Harley 1117 is written by Bishop's 'scribe i'; the second by his 'scribe xviii'. It has been suggested that another manuscript of this group, London, British Library Roy. 12 C. XXIII, which was also written in part by Bishop's 'scribe i', is a book of Glastonbury provenance. See J. P. Carley, 'The Pre-Conquest Manuscripts from Glastonbury Abbey', *Anglo-Saxon England* 16 (Cambridge, 1987), 203. For Glastonbury's interest in Guthlac, see J. P. Carley (ed.), and D. Townsend (transl.), *The Chronicle of Glastonbury Abbey* (Woodbridge, 1985), 275.

representing a book-production style which must have been widely sought after.[35] Until there is evidence to the contrary, it seems reasonable to conclude that Harley 1117 is the library copy of three *libelli* containing the 'authorized' versions of the lives and histories of these three saints, made for a centre (I am inclined to believe Glastonbury) which expected that it might be called on to supply such material. If one is to tie into all this the manuscript Paris 12036, it can clearly not be on the evidential level of the physical source itself; it will, rather, concern the pedigree which lies behind the book, perhaps several generations behind it. It may be possible to speculate upon the nature of the authority behind this version of *Fuit vir vite venerabilis*, but there is no evidence for how widespread was its distribution. This, however, is primarily a problem in accounting for what seems to be a witness to it in Paris 12036. It is not necessary to anticipate the same difficulties with Oxford c36. We need only note that the evidence we have suggests that, before the Conquest, a monastic form of this version seems to have been put out from an influential house in south-western England.[36]

The Office for Mary Magdalene

The second of the two notable histories in c36 which I wish to consider is that for Mary Magdalene. The basic work on her cult and its liturgical manifestations has been done by Monsignor Saxer in two books.[37] As with Benedict, there are a number of recognizable histories, together with many tiresome hybrids, and two feasts—the Birthday in July and the Translation in March. With the exception of the early fourteenth-century Cluniac Breviary of Pontefract (Oxford, University College 101), English sources do not, so far as I am aware, cater for the Translation.

[35.] The situation about these books is a complicated one, and I am most grateful to Mr T. A. Heslop for discussing it with me. He has identified a book style which he describes as 'Dunstanesque', whose origin is in a Canterbury scriptorium (not necessarily exclusively that of Christ Church) and which may have later migrated to shops outside Canterbury; it seems to have been predominantly employed in the production of library books. See now T. A. Heslop, 'The Production of *de luxe* Manuscripts and the Patronage of King Cnut and Queen Emma', *Anglo-Saxon England* 19 (1990), 151–95.

[36.] I have confined myself in this paper to broad matters of the arrangement of chant items, but in the context of this argument a matter of detail might be noted. Harley 1117 and Oxford c36 share a comparatively rare reading of the first matins antiphon *Fuit vir vite venerabilis gratia abba benedictus*, found also in the MSS C and S of *CAO*, against the majority of English sources which give . . . *gratia benedictus et nomine*. Paris 12036 adopts a hybrid version, . . . *gratia abbas benedictus et nomine*, which retains both Benedict's title and the pun on his name, and which I have not otherwise noted.

[37.] V. Saxer, *Le Culte de Marie Madeleine en Occident*, Cahiers d'Archéologie et d'Histoire 3 (Auxerre and Paris, 1959); *Le Dossier Vézelien de Marie Madeleine*, Subsidia Hagiographica 57 (Brussels, 1975).

In the earlier of his two books, Monsignor Saxer established the existence of a 'type commun' of office for the July feast.[38] This type, established from about twenty monastic books and forty-five secular ones, was shown by Saxer to relate so closely to that of the only surviving breviary of Vézelay, Lyon, Bibliothèque municipale 555 (fourteenth-century), that he postulated its archetype as the official version published by the Burgundian house, inferentially during the eleventh century. This is the history with R′ 1 *Letetur omne seculum*, and as may be anticipated from this pedigree, it has wide circulation in northern Europe. It is the first of the three offices which need concern us if we are looking at the cult of the Magdalene in England, where its most notable witness is the Use of Sarum.

The second of the offices, that with R′ 1 *Gloriosa es Maria Magdalena*, is designated by Saxer as 'the English Office', and that name conveys its general distribution. There is evidence for it in the books of four English Benedictine houses,[39] and it is widely found among the Austin Canons.[40] It is, in addition, the history for the Magdalene used by the Hereford Breviary. On the Continent, it seems only to be found in secular form in the Use of Nidaros, who will have derived it from an English source, and in monastic form in the Breviary of Saint-Bertin.[41]

The office for the Magdalene's July feast in Oxford c36 is the third of this trio, that with R′ 1 *Gloriosa diei huius sollempnia*, and in the context of an English secular book it is a most unexpected find. In Appendix 3 is the tabular evidence for the arrangement of the matins of this history. Sources A, B, and C of Section 2 are continental monastic manuscripts used by Saxer in his study; columns D and E are the English secular sources; columns F, G, and H are English monastic sources; column J is the York Breviary; and K is the arrangement at Bayeux. I have omitted from this table one other source which shows evidence of this history. The manuscript Oxford, Jesus College 10 is a late twelfth-century monastic antiphoner from St Peter's, Gloucester, containing mainly the diurnal hours, and in this particular office transmitting nothing for matins. It does, however, have the *Annua Magdalena* antiphon sequence for the hours,

[38] Saxer, *Le Culte*, 309 ff.

[39] Those of Durham, Worcester, and Peterborough already cited (nn. 1, 15, 16), and, inferentially, in Norwich books, to judge from the presence of the vespers antiphon sequence *Adest preclara* in J. B. L. Tolhurst (ed.), *The Customary of the Cathedral Priory Church of Norwich*, Henry Bradshaw Society 82 (London, 1945–6), 151.

[40] The manuscripts are London, British Library Add. 35285 (Guisborough, Missal/ Breviary); Cambridge, St John's College D.21 (Westacre, Antiphoner); London, British Library Add. 5284A (?Cirencester, Breviary).

[41] Gjerløw, *Antiphonarium Nidrosiensis* 179–80, using the late 12th-C. Breviary (*Pars Hiemalis*) of St-Bertin: St-Omer, Bibliothèque municipale 354 (Leroquais, *Les Breviaires*, IV, 135–6).

which is a characteristic of this history, and brings the total of insular monastic sources to four. From no more than a superficial glance at the table, the widespread agreement of the sources over the arrangement here is in sharp contrast to the situation with the Benedict history of Appendix 2. Doubtless one part of the explanation for this must lie in the comparatively recent composition of this history, and also in the establishment of it within a relatively tightly defined group of centres—a point to which I shall shortly return. Some of the more substantial deviations from what is the apparent norm may be explicable by special circumstances. At Bayeux, for instance, the lessons of the second nocturn are taken from the legend of St Wandrille, who shares the day with the Magdalene. Though he has no proper history at Bayeux, it was clearly felt that the lessons should be accompanied by responds with texts appropriate to him rather than to the Magdalene.[42] The case of the York Office (column J) would seem to be one of extreme hybridization.[43] With the Ely Office (column H) we could perhaps be dealing with a source which for some reason did not receive the complete history.

Once again, however, to return to the theme of Oxford c36, what stands out here once more is the pairing of Oxford c36 and Paris 12036 (columns D and E), and the apparent closeness of these to at least one of the monastic sources: again purely hypothetically, one could see these two as slightly different models of the secularizing of the arrangement transmitted by the Winchester source F. Saxer has dealt in the second of his two books with the possible origin and diffusion of this history *Gloriosa diei huius*.[44] It appears to be a borrowing for the Translation feast, instituted in the thirteenth century, of material originally composed for the Birthday in July. Of manuscripts whose physical date is twelfth century and which have this history for the Birthday, Saxer gives, besides the Gloucester Diurnal referred to above, books from Saint-Germain, Saint-Denis, Jumièges, and Fécamp.[45] As he says, 'L'origine monastique de l'office paraît assurée', and he goes on to suggest a genesis for it in the diffusion of the cult of the Magdalene which attended upon the monastic reforms of the

---

[42.] The RR′ are *Magnificat eum, Posui adjutorium*, and *Justum*. This phenomenon at Bayeux should suggest the investigation of any tendency for responds (at least) to follow particular lessons.

[43.] This level of hybridization often makes the Magdalene's histories difficult to categorize. Mr Hohler tells me that the York history is basically that which he has classified as R′1 *Soror Marthe*, but which at York (as in the books of Prague and Olmütz) has R′ *Maria Magdalena que fuerat* at its head. The antiphons of the 3rd nocturn are from the history R′1 *Gloriosa es*. It is notable that the 'regular' items of *Gloriosa diei* fall in the places in which one would expect them to be.

[44.] Saxer, *Le Dossier*, 57–60.

[45.] That from St-Germain is the fragmentary Paris, Bibliothèque nationale lat. 13239; Jumièges and Fécamp are Rouen, Bibliothèque municipale A 145 and A 261 respectively.

mid-eleventh to mid-twelfth centuries. One might now add that there are two English secular sources of this history which cannot be more than a few years younger than these early monastic sources—Oxford c36 may well, indeed, be itself a twelfth-century manuscript.

Once more we are dealing with secular versions of a history whose manifestations are predominantly monastic. If we leave aside Paris 12036, which as I hope I have now shown must be the result of a particularly complex set of genetics, could not this chronological closeness suggest that with Oxford c36 we have evidence of the secularizing of a Use derived from a monastic cathedral?

Other Offices

I have spent some time dealing with the histories of Benedict and Mary Magdalene in c36 since they seem to me to be both critical pointers to what might be the nature of this antiphoner, and also illustrative material for the problems involved in handling evidence of this sort. Before I move towards a conclusion I will summarily deal with some other noteworthy features of the manuscript.

Firstly, there is here the proper history for St Giles, R' 1 *Fidelis Christi confessor Egidius*, which may be one of the liturgical compositions of the eleventh-century so-called 'School of Chartres', and is transmitted by Oxford c36 essentially in the form in which it is found on the Continent.[46] This history is rare in England, and I have noted it only from the secular Use of York and from the late thirteenth-century monastic breviary of Muchelney, Somerset (diocese of Bath).[47] The latter may be significant, in view of the fact that all evidence about the Use of York, with the exception of parts of the missal Manchester, Rylands Library 186,[48] is fourteenth-century or later. Although it is reasonable as a working hypothesis to take this evidence as indicative of earlier practice, this cannot be taken as necessarily true in detail.

My second point concerns the history for Lucy in this book. As *CAO* reveals, Lucy's Office is one for which the great majority of the 'classic' sources transmit incomplete histories, although there is broad-scale agreement between them. The exception is the 'Silensis' of *CAO* Volume II, which gives her a full history. I am not aware of another English source

---

[46.] Printed from MSS from St-Étienne (Loire), Chartres, and Beauvais in R. Merlet and l'Abbé Clerval, *Un manuscrit Chartrain du XIᵉ siècle* (Chartres, 1893), 198–229, and, with facsimiles, from Rouen U 135, a Jumièges book, in R. Hesbert, *Les Manuscrits musicaux de Jumièges*, Monumenta Musicae Sacrae 2 (Mâcon, 1954).

[47.] See n. 16 *supra*.

[48.] W.H. Frere, *Bibliotheca musico-liturgica* (London, 1894–1932), II, 43, s.v. no. 659.

which will give a convincing parallel to the composition of c36. So, for instance, the matins responds in Oxford c36 are drawn from the Silensis set which is also used by the monastic sources of Winchester and Worcester and from which the York Breviary compiles its history, although Oxford c36 does not correspond in either selection or in sequential arrangement. For lauds, on the other hand, where York continues to take its material from the Silensis, Oxford c36 adopts a quite different set of antiphons, a series found also in the Uses of Hereford and Sarum, and in the books of two Augustinian houses.[49] The point I would wish to make here is the apparent independence of Oxford c36 from other surviving office anti-phoners from England.

My third point is to draw attention to the only surviving *prosa* in this book. The R' *Cornelius centurio*, used here for first vespers of the 29 June feast of Peter and Paul, has a three-verse *prosa* (V'1 *Cornelius vite eterne te heredem noveris esse*) which so far seems not to have been found elsewhere.[50] *Prima facie* it might suggest some special attention being paid to St Peter, although this is not borne out by any apparent stressing of the feasts of his Chair and Chains. To this observation I shall return when I conclude.

I would, finally, in this section like to draw attention to the fact that this book was modernized by various hands over the course of perhaps two hundred years. The successive stages of emendation, always in the form of marginal additions or corrections, would be an object of special study. Confining the issue to modifications which could reasonably be said to have been made within a generation of the book's creation, we have, for example, a marginal renumbering in cursive of the matins responds for the Assumption to bring them into line with the order used (for example) by Sarum. In the same way, matins of the Purification have been 'modernized' (see Figure 1). The original text (which is left intact) uses the *Benedicta tu in mulieribus* antiphon series found in some English Benedictine sources (Ely, Evesham, Worcester, and—rather casually—Hyde) and in one Augustinian book.[51] In the margin has been added the (quite different) metrical antiphon series *Specialis virgo*, characteristic of the three major English secular Uses and of the majority of Augustinians'.[52] What, however, have not been emended are the lacunae in the music. There are several

---

[49] The Westacre book already referred to (n. 41) and in Oxford, Bodleian Library Bodley 547, the breviary of an unidentified house.

[50] This *prosa* is not listed in H. Hofmann-Brandt, *Die Tropen zu den Responsorien des Officiums* (Erlangen and Nuremberg, 1971). The respond *Cornelius centurio* is one which Michel Huglo has been studying for many years, and which he considers to have been composed at St-Pierre- (later St-Maur-) des-Fossés. I am very grateful to M. Huglo for telling me that he has not encountered this *prosa* in any antiphoner or processional which he has consulted.

[51] Oxford, Bodleian 547, already referred to (n. 49).

[52] The books of Westacre, Cirencester, and Guisborough.

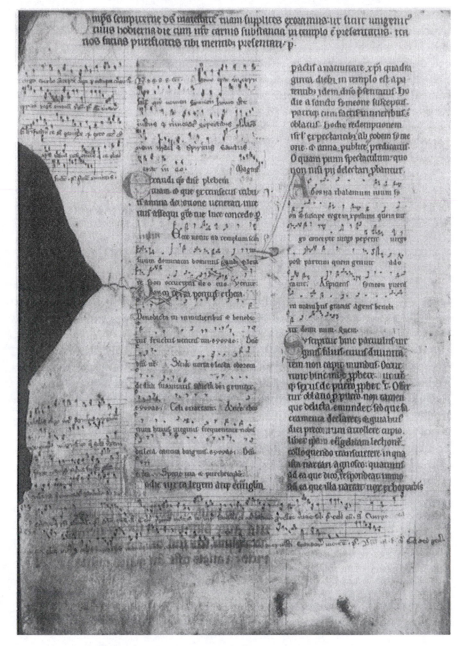

Figure 1. Oxford, Bodleian Library Lat. liturg. c36, fol. 27v

instances of text below blank staves, and they include (rather infuriatingly) the *prosa* just mentioned and the whole of the offices for Benedict and Mary Magdalene which I have discussed above. Had the book not contained the evidence of continued use, it would be simple to dismiss it as 'unfinished'. Once again, this is a point I shall resume in my conclusion.

The Nature and Provenance of Oxford c36

I would like finally to draw together some of these threads and move towards finding a convincing home for this book. The kalendar which lies behind the Sanctorale (as opposed to the *in situ* kalendar) will define the broad area. It includes Guthlac (to whom I shall return shortly); Vincent with an extra antiphon and called *patronus*; Wulmar; and Ouen (not called *patronus*). There seem to be no northern British saints save Cuthbert (who is, in this context, not 'northern' at all)—that is, no Wilfred, John of Beverley, or Oswald. The absence of Chad and Werburga will rule out the diocese of Lichfield. The loss of the end of the book means that we cannot know what was done for St Edmund of East Anglia, but the feast on 8 March of Felix of Dunwich is not marked in any way. This should suggest somewhere other than the eastern counties of England. We seem to be left with the southern part of the island.

One feature of Oxford c36 not so far dealt with is its selection of collects. Those for English saints are a most interesting collection, suggesting once again a use for which there is no parallel in surviving insular sources. The collect for St Dunstan relates to a cue in the Ordinal of the nuns of Barking Abbey, and is, in fact, an expanded version of the collect for him transmitted by the Missal of St Augustine's Abbey, Canterbury.[53] The collect for St Alphege, which describes him as *patronus*, is so far unique to this manuscript.[54] That for St Guthlac occurs, to my knowledge, in only

[53] The prayer in c36 is 'Deus placabilis indulgencie auctor potentissime. qui beatum antistitem confessoremque tuum dunstanum in regnum eterne beatitudinis voluisti assumere. concede quesumus familie tue: ut ipsius adiuvantibus meritis. sanctorum mereamur adiungi consorciis. per.' The cue 'Deus placabilis' is found in J. B. L. Tolhurst (ed.), *The Ordinale and Customary of . . . Barking Abbey*, Henry Bradshaw Society 65–6 (London, 1926–7), II, 228. For the shortened version of the full prayer see M. Rule (ed.), *The Missal of St Augustine's Abbey, Canterbury* (Cambridge, 1896), 89.

[54] 'Deus qui beatum elfegum post pontificalem apostolici honoris stolam martirii purpurea et gemmis celestibus decorasti; fac nos tam lucidi patroni documentis. tantique magistri glorie interesse disciplinis. per.'

one other liturgical book, the monastic Breviary of Evesham which I have already used elsewhere in this paper, and which transmits this prayer in a form shortened by about one half of the Oxford c36 version.[55] According to John Wickham Legg's collation in his edition of the Westminster Missal, the prayer *Deus qui nos beati Guthlaci* which that book gives is almost universal, so the collect in Oxford c36/Evesham is something of a curiosity.[56] However, there are two points to be made about it. The first is that it is based on a prayer which is transmitted by both the Bangor Antiphoner and the Stowe Missal, where it is 'de martyribus'.[57] In terms of the surviving British evidence, this should make it 'ancient and Irish', and in looking for a centre which might have circulated it, Glastonbury must be a strong contender. The second point to make about this prayer is that, in the form specific to Guthlac, it turns up once more, though not in a liturgical book. The manuscript Boulogne, Bibliothèque municipale 637 contains Felix's *Life* of St Guthlac, to which this collect is added as a postscript. In his edition of this *Life*, Colgrave argued that although this manuscript belonged to and was in part written at the monastery of Saint-Bertin at Saint-Omer, the part containing Felix's *Life* is in a hand very similar to that which copied the same work into Arras, Bibliothèque municipale 812, a book which is known to have been among those presented to Saint-Vaast by Abbot Seiwold of the Bath when he fled to Arras after the Conquest.[58] Colgrave therefore goes on to suggest that this part of the Boulogne manuscript, containing the *Life* with the appended collect, may well be the product of the Bath scriptorium.

Could the antiphoner of Oxford c36 be a secular book of Bath diocese? Such an explanation would take up the possible south-western connections which have already been laid out. It would make sense of the unique prayer

[55] The Oxford c36 reading is: 'Omnipotens sempiterne deus qui omnes sanctorum tuos cum mensura probas et sine mensura glorificas; concede quesumus ut gloriosi confessoris tui sacerdotisque guthlaci precatu uitam consequi mereamur perpetuam et despiciendo calcare presentem; ut per illius merita et intercessiones de tuis preceptis salutaribus muniamur. et a nostris peccatis plurimum in hoc mundo abluamur. per.' Evesham (fol. 318v) curtails this version at 'mereamur perpetuam'. Other disagreements between these two forms are slight.

[56] J. W. Legg (ed.), *Missale ad usum ecclesie Westmonasteriensis*, Henry Bradshaw Society 1, 2, 12 (London, 1891, 1893, 1897), III, 1543.

[57] F. E. Warren (ed.), *The Antiphonary of Bangor*, Henry Bradshaw Society 4 and 10, (London 1893–5), I (facs.), fol. 22v; II (edn.), 24, s.v. no. 61. G. F. Warner (ed.), *The Stowe Missal*, Henry Bradshaw Society 32 (London, 1915; repr. 1989), 20.

[58] The edition is B. Colgrave, *Felix's Life of Saint Guthlac* (Cambridge, 1956), with the prayer on p. 179 n. 18. For the argument about Boulogne see ibid. 35–9, and further on Seiwold, P. Grierson, 'Les Livres de l'Abbé Seiwold de Bath', *Revue bénédictine* 52 (1940), 96–116.

to Alphege as *patronus*, and also the comparative rarity of the prayer to Dunstan, for Alphege was the abbot appointed to the reformed house of Bath by Dunstan in 980; and it would explain the prayer for Guthlac. What is more immediately a problem is the inclusion here of Wulmar with a collect not otherwise known in English sources.[59] Bath Abbey had a relic of Wulmar by the time its earliest surviving relic-list was compiled, though in this it was not particularly unusual.[60] By 1200, any cult which he may have enjoyed will have tended to be overtaken by the popularity of devotion to St Margaret, who shares a day with him (20 July). His presence in Oxford c36 with a collect alone, embedded in the office for Margaret, is testimony to this process.[61] That he should have this attention paid to him is, however, a fact not easily passed over, and I would be inclined to see this prayer as the relic of a fairly old proper office for him. The problem is where such an office might have originated. The answer to that will have to await further investigation. I would only say now that the obvious focus of Wulmar's cult is in the Pas-de-Calais region, with which Bath Abbey had some connection; most notably, perhaps, when in the mid-tenth century it

---

[59] 'Omnipotens sempiterne deus qui beato Wlmaro confessor tuo atque abbati eterne beatitudinis gloriam contulisti; da quesumus ut cuius sollempnia celebramus. eius meritis et precibus adiuuemur. per dominum.'

[60] The Bath relic-lists are printed from Cambridge, Corpus Christi College MS 111, in W. Hunt (ed.), *Two Chartularies of the Priory of St. Peter at Bath*, The Somerset Record Society 7 (London, 1893), pp. lxxv–lxxvii. The two leaves on which these lists were written were originally blank leaves of Cambridge, Corpus Christi College MS 140. The entry for this latter in N. R. Ker, *Catalogue of Manuscripts containing Anglo-Saxon* (Oxford, 1957), 48, s.v. no. 35, refers to 'two lists of relics at Bath'—that is those of Ælsige (abbot, died 1087) and Wulfwine. It would seem, however, that there are at least three lists—there is a list of Heorstan's gift between the two cited, and it may be that the sections in Latin at the end of the Ælsige and Wulfwine catalogues are separate lists. The relic of Wulmar is in the Ælsige list. These lists are not dissimilar to that in the Leofric Missal, which also includes Wulmar and Malo.

[61] A rough and ready view of the pattern can be ascertained to some extent by comparing the kalendars edited by F. Wormald in *English Kalendars before A.D. 1100*, Henry Bradshaw Society 72 (London, 1934; repr. Woodbridge, 1988) with those in his *English Benedictine Kalendars after A.D. 1100*, Henry Bradshaw Society 77 (London, 1939). Of the 19 kalendars in the former, Wulmar is alone on his day in five; the 1st mentioned in six; and the 2nd mentioned in two. In the latter volume, he is not mentioned in eight of the 11 texts printed, and the other three give him a commemoration. One of the post-Conquest texts (no. 10 of Wormald's edition) is from Dunster, and has been usually regarded as the only surviving liturgical evidence of Bath diocese. It is, regrettably, not a particularly useful contribution to the hypothesis I have been pursuing about c36, not least because of its comparatively late date. It does, however, grade Vincent and Alphege as 'two copes' (the only higher grading is 'four copes'). Eufemia, who is absent from c36, is likewise graded 'two copes'—most unexpectedly—at Dunster, a phenomenon explained by Wormald (p. 147) as the result of the gift of a relic to Bath by Bishop Reginald Fitzjoscelin (d. 1191). I would not be surprised if this had failed to get into an exemplar being used c.1200.

offered refuge to monks of Saint-Bertin fleeing from the reforms of Gerard de Brogne.[62]

In one further respect, a Bath provenance would suit a peculiarity of this book. I remarked above that the presence of the *prosa* to the respond *Cornelius centurio* suggested a stressing of St Peter not otherwise indicated. This observation, taken at face value, involves an assumption about the process of compiling liturgical books of this kind which I believe to be simplistic. A book of Bath Abbey, whose church was dedicated to St Peter, will certainly have stressed his feasts. This, however, need have been of no compelling interest to a secular of the diocese involved in compiling books for his own church. On the other hand, such a person—a person, quite clearly, with a developed taste for liturgical music—might well, around 1200, have found a *prosa* to be quite irresistibly fascinating, just as he would have found histories for Benedict and the Magdalene. The processes by which each 'petite édition critique' was formed are likely to have been multifarious and subtle, especially in a situation where some form of 'critical' activity (as in the adaptation of monastic to secular Use) was inevitable, and standardization not yet common. Perhaps here too we may look for an explanation of those pieces—or sometimes whole histories— which lack their music notation in this manuscript. We do not know what the compiler of our book had in front of him as he worked, but it is most unlikely that it was *tabula rasa*. It is not outside possibility that he was emending, correcting, and amplifying books which he already used, referring for authority and guidance to an exemplar from his cathedral which was not itself a noted book, or which perhaps did not have its music notation on staves. In this context, it may not be without significance that the two histories with which I have been predominantly concerned— histories which would seem to have a clear monastic background—should be among those items to have been copied without their notation.

At some point in the process of this argument we move from the testing of a hypothesis into realms which seem uncomfortably like those of speculation. It is not only through the partiality of our knowledge of liturgical Uses and their transmission that we experience difficulties in assessing the meaning of manuscripts such as ours. Faced with issues where such mundane but perennial matters as choice and circumstance are

---

[62.] The story of this migration is in Folcwin's *Gesta abbatum S. Bertini Sithiensium*, ed. O. Holder-Egger in G. H. Pertz (ed.), *Monumenta Germaniae Historiae . . . Scriptorum* (Hanover, 1854), 13. 628–9, cap. 107. Until avenues such as this have been exhausted, it might be wise not to play the rather long shot of St Peter's, Ghent, where (as William of Malmesbury tells us in his *Life* of Dunstan) Count Arnulf installed relics of Wandrille, Ausbertus, and Wulmar (W. Stubbs (ed.), *Memorials of St Dunstan*, Rolls Series 63 (London, 1874)). Such a line makes large assumptions (about the extent and nature of Dunstan's reforming activities, among other things) which would need detailed justification.

concerned, we lack a grasp of the *mentalité* which makes one course of events more likely than another. We might erect a further hypothesis which would explain this book by postulating as its original owner a music-teacher in the diocese of Bath who obtained the post of precentor at the Augustinian house of Stone. He took with him his working collection of books—portably arranged in separate sections, as the books of such men must have been—and he prefixed the kalendar of his new employers to the sanctorale of his Breviary, where the information it contained would have been of most use. What was now 'wrong' in his books he corrected marginally. What he no longer needed he ignored. The material that was necessary in his new job but which his old books did not contain would, if at all extensive, have gone into an appendix. Such a hypothesis as this, without a body of precedent material, is in the realms of fiction. Yet so much in history must eventually be reducible from theorems to people— the kinds of conventional opportunities and restraints within which their careers operated; how they thought, and worked, and organized their lives.

APPENDIX 1

The Contents of Oxford, Bodleian Library Lat. liturg. c36

The abbreviations used are:

a'/aa'	=	antiphona/antiphonae
R'/RR'	=	responsorium/responsoria
or'	=	oratio(nes)
lc.	=	lectio(nes)
P	=	Proper history
[*]	=	blank staves for some chant item(s)
[†]	=	blank staves throughout history
[...]	=	lacuna in the manuscript

Date	Fol.	Feast	Remarks
31. 11	3	Andrew	P
06. 12	6	Nicholas	P
13. 12	10v	Lucy	P
21. 12	12v	Thomas (apostle)	or', 9 lc., Common cues
14. 01	14v	Felix	or' & 3 lc.
15. 01	14v	Maur	or' & 3 lc.
16. 01	15	Marcellus	or' & lc.
18. 01	15v	Prisca	or'
20. 01	16	Fabian & Sebastian	a' ad Magn. (1st vesp.), 2 or' & 9 lc.
21. 01	17	Agnes	P
22. 01	20	Vincent	P (with extra a')
25. 01	23v	Conversion of St Paul	P
02. 02	27	Purification of BVM	P
03. 02	30	Blaise	9 lc. (only)
05. 02	33	Agatha	P
22. 02	35v	Peter's Chair	9 lc., Inv. & occasional aa' [†]
24. 02	37	Matthias	or', 9 lc., Common cues [†]
12. 03	38	Gregory	or', 9 lc., Common cues [†]
20. 03	39v	Cuthbert	or' & 6 lc.
21. 03	40v	Benedict	P [†]
25. 03	43v	Annunciation of BVM	P
04. 04	45v	Ambrose	or'
11. 04	45v	Guthlac	or', 3 lc., Common cues
14. 04	46v	Tiburtius etc.	or'

Date	Fol.	Feast	Remarks
19. 04	46v	Ælfege	or'
23. 04	46v	George	or', 6 lc., Common chants
25. 04	48v	Mark	or', 9 lc., Common cues
28. 04	49v	Vitalis	or', 3 lc., Common cues
01. 05	50	Philip & James	or', proper aa' (1 vesp.), Common cues [*]
01. 05	52	Alexander etc.	or' (during 1 vesp. of Finding of Cross)
03. 05	51v	Finding of Cross	P
06. 05	53v	John *ante porte Latinam*	or' & Common cues [†]
10. 05	53v	Gordianus etc.	or'
12. 05	53v	Nereus etc.	or' & 3 lc.
19. 05	54	Potenciana	or'
19. 05	54	Dunstan	or' & 3 lc.
25. 05	55	Urban	or'
26. 05	55	Augustine (angl.)	or' & 3 lc.
19. 06	56	[. . .] Gervasius etc.	end of final lc. only
21. 06	56	Leufred	or'
22. 06	56	Alban	or' & 3 lc.
23. 06	56v	Etheldreda	or' & 3 lc.
24. 06	57	John the Baptist	P (with extra RR' [*])
26. 06	61	John & Paul	P
28. 06	62v	Leo	or'
29. 06	62v	Peter	P [*]
30. 06	67	Commem. Paul	P (6 lc) [*]
01. 07	70	Octave of John	3 lc.
02. 07	70v	Processus etc.	or' & 3 lc.
04. 07	70v	Martin [. . .]	First of ? lc. only
06. 07	71	[. . .] Octave of Peter	9 lc (MS recommences during lc. 8)
10. 07	71	Januarius etc.	or'
11. 07	71	Transl. Benedict	or' & 6 lc.
15. 07	72	Transl. Swithun	or'
20. 07	72	Margaret	or' & 3 lc.
20. 07	72	Wulmar	or'
21. 07	72v	Praxedis	or'
22. 07	72v	Mary Magdalene	P [†]
23. 07	75v	Apollinaris	or'
25. 07	75v	James	or' & 9 lc.
25. 07	75v	Christopher etc.	or' (rubric *Memoria*)
27. 07	77	Seven Sleepers	or' & 3 lc.
29. 07	77v	Felix etc.	or' & 3 lc.
30. 07	78	Abdon etc.	or' & 3 lc.
01. 08	78	Peter's Chains	P [*]
03. 08	80	Finding of Stephen	P [†]
06. 08	83v	Sixtus etc. [. . .]	or' & ? lc. (MS breaks during lc. 3)

Date	Fol.	Feast	Remarks
10. 08	84	[. . .] Lawrence [. . .]	P
13. 08	86	[. . .] Hippolytus	P (3 lc.) [*]
14. 08	86v	Eusebius	or'
15. 08	86v	Assumption of BVM	P (+ aa' *infra octavas* [*])
22. 08	92	Octave of Assumption	6 lc.
23. 08	92	Timothy etc.	or'
24. 08	92v	Bartholomew	or' & 9 lc.
24. 08	94	Ouen	or'
27. 08	94	Rufus	or'
28. 08	94	Hermes	or'
28. 08	94	Augustine of Hippo	or' & 6 lc.
29. 08	95	Beheading of John Baptist	P
29. 08	95	Sabine	or'
30. 08	98	Felix etc.	or'
01. 09	98	Priscus	or'
05. 09	98	Bertin	or'
01. 09	98	Giles [. . .]	P [†]
08. 09	100	Nativity of BVM	P
08. 09	102	Hadrian	or'
09. 09	102	Gorgonius	or'
11. 09	102	Protus etc.	or'
14. 09	102	Raising of Cross	P (defective in middle)
14. 09	102v	Cornelius etc.	or'
21. 09	104v	Matthew	or' & Common chants
22. 09	106	Maurice etc.	or' & ? lc. (MS ends during lc. 6)

APPENDIX 2

The History *Fuit vir vite venerabilis* (St Benedict)

1. PROPER ITEMS

Chants are arranged alphabetically and enumerated.

Abbreviations used are:

B.	= Benedictus	R′	= responsory
a′	= antiphon	Inv	= Invitatory

1.	a′	Ab ipso pueritie
2.	a′	Aqua de montis
3.	R′	Ante sextum vero
4.	Inv	Adoremus Christum regem
5.	R′	Beatus B. cum iam
6.	R′	Beatus B. dum iam
7.	a′	Beatus vir B. plus
8.	R′	Beatus vir B. qui
9a.	a′	B. dei famulus
9b.	R′	B. dei famulus
10.	R′	Ceperunt postmodum
11.	a′	Compassus nutrici
12.	a′	Confessor dei B.
13.	Inv	Confessorum regem
14.	R′	Convocatis fratribus
15.	a′	Cum cognovisset
16.	a′	Cumque in specu
17.	R′	Cumque sanctus B. in cella
18.	a′	Cumque sibi
19.	a′	Cumque vir domini
20.	R′	Domine non aspicias
21.	a′	Diuturnis inopia
22.	R′	Dum beatus B.
23.	R′	Dum beatus vir oraculo
24.	a′	Dum in hac terra
25.	a′	Dum in heremum
26.	a′	Dumque super undas

27.	a′	Ecce vir dei B.
28.	a′	Electus a fratribus
29.	R′	Eodem vero anno
30.	a′	Erat vir domini B.
31.	R′	Erat vultu placido
32.	a′	Euge beate pater
33.	a′	Expetitus a fratribus
34.	a′	Exultet omnium turba
35.	R′	Factum est post obitum
36a.	a′	Fuit vir vite venerabilis
36b.	R′	Fuit vir vite venerabilis
37a.	a′	Frater Maure
37b.	R′	Frater Maure
38.	a′	Gloriosus confessor domini
39.	a′	Hec est via
40.	a′	Hodie sanctus B. per
41a.	a′	Hic itaque iam
41b.	R′	Hic itaque iam
42.	a′	Hic vir despiciens
43.	a′	Immensi regis
44a.	a′	Inito consilio
44b.	R′	Inito consilio
45a.	a′	Intempesta nocte
45b.	R′	Intempesta nocte
46.	R′	Iste sanctus
47.	R′	Iustum deduxit
48.	R′	Igitur beatus B.
49.	R′	Laudemus dominum in beatus
50.	Inv	Laudemus dominum in hac
51.	R′	Letemur omnes
52.	a′	Liberiori genere
53.	R′	Misereatur vestri
54.	a′	Mulier quedam
55a.	a′	Non aspicias
55b.	R′	Non aspicias
56a.	a′	Nursia provincie
56b.	R′	Nursia provincie
57.	a′	Nutrici in auxilium
58a.	a′	O beati viri B.
58b.	R′	O beati viri B.
59.	R′	O laudanda sanctus B.
60.	a′	Oramus te
61.	a′	Oravit sanctus B.
62.	a′	O quam venerandus
63.	R′	Pater insignis
64a.	a′	Pater sanctus dum
64b.	R′	Pater sanctus dum

65.	R′	Preciosus confessor
66a.	a′	Predicta nutrix
66b.	R′	Predicta nutrix
67.	R′	Puer domini B.
68.	a′	Puer quidam parvulus
69.	R′	Quidam rusticus
70.	a′	Qui dum heremum
71.	a′	Recessit igitur
72.	Inv	Regem confessorum
73.	a′	Relicta domo
74.	a′	Rex seculorum
75.	R′	Sanctus B. Christi
76.	R′	Sanctus B. plus
77.	a′	Sanctimonialis autem
78a.	a′	Sanctissime confessor
78b.	R′	Sanctissime confessor
79.	R′	Sexto namque
80.	a′	Sicut discipulus
81.	a′	Similabo eum viro
82.	R′	Sancte B. confessor
83.	a′	Tantam gratiam
84.	a′	Tunc ad locum
85.	R′	Via recta orientis
86.	R′	Vir dei mundum
87.	a′	Vir domini B. omnium
88.	R′	Vir enim domini
89.	a′	Vix obtinui

2. MATINS AND LAUDS IN CONTINENTAL SOURCES

Of the eight sources given, the first seven are those of *Corpus Antiphonalium Officii* (where full details are given), using the sigla employed by Hesbert. They are:

H   = Hartkerii (Saint-Gall, Stiftsbibliothek MS 390–1)
R   = Rhenaugiensis (Zurich, Zentralbibliothek Rh. 28)
D   = Sandionysianus (Paris, Bibliothèque nationale lat. 17296)
F   = Fossatensis (Paris, Bibliothèque nationale lat. 12584)
S   = Silensis (London, British Library Add. 30850)
L   = S. Lupi Beneventani (Benevento, Biblioteca Capitolare V. 21)
C   = Compendiensis (Paris, Bibliothèque nationale lat. 17436).

The eighth source used (with the siglum X) is London, British Library Add. 18496, a book of some monastic house in north-western Germany, possibly in the diocese of Bremen, which I date *circa* 1200.

		H	R	D	F	S	L	C	X
Mat.	Inv.	72	13	13	13	13	50	—	13
	a′1	36a	36a	36a	36a	36a	36a	36a	36a
	2	1	1	52	1	1	1	1	1
	3	24	24	1	24	24	56a	24	24
	4	56a	56a	24	52	56a	73	56a	52
	5	73	73	73	73	73	71	73	73
	6	41a	41a	71	71	71	9a	71	71
	7	66a	66a	11	41a	41a	27	41a	41a
	8	57	57	33	11	66a	16	66a	11
	9	71	71	68	33	11	37a	11	33
	10	25	25	61	18	70	2	9a	18
	11	16	16	83	44a	61	45a	70	44a
	12	18	18	78a	84	9a	54	16	84
	ad cantica	44a	44a	87	77	81	89/ 55a/ 43	—	83/ 77
	R′1	36b	36b	36b	36b	36b	36b	36b	36b
	2	6	6	76	76	44b	56b	41b	41b
	3	5	5	44b	44b	69	41b	48	76
	4	—	64b	75	20	20	67	44b	44b
	5	66b	66b	20	17	64b	96b	14	17
	6	69	69	64b	45b	17	86	69	45b
	7	20	20	17	64b	31	53	20	64b
	8	—	58b	58b	78b	29	10	64b	78b
	9	37b	37b	8	29	3	22	29	29
	10	29	29	31	79	79	55b	3	3
	11	3	3	45b	31	58b	45b	79	79
	12	79	65	78b	85/ 58b	46	88	40/ 35	65

		H	R	D	F	S	L	C	X
Lauds	a′ 1	55a	55a	7	7	28	41a	—	7
	2	61	61	25	30	18	66	—	30
	3	89	89	16	38	44a	44a	—	38
	4	45a	45a	30	68	16	21	—	68
	5	77	77	60	87	7	64a	—	87
	R′	—	—	76	—	76	9b	—	47
	a′ ad Ben.	40	40	64a	64a	64a	40/	—	78a
							78a		

3. MATINS AND LAUDS IN THE INSULAR SOURCES

A = London, British Library Harley 1117
B = Oxford, Bodleian Library Lat. liturg. c36
C = Paris, Bibliothèque nationale lat. 12036
D = Hyde Breviary, edited from Oxford, Bodleian Library Rawl. liturg. e 1* and Gough liturg. 8 in J. B. L. Tolhurst, ed., *The Monastic Breviary of Hyde Abbey, Winchester*, Henry Bradshaw Society 78 (London, 1939)
E = Oxford, Bodleian Library Barlow 41 (Evesham Breviary)
F = Paris, Bibliothèque nationale lat. 16304
G = Worcester Antiphoner, published in facs. from Worcester, Chapter Library F. 160, in Paléographie musicale 12 (Tournai, 1922)
H = Valenciennes, Bibliothèque municipale 116 (109) (Winchcombe Breviary/Missal)
J = Oxford, University College 101 (Breviary of Pontefract Cluniacs)

		A	B	C	D	E	F	G	H	J
Mat.	Inv.	4	13	13	13	13	13	13	13	13
	a'1	36a	36a	36a	36a	36a	36a	36a	36a	36a
	2	1	1	1	56a	1	56a	52	1	1
	3	24	24	24	73	24	73		24	24
	4	56a	56a	56a	71	52	71	24	52	52
	5	73	73	73	11	73	11	73	73	73
	6	71	71	71	28	71	28	71	71	71
	7	41a	7	7	18	41a	18	11	41a	41a
	8	66a	11	11	24	11	24	33	11	11
	9	11	28	28	1	33	1	68	33	33
	10	7			61	18		61	18	18
	11	70			68	44a		83	44a	44a
	12	16			83	84		78a	84	84
	ad cantica	28			7	77		45a	77	77
	R'1	36b	36b	36b	36b	36b	36b	36b	36b	36b
	2	44b	44b	44b	31	41b	695	76	41	76
	3	69	69	69	69	76	20	44b	76	44b
	4	20	20	20	20	44b	44b	58b	44b	20
	5	17	17	17	44b	17	64b	20	17	17
	6	64b	64b	64b	64b	45b	17	64b	45b	45b
	7	29	29	29	51	64b	31	17	64b	64b
	8	3	3	3	63	78b	29	78b	78b	78b
	9	79	51	51	29	29	82a	—b	29	29
	10	31			3	79		—	79	79
	11	51			79	85		—	85	85
	12	58b/ 49/ 82			78b	58b		—	58b/ 63	58b

		A	B	C	D	E	F	G	H	J
Lauds	a′ 1	18	41a	41a	41a	7	41a	9a	7	7
	2	44a	66a	66a	66a	30	66a	70a	30	30
	3	37a	70	70	70	38	70	16	38	38
	4	68	16	16	16	68	16	44a	68	68
	5	61	44a	44a	44a	87	44a	87	87	87
	ad Ben.	77ᶜ	77	77	19	78a	77	64a	78	64

ᵃ The text is: R′ *Sancte benedicte confessor domini audi rogantes servulos et impetratam celitus tu defer indulgenciam* V′ *O benedicte sidus aureum domini gracia servorum gemitus solita suscipe clemencia*. Compare *CAO* IV, no. 7579 (Common), which uses this R′ text only, divided as V′ *Et impetratam . . . indulgenciam*. I know only of this manuscript and Harley 1117, where it appears as a 'spare' respond (see column A *supra*), as sources of the longer version.

ᵇ The final nocturn in the Worcester Antiphoner uses RR′ 2, 5, 11, 12 of rhyming office *Florem Mundi* (AH 25).

ᶜ With 'supplement' of nos. 83, 19, 64a, 15, 40.

APPENDIX 3

The History *Gloriosa diei huius* (St Mary Magdalene)

I. CONSTITUENT ITEMS

The numbering of items is taken from the list in Saxer, *Dossier*, 48–52.
M M = Maria Magdalena; M = Maria.

2.	R′	Accinxit beata M M	87.	a′	M M et M Iacobi
6.	R′	Ad suum igitur	89.	a′	Martha inquit dominus
17.	a′	Capillis quoque capitis	97.	R′	Nequissimo Iude
21.	R′	Completum est	101.	R′	O felix felicis
26.	a′	Cum discubuisset	103.	R′	O felix verbi
38.	R′	Diluculo valde	110.	a′	Optimam ergo partem
42.	a′	Dixit itaque Martha	134.	R′	Rediens a monumento
48.	a′	Eterne iocunditatis	135.	R′	Regnum mundi
50.	Inv	Eternum trinumque	136.	a′	Remittuntur ergo ei
60.	R′	Fortis ut mors	137.	a′	Respondens autem
62.	R′	Gloriosa diei huius	145.	a′	Sedens ergo ad
65.	R′	Hec est illa M	155.	a′	Stans autem retro
75.	a′	Intrantem Iesum	161.	R′	Videns ergo flentem
81	R′	Letetur omne seculum	162.	a′	Videns hoc Phariseus
83.	R′	Lugens pie defunctum	163.	Inv	Unanimes regem

Supplementary list (not in Saxer, *Dossier*)

α	R′	Congratulamini	ι	a′	Magdalenam sua crimina
β	R′	Cuius ergo vel saxeum	κ	a′	Noli me tangere
γ	a′	Exquirebat M quem non	λ	R′	O diligens Christum
δ	a′	Hanc ergo toto corde	μ	a′	O quanta vis amoris
ε	R′	Hanc vero quam lucas	ν	a′	Rogabat Iesum quidam
ζ	a′	Lavit M lachrimis	ξ	a′	Solennitatem Magdalene
η	R′	M M et altera M	ο	R′	Tulerunt dominum
θ	R′	M M que fuerat			

2. THE ARRANGEMENT OF MATINS CHANTS IN THE SOURCES

A = Le Mans, Bibliothèque municipale 188 (Breviary of La Couture, s. xv: source *LM* of Saxer, *Dossier*)

B = Paris, Bibliothèque nationale lat. 13239 (Breviary of Saint-Germain-des-Prés, s. xiv: source *PP* of Saxer, *Dossier*)

C = Paris, Bibliothèque nationale lat. 17296 (Antiphoner of Saint-Denis, s. xiii init. (this Office): source D of *CAO*)

D = Oxford c36

E = Paris, Bibliothèque nationale lat. 12036

F = Oxford, Bodleian Library Rawl. C 489 (Sanctorale of Breviary, St Swithun's, Winchester, 1424)

G = Oxford, Bodleian Library Lat. liturg. e39 (Breviary of Chertsey, s. xv)

H = Cambridge, University Library Ii. iv. 20 (Breviary/Missal of Ely, s. xii)

J = The 1533 edition of the York Breviary, in S. Lawley (ed.), *Breviarium ... Eboracensis*, Publications of the Surtees Society 71 and 75 (Durham etc., 1880–2)

K = U. Chevalier (ed.), *Ordinaire et Coutumier de ... Bayeux (XIII-s)*, Bibliothèque liturgique 8 (Paris, 1902)

		A	B	C	D	E	F	G	H	J	K
Mat.	Inv.	163	163	—	163	163	163	—ᶜ	163	50	50
	a' 1	26	26	26	26	26	26	—	26ᵈ	v	26
	2	155	155	—	155	155	155	—	—	155	155
	3	17	17	—	17	17	17	—	—	κ	17
	4	162	162	—	162	162	162	—	—	μ	162
	5	137	137	—	137	137	137	—	—	γ	137
	6	136	136	—	136	136	136	—	—	δ	136
	7	75	75	75	75	75	75	—	75	ζ	75
	8	145	145	—	145	145	145	—	—	ξ	145
	9	42	42	—	42	42	42	—	—	ι	42
	10	89	89	—			89	—	—		
	11	103	103	—			103	—	—		
	12	110ᵃ	110ᵃ	—			110ᵃ	—	—		
	ad cantica	48	48	48			48	—	48		
	R'1	81	65	62	62	62	62	—	62	θ	62
	2	62	83	65	65	65	65	—	65	β	65
	3	65ᵇ	161	83	83	83	83	—	83	ε	83
	4	83	135	161	161	161	161	—	161	161	—ᵉ
	5	161	97	97	60	97	97	97	21	97	—ᵉ
	6	97	60	60	21	60	60	60	2	60	—ᵉ

	A	B	C	D	E	F	G	H	J	K
7	60	21	21	2	21	21	21	6	λ	21
8	21	2	2	101	2	2	2	135	21	134
9	—	38	38	38	101	38	38	η^{f}	101	101
10	—	6	6			6	6	o^{f}		
11	—	134	53			134	134	α^{f}		
12	—	101	101			101	101	101		

[a] Saxer, *Dossier* gives these as no. 111, in error.
[b] Saxer, *Dossier* gives this as no. 64, in error.
[c] This office is defective in Chertsey Breviary, and begins during R' 5.
[d] After R' 1 is the rubric 'et cetera sicut unius virginis': i.e. the missing responds were taken from the Common.
[e] These three RR' taken from the Common of confessors 'quando fit sine festo' (p. 280 of edition). See text.
[f] These three RR' given as cues with rubric 'Require in feria ii ebdomade pasche'.

9

British Rhymed Offices

A Catalogue and Commentary

ANDREW HUGHES
(University of Toronto)

A general introduction to rhymed offices, still quite the most extensive survey of the repertory, has appeared in the R volume of the *Dictionary of the Middle Ages*.[1] The repertory consists of poetic texts and chants in thousands of proper offices for new feast-days and saints' days of the later middle ages, mostly between the tenth and sixteenth centuries, from all over Europe. The texts, newly compiled, are for the antiphons and responsories of the canonical hours: often the chants that accompany them are also newly composed or borrowed and adapted from earlier models. Of the hymns, lessons, prayers, and dialogues that also form a part of these new offices, only the hymns are always poetic. They are normally not newly-composed but are standard hymns appropriate to the saint or feast; although occasionally a new antiphon text is identical with a stanza of a hymn, various features make it clear that hymns are not regarded as a part of the rhymed office proper. New lessons and prayers are often closely related to the texts of the new office chants and would have to be taken into account in any detailed study of an individual office.

For reference to liturgical items and services, the following abbreviations will be used:

Services
V = first vespers
M = matins
L = lauds
W = second vespers

Genres
A = antiphon
R = responsory
I = invitatory
E = Magnificat or Benedictus antiphon (i.e. the antiphon *ad Evangelium*) and the monastic canticle antiphon at matins.

[1.] Andrew Hughes, 'Rhymed Offices', *The Dictionary of the Middle Ages* 10 (New York, 1988), 366–77.

Compline rarely has proper texts and chants, and the little hours (prime, terce, sext, nones) usually repeat the antiphons of lauds. Two-letter abbreviations, sometimes with a numeral, represent service and genre, thus: LA3 signifies the third antiphon at lauds, WE the Magnificat antiphon at second vespers. With considerable variation possible, offices for secular and monastic institutions are structured in this way:

VA1(–5) VR VE

    MI MA1–3 MR1–3 MA4–6 MR4–6 MA7–9 MR7–9   (secular)

or MI MA1–6 MR1–4 MA7–12 MR5–8 ME   MR9–12 (monastic)

LA1–5 LE

WE1(–5) WR WE

Secular offices thus have some twenty-eight antiphons and about ten responsories, monastic offices some thirty-two antiphons and more than a dozen responsories, but in each case alternatives for ferias after the feast may be provided. Offices therefore have anywhere from nearly forty to fifty or sixty rhymed items sung to chant.

    A research report, giving more details of the repertory and describing the unpublished 'Catalogue of Offices' and other reference tools and indices from which this article was prepared, has appeared in the *Journal of the Plainsong & Mediæval Music Society*.[2]

    These abbreviations will be used:

AH   Analecta Hymnica,[3] where 2. 21 refers to volume and office number;

CAO *Corpus Antiphonalium Officii;*[4]

cd   canonized;

tr.   translated—the date given not necessarily the first or only translation.

    Various standard methods for reporting poetic schemes are in common use. None is adequate for dealing with liturgical items, especially when the phrasing of the chant must be taken into account and, as will be argued below, sometimes the organization of the chant is the only method of determining whether an office can be regarded as poetic and rhymed. After much experimentation, I am developing an extension of the system used by Dag Norberg in his standard study of late Latin poetry, *Introduction à l'étude de la versification latine médiévale*.[5] This system essentially cites the number of syllables in a line, using p or pp for paroxytone or proparoxy-

---

   [2.] 8 (1985), 33–49.

   [3.] Ed. G. M. Dreves *et al.*, 55 vols. (Leipzig, 1886–1922); M. Lütolf *et al.*, *Analecta Hymnica: Register*, 3 vols. (Bern and Munich, 1978).

   [4.] R.-J. Hesbert (ed.), *Corpus Antiphonalium Officii* I: *Manuscripti 'Cursus romanus'*, II: *Manuscripti 'Cursus monasticus'*, III: *Invitatoria et Antiphonae*, IV: *Responsoria, Versus, Hymni et Varia*, V: *Fontes earumque prima ordinatio*, RERUM ECCLESIASTICARUM DOCUMENTA, ser. major, Fontes 7, 8, 9, 10, 11 (Rome 1963, 1965, 1968, 1970, 1975).

   [5.] Acta Universitatis Stockholmiensis, Studia latina 5 (Stockholm, 1958).

tone accentuation of the final syllables, where the accentuation is regular. Thus, the standard twelfth-century sequence stanza is 8pp8pp7p × 2 rhymed aabccb, and the goliardic stanza alternates 7pp and 6p. When the accentuation frequently varies, the formula is limited to the number of syllables. The sign + identifies the caesura (here taken to be rhymed). For the purposes of this article it will be necessary to add to this system the following signs:

—   identifies the caesura without rhyme
/   separates responsory and verse
:   indicates the place to which the *repetenda* of a responsory returns, and supersedes the signs below
.   indicates punctuation or a capital letter in the manuscript
,   indicates similar musical punctuation, a clef or an accidental.

Thus, a responsory in hexameters with a stanza in goliardic metre might be represented as:

$$\text{h } 6 + 9.5 - 10{:}7 + 8/4 + 3pp6p \; 7pp6p \; aa{:}b/aabb \; (\text{or } aaxa{:}bb/aaabb).$$

As the preceding text suggests, much of what can be said is in the nature of work in progress. In a repertory involving more than 1,300 offices, of which perhaps a score have been edited or described adequately, what is presented here is but a small part. Furthermore, the small part has not been the subject of detailed investigation but is merely extracted from a general survey of the whole repertory. This study must be regarded as though it were extracting Dickens's novels from the *very first* examination of the modern novel. As work in progress, it is as much a request for additional information as a revelation of what is known. What is in fact revealed may not be applicable particularly to British rhymed offices, but to the repertory in general.

Most offices are very local. But the chant style seems reasonably universal across Europe. From these two assertions we could infer that there must have been some mechanism by which the style was understood and transmitted, a common way of constructing or borrowing phrases that supersedes local styles. At the moment, we can only glimpse the general style. Here, limitations of space make it impossible to trace more than the most obvious of borrowings, reuse of items from the Common, or from other offices. Until we have a method by which we can trace the borrowing of chants, it will remain difficult to see how local musicians adapted and revised them, and to see whether they did so because of differences in the text or because regional styles were important. The study of individual repertories, whether national or by ecclesiastical order such as Franciscan or Benedictine, will certainly eventually lead to a better understanding of their similarities and differences, and to an identification of the minute dialects by which they can be distinguished. With respect to the texts, it would seem likely, judging from the desire of Latin scholars to isolate local vocabularies, that a national style, or at least a set of national ingredients, might be discernible. But with respect to the chant, we are a long way from being able to distinguish styles and elements adequately. At the moment we have no method by which such fine discrimination could be achieved systematically. Indeed, many features discussed here were raised to conscious observation only for the first time during the research and analysis of these offices, and such things have not been investigated in the remainder of the repertory.

The preferred literary genre of the ninth century, the *prosa*, used structured and perhaps rhymed phrases, often with a metrical cursus at the end. By the twelfth century, this style had largely been replaced, in many literary genres, by accentual poetry in regular metre and rhyme.[6] In late medieval offices, structured prose remains common, especially for responsories, even when the remainder of the office is regular. Classical poetry, mostly in hexameters, by and large disappears after the twelfth century, except perhaps in offices from more peripheral regions: some Irish offices use hexameters prominently. Hexameters, too, are a notable feature of the mid-fifteenth-century office of St Osmund. Even though the evidence suggests that the poets of these offices were also usually responsible for the chants, I sometimes sense that the music did not always keep pace with these literary changes. Musical analysis of a chant may suggest that it is proper to a rhymed office when the corresponding analysis of the texts reveals little that is metrical. Such a discrepancy may have been the result of adapting a rhymed chant to a prose text or to one with a different poetic form. Conflicts between the structure of the chant and of the text, then, make it exceedingly difficult to define what a rhymed office is. I have been somewhat liberal.

The case cannot be argued in full here. The concept of rhyme often demands a definition less rigorous than ours: single-syllable rhymes such as -ia/-era, and assonant rhymes such as -am/-era/-ans are not uncommon. Rhymes such as -am/-em may even be tolerated. Nevertheless, in the most regular of rhymed texts, at least two syllables, and often more, are involved. The true number of syllables in the line, too, is sometimes difficult to determine: hypermetric syllables are used; elision is commonly a method of achieving strictly regular lines, yet is almost never allowed by the chant, which supplies pitches for both syllables. Weighing all these factors, and allowing for other minor poetic licences, we may conclude that when all texts have rhymed lines of regular length, they must constitute a rhymed office. An occasional item in prose or less than strict poetry would

---

[6.] See Andrew Hughes, 'Literary Transformation in post-carolingian Saints' Offices: Using all the Evidence', in *Acta: The Cult of Saints*, ed. S. Sticca (Center for Medieval and Early Renaissance Studies, Binghampton), in press.

not affect the issue: indeed, responsory verses or even the whole responsory are often excluded from the poetic parts of the office. Nor should the setting of such poetic texts to unstructured chant affect the issue, although one might question the competence of the composer. But what if all or most of the texts consist of lines of very irregular length? Were this prose arrangement not rhymed, the office would stand no chance of being included in the rhymed repertory. But even if rhyme is lacking, we should dismiss items as prose only after considering the chants.

Often, however, even with irregular texts there is some rhyme; the inflections of Latin make rhymed endings difficult to avoid. In controversial cases, other criteria are needed to determine whether the text is deliberately structured. Does the rhyme coincide with other textual divisions? A major break in the text of course occurs at the *repetenda* in responsories, items that are often very contentious. Decisive factors in other cases may be, for example, whether the chant is structured so as to reinforce the text; whether there are visual clues to suggest that the scribe was aware of the structure, and whether these reinforce the rhymes. If the chant phrases end at textual rhymes with the same series of pitches, forming a musical rhyme (a not very common occurrence), an intention is clear. More often, indeed normally, at textual rhymes, chant phrases end on the final or reciting note, usually with a stereotyped cadential figure such as a rise of a step to a repeated note, or a fall of a step or a third to a repeated note, or a repeated (or doubled) note falling to the cadence pitch. Phrases ending on the plagal reciting note in either authentic or plagal modes are less common, but often reinforce the rhyme of the text equally strongly. By convention, too, the penultimate phrase, in regular and irregular text, is marked by a chant cadence to the tone below or above the final. The opening motives of individual phrases are to some extent stereotyped, reinforcing textual divisions. Visual clues occur in both text and chant. The point to which the *repetenda* returns may be marked with a capital letter, often with a highlight, even if the cue is not noted after the verse; punctuation often follows rhymes. In the chants, changes of clef often reinforce the purely musical gestures, often because individual phrases of rhymed chants exploit pitches higher or lower than the adjacent stave can allow; accidentals, which may serve as clefs and which need not stand immediately before the pitch they affect, often mark rhymes; incises (vertical lines on the stave) are perhaps used for a similar purpose. In Figure 1 a flat stands between *auctor* and *Christo*, column 1, stave 3; a stop, capital letter, and incise separate the hexameters in the invitatory, column 2, stave 2; a clef separates lines in MA1 (column 2, stave 5, after *lotus*). It is true that visual reinforcements of a structure are more likely to occur in a manuscript whose palaeographical qualities are good.[7] One other musical

---

[7] Ibid.

Figure 1. Salisbury, Cathedral Library 152, fol. 374r
(by courtesy of the Dean and Chapter of Salisbury Cathedral)

matter can also help to resolve the structure of the textual line. In some cases, it seems that the intonation is set apart from the poetic scheme, so that syllable and rhyme counting must start after the intonation: reversing the procedure, to determine where the latter in fact ends, may require analysis of the poetic scheme.

Often the co-ordination between text and chant is quite subtle, and a casual analysis can be misleading. Some idea of the difficulty may be illustrated by the fourth responsory of the office of St Osmund (Example 1). Responsories, because of their elaborate melismatic style, are often problematic. Here, the chant does not seem highly structured. Cadential figures in the responsory are on -*sito, magna, manus,* and *ei.* Before the *repetenda* a cadential figure moves to a pitch modally justifiable but unusual in this repertory. The text is not obviously poetic. Analysing it with these cadences in mind, one could arrive at neatly balanced and perhaps rhymed halves with some internal phrasing: 4pp 4 + 6p: 4p 10p.

Example 1. St Osmund, Matins responsory 4

Accepting the cadence on *magna*, but not that on *manus*, one could force the text into even more balanced segments of 8p6p7pp7p, in which the chant neatly ends on a modally dissonant pitch for the penultimate phrase. Clearly, this arrangement distorts the text, but could it suggest that the chant originally set a regular accentual poem of 8pp7p8pp7p and was adapted for a prose text? Such a possibility seems unlikely in this case, because an alternative analysis suggests that the chant and text are extremely well co-ordinated. The responsory is of course an elegiac couplet, the verse a hexameter. The opening four syllables, defined by the cadence on *-sito*, set off the intonation; the caesura is to the pitches CDF on *plebi*; the cadence on *magna* was quite weak in any case and is easy to elide. In the second hexameter the cadence on *manus* is quite strong, but the following notes CDF at the caesura on *domini* rhyme with the pitches of the earlier caesura. Since the poem is rhymed at the caesura, giving *plebi*, *potenti*, *domini*, and *ei*, the chant is rhymed (although not on modally consonant pitches) to correspond. The setting of the verse as a hexameter is uncomplicated. Is this a case of the adaptation of chant for one rhyme scheme to another, or deliberate subtlety, a dissonance or 'polyphony' of chant rhymes, cadences, and textual rhymes?

To reinforce my belief that this is subtlety and not accident, I cite responsory 11 from the office of St Wulstan (Example 2). It is easy to perceive similar dislocations of chant and text because of the positions of rhyming words.

R.	Regis iram non formidans baculum non tradidit	15pp	a
	apud regem sed defunctum baculum deposuit	15pp	a
	Quam iacentis virtus servat redit† ut Wulstanus voluit	17pp	a
V.	Viri usque gloria meritum	10pp	b
	et gratia cunctis hinc innotuit	11pp	a

† the MS has *reddit*.

Many would dismiss this text as rhymed prose. But once the influence of the heavily repeated *baculum* and the misleading concatenation of *defunctum* with *baculum* can be set aside, the natural punctuation of lines 1 and 2 allows a subdivision into 8 and 7 syllables. In line 3, the hypermetric word *redit* sits between similar lines of 8 and 7 syllables. The syntax of the verse is quite convoluted, and despite its apparently balanced halves, is clearly designed to produce three 7-syllable lines. The poem should be presented thus:

Example 2. St Wulstan, Matins responsory 11

R.	Regis iram non formidans	8pp	a
	baculum non tradidit	7pp	b
	apud regem sed defunctum	8p	c
	baculum deposuit	7pp	b
	Quam iacentis virtus servat	8p	d
	redit		
	ut Wulstanus voluit	7pp	b
V.	Viri usque gloria	7pp	e
	meritum et gratia	7pp	e
	cunctis hinc innotuit.	7pp	b

(R. Not fearing the wrath of the king, he did not hand over the sceptre, but placed it near the dead king. The virtue of the dead king, which he protects, returns, as Wulstan wished. V. After this, the worth of the man became known continually to all because of his glory and grace.)

The end of every line is emphasized in the chant with cadences, incises, and clefs. Even the hypermetric word is set off, almost parenthetically (as it is by punctuation in the translation), by the suddenly higher pitch of the phrase.

As for the general musical style of the chant, many of the appropriate questions have yet to be formulated. Superficially, chants for the rhymed repertory can look seductively like those of the standard repertory. But matters of range and modal transposition, especially of individual phrases, need to be examined more closely. We need to know how phrases are constructed from stereotypical chant formulas, and what modern elements of melodic composition are incorporated. We need to ask what constitutes musical accent, and how it is used to reinforce the text. We need to ask by what methods chants are adapted: are conventional explanations, evolved for the standard repertory, suitable for this repertory? I shall limit myself here primarily to matters of tonal organization, because that is what helps to determine the rhymed nature of each item. Within an overall framework of modes arranged in sequential order, each chant is constructed from discrete phrases, each often using a segment of the modal range different from adjacent phrases, and with clear tonal direction. I have discussed this aspect in more detail elsewhere.[8] Obviously, as the previous example demonstrates, the phrases are co-ordinated extremely closely with those of the text, and with the semantic, grammatical, and syntactic structures of the poem. The music cannot be analysed independently of the words.

Omitted in the following descriptions are features specific to the actual source used that have no bearing on the office as such, for example the later addition of alleluias to the office of William of York, and the crossing out of that office in the manuscript cited. On the other hand, elements of textual or musical punctuation to be described may be very specific to individual sources and different applications of these in different manuscripts may lead to different conclusions as to the status of the text as poetry. In most cases, only a single manuscript source has been used: usually there is no more than one. Nevertheless, a more detailed study would have to account for the variants, especially in order, amongst sources. The model for this exercise, apart from its failure to consider the chant, is Christopher Hohler's account of the office for St Cuthbert.[9]

British Rhymed Offices

We begin in the early tenth and end in the mid-fifteenth century, taking into account some thirty-eight saints and fifty offices: the thirty-two offices for which all, or a substantial amount of, music remains will be described. We begin in the 930s with the office for St Cuthbert, in which the word *scandit* occasions no particular musical gesture, and end about 1457 with

[8.] 'Modal Order and Disorder in the Rhymed Office', *Musica disciplina* 37 (1983), 29–51.
[9.] C. Hohler, 'The Durham Services in Honour of St Cuthbert', *The Relics of St Cuthbert*, ed. C. F. Battiscombe (Durham, 1956), 155–91.

the canonization and translation of St Osmund, in whose office the word *scandere* occasions the most obvious visual motive on the leaf, a stepwise scale passage from C to d and down again (see Figure 1). But such word-painting is rare and, apart from a general expansion and more active use of the range, and an even more clearly defined tonal direction within phrases in later offices, the general plainsong style changes little over the centuries. We can detect a greater change in the textual styles.

What constitutes a British rhymed office? The chronological and stylistic limits outlined allow the inclusion of almost all known late British offices for which the chant exists. The nationality of saints or regional cultivation of feasts is usually easy to ascertain and minimum biographies or descriptions are given below. For detailed work they must of course be supplemented from standard reference works or original research. A few offices used outside the British Isles have been included when they are known to be of insular origin or by a British author. The office *Felix Anna cella* for St Anne is one such. The main office for Thomas Becket, distributed almost universally over Europe, is by an English abbot and we can probably assume that the office for his translation is of similar origin. When the nationality of the saint or feast is in doubt and we do not know where the office originated, the preservation of the text principally in British manuscripts may be the deciding factor.

Many feasts kept only in European churches, of course, venerate saints of actual or supposed British birth: these are not included. On the grounds that very few of its texts seem remotely structured and no source with chant survives, the office for the Relics at the Cluniac monastery of St John the Evangelist in Pontefract, Yorkshire, although obviously local, is excluded (Oxford, University College 101, kept in the Bodleian Library). In the same manuscript is the rarely found rhymed office for St John at the Latin Gate (AH 26. 53), known elsewhere only in continental sources. No evidence suggests English provenance for this office, or for the elaborate monastic office venerating St James the Greater (AH 26. 45), for which a twelfth-century noted version exists: although the manuscript of that version (Oxford, Bodleian Library Rawl. A 416) is said to be of English origin, and Reading Abbey supposedly had a relic of the saint, the five sources listed in AH are associated with Switzerland.

In the absence of evidence for British origin, offices for standard feasts such as the Conception of the Blessed Virgin have not been included. One of the texts for that feast may be of English or northern French provenance. Two feasts of the Visitation must also be mentioned.

The feast of the Visitation was kept by the Franciscans, and extended to the universal church in 1389. It appears in a fifteenth-century manuscript of new Sarum feasts (Cambridge, Emmanuel College 248), and is often appended separately to English books already complete. In the Salisbury noted breviary (Salisbury, Cathedral Library 152) shown in Figure 1, for example, it is before St Osmund in leaves added at the end of the book. Lacking films, I cannot ascertain which of the many texts such sources might transmit, except for the case described in the next paragraph. One of the most widely distributed rhymed offices of all, *Accedunt laudes/Surgens Maria/Sacra dedit* (AH 24. 29), was written by Adam Easton (cardinal *tituli S. Ceciliae*, d. 1397) and was confirmed by Pope Boniface IX (1389–1404): so much two of the manuscripts cited in AH tell us, and one adds that it was composed 'juxta cantum beati Francisci'. Another source refers to its barbarisms and ineptness, the cause of its later replacement. Despite its very wide distribution, not a single English source is cited in AH, and the frequency of its location in Roman/Franciscan books suggests that the office belongs with a Franciscan rather than a British group.

A different office for the Visitation (AH 24. 37) appears in early sixteenth-century printed breviaries of York and Aberdeen, and is said to be by a John Horneby. It also appears in an appendix to Oxford, Bodleian Library Laud misc. 299, a Sarum noted breviary; at a cursory glance the hand appears to be the same as that in the main body of the book. This office is described at the end of the Catalogue.

No account of late medieval British music would be complete without some allusion to the four important offices by Radulfus Niger, uniquely preserved in Lincoln Cathedral 15, fols. 33–43 (not 42). Radulfus was of Bury St Edmunds, and Archdeacon of Gloucester, born *circa* 1140 and died *circa* 1217. Apart from mentioning that notation exists, the only recent note of his work omits all discussion of the chants.[10] Furthermore, in·asserting that Radulfus wrote these offices for some Cistercian house, this study fails to consider that all of them are secular, and thus quite unsuitable for use in a monastic setting. The offices are for the Nativity, Annunciation, Assumption, and Purification. Although none can qualify as a rhymed office, or even as a structured office as discussed above, the chants and texts are newly composed, as Radulfus tells us in an introduction, a small treatise on the feasts themselves: 'Novum enim cantum antiphonis et responsoriis conquesivi ut et concentus redimeret scripture ruditatem'. They thus provide us with a superb opportunity to compare chants, known to have been composed within a half-century to new prose texts, with those of the rhymed repertory. They offer a control against which the determination of structured or rhymed can be measured. A few pointers can be offered. The texts are often balanced, the antiphons in rhymed halves, and the responsories similarly divided at the *repetenda* and concluded by a verse which itself may be balanced in the same way. Lacking more of a stanzaic structure, most texts are shorter than those of

---

[10] G. B. Flahiff, 'Ralph Niger', *Mediaeval Studies* 2 (1940), 104–26.

the structured repertory. If poetic at all, they are so only in so far as psalmodic texts with balanced hemistichs are poetic. Furthermore, none of the structural clues occurs: cadences and rhymes do not strongly coincide, and *repetenda* and other divisions are never emphasized by capital letters or clef changes. Perhaps most important, but very difficult to analyse, the word order is subtly different, phrases ending with words like *suam* or *est* that carry little semantic weight. In fact, the texts seem exceedingly uninteresting, mostly quite repetitive paraphrases of standard biblical or liturgical texts common to the feasts in their usual setting. One or two are almost verbatim reproductions of common items: but *Ascendit Christus* and *Tota pulchra*, for example, do not use the standard chants. Although mostly in strict numerical order, the chants themselves are obviously less articulated than those of the rhymed repertory. Stylistic oddities occur. The *differentiae* are unusual, that for mode 8 being used for mode 3, which recites on the same pitch. And, for example, descending major sixths, in the rhymed repertory reserved for dead intervals between phrases, here sometimes occur even within the same word. In short, almost everything about these offices highlights what makes the structured and rhymed repertory distinctive.

For saints of local importance in the British Isles (other than those in the Catalogue), and there are many, I know of no rhymed texts.[11] Indeed, few proper offices of any kind are extant, the celebration being limited to suffrages or proper lessons and prayers with the sung items drawn from the Common of saints.

Catalogue

Below are listed in alphabetical order saints for whom a full office exists or is known to have existed. An office for the Blessed Virgin Mary follows the main alphabetical sequence. The format of the entries is as follows:

Feast

    possible dates or occasions for composition of the items, e.g. translation
* type of office: published text source: date of earliest noted source
    (number of sources known)   [rc]
—type of office: published text source: /date of earliest unnoted source/   [rc]
    incipits: first item, MR1, LA1
    manuscript source
    notes

[11.] See Andrew Hughes, 'Offices (new liturgical)', in *The Garland Encyclopedia of Medieval England*, in press.

Main offices and translations are distinguished. An asterisk in the left margin signals the existence of one or more noted sources; normally at least one of these is specified. A dash in the left margin denotes sources without musical notation; those on this line shown between // derive from AH and are not further identified, unless necessary. The indication [rc] relates to the reference code for the computer file in which the data are stored, and is included for future convenience. When no manuscript is cited, the sources may be ascertained through the notes in AH, or from the bibliography mentioned with each office. Bibliographical references are limited to those which bear on the liturgical office. Offices are secular unless otherwise noted.

Alban, martyr (*protomartyr anglorum*)

    tr. 1129
* main office: AH 13. 7 (prints the secular form of the monastic office transmitted
    in the manuscript noted below):
    11th C. (1 source and later fragments)   [AL21 and 23]
    Inclita martyrii/Sacrosanctum venerando/Suscipiens martyr
    New York, Pierpont Morgan Library 926

The chants in this manuscript are written in Anglo-Saxon neumes *in campo aperto*, and are untranscribable as they stand. This office and manuscript have been described by Drew Hartzell.[12] Unfortunately, Professor Hartzell was not aware of the several fragmentary manuscripts, discussed by John Bergsagel,[13] that have parts of the chant on staves. Dr Bergsagel also refers to obvious reworking of the office in offices for St Kanutus Lavard (Canute, Knud), *dux*, for which we have a complete musical setting, and other Scandinavian saints, including the other St Kanutus, *protomartyr danorum*, for which no musical sources are known.

    Thus, five chants can be recovered complete, or nearly so, together with the opening of a sixth. Bergsagel also identifies two antiphons in common with the office for St Cuthbert, whose melodies are likely to be the same.

    The question of authorship is extremely complex and confused, and Hartzell and Bergsagel, reviewing the evidence, come to different conclu-

    [12] K. D. Hartzell, 'A St Albans Miscellany in New York', *Mittellateinisches Jahrbuch* 10 (1975), 20–61, with three plates.
    [13] J. Bergsagel, 'Anglo-Scandinavian Musical Relations before 1700', *Report of the Eleventh Congress of the International Musicological Society* (Copenhagen, 1974), 263–71; 'Liturgical Relations between England and Scandinavia: as seen in Selected Musical Fragments from the 12th and 13th Centuries', *Föredrag och diskussionsinlägg från Nordiskt Kollokvium* 3 (Helsinki, 1976), 11–26, with facsimiles.

sions. In any case, the author also provided the music, 'et eidem notam melicam adaptavit': the choice is between Leofric, abbot of St Albans, after 995 (Hartzell) or Ælfric, the early eleventh-century abbot of St Albans (Bergsagel). Without access to all the original chroniclers' statements (and perhaps not even then), it is not possible to arbitrate safely: on the evidence presented, a better case can perhaps be made for Leofric.

In view of the importance of St Alban as *protomartyr anglorum* it is exceptionally unfortunate that no source is known from which the chants could be recovered complete. Chants are used as tenors in a number of polyphonic works, from Dunstable's isorhythmic motet, *Albanus roseo rutilat*, which uses MA1, to works by Fayrfax.

The antiphons are in elegiac couplets or hexameters and few are really rhymed: most of the responsories, on the other hand, are characterized by rhymed prose, although a few have completely regular schemes (e.g. MR3/V3 $6 + 5$p $\times 5/ \times 2$ without rhyme; and MR6/V6 10p $\times 4/ \times 2$ with rhyme aa:bb/cc, in which the first pair is clearly rhymed in the chant also).

—invitatory and two antiphons: AH 28 app. [AL22]

—one antiphon, *Ave protomartyr Anglorum*, is the only chant proper for St Alban in the Sarum breviary: it is modelled on the well-known antiphon *Ave rex gentis* and was presumably sung to the same chant.[14]

Anna, mother of the BVM

    circa 1382: cult made obligatory in England
* main office: AH 5. 39: late 14th C. (several)   [AN26]
    Felix Anna cella/Felix Anna flos/Omnis sanctorum

This office was probably written by the English Dominican, Thomas Stubbs, *circa* 1320–83. In the source from which the transcription was made, Oxford Bodleian Library Lat. lit. b14, a Sarum antiphonal, it is extremely regular: the modes appear in a completely sequential order; responsories are 8pp7p $\times 3/ \times 1$ abab:ab/ab; all antiphons are 8pp $\times 4$, rhymed abab or abcb, except for VA1, MI, and the Gospel antiphons. VA1 and WE are more elaborate, using $4 + 6$pp $\times 4$ aaaa, while VE and LE are identical textually with two stanzas of the sequence *Gaude mater Anna* and use 8pp7p $\times 2$ aabccb. In most of these characteristics, the office resembles that of St Dominic, and indeed seven of the antiphon chants are related to the corresponding chants in the Dominic office, one or two quite exactly, the others in adaptations that could almost qualify them as different tunes (see Example 3).

[14] See below, under St Edmund, king and martyr, where the source of this information is acknowledged.

Example 3. SS Dominic and Anna, Lauds antiphon 3

Dominic

Sca - la ce - lo pro - mi - nens fra - tri re - ve - la - tur

Anna

Ex Jo - a-chim quem ha - bu - it vi - te vi-rum ex - i - mi-um

per quam pa - ter trans - i - ens sur - sum fe - re - ba-tur

An - na Ma - ri-am ge - nu - it ma-trem re - gis ju - sti - ti - e.

—main office: AH 25. 20: /Carmelite, 1489/   [AN30]
one Irish source
—main office: manuscript: /?1270/   [AN42]
monastic, in the Coldingham Breviary, London, British Library Harley 4664

Augustine, archbishop of Canterbury

tr. 1240
—main office: AH 13. 17: /13th–14th C./   [AU21]
—one antiphon: AH 28 app.   [AU22]

Birinus, apostle of Wessex, bishop of Dorchester

tr. to Winchester, *circa* 690
* main office: manuscript: 11th C. (1)   [BI81]
[missing]/ . . . *celebret specialius/Dominator domine Birinus*
New York, Pierpont Morgan Library 926

This manuscript is discussed and the text edited by Drew Hartzell.[15] It is
laid out as a series of nine responsories, the first of which is incomplete by a
few syllables, the five antiphons and Benedictus antiphon of lauds, and the
Magnificat antiphon of second vespers. Eight antiphons follow, in a
different format, but a marginal rubric notes that they are the antiphons of
the little hours, and four for second vespers. Lacking of a complete office,
then, are the antiphons of first vespers and matins. The provision of

---

15. K. D. Hartzell, 'A St Albans Miscellany in New York'.

separate antiphons for the little hours suggests a celebration of considerable importance. Hartzell suggests that other marginal incipits, now almost invisible, probably indicated to the monks of St Albans by whom the manuscript was used, how the secular office (probably written for Dorchester) was to be done.

The eight antiphons at the end are clearly separate, both in the way they are laid out, and textually. The other items are in rhymed and very highly structured prose, often with quite regular lines (e.g. MR4/V4 *Sancto regente* 8pp × 5/7p × 2 rhymed abc:cd/ee). The eight antiphons, however, are in leonine hexameters, rhymed at the caesura: furthermore each is provided in the margin with a roman numeral and the end of the *differentia* appropriate to modes 1–8 in order. Unfortunately, these tiny motives, not even the complete *differentia*, are of little help in transcribing the neumes.

Blaanus, bishop of Kingarth, confessor

—main office: AH 13. 27: /pr. 1510/ [BL01]

Botulph, abbot, associated with East Anglia

* I do not know whether the office in a fragmentary manuscript in the Riksarkiv, Stockholm (with another leaf in London, British Library Add. 34388) is rhymed or complete, but it has the chant.[16]

Breowa, virgin martyr

—nine poems, perhaps the matins antiphons: AH 25. 63: /12th C./ [BR31]

Brigid, abbess and founder of nunnery of Kildare

tr. with Columba and Patrick, 1185/6
* main office: AH 13. 29: 14th/15th C. (2) [BR41]
Virgo sancta Brigida/Felix Hiberniam/Thalamum sponsi
Dublin, Trinity College 78 (B. 1. 3)

The office is fairly regular, mostly in goliardic metre, 7pp6p, for both antiphons and responsories, except for MR1–4 which all have lines of 6pp. The modal order is regular up to lauds, where modes 3 and 4 are omitted. MR9, *Regnum mundi*, takes its first chant phrase from the responsory of the Common of virgins with the same incipit. Unlike the offices for Cannicus and Patrick in the same manuscript (see below), only a single antiphon for first vespers is provided.

[16.] Bergsagel, 'Liturgical Relations'.

—main office: AH 13. 30: *circa* 1200 (1)   [BR42]
  Paris, Bibliothèque nationale lat. 12036

This manuscript, a breviary possibly for St Andrews (Scotland) or nearby non-monastic church, has the musical incipits and *differentiae* in the margin, but unfortunately for this office the marginal staves are empty. The office is metrically quite regular, mostly 8pp7p, but the number of lines in adjacent antiphons often differs. The antiphons, in fact, are unusually long, sometimes with eight lines.

Cannicus (Kenneth), abbot of Achad-Bó (Kilkenny), confessor

* main office: AH 25. 65: 15th C. (1)   [CA41]
  O pastor pie/ [missing]/*Decantemus Cannici*
  Dublin, Trinity College 78 (B. 1. 3)

Most of the first and second nocturn of matins are missing from the manuscript. Like the office of Brigid, this is in quite regular goliardic metre, excepting the Magnificat antiphons, which have 6-syllable lines, and three additional antiphons listed at the end and presumably for the ferias, which have 8- and 7-syllable lines. The modal order is mostly regular.

Cedda (Chad), bishop of York and Lichfield, confessor

  tr. 1148
—main office: AH 13. 33: /pr. Sarum breviary, 1494/   [CE21]

Columba (Colum Cille), abbot of Iona (see Patrick)

  tr. 849. Also apparently translated in 1185/6 with Brigid and Patrick.
—main office: AH 13. 35: /15th C./   [CO21]
* main office and octave: manuscript: 14th C.(1)   [CO22]
  (MR9) . . . *ancta quoque*/ (LA1) *Dei potens*
  Edinburgh, University Library 211. iv

About twenty items survive, beginning with MR9 (incomplete) and including several responsories and Gospel antiphons for the octave.[17] Of these I have seen only four.[18] They are highly structured: the antiphon *Pastor oves* is 10pp × 3 aaa. The Benedictus antiphon *Pater Columba* is 9p × 2 8p × 3 aaaaa: it refers to English incursions and thus may post-date the years 1335/6. The extremely long Magnificat antiphon *Sanctorum piisime* begins as rhymed prose and becomes more regular.

[17.] I owe most of my knowledge of this office to Isobel Woods, 'Our Awin Scottis Use: Chant Usage in Medieval Scotland', *Journal of the Royal Musical Association* 112 (1987), 21–37.

[18.] These were reproduced by Isobel Woods in a hand-out for the AMS annual meeting, 1986.

Cuthbert, bishop of Lindisfarne, 685–7

circa 930 (see below); tr. 999, and to the Norman monastic cathedral of Durham in 1104
* main office: AH 13. 36: late 10th C. [CU71–3]
Ave presul gloriose/Cuthbertus puer/Christi fortis
London, British Library Harley 1117 (neumes *in campo aperto*); also in the Worcester Antiphonal and numerous later sources

The basic information about manuscripts and the texts, including a comparative edition, were published by Christopher Hohler in 1956, although without discussion of the music for the office.[19]

In the 930s, King Athelstan gave gifts to the church of Chester-le-Street, including a *vita* and this office (the actual book survives as Cambridge, Corpus Christi College 183, without notation). Hohler suggests that the office was composed by a clerk from the Low Countries. The obvious poetic structure makes this one of the very earliest rhymed offices. The chant need not originate from this early date. Not known to have been used in the North before its revival by the Normans, the original secular office was adapted for monastic use by the composition of additional items between 1083 and 1150.

The additional monastic items are in a thirteenth-century breviary from Ely without music (Cambridge, University Library Ii 4. 20), and with chant as VA1–4 and MA9 in a secular office (in the Antiphonal Edinburgh, National Library 18. 2. 13A), and in their proper monastic position, in a mid-twelfth-century liturgical *libellus* (Cambridge, Trinity College o. 3. 55). I have not seen the last manuscript.[20] The monastic Worcester Antiphonal adds different items, some drawn from the office of the Common. The additional items are mostly distinct in poetic form, being more complex than the original secular antiphons, all of which are 8pp (or 8p) × 4, usually aaaa or aabb. The original responsories are structured in a very complex way, with lines of irregular length but with consistent rhymes. Thus, MR4/V4 *Vir Domini* and MR5/V5 *Merito sanctitatis* are 7p6p7p13p:10p8p8pp/15p12p abac:dec/cc and 7pp7pp11p9p:10p10p/8p8p aabb:aa/cc respectively. The original secular items, too, are strictly in modal order. Even in the secular offices, however, lauds begins from mode 2, continuing from mode 1 of MA9: this feature is characteristic of Benedictine offices.

Noteworthy, of course, are the very early date of the text (not necessarily the chant) of this office, its Norman monastic revisions, and the complete absence of classical metres.

---

[19] Hohler, 'The Durham Services in Honour of St Cuthbert'.
[20] See the description and discussion by S. Rankin in *Cambridge Music Manuscripts: 900–1700*, ed. I. Fenlon (Cambridge, 1982), 33–7.

David, bishop and patron of Wales

> tr. 1275: into Sarum Kalendar 1398, made obligatory in 1415
> * main office: manuscript: late 14th C. (1)   [DA71]
> *O desiderabilis/Tractavit Patricio/Dictus est Patricio*
> Aberystwyth, National Library of Wales 20145 E

This is a quite elaborate office, including an alternative invitatory abbreviating the text and chant of the main one, and the beginning of services for the commemorations during the octave, unfortunately incomplete in the manuscript.[21] It is quite regular, using goliardic poems for the antiphons and more complex catalectic poems for the responsories. The modal order is correct, except for MR3, which is in mode 5, and MR9, in mode 2.

The most interesting feature of the office is its close relation to that of Thomas of Canterbury, for which the manuscript provides one of the most elaborate offices known to me. The textual borrowing is limited almost entirely to the single, but striking word *Studens* which opens the important first responsory of the Thomas office, and the second responsory here. The musical borrowings are often heavily varied, and in isolation might be discounted as merely resemblances of the modal family: the following describes the relationships, which are usually to the corresponding item in the Thomas office.

Nothing before MA2 and MR2 seems related. Antiphons of matins and lauds are borrowed quite exactly, except for MA1 and 6; the six-line MA9 is related to the important Thomas antiphon *Felix locus* by replacing and rearranging the phrases thus—abcdef becomes axbyef. Responsories 2 and 4–9 are borrowed with a great deal more variation, at least in parts of the chant, especially at the beginnings; sometimes the distribution of textual phrases differs, especially when the metre is different. MR1 is quite remotely related. MR3, as noted above, is out of modal order, serving for a chant in mode 3, and its mode 5 chant is related to the mode 5 Thomas responsory only by family resemblances. The fourth responsory of matins is an adaptation of the chant usually appearing as MR9 in the Thomas office.[22] As I have pointed out elsewhere in connection with modal order, modes 3 and 4 seem to be avoided or to cause some embarrassment in rhymed offices. The Benedictus antiphon and Magnificat antiphon of second vespers are related to those of the Thomas office, the former by way of adjustments for a different metre (see Example 4).

---

[21] On this office see O. T. Edwards, 'In festo sancti David', *National Library of Wales Journal* 21 (1980), 229–40, and id., *Matins, Lauds and Vespers for St David's Day* (Woodbridge, 1989).

[22] I thank Professor Edwards for drawing my attention to this.

Example 4. SS Thomas of Canterbury and David, Benedictus antiphons

In view of the close association between the David and Thomas offices, it may be worth speculating as to the author of the former. Gerald of Wales (Giraldus Cambrensis), 1146–1223, is known to the musicological world for his famous description of music in Wales and the sweetness of B flat. A Welsh literary connection between Gerald and a verse life of Thomas is described by Pauline Thompson.[23] This connection exists also with the Thomas office. In addition to his literary skills, Gerald was chaplain to

[23] 'An Anonymous Verse Life of Thomas Becket', *Mittellateinisches Jahrbuch* 20 (1985), 147–54.

Henry II, and had close connections with Canterbury. Although elected as bishop of St Davids, he was prevented from taking office, and spent several years trying to secure papal approval for the elevation of St Davids to an archbishopric. Could the rhymed office to David be connected not with the promotion of the saint but to the institution that housed his shrine? Could Gerald have adapted the Thomas office, of quite recent composition, for this purpose?

Ebba, abbess of Coldingham, virgin

   vita by Reginald of Durham, after 1188
—main office: AH 13. 42: /13th–14th C.   [EB11]

Edmund, king and martyr

   late 11th C.; tr. 1095
* main office: manuscript: late 11th C. (1)   · [ED62]
   Ave rex gentis/Sancte indolis/Quidam maligne
   Copenhagen, Det Kongelige Bibliotek 1588
   shortly before 1087, Abbot Warner of Rebais (Normandy) composed four
   additional antiphons, text, and music
* . . . additions: manuscript: before *circa* 1125 (several)
* . . . and a vigil office: manuscript: before *circa* 1125 (several)
   Prepollens magnifice/Animis invigilantes/Devotus Egilwinus

The earliest manuscript is New York, Pierpont Morgan Library 736, with the vigil and the main monastic office; the other important source used here is Oxford, Bodleian Library Digby 109, which transmits a secular version and lacks the vigil.[24]

With an associated vigil office, and being monastic, this is a very long and elaborate office, deserving of a major study by someone expert in both the rhymed and standard repertory of chant. It is a classic case in which both texts and chants fall between prose, standard chant, and poetic, rhymed chant. As for the texts, very few are regularly structured. In fact, only three of the four antiphons added (and composed) by Abbot Warner (VA1, 3, 4) are regular, in 8-syllable lines mostly with a single rhyme: the fourth antiphon, *O purpurea*, is in prose. The first of these antiphons is the famous *Ave rex gentis*, discussed in a classic article by Manfred Bukofzer.[25] As Rodney Thomson points out, this antiphon was quite widely used in a number of late medieval English offices, including Alban, Edmund Rich, Ethelbert, and Oswin (all discussed here).[26] In other texts, the line lengths

---

[24.] Much of this information and a brief description of the music for this office is in R. M. Thomson, 'The Music for the Office of St Edmund King and Martyr', *Music & Letters* 65 (1984), 189–93. Thomson erroneously identifies the vigil office as that for the translation.

[25.] 'Two fourteenth-century Motets on St Edmund', *Studies in Medieval and Renaissance Music* (London, 1951), 17–33.

[26.] Thomson, 'The Music for the Office of St Edmund King and Martyr', 193.

Example 5. St Edmund, king and martyr: passage from the Magnificat antiphon

(*Exultet* chant): Paris, Bibliothèque de l'Arsenal 135 (an English missal)

are so irregular that they must be described as rhymed prose. Isolated hexameters are surely not intentional. On the other hand, the frequent rhyme schemes correspond both to the *cola*, or phrases of the text, and to musical phrases: in addition the later source, the Digby manuscript, seems to make a real attempt to delimit the phrases with the signs of musical and textual punctuation which often characterize structured chant (see Example 5 above). Unlike Dr Thomson, who expects the bulk of the chant to be pre-existing plainsong, I think it is distinctly characteristic and different from the standard repertory, but this judgement at the moment must remain subjective until the appropriate analytical tools for comparing standard and later repertory have evolved. In any case, I recognize phrases, cadences, and other motives which remind me of gestures commonly occurring in the rhymed repertory and which seem more artificially structured than those of standard chant, but the sense of balanced phrasing is missing. Example 6 shows typical passages. Apart from obvious family resemblances to be expected in chants of the same mode, I have noted only one phrase obviously drawn directly from the standard repertory, from the *Exultet* chant of Holy Saturday, presumably because of its textual suitability (see Example 5).

Example 6. St Edmund, king and martyr: passages from a Matins antiphon and responsory

As Bukofzer noted, texts and chants from this office are used in a number of fourteenth-century polyphonic works in English manuscripts.

Edmund Rich (Canterbury), bishop and doctor

> exiled, like Thomas of Canterbury, in the Cistercian Abbey of Pontigny, where
> he also died; cd 1246
> —main office: AH 13. 43: /14th C./   [ED51]
> * main office: AH 25. 88: 13th C. (several)   [ED52]
>   *Gaude Sion ornata/Primus iaspis lapidum/Ad laudandum celi regem*

The office ED51 is probably the standard English office, for which no
music survives. ED52 is perhaps more associated with France, emanating
as it does from French Cistercian sources. ED54 is in a manuscript also
containing the office for Richard of Chichester, with *vitae*, passions, and
letters relating to Thomas of Canterbury and others: it would seem
therefore to be closely associated with England.

Unfortunately, the only source of ED52 with the chant that I have
available is incomplete, beginning with MR3: Paris, Bibliothèque nationale
lat. 8882, a Cistercian antiphonal from the Pontigny area. The office also
occurs with chant in the Cistercian antiphonal, Vallbona Monastery
Library 21. A very clear relationship to the office of Thomas of Canterbury
exists in MR6, 9, and 11, and LA2 and 3, where the responsory texts of
Thomas are adapted from lines of 10pp to goliardic metre, 7pp6p, or to
8pp7p stanzas. Since the texts of VA4 and VR are identical to those of the
other main office, ED54 below, we can perhaps recover the chants from
that office, in which they are not borrowed from the Thomas of Canterbury
office. More evidence of the continental associations of this office are
apparent in its very close textual connection to the office of St Claudius,
Benedictine bishop of Besançon.

> —one antiphon: AH 28 app.   [ED53]
> * main office: manuscript: 14th C. (1)   [ED54]
>   *Iste pastor* (or *Ave speculum*)/*Gaudet mundus*/*Novi solis*
>   Rome, Biblioteca Alessandrina (Universitaria) 120[27]

Poetically and musically this is almost the same as the main office to
Thomas of Canterbury, borrowing the schemes and chants of the corresponding items. Even its modal order has the same omissions and re-
arrangements that many of the Thomas versions demonstrate. Textually,
too, many of its phrases are borrowed verbatim from Thomas, although
not always from corresponding items. Only the VA and VR are not
borrowed from Thomas, and these items are textually identical to VA4 and
VR of the office ED52 above. For the VA in London, British Library
Stowe 12, without the chant, is the antiphon *Ave speculum Anglorum*, as
noted below. The Magnificat antiphon of first vespers, VE, in that source

---

[27.] I must thank Professor David Hiley for drawing my attention to this manuscript and
previously unknown office, and for sending me photographs and information.

differs too, but its relation to the VE of the Thomas office is so close that the same melody was obviously used:

VE *Thomas of Canterbury*		*Edmund Rich*	
Pastor cesus	in gregis medio	Pastor ingens	in gregis medio
pacem emit	in cruoris precio	pacem docet	oris eloquio
letus dolor	in tristi gaudio	letus regnat	in celi solio
grex respirat	pastore mortuo	celi fruens	eterno gaudio
plangens plaudit	mater in filio	gaudens gaudet	mater in filio
quia vivit	victor sub gladio	quia carus	caret supplicio

(an erroneous 'o' before 'letus' is common).

—the antiphons *Ave speculum Anglorum* and *Ave primus Anglorum* appear in various English manuscripts as a replacement for one antiphon of a complete office, or as a suffrage text, without music, as noted by Christopher Hohler and Rodney Thomson. They are both modelled on *Ave rex gentis*.

Ethelbert of England (East Anglia)

> not the same as Ethelbert of Kent
> * main office: manuscript: 1254–58 (1)   [ET12]
> *Diem festum/Illustris regis/Innocentem dolo*
> Hereford, Cathedral Library P. 9. VII

Since the feast-day was on 20 May, this office has only a single nocturn, suitable for Easter time, apparently with only a single antiphon, but three other antiphons are provided for years when the feast falls after Ascension, and six more for a normal matins of nine antiphons when it falls after Trinity, making ten in all. Nevertheless, only three responsories are given. The antiphons of lauds and the single Easter antiphon of matins are poetic, mostly 8pp7p in stanzas of four lines, or more for the Gospel antiphons. The 'subsequent' antiphons for matins are mostly in rhymed prose. Modal order is preserved for the antiphons, including the 'subsequent' alternatives. The three responsories are much less regular, in modes 1, 5, and 8, suggesting that others may have existed for the service outside Easter time. The antiphons beginning *Regali ex progenie* and *O radix* do not borrow from the standard plainsong melodies of the antiphons which begin with those words. The Benedictus antiphon, however, is yet another modelled on *Ave rex gentis* (see Edmund, above). To obtain lines of consistent 8 syllables, as usual with this item, *o Ethelberte* must be elided, but the chant allows five clearly separate neumes for the text. At another point, *Ethelberte* rhymes with *detur per te*.

The chants for this office seem like fairly conventional rhymed chants, with rather elaborate alleluia terminations which as usual fall outside the poetic scheme. Even in the prose-like 'subsequent' antiphons, the chants resemble rhymed melodies whose phrases correspond to the main textual divisions, thus enhancing the effect of any structure.

—two antiphons: AH 28 app.   [ET11]

Ethelwold, bishop of Winchester, Benedictine monk

* main office: manuscript: *circa* 1300 (1)   [ET51]
  Sancto Dunstano/Signifer Christi/In pagina
  Cambridge, Magdalene College F. 4. 10

Many items of this monastic office are highly structured, although few can be counted as regularly poetic, and I can find no classical metres: *Sensit puerpera*, MA5, has two lines of 6 + 5pp, but without rhyme, the matins canticle antiphon *Fundator* has five lines of 8pp with a single rhyme. In general, however, the antiphons are characterized by two parallel halves, more typical of the standard repertory, and are rather short: a number of them begin rather oddly, too, in a way which does not resemble rhymed chant. This office must certainly be considered marginal with respect to the rhymed repertory.

Finian, abbot of Clonard (Co. Meath), confessor

  circa 1287–1320
—main office: AH 13. 51: /15th C./   [FI41]

Gilbert of Sempringham, confessor

  cd 1202
—main office: Henry Bradshaw Society 59:[28] /13th C./   [GI31]

Gregory I, pope, apostle of the English

* main office: manuscripts: 12th–14th C. (3)   [GR34]
  Gaudeamus universi/Fulgebat in venerando/O admirabile beati
  Worcester, Cathedral Chapter Library, F 160, fols. 209v–212r[29]
  Oxford, Bodleian Library Gough lit. 1, fols. 86v–89r, a noted breviary of York, *circa* 1400
  Cambridge, Magdalene College F. 4. 10, fols. 211r–214v, Benedictine antiphonal of Peterborough Abbey, *circa* 1300

Despite Gregory's certain importance both in and for England, and assertions (as in the *Oxford Dictionary of Saints*) that his principal feast was celebrated universally and given a high rank, in the Sarum books I have been able to examine the feast is drawn either entirely from the Common of

---

[28] R. M. Woolley (ed.), *The Gilbertine Rite*, 2 vols., Henry Bradshaw Society 59–60 (London, 1921–2), 115–26.
[29] *Antiphonaire monastique, XIIe siècle. Codex F. 160 de la Bibliothèque de la cathédrale de Worcester*, Paléographie musicale 12 (Tournai, 1922), plates 287–92.

saints or has only proper lessons. As far as I can determine without a re-examination of dozens of books all over England, a proper office for the saint occurs mostly in books for York and dioceses other than Sarum, and in English monastic books: this office, however, may well be the more common rhymed office, mostly known in its secular form, *Gloriosa sanctissimi*, published in AH 5. 64 (for which there are no particular insular associations).

The relations among *Gaudeamus universi* (GR34 above), *Gloriosa sanctissimi* (GR31), and the several others published in *CAO* are far too complex to describe in detail. Between *Gaudeamus universi* and *Gloriosa sanctissimi*, however, eight responsories are in common, although not in the same order. In the Worcester arrangement all are strictly in modal order up to the monastic additions, suggesting some priority for this version. Three of the monastic responsories are in common with the monastic antiphonal of Saint-Denis (Paris, Bibliothèque nationale lat. 17296), manuscript D in *CAO*. Also in common with the Saint-Denis antiphonal, but not with the *Gloriosa sanctissimi* office, are the Magnificat antiphon for first vespers and several of the antiphons for lauds, not in modal order. The reasons for these relationships and for the gaps in them need exploration. In general, all of the material in common with the standard office is rhymed (verses are prose) and that in common with Saint-Denis is in prose.

The other items in the office in English manuscripts are poetic, mostly in Victorine sequence stanza, and as far as I know are unique to these English sources. In strictly modal order, they are certainly English in usage, if not origin: there are references to England, or to the English (not merely the usual *angli/angeli* cliché), in six of them. Other signs are the replacement of the word *Rome* (with *ergo*) in MR3, one of those in common with the *Gloriosa sanctissimi* office, and the omission or erasure of the word *papa* on several occasions in the Worcester manuscript, even where this destroys the metre or the sense.

How Gregory was celebrated in England, where, and why, and when, could well form the basis for a most interesting monograph.

Helen, empress, mother of Emperor Constantine; associated with the discovery of the True Cross

> venerated in various areas of England, especially the North-East; Geoffrey of Monmouth (d. 1154) claimed she was of British origin
> There are numerous main offices in continental manuscripts. The office below seems unique to England.
> * main office: manuscript: mid-15th C. (1)   [HE16]
> *Collaudantes et dignam/Beatissime regine/Congaudendum*

This office is unique to the Ranworth Antiphonal, once kept in the church of St Helen's, Ranworth, Norfolk, now in the Library of the University of

East Anglia. The texts vary from quite regular to irregular but clearly structured and rhymed. The following example, MA9, is typical:

Virtutum humilitatis imbuta	11pp	a
hec femina religiosa	9p	a
regni spernens insignia	8pp	a
ancillarum Christi fit famula	10pp	a
aquam eis ministrans manu propria	12pp	a

The modes are strictly in numerical order. The chants are fairly conventional, although the responsory melismas are moderately elaborate, and one or two phrases range widely within a few notes: from (*humilita*)*tis* to *re*(*ligiosa*) in the above text, for instance, is set to these pitches, in mode 8— F A CDE D DE E C A AGF. The melisma in MR6 has these pitches, in mode 6—GA CDEg agFEDC—spanning a ninth.

John, prior of Bridlington, confessor, Order of St Augustine

    cd 1401, tr. 1404
* main office: manuscript: *circa* 1460 (1)   [IO61]
    Ioannis sollemnitas/Quem malignus spiritus/Vexatos a demone
    Wollaton Antiphonal (now in Nottingham University Library)

This is a very regular office, mostly in modal order, and would represent a typical composition of the thirteenth century or later, in this case early fifteenth century. Lauds begins with mode 2: I do not think this is a characteristic of Augustinian offices. Antiphons are mostly in goliardic metre, 7pp6p, and the Gospel antiphons as usual are longer. Responsories are in the same metre or in lines of 10pp or occasionally 6pp syllables.

    The chant of the first matins responsory, *Quem malignus spiritus*, provides the tenor for a fifteenth-century cyclic mass.[30]

—one antiphon: AH 28 app.   [IO62]

Kentigern, bishop of Glasgow, confessor

—main office: AH 26. 76: /pr. Brev. 1509/   [KE51]
* main office: AH 45. 55: 13th/14th C. (1)   [KE52]
    (VR) *In septentrionali/Christi miles/Eya laudes*
    Edinburgh, National Library 18. 2. 13B

Because the feast date is 13 January, during the difficult kalendar adjustments for the weeks after Epiphany, this office is recorded in the Temporale. It is a normal secular office, quite simple and regular, most items having either 8- or 7-syllable lines, or alternating lines of 8pp7p. The

---

[30.] Ed. M. Bent, *Fifteenth-Century Liturgical Music II: Four Anonymous Masses*, Early English Church Music 22 (London, 1979), 35–77.

modal order is considerably upset: the matins antiphons and responsories run thus—123 474 876 and 128 385 741. The style of the chant varies from being quite elaborate and moving rapidly over a large range (see Example 7 (*a*)) to very conventional rhymed chants (Example 7(*b*)) to simple syllabic settings which approximate the style of hymns, often being in mode 6 transposed to sound like a major scale, and with repeated phrases (Example 7(*c*)).

—two antiphons: AH 28 app. [KE53]

Example 7. Passages from the office for St Kentigern

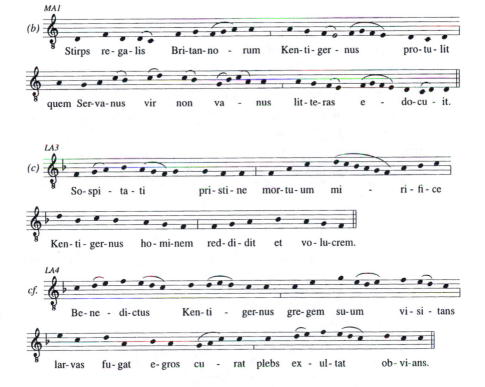

Kyneburga, Kyneswitha, and Tybba, two sisters and a relative, whose relics were translated to Peterborough; Kyneburga founded and was abbess of the convent of Castor (Northants)

* main office: manuscript: 14th C. (1)   [KY41]
   A sanctarum oraculo/Auctor virginitatis/Laborantibus
   Cambridge, Magdalene College F. 4. 10

This monastic office is textually on the border between prose and poetry, but the chant formulas reinforce the textual structure in a deliberate manner. Matins antiphons 9–12 are clearly prose, 1–8 are highly structured in irregular rhymed lines: the antiphons for lauds are rhymed and roughly metrical. The canticle antiphon is similar, mixing accentual poetry and a hexameter:

A sanctarum oraculo	8pp	a
annunciatum et reo	8pp	a
hunc occidendum sed martyribus socianda	hexameter 5–9	
quia ubi abundavit	8pp	b
iniquitas peccatoris	8pp	c
superabundavit	6p	b
gratia salvatoris	7p	c

(the short line at 'superabundavit' is marked by a clef sign).

Like the antiphons, the responsories are separated into those (MR6–8) that are structured prose at best, and the nine others (MR1–5 and 9–12) that are more or less structured. With these nine items, three doxologies are provided, and one is attached to MR8 of the other group. Although I can provide no explanation, these circumstances suggest that a more or less structured secular office has been converted into a monastic one by the addition of items in prose.

Macharius (Maurice), ?bishop of Tours, cult in Scotland (Aberdeen)

   a Gaelic *vita* from the 14th C.
—main office: AH 28. 23: /pr. 1510/   [MF71]

Magnus, count of Orkney[31]

   tr. 1136
—main office: AH 5. 71: /pr. 1519/   [MA41]
—main office: AH 5. 72: /pr. 1510–17/   [MA42]

Mildretha, abbess of Minster-in-Thanet

   tr. to St Augustine's, Canterbury, in 1035, and the office probably written in the 1090s
* main office: manuscript: late 11th C. (1)   [MI41]
   Inter sidereos/Devota deo Mildretha/Regina a summa opulentia
   London, British Library Harley 3908, fols. 43r–50v (the Magnificat antiphon for first vespers occurs, without chant, as a suffrage in the Cologne manuscript edited in AH 28. 312)

[31.] See I. De Geer, *Earl, Saint, Bishop, Skald—and Music: The Orkney Earldom of the Twelfth Century* (Uppsala, 1985).

Occupying a complete gathering of 8 leaves that might once have formed a separate *libellus*, the office is included in a manuscript completely dedicated to Mildred. It appears after Goscelin's *Vita S. Mildrethe*, the lessons for matins, and a proper mass, and before material relating to *Translation S. Mildrethe*, also by Goscelin. Richard Sharpe proposes a date in the 1090s for the composition of this office. Goscelin, the hagiographer and precentor of St Augustine's, and author of the other liturgical material in the manuscript, may have been responsible for both words and music of the *historia*; William of Malmesbury speaks of Goscelin as one of the best musicians of his time.[32]

The chant is in a neat square notation on four dry-point lines with ragged edges. These 'staves' are between single dry-point lines that extend to the edges of the leaf and support the text. Clefs D, B natural, B flat, F, and E natural with B flat are used: several interesting note-shapes are distinctive. Evidence suggests that the scribe was careful and musically literate: before the end of the MI at a new line, for instance, he placed a quite unnecessary B natural clef needed only for the following antiphon. In the opinion of Drew Hartzell and Susan Rankin, the date proposed by Sharpe would make this the earliest insular source to exhibit such a clear notation on what amounts to a real stave.

The office is monastic, with four antiphons at first vespers. Its texts are extremely interesting from the poetic and musical point of view. The VE is completely poetic, as its transcription in AH 28 demonstrates. On the other hand, most of the other items, while often clearly rhymed, are metrically irregular. Nevertheless, that the rhymes are deliberate, and that the musical scribe was aware of them, is clear from the frequency with which clefs are placed at these poetically important points. The chants are in modal order. The monastic antiphons, MA9–12, are all in mode 8, as is MA8 itself: such a concentration on the G mode appears in other early offices. The four antiphons of first vespers begin with mode 2, an interesting oddity that would need investigation. The chant is well aligned with the text, and yet is not quite like that of fully metrical later offices. In MR2, for example, the text is:

R.   Respondit
    fortissima puella
    persecutrici sue
    'torque,

---

[32] I owe my discovery of this office to Richard Sharpe; he has since published 'Words and music by Goscelin of Canterbury', *Early Music* 19 (1991), 94–7. See also my 'Word Painting in a 12th-century Office', in *Beyond the Moon: Festschrift Luther Dittmer*, ed. B. Gillingham and P. Merkeley, Musicological Studies 53 (The Institute of Medieval Music, Ottawa, 1990), 16–27.

exure,
occide:
non potero
quicquam Christo
preponere.
  V.   Quis nos separabit
        a caritate Christi
        in quacumque tribulatione'.

(The most steadfast girl replies to her persecutors: 'Torture, burn, and kill: I will not substitute anyone for Christ. Who will separate us from Christ's charity, in whatever suffering we are?')

The poetic layout suggested above (or some more economical version of it) seems mandated by the intonation of the chant, the rhyming syllables, sometimes by the number of syllables (as in *non potero/quicquam Christo*), and by the cadences and contours of the chant. The phrase *quicquam Christo*, for example, is a typical rhymed office phrase ascending from the final by way of a repeated note cadence rising from below to the reciting note. But it sets not a phrase of eight syllables, as in a later office, but one of four syllables.

   In other words, poetically and musically this office has a wealth of interesting and important material, illuminating the crucial period when composers and poets were starting to write office chants and texts not structured in an earlier way but with balanced phrases and in strict rhyme and metre.

Ninian, bishop in Withern, Scotland

—main office: AH 28. 31: /pr. 1510/   [NI71]

Osmund of Salisbury, bishop and confessor

   cd/tr. 1456/7
* main office: AH 13. 80: *circa* 1460 (1)   [OS41]
   Suscipe cum gaudio/Presulis Osmundi/Hic Osmundus
   Salisbury, Cathedral Library 152

Osmund was the last medieval English saint to be canonized. The Salisbury manuscript is the unique source of the chant, but unfortunately music has not been provided for the antiphons of first vespers. Modal order is strict except at MR4 and 5, where modes 3 and 7 appear. Noteworthy, too, is the transposition of MA2, mode 2, a fifth up and MA5, mode 5, a fourth up. I know of few similar examples. All psalm antiphons and the Magnificat antiphon for second vespers are in rhymed goliardic metre, 7pp6p. All the other items are in hexameters, mostly rhymed at the caesura, and MR3 and 6 include elegiac couplets. The reappearance of classical metres in such profusion is surely a sign of the Renaissance revival of classical studies.

These oddities, and the brief use of word-painting mentioned earlier, make the chant of this office interesting. I judge that the general use of rhymed phrases in the chant is somewhat unusual, and some aspects of the notation suggest an unskilled scribe. But, as Example 1 demonstrates, in responsory 4, at least, the co-ordination of text and chant is highly sophisticated.

Oswald, king of Northumbria

> not to be confused with Oswald, archbishop of York, whose offices are in the Worcester Antiphonal
>
> tr. 909; after his death, one of his arms was stolen by a monk of Peterborough, an event that may have resulted in the office described here, OS93

* main office: AH 13. 81: 13th C. (several)   [OS91]
> This seems to be the continental office, found in manuscripts mostly from southern Germany.

—one antiphon; AH 28 app.   [OS92]

* main office; manuscript: *circa* 1300 (1)   [OS93]
> Cambridge, Magdalene College F. 4. 10
> *O martyr et rex/Rex sacer Oswaldus/Rex Oswaldus*

This is an elaborate monastic office, with extra responsories for the octave. Most antiphons have rhymed lines of irregular length, although the more important antiphons, for canticle and Gospel texts, are regular. Unusual poetic schemes, such as that of *Sol oriens* (WE)—4 + 5pp6p × 4—are difficult to detect in manuscript form, especially since some syllables must be elided. Responsories, however, for most of which doxologies are provided, are mostly hexameters rhymed at the caesura. As with the office of Osmund, above, we can suspect that the presence of hexameters causes difficulties of adjustment between standard rhymed chant phrases and poetic lines.

Among those items set apart by their poetic schemes are VA2, MR4, MR11, MR12, and *Sol oriens* (WE). All of these are also in the continental office, OS91: because they differ in style, we might infer that they were borrowed from that office rather than the reverse. But the dating of the two offices must be established before conclusions of this kind can be safely drawn.

Oswin, king of Northumbria, martyr

> tr. 1065

* main office and the   [OT01]
* translation: manuscript: ?12th C. (1)   [OT02]

Oxford, Corpus Christi 134: the kalendar is before 1173, because Thomas of
Canterbury is not included.

Unfortunately, this unique source for the music of the monastic offices for
St Oswin is damaged, so that many items are missing or incomplete. The
printed breviary of St Albans (1530) contains only the texts. The book is
for the Benedictine priory of Tynemouth, a dependency of St Albans. It is
about the size of a postcard. This fact, and the comprehensive nature of its
contents, raise interesting questions about the destination of the book and
the purpose of the rhymed office that cannot be addressed in this context.
A full study of the manuscript needs to be made. Here it will be possible
only to give a preliminary description of the office. The whole document is
devoted to St Oswin, giving a list of relics, a *vita*, a Passion, sermons, and
miracles about the saint. An extensive rhymed office (not known to the
editors of AH) has material for the feast-day, the ferias of the octave, the
octave itself, and the translation. Prayers, dialogues, lessons, and other
readings are given in full. Many items are repeated from one day to
another, subsequent appearances consisting of only the incipits again.

From the incipits one can reconstruct a few short passages of the missing
sections. The main service begins in the middle of MV6. But from the
incipits given for the ferias within the octave we can undoubtedly identify
the preceding five responsories, and the beginning of the sixth and its
verse. After terce the rubric *Ad missam* precedes a lacuna up to nones. To
emphasize the elaborate nature of this office, prime, terce, nones (and
presumably the missing sext) have proper antiphons, rather than repeating
those of lauds, and hymns written out in full. For the ferias within the
octave, fourteen antiphons are provided, mostly in incipits, including the
famous *Ave rex gentis Anglorum* given complete with the usual tune.
Incipits of twelve responsories follow, with the incipits of their verses, and
a complete doxology for each one. All this material has the music. We can
infer that the items in incipits repeat those of matins of the feast itself. The
translation gives us a Magnificat antiphon, and the incipit of the matins
invitatory.

The poetry is extremely irregular, both as to the number of syllables in
each line (within each item as well as from item to item), and as to the
rhyme schemes used. The fourth antiphon of lauds, for example, is:

Quem mare terra polus   7a
laudat benedicit adorat   9b
Oswinum magne merito   8c
virtutis honorat.   6b

Yet there is no doubt that the rhymes and the structure are intentional.
Nearly all poetic lines end with a full point in the manuscript, and are

reinforced by the shape of the musical phrases. The latter, too, are also usually separated graphically, occasionally by incises running through the stave, but more often by clefs.

Although more evidence would be needed to establish firmly the exact contents of the main office as it appears in this manuscript (and some difficulties have not been satisfactorily resolved), it would seem that the chants are in modal order. A very brief assessment suggests that they are stylistically interesting and varied without being extravagantly modern in range or melodic characteristics. The stereotyped cadence rising to a repeated note occurs, even though the office is a relatively early example of the genre. The general style ranges from syllabic to elaborately melismatic, with a single long melisma in responsories. Responsory verses do not use the standard tones. At second vespers a single-stanza item, *Gens laudum*, is called a hymn, although its tune is extraordinarily un-hymnlike, rising a sixth, falling a seventh, and rising an octave within the first six syllables. At terce is the famous two-part voice-exchange hymn *Nunc sancte nobis*, and at prime the hymn text *Iam lucis orto*, also appearing in some manuscripts as a voice-exchange hymn, is given an interesting melody that does not, however, seem to have voice-exchange potential. I have not yet been able to compare the chants with those of the rest of the repertory. *Ave rex gentis*, of course, is known in several other offices: that antiphon and the two following ones in the ferial list, *O purpurea* and *Princeps et pater*, are borrowed from the office to Edmund, king and martyr (ED62), to which they were added by Abbot Warner: the fourth one added there by the abbot was not borrowed. A detailed comparison of the two offices may enable other chants for St Oswin to be identified.

Patrick, bishop and apostle of Ireland

> tr. with Columba and Brigid, 1185/6; Columba and Brigid also have independent offices
>
> * main office: manuscript: 15th C. (2)   [PΛ71–3]
>   AH 26 intro.: 13th/14th C. (several)
> Dublin, Trinity College 79 and 80 (B. 1. 4 and B. 1. 5)
> *Veneranda imminentis/Egregius Christi/Beatus Patricius*

Some antiphons and an invitatory are printed in the introduction to AH 26. The complete office can be reconstructed, with some overlap, from the two manuscripts cited. It is highly structured, but few items are really regular, even amongst the antiphons. Modal order is mostly maintained.

The text is quite repetitive, motives being repeated between antiphons and responsories more than is typical. The chants, too, often seem to be quite unsophisticated, with a great deal of recitation and much strictly syllabic setting. Dislocations between rhymed chant phrases and the rhymes of the text are common, suggesting that this office should be relegated to the borderline of the rhymed repertory.

—tr. office: AH 13. 82: 13th/14 C. (several)   [PA74]

There is no known noted source for the chants. Goliardic verse for the antiphons alternates with hexameters for the responsories. The opening item *Veneranda imminentis* continues differently from that of PA71–3.

Raphael, archangel

—main office: AH 13. 86: /pr. 1505/   [RA61]
  written by Edmund Lacy, bishop of Hereford, 1417–20
—the other office, AH 18. 82, has no obvious connections with England.

Richard, bishop of Chichester

  cd 1262, tr. 1276; see Richard, martyr, below, under Rhymed Suffrages
* main office: manuscript: 14th C. (1)   [RI22]
  Letare Jerusalem/Factus Aaron/Digno dato sterilis
  Rome, Biblioteca Alessandrina (Universitaria) 120[33]

This is a tediously regular office, using goliardic stanzas almost throughout. Only the Gospel antiphons and invitatory are different. Modal order, however, is quite broken in the responsories: 826 717 711. Although a chant such as MV7 has a large range, the general style is one of quite simple settings, some of which are very similar, as with the third antiphons, all in mode 3, of vespers, matins, and lauds. The melodies are shared with another office (see William of York).

Richard of Hampole, hermit mystic

  d. 1349, cult from 1380, tr. by 1393
—main office: AH 52. 390: /15th C./   [RI31]

Simon de Montfort, earl of Leicester

  d. 1265, never cd
—fragments: AH 13 intro. etc.: none/14th C./   [SI61]

The Franciscans composed an office to Simon, of which the three surviving hymns and two antiphons in Cambridge, University Library Kk. iv. 20 may be part.[34]

Swithin, bishop of Winchester

  tr. 971, 1093
—main office: AH 13. 91: /13th–14th C.   [SU41]

[33.] On this manuscript, see under Edmund Rich and n. 27 *supra*.
[34.] See P. M. Lefferts, 'Two English Motets on Simon de Montfort', *Early Music History* 1 (1981), 203–23.

Thomas Becket, archbishop and martyr of Canterbury

cd 1173; tr. 1220; jubilees in England every 50 years

Denis Stevens has described numerous polyphonic pieces as well as monophonic chants composed to the saint, and Husmann has dealt superficially with the topic.[35] Apart from the half-dozen pages in these articles, only one other study in the massive bibliography of Thomas deals with the offices.[36] The relationships between the six or seven complete offices now known is so complex that a separate monograph will be required: some of these offices are known only in continental manuscripts (e.g. AH 17. 67 is known only in Spanish sources). Here only the main and obviously English office and one other office, also perhaps English (both published in AH) can be discussed, with the translation offices, both of which seem to be English. Despite the presence of continental offices, the standard English office TH21 was widespread over almost the whole of Europe.

* main office: AH 13. 92: many   [TH21]
   Pastor cesus/Studens livor/Granum cadit

As noted by Richard Hunt,[37] this monastic office and its chants were composed by Abbot Benedict of Peterborough (d. 1193). Is the defective version in the monastic Antiphonal of Peterborough Abbey cited so often above (Cambridge, Magdalene College F. 4. 10) closer to the original? Only a full textual and musical analysis could answer this question. Other material in the earliest known source, London, British Library Add. 16964, is associated with the Belgian church of St Remacle, in Stavelot. Although clearly not the original version, the secular form of the office is better known, because Sarum books were more widely used than monastic books. In most English manuscripts, the office has been torn out, crossed or blackened through, as a result of the attempt to eradicate Thomas's influence in the time of Henry VIII. Fortunately, many sources with and without chant still survive in complete or readable form. Even though it is a secular book, the Welsh antiphonal in which the office of David is found (see above) has one of the most elaborate versions, using monastic items (although without the chant added) for the octave.

[35.] D. Stevens, 'Music in Honor of St Thomas of Canterbury', *Musical Quarterly* 56 (1970), 311–48; H. Husmann, 'Zur Überlieferung der Thomas-Offizien', *Organicae voces: Festschrift Joseph Smits van Waesberghe* (Amsterdam, 1963), 87–8.

[36.] Andrew Hughes, 'Chants in the Rhymed Office for St Thomas of Canterbury', *Early Music* 16 (1988), 185–201.

[37.] 'Notes on the *Distinctiones monasticae et morales*', *Liber Floridus: Mittellateinische Studien Paul Lehmann zum 65. Geburtstag*, ed. B. Bischoff and S. Brechter (St Ottilien, 1950), 355–62.

The texts are very regular, antiphons being in goliardic metre, 7pp6p. Antiphons for the monastic canticles and for the Magnificat, Benedictus, and invitatory, have lines of 4–6pp, usually with a single rhyme. Almost all of the responsories also adopt this scheme. The sole exception is *Ex summa rerum*, which is usually MR6. This responsory also occurs in the other main office to be described here, TH22, and in at least one other office perhaps connected with Spain. Being out of place here, we can perhaps infer that it was borrowed from elsewhere, rather than being copied from TH21. As for the modal arrangement, it varies to some extent from manuscript to manuscript, but we can be fairly certain that originally the modes were in order. As is frequently the case, the responsories are often out of sequence. The musical style of this office in almost all respects impresses me as a sophisticated, careful setting of the rhymed texts, in which musical and textual phrases are matched, and the artistic level of composition high.[38] That it was widely distributed and imitated is perhaps as much a reflection of its literary and musical qualities as of the fame of the saint to whom it is dedicated.

The chants were used, verbatim or with considerable variation, for later offices. Apart from forming the basis for most of the offices of David and Edmund Rich, they were used for one of the Thomas translation offices, and individually or in a complete office were the model for the offices of many continental saints.

* main office: AH 13. 93: 13th C. (several)   [TH22]
   Martyr Thoma/Sacrat Thomas/O Thoma martyr

This office is normally transmitted in manuscripts for use in European churches, for example, Cambrai, Nantes, Beauvais, Toledo, and Braga. Nevertheless, it is also in Paris Bibliothèque nationale lat. 12036, a curious manuscript that current research suggests may be for St Andrews, Scotland (see Brigid, above), which has marginal staves for the incipits and *differentiae*. The whole chants are in several other manuscripts.

Although the poetry begins quite regularly, with antiphons of 8-syllable lines rhymed aabb, from LA3 the texts degenerate into structured prose. The responsories are less regular: *Ex summa*, mentioned in the discussion of TH21 does not follow the 8-syllable scheme of the other responsories but is matched by MR5. MR7–9, too, are different in poetic form. As we have seen before, this kind of irregularity suggests that the items were borrowed from elsewhere. Modally, the responsories and lauds antiphons are disordered. Like the previous office, however, the chants seem well matched to the texts, and interestingly varied in style.

---

[38] See Hughes, 'Chants in the Rhymed Office for St Thomas of Canterbury'.

—tr. office: AH 13. 94: 13th C. (several) [TH26]
 Adest Thome/Volens deus/Summa cum letitie

The situation regarding the feast of the translation of Thomas Becket is both confusing and interesting. Many manuscripts merely give the translation as *sicut in alio festo*, sometimes with the proper prayer or lessons. In this case, the chant items appear at most in incipit. What remains of the office in Oxford, Bodleian Library Laud misc. 299 is the main office TH21 given in full with its chants, thus perhaps duplicating what appears with the main office, most of which is also missing in this book. Several manuscripts transmit proper texts for the translation, published in AH 13. 94 (TH26). Even when the manuscript is noted and gives the chants for the main office, the translation texts have no chants, a circumstance which raises the interesting question as to how they were performed. The poetic schemes for this proper office are mostly quite different from those of the main office, and nearly all of the responsories involve rhymed hexameters, a metre which does not appear in the main office. Even where the metres are the same, as with the Magnificat antiphons of second vespers (4–6pp), the text of the main office has only five and that of the translation six lines. Adapting the chants of the main office for the translation texts would therefore not be a negligible task to be done at sight, unless of course we grossly underestimate the musical capabilities of medieval choirs, or grossly overestimate the quality of the results. In fact, we can perhaps recover the chant for the (normal) antiphon of first vespers, *Adest Thome*, because it appears in the same position in the following translation office, which then continues with unique texts.

* tr. office: manuscript: 13th C. (1) [TH27]
 London, British Library Add. 28598
 Adest Thome/Absorbetur/Granum qui

This office is in the Ely noted breviary, London, British Library Add. 28598, only slightly damaged and all readable. It is obviously modelled on the main office TH21, since apart from the vespers antiphon just mentioned it uses the chants from that office and it recalls various textual motives.

LA1 *main office*	*translation*
Granum cadit copiam	Granumque in tempore
germinat frumenti	moritur brumali
alabaustrum frangitur	frumentum multiplicat
flagrat vis unguenti	surgens estivali

It is a secular office, but using some chants from the monastic rather than secular version of the main office. Making adaptation of the chant very easy, the metres are those of the main office, except for the antiphon of first vespers, the invitatory, and the fifth matins responsory: this item uses the chant but regularizes the text of *Ex summa*, the irregular sixth responsory of matins of the main office, already mentioned. In addition, since its chant also appears in the David office, closely modelled on Thomas's main office, we can infer that the eighth matins responsory of this translation uses the chant of the mode 4 responsory, missing from Thomas's main office.

Thomas of Hereford, bishop and doctor

> cd 1320
> * main office: AH 13. 95: 1, incomplete   [TH51]
> *In celesti gloria/Pater pius/Christo laus*
> Gloucester, Record Office fragment 14

Transcriptions of this fragmentary source have been published by Brian Trowell and Andrew Wathey.[39] Oxford, Bodleian Library E Mus. 2 transmits a single memorial antiphon with music, so that what survives of the office printed in AH 13 is the Magnificat antiphon of second vespers, three Magnificat antiphons for the octave, and two additional responsories (the second incomplete) not published as part of that office. It was perhaps composed by Robert of Gloucester, canon of Hereford Cathedral, 1279–1322.

What remains appears very regular. The Magnificat antiphon *Sicut fragrant* has a most unusual repetition of the chant phrases thus: abab′cdc′e, followed by an alleluia.

Trinity

> after 1279
> * main office: AH 5. 1: several   [XT31]
> *Sedenti super solium/Confirmat hoc mysterium/Quam clara*

This office is based on the chants of the office to St Francis, with a monastic version, by John Peckham, Franciscan archbishop of Canterbury from 1279.[40] I know of no Franciscan books that can be attributed to England, and certainly none with chant. From Ireland a Franciscan breviary contains the office, but a similar antiphonal is incomplete. Continental manuscripts are common. Since Peckham's contribution seems to have been limited to the texts, the interest of this office as a contribution to British composition is minimal.

[39.] 'John Benet's "*Lux fulget ex Anglia—O pater pietatis—Salve Thoma*" ', *St Thomas Cantilupe, Bishop of Hereford: Essays in his Honour*, ed. M. Jancey (Hereford, 1982), 159–80, with photographs and reference to polyphonic pieces which use texts votive to Thomas Cantilupe.

[40.] The office is described by P. Wagner, 'Zur mittelalterlichen Offiziumskomposition', *Kirchenmusikalisches Jahrbuch* 21 (1908), 13–32.

Wereburga, abbess of Ely, virgin

tr. *circa* 875
—two antiphons and fifteen poems which perhaps derive from antiphons and responsories of a true office: AH 28. 98: /12th C./ [WE71]

William, archbishop of York, confessor

cd 1227, tr. 1284
* main office: AH 13. 99: 14th C. (several) [GU61]
In Guillelmi laudibus/Voluntate trutina/Claudi recti
transc. from Oxford, Bodleian Library Gough lit. 1, a noted breviary of York

With the exception of the Magnificat and Benedictus antiphons (8- or 10-syllable lines) and the invitatory (10pp), all poems are in regular goliardic metre, 7pp6p. Modal order in the antiphons is strict except for MA9, in mode 7: the responsories have this order—826 717 711. The whole office seems extremely conventional, although on several occasions the phrases of text and chant seem dislocated. As David Hiley has noticed, the music for this office is the same as that for Richard of Chichester.

—one antiphon: AH 28 app. [GU62]

Wulstan, Benedictine bishop of Worcester

tr. 1198 and more solemnly in 1218
* main office: manuscript: 13th C. (1) [WU61]
Ave pater Wulstane/Celebremus diem istud/Benedictus sit
Worcester Cathedral Chapter Library F. 160

The matins antiphons and the Magnificat of second vespers are quite regular schemes, usually of 8pp7p, but those of lauds, the other Gospel antiphons, and the responsories range from structured to rhymed prose. But responsory 11, at least, proves to be in regular poetic form (see Example 2). The invitatory and one or two of the responsory verses are in rhymed hexameters. As with so many offices in which the poetic schemes are thus varied and semi-structured, the co-ordination between phrases of rhymed chant and text seems muddled, cadences appearing in incorrect places, and obvious opening musical gestures occurring in mid-phrase. Antiphons are in strict modal order: responsories are arranged thus—1236 1536 1571— omitting modes 4 and 8.

Blessed Virgin Mary

Visitation, associated with the Franciscans and extended to the universal church in 1389
  * main office: manuscript: early 15th C. (1)   [YV50]
Eterni patris/Elisabeth ut virgini/Scandit montes
Oxford, Bodleian Library Laud misc. 299

This office is said to be by John Horneby.[41] It is closely related, at least textually, to monastic offices for the Visitation in manuscripts mostly associated with the north of Italy (AH 24. 32). Poetically, goliardic stanzas characterize most items, except in the last nocturn, which thus seems to stand out: there the antiphons and responsory 9 use the sequence stanza, 8pp7p, and the other two responsories use 10-syllable lines divided 4 + 6. Since modal order is not consistently followed in the responsories, and 2, 3, and 6 have doxologies, it is apparent that some shuffling or borrowing has taken place. Musically, the chants are quite simple, often one note to a syllable, and even the responsories are moderate in style, lacking long melismas. The chants, at least the antiphons, are instantly recognizable as standard melodies.

Although it is not possible, at the moment, to identify all the relationships, VA1 obviously borrows the chant of MA1 of the office for St Francis. Despite this immediate assertion of Franciscan connections, none of the later chants seems similar enough in both melodic and notational matters for the remainder of the office for St Francis to be cited as a model elsewhere. On the other hand, a number of chants are borrowed from the Thomas Becket office, usually with very little variation, as follows:

VA2 ←MA2 (*Monachus*)
MA3←MA3 (*Cultor agri*)
MA4←MA4 (*Nec in agnos*)
MA5←MA5 (*Flagrat virtus*)
MA9←MA9 (*Hosti pandit*)
MR7←MR5 (*Jacet granum*).

The third phrase of LA1 is identical in both pitches and ligatures to that of VA1 of the Thomas office, but lacking other evidence one might dismiss this relationship as a coincidence.

[41.] K. Schlager, 'Reimoffizien', *Geschichte der katholischen Kirchenmusik* 1, ed. K. G. Fellerer (Kassel, 1972), 296.

The following are saints for whom only a rhymed suffrage exists, without chant, and without substantial evidence that the items derive from a lost office: most are in Cologne, Historisches Archiv 28, dating from *circa* 1480. This manuscript, which contains no chant, is edited in the appendix to AH 28. In most cases, one or two antiphons and an occasional responsory are supplied. Some saints for whom there are complete offices, listed in the main catalogue, also have suffrages in this manuscript.

Anselm, archbishop of Canterbury: cd ?1163 or on tr. 1174	[AN91]
Duchat (or Duthac), bishop	[DU21]
Dunstan, archbishop of Canterbury: *vitae* from the 11th C.	[DU61]
Edward, king and confessor: 1138 (*vita* by Osbert de Clare of Westminster); cd 1161, tr. 1163, 1269	[ED81]
Edward, king and martyr, 11th C: cult widespread	[ED91]
Erkenwald, bishop of London, confessor: tr. 1148, 1326	[ER31]
Ethelbert, king of Kent, confessor (not Ethelbert of England)	[AT51]
Etheldreda, abbess of Ely: tr. 1379/80 to Ely	[ET31]
Hugh, bishop of Lincoln, confessor: tr. 1280: several items: AH 28 app., and 43. 175	
(This is probably not part of a complete office, since Hugo was a Carthusian, and the Carthusians did not use rhymed offices.)	[HU51]
John of Beverley, archbishop of York, confessor: after 1415 his feast was kept throughout England	[IO91]
Mildred, abbess of Minster-in-Thanet, virgin: tr. 1035	[MI41]
Osith, virgin martyr	[OS31]
Richard, martyr (unknown) (The manuscript has *Richardi episcopi et martyr in Anglia* with no feast date, and after the antiphon is a collect which also includes the word *martyr*. The antiphon text itself, however, is used for the Benedictus at lauds in the office of Richard of Chichester, who was not a martyr (see above).)	[RI41]
Thomas of Lancaster, martyr	[TH71–2]

Chronology

As with the Viking invasions of northern France somewhat earlier, the Norman invasion of England in 1066 brought about considerable changes in English ecclesiastical life, especially in the monasteries. The question of whether unknown saints should be revered or not led to a spate of research and hagiography that helped to preserve the tradition of older saints. In the process, many relics of English saints were disturbed and no doubt, as in France, invented (in both ecclesiastical and everyday senses of the word) and translated. Both liturgical celebrations would probably have occasioned new liturgical texts. We might expect many offices to originate in the late eleventh and early twelfth century, but the extant manuscripts do not allow us to confirm this early date.

Abstracting information from what is given above, the following list sets out offices for which a date of composition is known or can be suggested. A question mark accompanies those for which there is no direct evidence. Perhaps when our analytical senses are sharper for this kind of music it will become possible to suggest more accurate dates. The case of the office of St David is particularly intriguing, since several dates can be suggested. If stylistic evidence cannot suffice to discriminate between them, it may be possible to arrive at the correct one through textual analysis of the chants of the office of Thomas of Canterbury: a number of manuscripts for that office can be dated, and through analysis of errors and variants a stemma might emerge. The chant in David's office may have been copied from or be closely related to an extant version of the Thomas office.

* *circa* 935: main office for Cuthbert, bishop of Lindisfarne, tr. 999.
—971: ? office for tr. of Swithin, bishop of Winchester
* 1065: ? offices for invention and tr. of Oswin, king of Northumbria
—1093: ? office for tr. of Swithin, bishop of Winchester
* by the 11th C.: office for Birinus, bishop of Dorchester; possibly pre-Norman, and eliminated after 1066 (Hartzell)
* pre-Norman (Hartzell) or late 11th C., and earlier than *circa* 1125: main office and additions, and complete vigil office for Edmund, king and martyr, tr. 1095
* 1129: ? office for tr. of Alban, martyr
—1136: ? office for tr. of Magnus, count of Orkney
—1148: ? office for tr. Cedda (Chad), bishop of Lichfield
* probably before 1173: ? offices for the invention and tr. of Oswin, king of Northumbria
* 1173–93: main office for Thomas Becket, cd 1173
* 1185/6: ? office for tr. of Brigid, Columba, and Patrick
—after 1188: ? office for Ebba, abbess of Coldingham
* 1198: ? office for tr. of Wulstan, bishop of Worcester
* *circa* 1200: ? office for David of Wales (? by Gerald of Wales)
—1202: ? office for Gilbert of Sempringham
* before 1217: four offices for the Blessed Virgin Mary
* 1218: ? office for tr. of Wulstan, bishop of Worcester
* 1220: ? tr. offices for Thomas Becket
* 1227: ? office for William, archbishop of York

—1240: ? office for tr. Augustine, archbishop of Canterbury
* 1246: ? two offices for canonization of Edmund Rich of Canterbury
* 1262: ? office for Richard, bishop of Chichester
—1265: ? office for Simon de Montfort, earl of Leicester, never cd
* 1275: ? office for tr. of David
* 1276: ? office for tr. of Richard, bishop of Chichester
* after 1279: office for Trinity Sunday
* 1284: ? office for tr. of William, archbishop of York
—*circa* 1287–1320: ? office for Finian, abbot of Clonard (Co. Meath)
* 1288: see 1456/7
* 1320–2: ? office for Thomas of Hereford
* after 1335/6: ? office for Columba of Iona
* *circa* 1382: ? office for Anna, mother of the BVM, whose cult was made
 obligatory in England
—after 1380: ? office for Richard of Hampole, d. 1349; tr. by 1393
* after 1389: office for the Visitation of the BVM
* 1398: ? office for David of Wales, who enters Sarum Kalendar
* 1401, 1404: ? office for John, prior of Bridlington, cd. 1401, tr. 1404
* 1415: ? office; David made obligatory in Sarum Kalendar
—1417–20: office for Raphael, archangel
* 1456/7: ? office for Osmund of Salisbury (but the canonization process
 was begun in 1288)

Conclusion

To replace texts of a generally prose nature, the sequence metre, 8pp7p, and especially the goliardic stanza, 7pp6p, with longer stanzas or longer lines of 4 + 6 syllables for important antiphons, emerge as predominant by the thirteenth century. Hexameters survive in Irish offices to some extent, and re-emerge in the incipient Renaissance in the Osmund office. Offices for Scottish and Irish saints are more likely to be extremely regular, and often the chants of their antiphons collapse into little more than entirely syllabic hymn melodies.

A more thorough examination would surely reveal many more relationships between offices: with some difficulty, this research could be done for the texts by means of tools already available. Relationships between the chants may be traced more systematically by means of tools in preparation. Even now, however, simple observation of poetic schemes, and perhaps dislocations of the modal order, can suggest the presence of borrowings. The notational habits of Sarum musical scribes and some characteristics of transmission in Sarum manuscripts have now been carefully described by

Diane Droste.[42] In the course of preparing this study I observed, unsystematically, similarities of notation in the manuscripts of offices for York, Ireland, and Ely, features of scribal musical practice that are not those of Sarum. By following this kind of hint, and by detailed comparisons of chants and text, we should be able more accurately to date and to place manuscripts of English chant.

A cursory review of the catalogue above will reveal the prominence of East Anglia and the south-eastern region of England. St Albans, Ranworth and Norwich, Peterborough, Lincoln, and Bury St Edmunds are the home of offices, the repository for relics, or the places where important surviving manuscripts were used. Winchester, Worcester, Hereford, and York are also important. Despite some prominent exceptions, secular offices and sources are in the majority. We can only guess at the treasure of monastic manuscripts, each with its own local and favoured saints, destroyed in the dissolution of the monasteries.[43]

[42.] 'The Musical Notation and Transmission of the Music of the Sarum Rite', Ph.D. diss. (University of Toronto, 1983).

[43.] My searches for rhymed offices, especially in European countries, have been mostly confined to the thousands of complete antiphonals and breviaries that survive. Consequently, I know less of offices in fragments, in *libelli*, or on flyleaves, or in other kinds of sources such as *vitae* or passionals. In order to make more complete my forthcoming catalogue of all rhymed offices, I am always anxious to receive basic information (e.g. incipits, sources, the presence of music, and secondary sources) about offices that are not in AH.

10

Relations between Liturgical and Vernacular Music in Medieval England

JOHN CALDWELL
(University of Oxford)

One of the effects of the Reformation in England (and doubtless elsewhere) was to create a mythology about the pre-Reformation liturgy according to which it was by virtue of its language and its musical adornment incomprehensible to and remote from ordinary people. This of course was far from being the case: the liturgy was not always clothed in elaborate music, or indeed in any music, and some of it, addressed primarily to the laity, had traditionally been in the vernacular: the dictation of the marriage vows, the Great Cursing, the Sunday bidding prayer, and above all the homily or sermon.[1] In any case, a good deal of trouble was expended in bringing home the Christian message through visual means: painted glass and walls, carved stone and wood, ceremony and drama. Translated texts of the bible and parts of the liturgy were available at certain periods and for certain purposes.[2]

A good deal of the surviving vernacular music of medieval England is connected in some way with the liturgy. Here a problem of definition arises, for unless the word is restricted to the technical sense still current in the East, that is, to mean the eucharist or mass, it is difficult to say at what point sacred music ceases to be liturgical. The most convenient definition for general purposes would be by means of some such phrase as 'formalized

[1] See e.g. the texts printed in the *Manuale et Processionale ad usum insignis ecclesiae Eboracensis*, ed. W. G. Henderson (Durham, etc., 1875), 119–22, 123–7 (from the York Manual), 86*–94* (from the Salisbury Manual), etc.

[2] See the references to sequences in n. 15 below; an English antiphon in honour of St Thomas of Canterbury (*English Lyrics of the XIIIth Century*, ed. C. Brown (Oxford, 1932) no. 42); the English paraphrases of hymns and other forms by J. Ryman (discussed in J. Stevens, *Music and Poetry in the Early Tudor Court* (London, 1961), 48–51); and, though not intended for liturgical use, the various 16th-C. Primers.

communal worship'. This in itself contains ambiguities, but it rules out private and domestic prayer while retaining, for example, monastic offices and most religious processions.

The very attempt to define the word 'liturgy' leads inescapably to the conclusion that nothing devised for a formal act of worship could properly be described as non-liturgical. This applies both to 'services', however defined (such things as independently delivered sermons and mystery cycles lie perhaps on the fringes of the topic), and to items within them such as tropes, conductus, or dramatic ceremonies. These latter are often described as 'paraliturgical', or as 'not part of the official liturgy'—but the distinction has little meaning for the middle ages. The Tridentine reforms created such a distinction, and it has been extrapolated back into the middle ages, where it is irrelevant. Medieval service-books may describe or prescribe, but they are rarely couched in such a way as to prohibit accretion. Such accretions may be highly localized and temporary, but their status, in the books in which they are recorded, is exactly that of the main liturgical stock.

These considerations should constantly be borne in mind by the historian of liturgical music. One of the phenomena most frequently met with, however, is that of music to sacred words found in sources in which no liturgical context is either stated or implied. This can apply even to whole genres: the *versus* and conductus of Saint-Martial and Notre-Dame, the motet, the carol, and so on. The fact that within such genres the texts are not always sacred only makes the problem more complex. Perhaps the genres are wrongly defined, and perhaps the notion of a single specific function for individual pieces of this type is misplaced. Some kinds of sacred music might be equally at home in church, in hall, or in chamber. But the quest for liturgical function must be pursued as far as it can be taken; and even if the answers are often speculative, the attempt to provide them can itself lead to new insights.

The Selden, Egerton, and Ritson manuscripts provide interesting examples of the interaction between sacred music with well-defined and less well-defined functions.[3] They are not strictly comparable, for while the Selden and Egerton manuscripts are uniform in repertory and appearance, the Ritson manuscript is the work of several contributors over many years. Each is an important source of carols in addition to other sacred music.

[3] Oxford, Bodleian Library Arch. Selden B 26; London British Library Egerton 3307; ibid. Add. 5665. The first two are from the first half or the middle of the 15th C.; the third is slightly later, with additions from the early 16th C. The Selden MS was published in facsimile and transcription in *Early Bodleian Music*, i–ii (Oxford, 1901), and Egerton 3307 by G. S. McPeek (London, 1963). There are better editions of all the carols by J. Stevens in *Medieval Carols*, Musica Britannica 4 (2nd edn., London, 1970) and of the Selden antiphons by Andrew Hughes in *Fifteenth-Century Liturgical Music* i, Early English Church Music 8 (London, 1968).

The carol is bound to be at the centre of any investigation of the links between vernacular polyphony and the liturgy. The first serious study of the English medieval carol was as a literary genre in the English language,[4] but it was subsequently realized that many comparable Latin pieces existed and that the polyphonic settings with which many of them were provided were as characteristic as the literary form.[5] Indeed, the verbal repetitions which are a defining factor are only explicable in the context of a musical setting, and comparative study leads to the conclusion that the carol was originally always sung, though not to begin with in polyphony.

The link between the carol (Latin or vernacular) and the conductus has long been recognized;[6] but with the conductus, as with the carol, the liturgical function (if any) is not always clear. A few conductus are freely composed tropes of the Benedicamus domino, as are some carols; but with a few exceptions the remainder are liturgically ill defined. The term conductus itself is of disputed validity after 1300, and a large repertory best defined by the very general term 'cantilena' came into being.[7] The polyphonic carol, whether English or Latin, is an offshoot of this, retaining its functional ambiguities and its stylistic approachability.

The definition of the carol and the appreciation of its formal characteristics were such a landmark of scholarship that the temptation nowadays is to assume that that work is done. But it is possible to exaggerate the significance of the form of the carol and to neglect its intrinsic qualities. Its refrain structure is paralleled in other forms and conversely there are stylistic analogies with non-refrain pieces. The indication of the feast in the Ritson carols (e.g. 'De nativitate') is couched in exactly the formula found

---

[4.] *The Early English Carols*, ed. R. L. Greene (Oxford, 1935; 2nd edn., 1977), with full descriptions of all the MSS. The continental prototype, a dance-song whose precise structure may have varied considerably, is nowadays usually spelt *carole*; for a recent discussion see C. Page, *The Owl and the Nightingale* (Cambridge, 1989), esp. 110–33.

[5.] M. F. Bukofzer, 'Holy-Week Music and Carols at Meaux Abbey', *Studies in Medieval and Renaissance Music* (New York, 1950), 113–75; J. Stevens, *Medieval Carols*. Bukofzer's attribution of the Egerton MS to Meaux is no longer generally accepted, however.

[6.] F. Ll. Harrison, *Music in Medieval Britain* (London, 1958), 416–21. A processional function for the carol, first put forward by M. Sahlin, *Étude sur la carole médiévale* (Uppsala, 1940), should certainly not be ruled out, however. The carol 'Pray for us that we saved be' has been connected with the procession for first vespers of St Stephen on the strength of the line 'circumfultus undique' in the 1st stanza, though as the line occurs primarily in the hymn from which the processional respond is taken no certain conclusions can be drawn. See J. Stevens, 'Carol', in *New Grove Dictionary*, where many of the points raised in the present article are addressed.

[7.] E. Sanders, 'Cantilena and Discant in 14th-century England', *Musica Disciplina* 19 (1965), 7–52. J. Stevens, *Words and Music in the Middle Ages* (Cambridge, 1986), 50–1, has argued for *cantio*. One important context for such later pieces would be the post-compline antiphon ceremony, where (in England at least) a wide variety of texts was admitted.

in certain motet manuscripts.[8] There is thus a range of cross-references from which it emerges that the carol is in exactly the same ambivalent relation to the liturgy as are the motet and the cantilena.

The Selden manuscript includes, besides the carols, a number of Latin pieces of which some, but not all, could properly be described as 'antiphons', and some further settings of English texts of which some are sacred and some not. The carols themselves, of course, fall linguistically into both camps. Those that are in Latin are analogous to the unversified antiphons and other cantilenas, while those in English (with or without lines of Latin interspersed) are analogous to other sacred works with English text. It is with one of these, 'Glad and blithe mote ʒe be', that this essay is principally concerned.

Glad and blithe is a two-part paraphrase, both verbal and musical, of the well-known Nativity sequence *Letabundus exultet fidelis chorus alleluya Regem regum* (so full a title is required to distinguish it from all other poems beginning similarly).[9] The metre of the Latin original is not retained, but the final line of each simple versicle is quoted in the first five pairs:

Letabundus	Glad and blithe mote ʒe be;
exultet fidelis chorus,	alle that euer y here nowe se;
alleluya.	Alleluya.
Regem regum	Kynge of kyngys lorde of alle;
intacte profudit thorus,	borne he is in oxe stalle;
res miranda.	Res miranda.

This pattern is maintained in both versions until the final versicle, in which the final Latin phrases are dropped from the paraphrase:

Infelix propera,	Vnhappy iewe come þu nere;
crede uel uetera;	Byleue ellys thyne eldere;
cur dampnaberis,	Why wold þu wrecche
gens misera?	ydampned be.
Quem docet litera	Whomme techethe þe letter
uatum considera:	Byholde the childe þe better;
ipsum genuit	Hym bere a maide
puerpera.	moder marye.

Neither the Latin nor the English texts are free of problems, and in particular the translator was hard put to it to make good sense of a delphic original that may well have been corrupt in the version before him. The

---

[8] e.g. Oxford, Bodleian Library New College 362, and London, British Library Add. 24198, both from the first half of the 14th C.

[9] Selden B 26, fols. 19v–20r. Apart from the transcription in *Early Bodleian Music*, II, a performing edition by C. K. Scott was published in the Fayrfax Series (London, 1949). There is a facsimile, with some discussion and both Latin and English texts, in W. H. Frere, *Bibliotheca Musico-Liturgica*, I (Nashdom, 1901), plates 11, 12.

last double versicle apparently means something like the following: 'Hasten, unhappy [people], believe rather the ancient [texts]; why will you be damned, O wretched people? Consider him whom the word of the prophets foretells; he himself was brought forth in childbirth.' But the translator's copy evidently had 'natum' rather than 'uatum', a reading that is on the whole less plausible. In line 5 of the first extract, on the other hand, he must have had the correct 'thorus' rather than the corrupt 'chorus' of some sources, though considerations of versification prevented a literal translation (the intended meaning is 'a childbed brought forth the King of kings without blemish'—the 'thorus' could hardly be the manger in which He was subsequently laid).

Interested readers may draw their own conclusions from the transcriptions of the Latin sequence and the English paraphrase given at the end of this article. The musical paraphrase, however, deserves further comment. The Latin sequence has recently been published in a version that raises no immediate questions,[10] but in some sources at least not all is straightforward. A fully critical edition of this widespread composition would be a daunting task, since the melody is not only found in innumerable sources with its original text but was also used for a number of other texts, some of limited currency, others widely used.[11] In the fourteenth-century 'Dublin Troper' (Cambridge, University Library Add. 710), for example, the melody occurs three times: once in a position that implies its use at the second mass on Christmas Day, again for the feast of the Annunciation (and as a textual incipit only for feria iv in the Octave of the Assumption), and finally with the text *Letabundus decantet* for St Patrick.[12]

The second and third versions of the melody agree with the usual reading, with only minor variants, in that the fifth double versicle rises to the note c' and requires a g clef. In the first version, however, though a g clef had been originally written, this has been deleted and a flat-sign substituted with the effect of transposing the entire double versicle down a third. One could hardly accept this as a legitimate reading, but it is of interest in that it relates to an oddity in the English paraphrase.

Comparison between the plainchant and the paraphrase reveals that the latter transposes the chant down not a third but a fifth at this point. This transposition is maintained for two lines only, however, after which the 'correct' pitch is resumed. The same procedure automatically occurs in the

[10.] Stevens, *Words and Music*, 91–7. Stevens, however, accepts the reading 'natum' in 6b, although 'uatum' would connect with 'uatibus' in 5b.

[11.] A recent discussion of the *Letabundus* sequence, with a survey of its sources, may be found in W. Arlt, 'Sequence and "Neues Lied"', in *Atti del Convegno Internazionale sulla Sequenza Milano 7–8 Aprile 1984*, ed. A. Ziino (Rome, 1992).

[12.] Cambridge, University Library Add. 710, fols. 42v–43r, 55r–v, 101v–102r; facs., *Le Tropaire-Prosaire de Dublin*, ed. R.-J. Hesbert (Rouen, 1966).

second versicle of the pair, since the music for these is written out only once. The arranger may have had before him a version in which the *c* clef was not replaced by the necessary *g* clef until two lines too late; and it may have been one in which the words of the individual versicles in a pair were laid out beneath each other as in the polyphonic setting (otherwise we should have to assume that the copyist made the same mistake twice—at all events this layout would seem to have occurred when the corruption was first transmitted).[13]

The transcription in the Appendix of the melody as first given in the Dublin Troper indicates the precise incidence of clefs and key-signatures, both original and substituted, from which it can be seen that the copyist (or a later scribe) for some unknown reason deliberately changed the authentic text. Possibly the change of tessitura was found impracticable; but the effect was to produce highly eccentric cadences at 'ceca' and 'predicta'. The originator of the version followed by the polyphonic paraphraser may have had a similar intention, more artistically satisfactory in spite of the leap of a seventh between lines two and three (mitigated in the polyphony by paraphrase).[14] The following table compares the cadential notes of the first Dublin version, the authentic text, and the polyphonic paraphrase in the verse beginning 'Ysayas cecinit'.

Cambridge 710		Selden B26
fol. 43r	fols. 55v, 102r	
e	*g*	*c*
c	*e*	*a*
c	*e*	*e*
a	*c*	*c*

The polyphonic composition is not without its own problems, chiefly of rhythmic interpretation. The music of the sections in major prolation cannot be brought into a completely regular metrical scheme and, this being so, the question of *alteratio* is not easily solved. In the transcription below some alternative readings are suggested for the doubtful passages; and some emendation seems inevitable.

Glad and blithe is not in itself a composition of great significance, but it illustrates the close links that existed between popular plainchant and vernacular interpretations. These had existed at least since the thirteenth century, from when there are monophonic paraphrases of *Stabat iuxta*

[13.] The same is true of the corruption in Cambridge 710, unless indeed this first arose in Cambridge 710 itself as a device to avoid the high notes.

[14.] The possibility that the paraphraser himself altered the melody can probably be discounted, given the generally schematic approach to paraphrase in this period.

Christi crucem as well as the polyphonic *Jesu cristes milde moder*.[15] We
should not assume that their use in the liturgy would have been unthinkable, either in the thirteenth century or later. As for *Letabundus*, its
influence spread beyond the sphere of the literal paraphrase, even within
the Selden manuscript, for the words of the carol *Now wel may we merthis
make* are clearly based on it and even its music, subject to the constraints of
carol form, is not unaffected.[16]

The implications of these vernacular links cannot be fully pursued here,
but two later instances may be mentioned. The first is the refrain-setting of
the Te Deum laudamus by Thomas Packe in the Ritson manuscript.[17] The
refrain consists of a plainchant intonation followed by a five-part setting of
the second half of the first verse, the latter being based on the faburden of
the chant. The 'verses' are set to a curious mixture of Latin and English, at
first in three parts, then in monophony, and finally without music at all
(though there is a polyphonic alternative given for the monophonic
passages, and either version could be adapted to the final stanzas without
undue difficulty). The conception looks over-ambitious, and its literary
style is of quite startling eccentricity, but it doubtless illustrates an attempt
to bring home the text to provincial people (the manuscript has Devonian
associations)[18] in a vivid way. Again, one wonders whether such a
concoction could have been used in the normal liturgical position of the Te
Deum, perhaps on some great feast and after a liturgical play. It is
analogous in some ways to the same composer's setting of the Nunc
dimittis with the antiphon *Lumen ad revelationem gentium* for Candlemas.[19]
Here the setting is in Latin throughout and the refrain-structure is
intrinsic to the liturgy, so that there is no conflict between the conception

[15.] The paraphrases are *Stand wel moder vnder rode* (Cambridge, St John's College E 8,
fol. 106v, and London, British Library Royal 12 E. i, fols. 193r–194v; the text, which is not
a translation of *Stabat iuxta Christi crucem* but an independent poem in dialogue form set to
the same melody, in C. Brown, *English Lyrics*, no. 49 and pp. 203–4); and . . . *stod ho þere neh*
(Oxford, Bodleian Library Tanner 169, p. 175; text in Brown, no. 4). *Jesu cristes milde
moder*, from London, British Library Arundel 248, fols. 154v–155r, is a textual but not a
musical paraphrase of *Stabat iuxta Christi crucem*: E. Sanders (ed.), *English Music of the
Thirteenth and Early Fourteenth Centuries*, Polyphonic Music of the Fourteenth Century 14
(Monaco, 1979), no. 1.

[16.] Selden B 26, fol. 10r; Stevens, *Medieval Carols*, no. 20. The later carol no. 105, from
London 5665, fols. 36v–37r, though textually similar, is more distinct musically from
Letabundus.

[17.] London 5665, fols. 95v–105v. I hope to publish a full study and transcription of this
strange work in due course.

[18.] Greene, *Early English Carols*, 316. On the other hand, the composer Sir William
Hawte, *miles*, who is also represented in the manuscript, has music in a source connected
with the diocese of Canterbury (Cambridge, Magdalene College Pepys 1236: see *Cambridge
Musical Manuscripts*, ed. I. Fenlon (Cambridge, 1982), 111–14); so the West Country
connections of Packe himself are far from certain.

[19.] London 5665, fols. 62v–64r.

and the liturgical requirement; but the link between an intrinsically 'popular' ceremony and the 'popularization' of an essentially monastic or clerical one cannot be overlooked.

Our final example brings us very close to the Reformation itself. Thomas Cranmer's English Litany, published in 1544, has often been looked on as an isolated service, imbued with the spirit of reform. Certainly it is highly reformist and anti-papal, but it can only be properly understood as being part of an essentially Latin rite, the Salisbury procession and mass 'in time of need'.[20] The Litany is by no means the only processional text in that rite (though it is certainly of central importance), and Cranmer's phrase 'to be said or song in the tyme of the said processyons' clearly indicates its contributory role. He had also translated the festal processions for the mass, which he planned to set to music 'as nere as may be, for every sillable, a note';[21] but these have not survived, and his Litany of 1544 became the basis of the only official processional text the Anglican church has ever had.

Historians of English church music have been right, of course, to see Cranmer's Litany in the context of later developments; but at the same time his initiative can be interpreted as belonging to an existing tradition of vernacular aids within the liturgy, analogous perhaps to the reading of the biblical lessons in English at the daily office.[22] If with hindsight it can be seen to have immediately preceded the invention of a wholly vernacular liturgy, it was also a response to a long-felt concern that had been addressed in a number of ways long before the advent of continental Protestantism in the sixteenth century.

The actual survivals of sacred vernacular texts in musical settings are few in number except for the carols themselves. Here, however, is an extensive field for future research. Progress will best be made if a wide view of liturgy is kept in mind and if the analogies with the conductus, motet, and cantilena are taken fully into account. Of these, it is the cantilena or *cantio* that provides the closest connection, simply because it is a term that satisfactorily describes so much of the music cultivated in the fourteenth and fifteenth centuries. Scholars have indeed applied it to the Latin 'carol';

[20.] See the Processional of 1502, published in facsimile by the Boethius Press (Clarabricken, 1980), fols. 162r–165r. The Litany was intended to be sung on the return journey from the church in which the mass had been celebrated. Cranmer's version was published in facs. by J. E. Hunt, *Cranmer's First Litany* (London, 1939). An earlier translation, without music, had appeared in Marshall's Primer (1535).

[21.] For the full text of Cranmer's letter of 7 Oct. 1544 to Henry VIII see R. A. Leaver (ed.), *The booke of Common praier noted* (facs., Oxford, 1980), 77–9. The music of *Salve festa dies* he regarded as 'sobre and distincte enoughe'.

[22.] As ordered by a Royal Injunction of 1543. See P. Le Huray, *Music and the Reformation in England 1549–1660* (London, 1967), 1–30, for a comprehensive review of the early Reformation experiments with the use of the vernacular in the liturgy.

but it is time to recognize that the linguistic distinction does not justify the terminological one, and that all carols belong within the framework of the broader concept of the cantilena. It will then be seen that the question of their function has to be looked at from the same angle as that of any cantilena, whether the subject-matter is sacred or secular, the music monophonic or polyphonic, and the language Latin or English.

APPENDIX

LETABUNDUS

A void note signifies a liquescent: but the pitch of the liquescent element is conjectural. Not every detail of the version on fols. 55r–v is cited in the notes, but all the more important differences are recorded. The version on fols. 101v–102r (*Letabundus decantet*) is cited only to clarify one point: in the main it agrees with that of fols. 55r–v. Word-division is editorial; italics signify expansion of contractions.

1. Liquescent added later; liquescent present on fol. 55r.
2. fols. 42v, 55r: chorus *sic*.
3. fol. 55r *c d* for *e d c d*.
4. fol. 55r *g* (no liquescent).
5. *sic*.: fol. 55r *rutilans*.
6. fol. 55v: *a' g f* for *a' f*.
7. fol. 55v: *g* (no liquescent).
8. fol. 55v: *c*.
9. fol. 55v: *altissimi comparari*.
10. fol. 55v: *d d c* for *e e (d) d*.
11. fol. 55v: clef G3: 3rd note *sic*, but *b'* on fol. 102r (*Letabundus decantet*). fol. 43r: clef G3, erased.
12. Clef G3 erased; flat in first space substituted.
13. Clef C2.
14. Clef G3.
15. Clef G3, erased; no flat (but retained in transcr.).
16. Flat in 2nd space (both sources).
17. Flat in 2nd space reiterated.
18. Flat in 1st space to end.
19. Flat reiterated.
20. Flat in lowest space.

Example 1. Cambridge, University Library Add. 710, fol. 42v

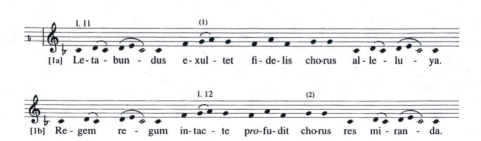

[1a] Le - ta - bun - dus   e - xul - tet   fi - de - lis   cho-rus   al - le - lu - ya.

[1b] Re - gem   re - gum   in-tac - te   *pro*-fu-dit   cho-rus   res   mi - ran - da.

Example 1—*cont*.

[2a] An - ge - lus con - si - li - i na-*tus* est de uir-gi - ne sol de stel - la.

[2b] Sol oc - ca-sum ne - sci - ens stel- la sem-*per* ru-ti - lens s[em]-*per* cla - ra.

[3a] Sic- ut sy - *dus* ra-di-um *pro*-fert uir - go fi- li - *um* pa-ri for - ma.

[3b] Nec- *que* sy - *dus* ra-di-o ne - *que* ma-*ter* fi - li - o fit cor-rup - ta.

[4a] Ce - drus al - ta li-ba - ni con-for-ma-*tur* y - so-po ual-le *nos* - *tra*

[4b] Ver-bum ens al-tis-si - mi cor - po-ra-li pas - sum est car-ne sump - ta

[5a] Y-sa-i-as ce-ci-nit sy-na-go - ga me-mi-nit nun*quam* ta-lem de - sinit es - se ce-ca

Y-sa-y-as ce-ci-nit sy-na-go - ga me-mi-nit nu*mquam* ta-men de - sinit es - se ce-ca

[5b] Si non su-is ua-ti-*bus* cre-dat uel gen-ti-li-*bus* si - bi - li-nis uer - si*bus* hec pre - dic - ta.

Si *non* su-is ua- ti-*bus* cre-dat uel gen-ti-li-*bus* si - bi - li-nis u*er* - si*bus* hec pr*e* - dic - ta.

Example 1 —*cont.*

[6a] In - fe-lix pro - pe-ra. Cre- de uel ue-te-ra. Cur damp-na - be - ris gens mi-se-ra.

In - fe-lix pro - pe-ra cre - de uel ue-te-ra cur damp-na - be - ris gens mi-se-ra.

[6b] Quem do-cet lit-te-ra Na- tum con-si-de-ra. Ip- sum ge-nu - it pu-er-pe - ra.

Quem do-cet li- te-ra ua-tum con-si-de-ra ip- sum ge-nu - it pu-er-pe - ra.
? na- tum

GLAD AND BLITHE

In the original, both texts of each pair are beneath the score. In this transcription, angle brackets are used for accidentals (including cancellations) implied by but not stated in the original notation. Underlay is as nearly as possible that of the manuscript, subject to the principle of simultaneous change of syllable where possible. Word-division is editorial; italics signify expansion of contractions.

1. Clef changes to C1 in upper staff.
2. Clef changes back to C2 in upper staff.
3. Flat added to signature in lower staff.
4. Flat removed from signature in lower staff.
5. Flat added to signature in upper staff.

Example 2. Oxford, Bodleian Library Selden B 26, fol. 19v

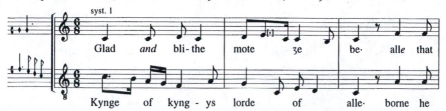

syst. 1

Glad *and* bli- the mote ʒe be- alle that

Kynge of kyng - ys lorde of alle· borne he

euer y here nowe se· Al - le - lu - ya.

is in ox- e stalle· Res mi - ran - da.

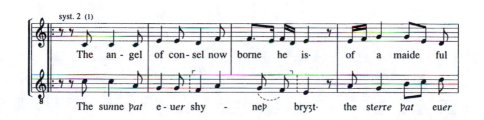

syst. 2 (1)

The an - gel of con - sel now borne he is· of a maide ful

The sunne þat e - uer shy - neþ bryʒt· the sterre þat euer

cle - ne y wys· Sol de stel - -

ʒe- ueth his lyʒt· Sem - per cla - -

syst. 3 (2) or ?

la. Ryʒt as þe sterre bryngthe forthe his

ra. No - ther þe ster - re for his

Example 2—*cont.*

beme· So þe   maide here   barn   teme· pa - ri

beme· no-*per* þe   maide for here   barne   teme· ffit cor -

syst. 4

for   -   -   ma.   The ce - *dure* of li - ban

rup   -   -   ta.   God -ys sone of he - uen

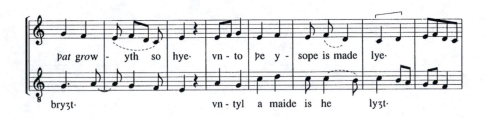

þat grow - yth so hye·   vn - to þe y - sope is made lye·

bry3t·   vn - tyl a maide is he ly3t·

fol. 20r
syst. 1 (3)

Val - le   nos -   -   tra.   Y - say - e

Car - ne   sump -   -   ta.   Yf they leue

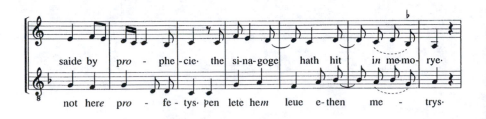

saide by pro - phe -cie· the si-na-goge hath hit *in* me-mo- rye·

not here pro - fe - tys· þen lete he*m* leue e-then me -   trys·

Example 2—*cont.*

III

Liturgical Polyphony
in
Later Medieval England

Plainsong into Polyphony
Repertories and Structures *circa* 1270–*circa* 1420

FRANK Ll. HARRISON
(†Canterbury, 1988)

The purpose of this essay is to discuss processes of composition used in England during the time indicated, in cases where a primary component in design was material from the plainsong repertory. The publication of four volumes of English polyphonic music of *circa* 1270 to *circa* 1400,[1] together with editions of the early fifteenth-century 'Old Hall' manuscript,[2] makes it possible to survey this aspect of the composition process and to observe some of its continuities and changes over this extended period.

From circa *1270 to* circa *1320*

Broadly speaking, plainsong was incorporated into polyphonic compositions either integrally or partially; in the former case usually in a ritual item, in the latter case in a motet (which was occasionally based on a complete chant). Table 1 shows polyphonic ritual items incorporating plainsong during this period. Of eleven settings in the category alleluia, seven occur in the context of troping preludes and interludes. One of these

---

[1] E. H. Sanders (ed.), *English Music of the Thirteenth and Early Fourteenth Centuries*, Polyphonic Music of the Fourteenth Century—hereafter PMFC—XIV (Monaco, 1979); F. Ll. Harrison (ed.), *Motets of English Provenance*, PMFC XV (Monaco, 1980); F. Ll. Harrison, E. H. Sanders, and P. M. Lefferts (eds.), *English Music for Mass and Offices (I)*, PMFC XVI (Monaco, 1983); E. H. Sanders, F. Ll. Harrison, and P. M. Lefferts (eds.), *English Music for Mass and Offices (II) and Music for Other Ceremonies*, PMFC XVII (Monaco, 1986). References to PMFC in this article give volume and item number.

[2] A. Ramsbotham, H. B. Collins, and Anselm Hughes (eds.), *The Old Hall Manuscript* (Nashdom and London, 1933–8); Andrew Hughes and M. Bent (eds.), *The Old Hall Manuscript*, Corpus Mensurabilis Musicae 46 (n.p., 1969–73). We follow the numbering in the latter edition.

TABLE 1. *Polyphonic ritual items, c.1270–c.1320*

Genre	Frequency	Comment
Kyrie	1	'motetized'
Gloria, troped	2	trope *Spiritus et alme*
Sanctus	2	one troped *Sancte ingenite* and 'motetized', one untroped
Introit *Salve sancta parens*	2	both 'motetized'
Alleluia	11	see below
Offertory trope	1	*prosula*/prose; see below
Hymn *Sponsa rectoris*	1	on tune of *Veni creator spiritus*
Prose	1	*Inviolata*, 'motetized', with one parallel troping text in two upper voices

(PMFC xiv, 70), which may be by W. de Wycombe,[3] who was active in the 1270s, comprises a complete scheme of the troped Alleluia and Verse *Dies sanctificatus*, with, in addition, a shortened return after the verse, should lack of time require this. It consists of:[4]

1. Prelude-trope in rondellus.
2. Beginners' incipit, motetized.
3. Choral plainsong: incipit and jubilus.
4. Interlude-trope.
5. Parallel-troped verse, over partly motetized chant.
6. Choral plainsong: ending of verse.
7. Interlude-trope in rondellus.
8. Replacement for 7, 'si brevitas hore deposcit'.
9. New setting of 2; this would be followed by the sequence (not by the choral plainsong shown in the edition).

This kind of extended alleluia and verse may have been a short–lived speciality of Worcester Cathedral Priory. The setting of the Alleluia *Nativitas* (PMFC xiv, App. 16), though made on orthodox 'Notre-Dame' lines, is formally unique in its encapsulation of Perotinus' *Ex semine* motet. The untroped Alleluia *Virga ferax Aaron* (PMFC xiv, 63) has a rhythmicized deployment of its chant. This manner of treatment is distinguishable from deployment in a 'motetizing' manner, i.e. one using one or a few reiterated rhythmic patterns. This latter procedure was applied

---

[3.] If so, it is the only entirely restorable setting in a cycle of over 40 alleluia settings listed in London, British Library Harley 978. In the opinion of Ernest Sanders, all were probably composed by William (see *New Grove*, 'Wycombe, W. de').

[4.] This scheme varies in some details from the edition, for instance in respect to the *dal segno* sign on p. 145.

to the parallel-troped Alleluia (*A laudanda*) and its Verse *Ave Maria* (*Ave mater veritatis*) (PMFC XIV, 69). A further procedure is that of basically monorhythmic chant, which may have momentary doubling and occasional rhythmicizing. This occurs in the Alleluia *Ave dei genitrix* (PMFC XIV, 62), which thus ranks as a prototype of a common fourteenth-century practice.

The composition with the single text beginning *Singularis et insignis* (PMFC XIV, App. 14), whose final section is not transcribable, is a *prosula* to the offertory *Recordare virgo mater*. Its text is applied to the neuma on the penultimate word *a [nobis]* of the offertory, with many note-repetitions to accommodate the long lines of the text. While conforming to the usual design of the English *prosa* (trope to an office-respond), this item is an addition to polyphonic tropes of this offertory known elsewhere.[5]

In all but two cases of plainsong use in the volume under consideration, the chant is deployed in the lowest voice; both exceptions concern the *Spiritus et alme* trope of the Gloria. A not quite complete four-part setting (PMFC XIV, App. 15), which may be by R. de Burgate, abbot of Reading Abbey from 1268 to 1290, has its chant, rhythmicized and at times considerably extended, mainly in the duplum, next above a supporting tenor. In the phrase 'Mariam sanctificans', however, it is in the tenor, though its notes, after an initial pedal point, are pitched above those of the duplum. The other exceptional composition (PMFC XIV, 73) is a hybrid, a three-part setting in which the trope *Spiritus et alme*, in the highest voice, has its contour rhythmicized and slightly extended. Below it as middle voice is a setting of two metrical stanzas beginning *Gaude virgo salutata . . . gaude mater iniocunda*; the piece is thus a parallel-troped trope. These two compositions provide early examples of the technique of contour-infill applied to plainsong.

The twenty-nine items in the volume under consideration that belong to the genre motet fall into two general categories.[6] Fifteen use a part (neuma) of a chant, whether identified or not as to its liturgical context; fourteen are based on an ostensibly *ad hoc* theme. The term *pes* appears occasionally (eleven times in the volume considered here) to indicate the tenor of a composition, though not where the tenor is identified by a liturgical cue. Not all instances apply to motets; two occur in an alleluia prelude and an alleluia verse (PMFC XIV, 70, 71) and one in a largely homorhythmic rondellus (PMFC XIV, 53).[7] Turning to the motets based on chant, or

---

[5.] See G. Björkvall and R. Steiner, 'Some prosulas for offertory antiphons', *Journal of the Plainsong & Mediaeval Music Society* 5 (1982), 28–30, and the references there in n. 36.

[6.] Excluding the inserted *Ex semine* by Perotinus, but including the new composition (PMFC XIV, App. 27) over the tenor *Mors*.

[7.] The foregoing information is based on the PMFC edition; it does not take into account incomplete items (for which see E. Sanders in *New Grove*, 'Pes'). An identifying cue and the indication *pes* seem not to occur together in motets; this suggests that the use of the term 'pes' was not normative.

assumed chant, germane to their structure is the numerical relation of the
cantus firmus to the rhythmic pattern or patterns (*taleae*), and the number
of statements allotted to the cantus firmus (*color*). On the latter point, six of
these motets have one statement of their tenor, while three have two
identical statements. Divergence from these regularities could be caused by
offsetting of *talea vis-à-vis color*, and by acceleration (in notational terms:
'diminution') of the *talea*. Both may be observed in the disposition of the
tenor *Veritatem* in *Tu capud ecclesie/Tu es Petrus* (PMFC XIV, 78). In such
cases the rhythm in diminution does not bear an exact proportion to the
preceding rhythm.

The Fourteenth Century: Ritual Music

It will be most convenient to consider here the succeeding volumes of
Polyphonic Music of the Fourteenth Century in the order XVI and XVII,
containing ritual items for the mass and offices, before volume XV,
containing motets. Those in the former category in which an identified or
presumed chant was used, with their frequencies, are shown in Table 2.[8]
The chief features of interest in the present context are: (1) the placing of
the chant predominantly in the middle voice of three, with fairly frequent
crossing; (2) its deployment in monorhythm with occasional small depar-
tures; and (3) its mirroring by the other voices in predominantly parallel
motion in basic homorhythm, definable in anticipation as proto-faburden
(e.g. XVI, 24, 25, 43). This last occurs also in a case where a Sanctus chant is
in the highest voice (PMFC XVI, 47). A more elaborate enclosure-
framework for a monorhythmic cantus firmus may be observed in the
ending 'Osanna in excelsis' of a Sanctus (PMFC XVI, 53).

In the manuscript New York, Pierpont Morgan Library M. 978,[9] there
are two voices of an Agnus Dei which proved to enclose as cantus firmus,
not there notated, a Sarum Agnus Dei chant (PMFC XVI, 67). Uniquely in
this repertory, its three sections have in succession three different mensurations of the breve. Of the two exceptions in PMFC XVI to middle-voice
deployment of the chant, a Kyrie (12) has the *Orbis factor* tune rhythmicized in the highest voice, and a Sanctus (58) has its cantus firmus in the

---

[8.] The identifying numbers of Sarum Ordinary chants given in this essay are those in N.
Sandon, *The Use of Salisbury: The Ordinary of the Mass* (Newton Abbot, 1984).

[9.] I would suggest that the manuscript was probably made for Edward's household
chapel between his effective declaration of war on France in late 1337 and *c.*1355, when
building works were in progress at St George's, Windsor, presumably with concomitant
changes in musical style. [However, see also the discussion of this source by R. Bowers in
'Fixed Points in the Chronology of English Fourteenth-Century Polyphony', *Music and
Letters* 71 (1990), 313–35, with references to previous literature.]

TABLE 2. *Music for the mass and offices* (*PMFC* XVI *and* XVII)

Genre	Frequency		Comment
	PMFC XVI	PMFC XVII	
Ordinary group	1		A pioneer grouping of Kyrie VI, Sanctus VIII, Agnus IX
Kyrie	13		Seven (PMFC XVI, 15–21) are unidentified
Kyrie, troped		1	Two parallel-troping texts over an untexted, unidentified chant
Gloria, troped	1		Based throughout on IX, with trope *Spiritus et alme*
Credo	2		On chant: Sandon, pp. 74–5
Sanctus	13		On chants II, III, IV, VII, VIII, X, and one unidentified
Agnus Dei	8		On chants II, IV, VI, X, XI, XII (no. 63 is a variant of no. 62)
[Ite missa est] Deo gracias	3		No. 68 on XIII; 69 on *Benedicamus* XXVI; 71 unidentified
Gradual [Benedicta] V. Virgo dei genitrix	1	2	For special treatment of chant in PMFC XVII, 15a, b, see below
Alleluia	4	2	PMFC XVII, 64 is a parallel-troped initium
Sequence	1		
Lesson trope	1		
Respond	5		
Te Deum	1		Conclusion only
Magnificat	2		
Hymn	2	1	In PMFC XVII, 13, are two parallel tropes above and below the untexted hymn *Jesu redemptor omnium*
Psalm tone	1		
Votive sequence		2	PMFC XVII, 1, on tune of *Victime paschali laudes*, is without text
Votive antiphon[a]		6	Nos. 4a, 4b, 7, 8, 10, 11, 12

[a] A canonic three-voice *Salve regina*, transcribed by N. Sandon (*Early Music* 10, 1982, 50–1) from one voice in British Library Royal 7. A. VI, of Durham Cathedral provenance, has a rhythmicization of the chant of the first two words.

lowest voice, rhythmically ordered in quasi-motet fashion, though not rhythmically patterned in that wise.

For the proper, the Verse *Virgo Dei genitrix* of the Gradual *Benedicta et venerabilis* has an orthodox monorhythmic setting, as well as two further workings of an unusual kind. One of these (PMFC XVII, 15a), coming from the late thirteenth century, has two troping voices over the monorhythmic cantus firmus, whose ending, omitting the chant of the last two words 'factus homo', suggests that it may have been liturgically destined. The other (PMFC XVII, 15b) has the same musical substance, with rhythmicizing and some infilling of the cantus firmus, and with the upper text only of the former version, written below the score notation for singing by all three voices.

Another alleluia setting, that of *Virga Jesse floruit* (PMFC XVI, 78), has its cantus firmus in the highest voice. The setting of the Alleluia *Hic est vere martir* (PMFC XVI, 79), with its monorhythmic chant in the lowest voice, is remarkable for a high incidence of pitch inflection, affecting at times all three voices.

Settings of office responds do not include the initium, as they regularly did in the Notre-Dame repertory, and two do not include the *Gloria patri*. One is exceptional in having the cantus firmus in the lowest voice. Shared disposition of the cantus firmus characterizes the hymns. In one (PMFC XVI, 88) all three voices participate; in the other (PMFC XVI, 89), with largely mirror-image movement, the outer voices interchange the notes of the chant. An eccentric use of the lauds hymn for a confessor-bishop, *Jesu redemptor omnium, perpes corona presulum* (PMFC XVII, 13), has the cantus firmus, which provides for the four stanzas but not the doxology, in the middle voice. It is framed by two troping texts containing praises for Jesus and for Augustine of Hippo. One of the two Magnificat settings (PMFC XVI, 90) has a formulaic lowest voice in every verse, supporting the chant in the middle voice of three. This same complementary voice recurs in settings of the canticle in the late fifteenth and sixteenth centuries, and is also listed among a series of faburdens for the Magnificat.[10]

The Fourteenth Century: Motets

English composers of motets in the fourteenth century cultivated a greater variety of techniques than did their French contemporaries. Instances of 'hybrid' design and of basing on apparently *ad hoc* tenors, thus not strictly

---

[10.] See F. Ll. Harrison, 'Faburden in Practice', *Musica Disciplina* 16 (1962), 20–1, 32.

within our subject, are a St Katharine motet (PMFC xv, 25) in paired-variation form, and a motet (PMFC xv, 26), with prayers to the Holy Spirit, in refrain form, on a rhythmically varied *pes*.[11] A decidedly insular technique was the framing of a plainsong cantus firmus by outer voices in mirror-image (PMFC xv, 3, 10, 13, 31). A tenor could be a middle voice to non-parallel outer parts; as if to underscore this, the scribe of the Durham leaves indicated such a tenor (PMFC xv, 30; facs., Early English Church Music 26, 168) as '*Medius cantus. Manere*'.[12] Two rare instances of middle-voice tenor in the continental motet-repertory are Philippe de Vitry's *Tribum quem non abhorruit/Quoniam secta latronum* on the tenor *Merito hec patimur* (PMFC I, 27) and B. de Cluni's *Apollinis eclipsatur/Zodiacum signis* on the tenor *In omnem terram* (PMFC v, 9). Also insular was a synthesis of motet and rondellus (PMFC xv, 2, 11, 20). It is notable that in each of the three cases of this the composer used a plainsong as his cantus firmus. In the first and second its genre was sequence, in whole or in part; in the third it was an antiphon divided into sections with each portion repeated. Again, a liturgical tenor was sometimes deployed complete in one statement over a whole motet (PMFC xv, 1, 10, 11, 13, 19, 20), a usage it would be difficult to find in the continental repertory.

The tenor *Petre, amas me* of the motet *Petrum cephas ecclesie/Petrus pastor potissimus* shows a layout resulting from tune-to-rhythm offset, treated in such a way that its fourteen units have a symmetrical pattern. In this diagram each digit represents a number of *longae* and each horizontal line represents four *longae* rests.

```
Statement  I      3——5——5——1
           II       4——5——5
           III      5——5——4
           IV   1——5——5——3
```

Palindromic motion was also used. The composer of a motet (PMFC xv, 13) used the tone of the psalm-verse *Quare fremuerunt* of the Introit at first mass of Christmas as tenor (not so indicated in the manuscript): he disposed it in three isorhythmic periods, followed by their retrograde form, the whole stated twice. The tenor (if correctly identified) is therefore closely allied textually to the single text *Quare fremuerunt gentes* in the mirror-image outer voices, while the lowest voice has textual links between units. Retrograde motion occurs also in the tenor of the reconstructed

---

[11] The 13th-C. term may conveniently be used in this sense. It is not in 14th-C. documents, though Johannes Alanus used it in the duplum poem of his motet (PMFC v, 31) to denote its plainsong tenor.

[12] For contents and concordances of the Durham leaves see F. Ll. Harrison, 'Ars Nova in England: A New Source', *Musica Disciplina* 21 (1967), 80–1. The concordance Switzerland, Freiburg Bibliothek Cantonal 260 should be added to no. 12.

motet *Regne de pité* (PMFC XVII, 57), apparently in a symbolic sense, since the text has the familiar medieval reversal Eva/Ave. It also features in the unidentified tenor, which may be from plainsong, of the motet *Inter usitata/Inter tot et tales* (PMFC XVII, 56), which bears the instruction *Hoc ter cantetur medio retro gradietur*, and in the cryptically notated tenor of a curious textless piece (PMFC XVII, 67).

There are two instances, perhaps the only ones in the international motet repertory, of pseudo-cantus-firmus tenor. The case involving plainsong (PMFC XV, 27) has the true *cantus prius factus* in the middle voice; it is a rhythmicized form of the chant of the words beginning *Absalon fili mi* in the antiphon *Rex autem David*, with its full text. The lowest voice is an illusory pseudo-tenor, isorhythmic, stated twice. The other instance (PMFC XV, 5) is a Latin contrafactum, *Virgo mater et filia*, of a French-language chanson, *Mariounette douche*. This is the true tenor, as middle voice over a quasi-motetized free voice masquerading as the tenor. The chanson was used as true tenor, so indicated, in another motet in the same group of leaves (PMFC XV, 6).

Two motets are special cases, in the sense that neither seems to have been destined for use in choir. In one (PMFC XVII, 53) the pietistic text *Worldes blisce have god day*, apparently the only surviving case of an English vernacular text as an upper voice of a motet, was set, probably in the late thirteenth century, over three statements of the 'Clemenciam' tune of Benedicamus domino. The other (PMFC XVII, 54), which appears not to involve plainsong, has two voices in ingenious reiterations of the same rhythm mutually offset, with texts on the Virgin Mary's influence on the lives of two of her devotees. These are set over offset statements of a *pes* deployed in successive isorhythmic units.

The device of restatement with rhythmic acceleration of the tenor of a motet has been observed in a thirteenth-century instance. An early fourteenth-century example is in a St Katherine motet (PMFC XV, 7) whose tenor *Agmina* is given a series of diminutions having patterns in imprecise proportion. They follow a first statement of the *color*, which is divided into ten three-note *taleae*. In France, Philippe de Vitry (d. 1361) was accustomed to use the device of diminution as a structural determinant, whereby he effected designs whose units were unfolded in lengths expressible in simple proportions. His profane motet *Vos quid admiramini/Gratissima virginis species* on the sacred tenor *Gaude gloriosa* (PMFC I, 76) may serve as an example.[13] Its tenor is deployed in two state-

---

[13.] For the texts of this motet, the edition by P. Dronke in *Medieval Latin and the Rise of European Love-Lyric* II (Oxford, 1968), 406–8, with English translation, should be followed. Dronke shows that the texts are on earthly love, not on a 'Marian theme', as proposed by E. H. Roesner in his Introduction to *Philippe de Vitry: Complete Works* (Monaco, 1984), v.

ments,[14] the first in a rhythmic pattern of the length of five perfect longs stated six times, the second with a different pattern of the length of three perfect longs stated seven times, plus two longs to accommodate the last two notes of the *color*. The dimensions of the motet are therefore (6 × 15 breves) + (7 × 9 breves), that is, 90 breves plus 63 breves, and its essential overall proportions are 10 : 7.

This is one of the ten motets of French provenance that were copied into the Durham leaves (facsimile in Early English Church Music 26, 149–64), presumably used in the fourteenth century by the Benedictine monks of the cathedral.[15] This motet was known also to John of Tewkesbury, author of the treatise entitled *Quatuor Principalia*. John

[14.] In Leo Schrade's edition (PMFC I, 76; Roesner, *Vitry*, 20) the lowest staff has the cue 'Tenor solus "Vivat iste" '. In fact the scribe wrote 'Vacat iste', i.e. 'ignore this part', which he broke off before finishing (see PMFC v, 194, 207). The staff should be deleted from the edition throughout.

[15.] N. Sandon has pointed out ('Mary, Meditations, Monks and Music—Poetry, Prose, Processions and Plagues in a Durham Cathedral Manuscript', *Early Music* 10 (1982), 55 n. 21) that the music leaves may have come from elsewhere, and have already been in the binding when the main manuscript was acquired for the abbey by John Wessington when prior between 1416 and 1446. The main facts about the manuscript may be briefly summarized. The volume contains two works: Hugutio, *Summa super derivationibus*, later 13th C., and Isidore, *Etymologiae*, mid-14th C. A note on fol. 5r reads: 'ex procuracione Joh. Wessyngton prioris eiusdem'. The writer was informed by Dr A. Piper of Durham University that between the two works there is a leaf, fol. 215, on which were written a number of caution-notes that record deposits in Oxford chests in the second decade of the 14th C. Three of the notes are dated 1312, 1313, and 1315. Professor R. B. Dobson of Christ's College, Cambridge kindly wrote that the volume 'clearly belongs to that not uncommon category of Durham manuscripts which seem to have been acquired by Durham monks at Oxford but were in pledge at various university chests on a number of successive occasions. The most precise reference perhaps is to John de Beverlaco on fol. 215r; he was prior of the Durham monks' *manse* (not a college until 1381) at Oxford in the 1330s.' Professor Dobson would suppose that the inscription on fol. 5r 'implies that Wessington had the manuscript brought up from Oxford (perhaps redeemed from a university chest where it had been pledged by a Durham student monk) either before he became prior in 1416 or (more probably) when he was himself an Oxford monk fellow between 1394 and 1407.' The question of whether or not the music-leaves at the beginning and end of the binding enclosing the two manuscript works had been part of a manuscript used by the Durham monks (probably between *c.*1358 and *c.*1400) hangs largely on the date and place of the binding. Professor Dobson writes further: 'it is quite possible that the manuscript in question was bound at Durham in the early fifteenth century'. He would not rule out the hypothesis—'hard' (he cautions) 'though it is to clinch on the manuscript evidence'—that 'the music-leaves had originally been part of a Durham motet-book'. The alternative possibilities for the home of the music-leaves before they were bound into the main manuscript are on this evidence Durham or Oxford, with a bias, in this writer's opinion, in favour of Durham.

referred to it as an example of the effective use of dots in notation:[16]

Posset tamen prima longa imperfici a parte ante per brevem precedentem vel per valorem, nisi punctus immediate eam sequatur, ut patet in tenore de Gratissima quem idem Philippus edidit.

French Motets in English Sources

The Durham leaves have two voices, triplum and tenor, of another de Vitry motet, *Rex quem metrorum* and its tenor *Rex regum*. The praise-poem of this triplum forms the single acrostic 'Robertus'; it was addressed to Robert of Anjou, whose coronation as king of Naples and Sicily took place at Avignon in 1309 and who died in 1343. Robert was a grandson of Charles count of Anjou and king of Sicily (d. 1309), brother of Louis IX of France, canonized 1297; he was therefore grand-nephew to the sainted king.[17] The other sainted Louis, bishop and confessor (1274–97), who was Robert's elder brother, renounced the throne of Naples and became a Franciscan friar. As bishop of Toulouse he observed the rule of poverty, and in 1317 was canonized by his friend Pope John XXII.[18] It was fitting, therefore, that de Vitry should select as the tenor of his motet in praise of Robert the opening of the first respond at matins on the feast of St Louis, king and confessor.[19] In the motet the *color* of the plainsong extract is divided into four isorhythmic *taleae*; this is stated twice, and then once in diminution by half (proportions 2 : 2 : 1).

In his references to de Vitry motets in *Quatuor Principalia*, John of Tewkesbury was not dealing with overall design, and his comments were made without illustrative notation. He need not have had access to manuscript copies of the motets; and he stated, in fact, that his treatise contained only what its writer had learned from 'skilled and approved authors and masters'. His observations are nevertheless germane to the

---

16. C.-E.-H. de Coussemaker (ed.), *Scriptorum de musica medii aevi nova series* IV (Paris, 1876), 268. The treatise has been connected with Simon Tunstede, called in the manuscript 'regent of the Oxford Franciscans who excelled in music and also in the seven liberal arts'. The manuscript, which carries the date of its completion as 4 Aug. 1351, has the information that Friar John Tewkesbury brought it with him in 1388 to the Franciscan community at Oxford. The late Neil Ker established that the handwriting of Oxford, Bodleian Library Digby 90, which contains the treatise, is the same as that of John Tewkesbury's *De situ universorum*. Tewkesbury may be assumed to have been the author/compiler of the treatise.

17. L. Schrade, in *Commentary Notes* to PMFC I, 118, made him a nephew of that saint.

18. For a motet in Louis's honour, see below, 'Compositions for the Ordinary on Other Plainchant Tenors'.

19. Not identified in Schrade's edition; see PMFC V, 207, where in col. 2, 1. 5, 'St Louis of Toulouse' should read 'St Louis, king and confessor'. The respond is printed, ibid. 215.

degree of knowledge among English composers of composition-practice in France.[20] The marked prevalence of major prolation in motets composed in France, and its rarity in those made in England, make this a usable criterion for discussion of the chronology and direction of changes in English methods.[21] It constitutes, for example, an observable distinction between two groups of motets on leaves in the binding of a manuscript from the Benedictine abbey of Bury St Edmunds (Oxford, Bodleian Library e Mus. 7). Those inside the front cover (edited PMFC xv, 18–22) clearly have English traits, though a surviving single voice *Frondentibus florentibus* and its tenor *Floret* (facsimile in Early English Church Music 26, 50) have a few major-prolation groups. Exceptionally, the St Edmund motet *De flore martirum/Deus tuorum militum* on the tenor *Ave rex gentis Anglorum* (PMFC xv, 21), indubitably an English product, has major prolation throughout; it may rank as the earliest such English motet to survive. One of the motets on leaves inside the back cover (PMFC v, 16a), which is based on the tenor *Concupisco*, is a sacred Latin contrafactum, presumably made at the abbey, of a motet with profane French texts in the Ivrea manuscript, and in leaves at Cambrai, Bibliothèque municipale 1328 (1176). Two others there have French text-elements; their rhythmic character and that of three others (PMFC xv, 22; facsimiles Early English Church Music 26, 54, 61) strongly suggest importation from France. The Durham leaves seem to show a parallel situation. Of seven motets on leaves inside the front cover (PMFC xv, 29–33; Early English Church Music 26, 152–3), all certainly English, one only (PMFC xv, 29), a sacred motet on a profane French-texted tenor, has major prolation, and may rank as the second earliest surviving English motet to do so. Of ten motets surviving in whole or part inside the back cover, all having major prolation, the two by de Vitry have been mentioned in respect to their structures, while three with profane French texts (PMFC v, 19, 21, 15) are in the Ivrea manuscript. French origin may be assumed for a surviving voice *O vos omnes* with its tenor *Locus iste*, as for *Virginalis concio* and its 'Contratenor. De Virgo sancta Katerina'. The latter has a special interest in that the poem *Virginalis concio* reappears with a different musical setting in a motet by Byttering in the Old Hall manuscript (London, British Library Add. 57950). Two of the remaining three Latin motets have continental concordances and presumably origins. The basic structures of motets

---

[20.] In that connection, it may be noted here that a page in York, Minster Library xvi. N. 3 (facs. Early English Church Music 26, 213), which has two voices of the English motet *Zelo tui langueo/Reor nescia* (PMFC xv, 14), also has the motetus of the *Roman de Fauvel* motet *Inter amenitatis/Reverlenti* (PMFC 1, 42; reprint in *Roman de Fauvel*, Monaco, 1984). The identification is due to P. M. Lefferts.

[21.] In England major prolation was used regularly, in a range of ritual genres, in one case (PMFC xvi, 76) with a measure signature, though not in motets.

based on an identified or presumed plainsong and known or assumed to be of French provenance that are preserved in English manuscripts are shown in Table 3.

French Motet-Structures: J. Alanus's Sub Arturo

The information in Table 3 may suggest some of the parameters of French motet-structure between *circa* 1320 and *circa* 1360. A survey of the whole known production tends to confirm these general lines. The relations of *color* and *talea* obtaining in the thirty-three motets in PMFC v have been tabulated in an analytical table in that volume (p. 201). They show a comparable range of practice, with twenty cases of integral relation and ten of offset. Two special cases call for notice in terms of structure. One is *Inter densas deserti/Imbribus irriguis* on the *ad hoc* tenor indicated as *Admirabile est nomen tuum* (PMFC v, 29). This is notable both for its dream-sequence poems in praise of Gaston Fébus, count of Foix and Béarn from 1343 to 1391, and for the disposition of its hexachord-based palindromic tenor. The transformations of the tenor constitute a *tour de force* of mensural practice, a veritable 'Art of the Motet', with eight mensurations of its theme demonstrated and eight others implied (see PMFC v, 216).

TABLE 3. *French motets in English sources: Structures*

Publication	Tenor	Relation of color/talea	Statements of that relation
PMFC xv, 22	Unidentified	$co = 4\frac{1}{2}$ ta	$1 + \frac{1}{2}$
PMFC xv, 24	Unidentified	2 co = 3 ta	$1 + \frac{1}{2}$
PMFC v, 16a	Concupisco	co = 2 ta	$2 + \frac{1}{2} + \frac{1}{2}$
EECM 26, 61	Relictis retibus	co = 4 ta	$1 + \frac{1}{2}$
EECM 26, 157	Unidentified	survives incomplete	$1 + \frac{1}{2}$[c]
PMFC v, 19	Dolor meus	co = 3 ta	2[b]
PMFC xv, 34	Dulcis virgo	co = 2 ta	3
PMFC I, 76	Gaude gloriosa	see above	
EECM 26, 160	Locus iste	co = 4 ta[a]	$1 + \frac{1}{2}$
PMFC I, 106	Rex regum	co = 4 ta	$2 + \frac{1}{2}$
PMFC v, 21	[Sicut fenum arui]	co = 3 ta	2
PMFC xv, 35	Avete	co = 4 ta	$1 + \frac{1}{2}$
PMFC v, 4	Alma redemptoris	2 co = 3 ta	1
PMFC v, 15	Tristis est anima mea	3 co = 5 ta	1

[a] With four-note '*introitus tenoris*' stated four times.
[b] Second *color* a fifth lower.
[c] Judging by the contratenor.

While the relation in French practice between the number of notes in a plainsong-derived tenor and the kind of units of notation chosen for its rhythmic deployment varied considerably, it is noticeable that any diminution used in repeats of that relation was virtually always in the proportion 2 : 1. Apart from the special mensural procedures of *Inter densas deserti*, there seems to be only one exception to this in the published repertory, including the motets of de Vitry and Machaut. The case is one in which overall proportions are complicated by combining diminution by half with a change of tempus—the relation of breve to semibreve. This happens in *Ida capillorum/Porcio nature* with contratenor and a tenor indicated as *Ante tronum* in Ivrea, as *Ante thorum* (recte *thronum*) *trinitatis* in Chantilly (PMFC v, 5, 5a). This motet is in honour of the sainted Ida of Lorraine, countess of Boulogne, two of whose sons, Geoffrey (Godefroy de Bouillon) and Baldwin (Baudouin de Boulogne) became kings of Jerusalem,[22] as is related in the duplum text. After Ida's eldest son Eustace, count of Boulogne, who is also named in the duplum text, returned from Palestine, she caused *circa* 1115 two churches to be built, at Wast and at Saint-Wlmer (Wulmar) in Boulogne.[23] Her foundation of a monastery, probably that in Boulogne, is noted in the triplum text ('in claustro quod stabilavit'), three lines before the maker of texts and music announces his name:

> Hoc tibi cantamen et dictionale gregamen
> offert laudamen Henricus, ovans rogitamen
> mortis in examen.

Henricus may plausibly be identified with Henricus Helene, who is named in the Ivrea manuscript in the triplum of the motet *Apollinis eclipsatur/ Zodiacum* on the tenor *In omnem terram* (PMFC v, 9) among a roll of twelve illustrious musicians, including Philippe de Vitry, Johannes de Muris, Guillaume de Machaut, and Egidius de Morino (elsewhere Murino). The maker of this motet named himself in the duplum, as both theorist and practitioner:

> B. de Cluni mittens energia
> artis practice cum theoria
> recommendans se subdit omnibus
> presentia per salutaria.

Henricus Helene was the author of a short treatise, headed *Summula musice*, that survives in a fifteenth-century copy. In 1335 he held a prebend as non-residentiary canon of Sens. The tenor instruction of his motet

---

[22.] Villehardouin, *The Conquest of Constantinople*, trans. M. R. B. Shaw (Harmondsworth, 1963), 95.

[23.] S. Runciman, *A History of the Crusades* III (4th edn., Harmondsworth, 1978), 379, 380 n. 1.

on St Ida prescribes change from perfect to imperfect breve[24] as well as diminution by half, in both tenor and contratenor:

primo dicitur [temporis] perfecte, secundo [temporis] imperfecte, tertio sese per semi de primo, quarto de secundo.

This sophisticated structure suggests a date very shortly before 1350, the probable last date for the commencement of the Ivrea manuscript.[25] The proportions that result from the instruction, namely 6 : 4 : 3 : 2, make this work almost unique structurally in the surviving French repertory of the fourteenth century. The only work comparable in this respect is the motet *Sub Arturo plebs/Fons citharizancium* on the tenor *In omnem terram* by the English composer J. Alanus, not preserved complete in any English manuscript but, like the two French motets just discussed, found in the prestigious Chantilly manuscript, and also in Bologna, Civico Museo Bibliografico Musicale Q 15 (PMFC v, 31).[26] Since the date of its composition and its possible historical relation to a motet not hitherto discussed, namely *Musicorum collegio/In templo Dei* on the tenor *Avete* (PMFC xv, 35)[27] preserved in the Durham leaves, will come into question, it will be appropriate to consider not only the structures but also the contents and contexts of these two motets.

The triplum text of J. Alanus's motet is a poem of praise to fourteen named musicians of an English choir who sing joyful songs ('musicorum vero chorus odas jubilat'). The poem of the duplum is a celebration of the great theorists of musical history, from Tubalcain to Pythagoras, Boethius, Gregory, Guido, and Franco. At its end J. Alanus commended himself with deep modesty to the singers named in the triplum, who by their impressive sounds ('sonis validis') defend the composer against envious critics. Between the theorists' roll of honour and his signing-off lines, Alanus drew attention to the structure of his motet, referring to its tenor as 'pes':

[24.] Such a change, from triple to duple subdivision, did occur, but within the confines of a *talea*, e.g. in de Vitry's motet no. 6, *Douce playsence/Garison selon nature* on the neuma of the fifth mode (PMFC I, 72; *Complete Works*, 16); it therefore did not affect overall proportions.

[25.] In the first item in the manuscript, the motet *O Philippe/O bone dux*, Philip VI of France is addressed as king, and John, who became king in 1350, is addressed as duke.

[26.] [An alternative reading of the first two words of the triplum is 'sub arcturo', i.e. 'under the north star'. However, a reference to King Arthur is in keeping with Edward III's purpose in founding the Order of the Garter. He himself announced in 1344 his intention to 'begin a Round Table in the same manner and conditions as the Lord Arthur, formerly King of England, appointed it'. For further discussion of this text see Bowers, 'Fixed Points'.]

[27.] Reprinted, with Alanus's motet and three other 'musicians' motets', including *Apollinis eclipsatur*, in *Musicorum Collegio* (Monaco, 1986).

Huius pes triplarii
bis sub emiolii
normis recitatur.

the tenor of this three-voice composition is repeated twice under the rules of *hemiola*.

Hemiola means the proportion of three to two. In the Chantilly manuscript the following instruction is given for the performance of the tenor:

primo de tempore perfecto maioris prolacionis; secundo de tempore imperfecto maioris prolacionis; tercio de tempore imperfecto minoris prolacionis.

The *color* is first deployed in three *taleae* each of the length of twenty-four perfect breves with major prolation; it is repeated with the breves made imperfect, also with major prolation, and repeated again with imperfect breves and minor prolation. Taking account of the change in prolation, which has not been encountered before, the overall dimensions in perfect semibreves are $144 + 96 + 64 = 304$. Thus the proportions are $9 : 6 : 4$, the rule of *hemiola* applying in the sense that the length of each section of tenor-repeat is in the proportion $2 : 3$ to the previous section.

While a main topic of this essay is the design function of plainsong when drafted as the tenor of a motet, discussion of Alanus's motet cannot but lead to the effect of the tenor's design on the course of the triplum and duplum. A possible concomitant of the change to minor prolation in the second repeat could be the same change taking place in the mensuration of the upper voices. The composer did not adopt this course, but with consummate craftsmanship maintained the mensuration of the upper voices unchanged. This was accomplished by adjusting the duplum to the tenor's motion by the deft interposition of red notes, making the semibreve imperfect. The major prolation of the triplum was carried through to the end, as far as its notation was concerned (it has no red notes). In doing so, its isorhythmic period, at twenty-one perfect semibreves, was made one minim shorter that those of the tenor and duplum, at thirty-two imperfect semibreves. The final flourish in this feat of craftmanship was to fashion a uniquely staggered ending.[28]

A Musicians' Motet from the Chapel of John II of France in England

It cannot be gainsaid that in relation to known previous practice Alanus's design and its execution marked an inspired leap forward in motet structure, and in the entry into composition-practice of sectional proportions at a new level. There has been general acceptance, though with some

---

[28.] In a transcription for present-day performance, it is practical to have common bar-lines, as in PMFC v, 176–7. For demonstration of the compositional process, the duplum may suitably be shown in 4/4 time, as in PMFC v, 217.

surprise at the 'advanced' elements in this motet, of Brian Trowell's theory that the occasion of its creation and first performance was connected with King Edward III's Order of the Garter, and in particular with celebrations around St George's Day (23 April) in 1358.[29] It is known that King John II of France, then prisoner of Edward III being held for ransom, was present at these proceedings. His stay at Windsor was prolonged at least until 8 May, when an agreement about territories was concluded between the two kings.[30] John II had arrived at Sandwich, escorted by the Black Prince, on 4 May 1357. His arrival in London via Canterbury on 24 May with the prince and members of his court was watched by great crowds and attended by unprecedented spectacle.[31] John and his household occupied Henry of Lancaster's palace of the Savoy, which was to be his habitual, though not constant, residence until 4 April 1359, when the household was moved to the castle of Hertford. John's presence at the Windsor celebrations of 1358, which were witnessed also by the King of Scotland, three queens, and the dukes of Brabant and Lüneburg,[32] was chronicled by John of Reading, as also was John's surprise that payments were made by tallies, without the passing of gold and silver.[33]

Quo anno apud Wyndleshoram, tam pro amore militari quam proprio honore ac presentia domini Johannis regis Francie aliorumque nobilium, festum Sancti Georgii martyris regaliter, nimis tamen sumptuose dominus rex celebrari procuravit. Quibus irridens, ipse rex Francie nunquam tanta solempnia cum taliis absque auri et argenti solutione se audivisse nec vidisse testatur.

Records of payments within John's household for a great part of the year 1359 (he was released at Calais in October 1360) have been printed.[34] An entry early in this period is 'pour asporter les orgues en Savoie vi^d' (with the word 'Chapelle' in the margin).

The following names of personnel of the chapel occur in these accounts:

[29.] B. Trowell, 'A Fourteenth-Century Ceremonial Motet and its Composer', *Acta Musicologica* 29 (1957), 65–75. [Bowers, however, now argues for a later date.]

[30.] J. Tait (ed.), *Cronica Johannis de Reading et Anonymi Cantuariensis 1345–1367* (Manchester, 1914), 130.

[31.] 'Circa eos tanta populi multitudo inauditum stupendumque intueri spectaculum ut vix post meridiem ad palatium pervenerunt'; ibid. 127.

[32.] Ibid. 273.

[33.] Ibid. 130.

[34.] H. D'Orléans (Duc d'Aumale) (ed.), *Notes et Documents relatifs à Jean, Roi de France, et à sa captivité en Angleterre*, Miscellanies of the Philobiblion Society 2 (London, 1855–6), 88 ff. The accounts are headed: 'Journal de la despense extraordinaire de l'ostel du Roy de France, faicte en Angleterre, paiee du commandement Jehan de Danville maitre d'ostel d'iceli Seigneur, par moy Denys de Callors, son chapellain depuis le xxv^e jour de decembre CCCLVIII'. De Callors was chaplain, notary, and secretary; he was also canon and precentor of the cathedral church of Meaux.

Chaplains

Denys de Collors

Arnoul de Grantpoint

Jehan Roussel

'Messire Gasse, premier chapellain, pour don fait a li . . . C escuz, valent xvi^l xiii^s iiii^d.' (This was Gace de la Buigne, author of a poem referred to below.)

Clerks

Baudement (e.g. 'Baudement, sommelier de la Chapelle, pour faire rapereiller une couroie des coffres de la chapelle et ii chemises de brévaire et du missel du Roy iii^d', and 'Baudement, clerc de la chapelle, pour demi C de crochez pour la chapelle vi^d. Pour i martel, viii^d. Pour parer v aubes, x^d. Pour i varlet qui apporta de Londres un autel benoist que l'on avait lessie a Savoie, viii^d, pour tout, ii^s viii^d.')

Barbatre

Climent (e.g. 'Barbatre et Climent, clercs de la Chapelle, pour leur livree, contenant les ii pars d'un drap . . . lxiii^s x^d obole.')

Caletot

Gopillet

Chaufecire

Mathelin (e.g. 'Mathelin pour une lampe de voirre, i lampier de fil d'archal et viii toises de corde pour mettre en la chapelle de Erthford, du commandement du Roy, xii^d.')

Denisot 'clerc maistre Yves'

Guillemin Dorge

Among other entries relating to the chapel are:

Climent, clerc de chapelle, pour ii varlet qui apporterent les orgues du Roy de Londres a Erthford, iiii^s.

Symon, boucher de Londres, pour xxxiii aunes de toile de Reims pour faire surpeliz pour la chapelle, achetez du commandement du Roy, lvii^s ix^d.

Marguerite, la custuriere, pour parer iii aubes et iii amiz pour la chapelle, vi^d.

Michiel Girart, pour le facon de vi surpeliz faiz pour Paques CCCLIX, qu'il a fait faire, et paie par li, xii^s.

Michel Girart, who ranked as a *valet de chambre*, was a distinguished painter whom John II had employed in 1356 to decorate the château of Vaudreuil in Normandy. During the captivity he made paintings, finished a chess-set, and decorated furniture. He was paid a very large sum for materials for paintings:

Maistre Girart d'Orleans, paintre et valet de chambre du Roy pour plusieurs otilz . . . pour faire certains tableaux . . . somme ii^c iiii^l vi^s viii^d.

Another entry records a payment on 24 March 1359:

Pour un grant pel de parchemin a escrire le traictie du Roy et du Roy d'Angleterre, et pour encre, a M. J. de Royer, xii^d.

The churchman and poet from Normandy, Gace de la Buigne, had been *maître chapellain* to Philip VI, and was retained in that position by John II.

It appears that he rejoined the king in England at the point when John moved to Hertford. An enthusiast for hunting and falconry, he there wrote a poem *Deduis de la Chasse*, on which its editor the Duc d'Aumale (H. d'Orléans) aptly commented:[35]

il est difficile d'imaginer une comparaison plus savamment musicale, toute grotesque qu'elle soit, que celle qui lui est suggerée par le bruit des chiens en pleine chasse.

Leo Schrade, in his commentary on Philippe de Vitry's motet *Douce playsance/Garison selon nature*, quoted a passage from Gace's poem that named de Vitry as its accomplished composer:[36]

> Car garison selon nature
> Desire toute creature
> de sa doleur, se comme dist
> un acteur, qui le nous escrist,
> en un motel qu'il fist nouveaulx
> et puis fu evesque de Meaulx
> Philippe de Vitry eut nom
> qui mieux seut motets que nul hom.

The main subject of the poem is an elaborate analogy between the music, plainsong and polyphony, to be heard in John II's chapel and the noises of the hunt in full cry in which the poet took such delight:[37]

> Adoncques y a telle noise
> qu'il n'est homs qui sur deux pieds voise
> qui onc oyt tel melodie;
> car n'est respons, ne alleluye,
> et feust chantée en la Chapelle
> du Roy, qui la est bonne et belle,
> qui si grant plaisance face
> comme est ouir une tel chace.
> Les uns vont chantans le motet,
> les autres font double hoquet,
> les plus grans chantent la teneur,
> les autres la cont-teneur;
> ceulx qui ont la plus clère gueule
> chantent la treble sans demeure,
> et les plus petits le quadrouble,
> en faisant la quinte sur double.
> Les uns font semithon mineur,
> les autres semithon maieur,
> diapenthe, diapazon,

---

[35] D'Orléans, *Notes et Documents*, 137.
[36] Commentary Notes on PMFC I, 103.
[37] D'Orléans, *Notes et Documents*, 174.

les autres dyathessaron.
Adonc le Roy met cor a bouche,
qui n'espargne n'estoc, ne souche.
Si commence fort a corner;
tantost a ouy fort huer
pres de luy.

The hypothesis of a historical relation between J. Alanus's motet and the motet *Musicorum collegio/In templo Dei* on the tenor *Avete* rests upon the text-content of the latter, whose *collegio musicorum* may have functioned in John II's chapel during his captivity, and on the further possibility that the two motets were written as *riposte* one to the other. This could have been occasioned by John II's singers being with him at Windsor in 1358, or by a meeting of the respective choirs at some other time. The triplum text begins:

Musicorum collegio
in curia degentium
Gallicorum zelo pio
Dei tantum zelancium
in sancto desiderio
Christi matris officium
quater in mense . . .

(To the company of musicians in the court of the French people, with their pious zeal for God so eagerly celebrating in holy devotion the office of the mother of Christ four times each month.)

It then records the names of seven choir-members: Hugo, the leader; Robertus de Hoyo; Johannes; Nichasius; J. Pallart; J. Anglici ('whom I cannot name more exactly'); and Stephanus. It continues with a tribute to their musicality:

O quanta delectatio
horum simul canencium!
O mira modulacio
sonorum musicalium!
O dulcis altercacio
acutorum et gravium
mediorumque vicio
discordie carentium!

Such delight in the polyphonic complexity of motet-sound recalls lines in Gace de la Buigne's poem.

In the duplum text the poet imagined an analogy between a seven-branched candelabra,[38] impossible to disunite, in the chapel where the

---

[38.] One is reminded that Mathelin, clerk of John II's chapel, was paid for the installation, and the materials needed therefore, of 'une lampe de voirre' in the chapel after the move to Hertford.

seven singers performed the polyphonic music of the Saturday Lady-mass, and their *collegium*, which he trusted would never be dissolved. He compared both to the biblical vision of the 'Son of Man' surrounded by seven golden candlesticks and holding seven stars seen by John the Divine.[39] It is highly likely that this *templum Dei* was the household chapel of John II during his English captivity. It is noticeable, however, that no name among its seven singers is among the clerks of John's chapel in the accounts for 1359 quoted earlier. It is conceivable that the Climent who was a clerk in John's chapel, and who was the medium for a payment to two 'varlets' who carried the chapel organ from London to Hertford, was the same Simon Clement named in Alanus's motet as one whose 'voice charmed the ears, and the clear voice of whose hand was outstanding on the organ':

> vox non parum
> mulcet auris Simonis
> Clementis, os cuius clarum
> manus nitet organis.

In sum, if the earlier date of Alanus's *Sub Arturo* be correct, the hypothesis seems sustainable that it was in the context of the presence in England of the court and chapel of John II during the period May 1357 to October 1360, and possibly during celebrations surrounding St George's day in 1358, that the two motets in question were composed, perhaps as in some sense complementary to each other. It may also be surmised that the singers charged with the solemn celebration of the Saturday Lady-Mass in John II's chapel were engaged only for that duty, and that the daily mass and offices there were carried out by the household's chaplains and clerks. That the former group does not appear in the household accounts for 1359 may or may not argue for their discontinuance by then. It is in either case possible that Simon Clement moved at one point from the *collegium* celebrated by Alanus to a clerkship, with responsibility for organ-playing, in the chapel of John II.[40]

Edward Roesner has remarked of the pieces in the Robertsbridge keyboard manuscript (London, British Library Add. 28550) that what makes them 'of special interest to us is the possibility that they may have reached England with the captivity there of Vitry's patron, John II, in

---

[39.] Revelations 1. 12–2. 1; see *Musicorum Collegio*, iv–v.

[40.] B. Trowell has summarized the material concerning Simon Clement, presumably the musician celebrated by Alanus, which shows him to have acquired several benefices in England after 1363, and to have been a member of the royal household chapel in 1377 (see n. 29). It seems unsafe, however, to assume that John II 'took with him to England in 1357' a 'Clement [*sic*, cited from J. Marix], clerc de chapelle'. The evidence so far shows only that a 'Climent' served John II in that capacity for a great part of the year 1359. [See also Bowers, 'Fixed Points'.]

1357–60'.[41] It will be recalled that intabulations of two motets by de Vitry are among the manuscript's contents.[42] Its origin in the chapel of John II while in England seems a probability, as does the origin there also of the ten motets at Durham, which include two by de Vitry, as well as the highly pertinent *Musicorum collegio*. The musical situation in Durham Cathedral Priory appears to have deteriorated between the monks' compilation,[43] presumably around 1358–9, of a collection of motets,[44] and the occasion of a visitation made about 1390. It was observed then that the custom of having clerks, apparently outside persons, who could sing polyphony (*cantantes organum*) to help the monks by singing treble parts (*adiuvantes monachos in cantu qui dicitur trebill*) had been discontinued, so that the singing of the brethren in choir was greatly hampered.[45]

The structure of *Musicorum collegio* does not bear comparison with Alanus's motet for enterprise. It has the orthodox design of a *color* announced in four *taleae* and then repeated in diminution by half; competently crafted in its realization, it has appropriately placed quasi-hocket passages. *Sub Arturo*, which stands alone in proposing a new form of proportionate design, was taken to France, and some thirty-five years later was copied with relatively few other motets into the Chantilly manuscript.[46] There it figured among a choice collection that has all the marks of having been chosen for high-level musical and textual interest, and for possible performance as part of the household music of an aristocratic connoisseur. In the next phase of musical history, Alanus's English successors adopted his concept of proportionate structure. By making use of the established mensuration-signatures, they eventually applied it to all parts of their polyphonic textures, particularly at the articulating points of their designs. In that important sense, Alanus laid one of the foundation-stones of much of the musical architecture of the two centuries to come.

The Old Hall Manuscript and the Fountains Leaves: Settings of Ordinary Chants

Many Sanctus and Agnus Dei settings in the Old Hall manuscript (British Library, Add. 57950: 'OH') and the Fountains leaves (Add. 40011B: 'LoF') show continuities with fourteenth-century settings,

---

[41.] *Complete Works*, Introd., p. vi.

[42.] The other contents are printed in PMFC XVII, 58–61.

[43.] But see n. 15 above.

[44.] There are also settings of *Virgo dei genitrix* and *Deo gracias*.

[45.] F. Ll. Harrison, *Music in Medieval Britain*[2] (London, 1963), 115, cited from W. A. Pantin, *Chapters of the English Black Monks* III, Camden Society 54 (London, 1937), 84.

[46.] The 13 Chantilly motets are edited in PMFC V, as nos. 4, 5a, 23, and 24–33.

with respect to the position of the plainsong in the texture and the manner of its treatment. This extensive repertory of compositions for the Ordinary of the mass and of votive antiphons in which plainsongs were used integrally or partially exhibits four distinguishable manners of treatment: (1) monorhythmic, with occasional deviation; (2) rhythmicized; (3) expanded, i.e. rhythmicized with infill and end-extension; and (4) motet-wise, in compositions for the Ordinary based on an external plainsong. Motetizing, with isorhythmic disposition, of an Ordinary chant itself, as in four movements of Machaut's *Messe de Notre Dame*, does not occur. The monorhythmic procedure had a long English history, its last splendid manifestation being in responds by John Sheppard in the last years of the Sarum rite.[47] From the fourteenth century on, the chant was notated in breves (e.g. PMFC xvi, 51; facsimile Early English Church Music 26, 9) which were generally imperfect, occasionally perfect (e.g. PMFC xvi, 57, 65, 66, and OH 106, by W. Typp; see Example 1). In this period the prolation was always major; modus did not come in question. Metrical bar-lines in modern transcriptions of such pieces are superfluous, though lines through the staff to indicate text-stresses do have validity. Rhythmic activity is on the whole less in Old Hall pieces of this kind than in some in the fourteenth-century repertory. Information relative to plainsong use is shown in Table 4; in all cases the plainsong is monorhythmic in the middle voice. An index figure to the Sarum chant number indicates an interval of upward transposition. All pieces were notated in score unless otherwise shown and are anonymous unless otherwise indicated.

Example 1. OH 106, W. Typp; plainsong from Sarum Sanctus VI (see above)

[47.] See D. Chadd (ed.), *John Sheppard: I, Responsorial Music*, Early English Church Music 17 (London, 1977).

TABLE 4. *Settings incorporating monorhythmic chant in Old Hall and Fountains leaves*

Number	Sarum chant	Lines of c-clefs	Comments
Sanctus			
OH 100	III	2 4 5	With trope *Marie filius*; exchanges between II and III
101[a]	V	2 4 5	Exchanges between II and III
103	IX^5	1 3 5	
104	IV^5	3 4 5	
105	IV^8	1 2 5	
106	VI^4	1 3 5	W. Typp
107	VIII^5	1 3 5	
110	X^5	2 4 5	W. Typp; crossing between II and III
LoF 5	III	1 4 5	
7	I	2 5 5	
8	IX^5	1 3 5	
Agnus dei			
OH 125	I^8	1 2 4	Crossing between I and II
128	III^4	1 3 5	Crossing between II and III
129[b]	VI^5	1 3 5	Crossing between II and III
130	V^5	1 3 5	
131	IV	1 4 5	Exchanges between II and III
134[c]	IX^5	1 3 5	
135	VIII^5	1 3 5	W. Typp; crossing between II and III
136	VIII^5	1 3 5	
138	X^4	1 3 5	Leonel; one setting for three strains
139	X^5	1 3 5 5	Voice III, indicated 'Contratenor de cantu feriali', is an active contratenor added to an orthodox setting
LoF 10	I	1 4 5	
11	II^4	1 3 4	
13	III^5	1 2 4	

[a] Also LoF 9.
[b] Also LoF 12.
[c] Also LoF 14.

TABLE 5. *Settings incorporating rhythmicized but undecorated chant in the Old Hall and Fountains leaves*

Number in OH	Sarum chant	Lines of c-clefs	Comments
Gloria			
5	V	2 4 5	Incomplete
20	V⁴	2 5 5	J. Excetre; chant in I, which changes to c³ clef; notated in separate parts, with sections in 2 and 3 voices; 'contratenor' and 'tenor' in 3-voice sections
Credo			
56	up a 5th	1 3 5	
57	up a 5th	3 3 5	Chant in I
58	up a 5th	1 3 5	
Sanctus			
95	I⁴,⁸	1 3 3	W. Typp; chant in I, II, and III
96	I⁵	1 2 4	Leonel
97	II⁵	1 3 4	Lambe
98	II²	2 4 5	W. Typp
99	III	2 4 5	Leonel
108	VII⁵	2 4 5	R. Chirbury; brief exchanges between I, II, III
109	X³	2 3 5	Leonel
118	V	1 1 3 4	Leonel; chant in III; III and IV indicated 'Tenor' and 'Contratenor'
121	→	2 4 5	Excetre; chant in Paris, Bibl. de l'Arsenal 135 (Sarum Missal etc., used in London or Canterbury)
122	V	1 1 3 3 (separate parts)	J. Tyes; notable for chant in Tenor, rhythmicized in quasi-motet fashion, though not rhythmically patterned in that wise (cf. PMFC xvi, 58)
123	III⁸	1 3 (separate parts)	Pycard; notable for chant in I made a canon a2 (?3)

In Table 5 similar information is given for the second category of chant treatment—rhythmicization, without significant infill or extension. It

TABLE 5—*cont.*

Number in OH	Sarum chant	Lines of c-clefs	Comments
Agnus dei			
126	II⁴	1 3 3	
127	III⁴	1 3 3	
133	→	1 3 4	Leonel; the initium of the chant, a tone lower than here, was quoted in Bishop Grandisson's Exeter Ordinal (ed. J. N. Dalton, ii, 1909, p. 465)
135	VIII⁵	1 3 5	W. Typp
137	VII⁴	1 3 5	Leonel
Votive antiphon			
43	Ave regina … ave domina	1 3 5	Leonel; up a 5th
44	Regina celi	1 3 4	Up a 5th
49	Beata progenies	2 3 5	Leonel; up a 5th
51	Regali ex progenie	2 3 4	Fonteyns; up a 5th

includes Glorias, Credos, and votive antiphons; in the last an occasional small degree of infill has been discounted. Where the chant is not in the middle voice of three, its disposition is shown in the fourth column, where certain other comments are also made. In the case of W. Typp's Sanctus, the chant is shown as being at times in any one of the voices, and as being transposed at times a fourth, at times an octave above its original pitch. This manner of chant deployment is generally called 'migrant', a term devised by Manfred Bukofzer. In his commentary on Old Hall in the form of an extended review of the first edition, and in his essay on the Fountains leaves (both fundamental to all later writing on the repertory), Bukofzer applied the term to this practice (which was not a usage in fourteenth-century Ordinary compositions), irrespective of whether it involved a few notes or a more or less complete unit of chant.[48] Many cases were mere momentary exchanges, opted for by composer or scribe;[49] they by no

[48.] See his *Studies in Medieval and Renaissance Music* (New York, 1950), 46–8, 101.

[49.] But see E. H. Sparks, *Cantus firmus in Mass and Motet* (Berkeley, 1963), 5–11, where a systematic construction was put on the practice.

means obviated crossings of parts, which were frequent, as they were in the fourteenth century. Such rare cases as Typp's Sanctus and Byttering's antiphon *Nesciens mater* (see Table 6) clearly constituted a particular resource in the process of composition. In both these cases there were concomitant transference of chant, and transposition of its pitch.

The nine cases of the third category, rhythmicized and expanded chant, are shown in Table 6. Here it seems appropriate to extend the scope of information in the fourth column. This includes the appearance of the indication 'contratenor', a term rare in English usage before Old Hall. Its appearance signals the entry of a fresh structural concept, that of a voice-line that complements the tenor, works above and below it, and threads its way around the tenor's previously determined contours. This is related, though at this juncture not inflexibly, to the indications of clef-placing given in Tables 4, 5, and 6. In all but a very few cases the clef placings are differentiated, e.g. 2 4 5 (c-clef is to be understood unless the letter f is shown); in a few cases the lower clefs are paired, e.g. 1 3 3. The latter formation had been for some time predominant in three-voice chanson composition in France, though less so in ritual music there. It is often found in association with the term 'contratenor'. To that extent, the term 'French chanson style' is a valid one, provided the factor of clef-disposition be taken in conjunction with melodic style, in the context of the structural and dialectical changes observable in the original layer of the Old Hall manuscript—changes which were part of a process of proximation, which eventually became mutual, of the two countries' styles. It is otherwise with the term 'English discant' when applied indiscriminately to the bulk of the three-part pieces in the original layer. Manfred Bukofzer used the term 'conductus', surely an anachronism here, of these Ordinary compositions. That he also remarked paradoxically on the 'scarcity of English discant' was due to his view that the term essentially involved the plainsong being in the lower or lowest voice. In spite of earlier and current usage, however, the term is unsatisfactory in reference to the repertory in question. Philologically, and in terms of time and place, the term 'discant' denoted a second voice to a given length of tune, in the context of a pedagogical exercise using the concept of 'sights'. Leonel Power's treatise on the subject has:

How thou shalt [t]hem [i.e. the sights] ymageyn betwene the playnsong and the discant, here foluythe ensample: Ferst to enforme a childe in his counterpoynt he most [using the quatreble sight] ymagyne his unisoun the 8te note fro the playnsong benethe.[50]

[50] Quoted from T. Georgiades, *Englische Diskanttraktate aus der ersten Hälfte des 15. Jahrhunderts* (Munich, 1937), 12.

TABLE 6. *Settings incorporating rhythmicized and expanded chant in Old Hall and the Fountains leaves*

Number in OH	Sarum Chant	Lines of c-clefs	Comments
Credo			
82	up a 4th	3 3 f³ (separate parts)	Chant in II ('cantus secundus'), with 'Tenor' and 'Contratenor'; I is a gymel in final section
Sanctus			
115	I⁴	1 1 5 (separate parts)	Leonel; expanded chant in I, II; II, III indicated as 'Contratenor' and 'Tenor'; very extended setting; 'new style phonemes'
116	II⁵	3 4 5 (separate parts; III changes to c⁴)	Leonel; expanded chant in I; II, III indicated 'Contratenor' and 'Tenor'; 'new style phonemes'
117	III⁴	3 3 5 (separate parts)	Leonel; expanded chant in I; III, IV indicated 'Contratenor' and 'Tenor'
119	II⁵	2 3 5	Olyver; expanded chant in I, momentarily II
120	V⁵	1 3 5	Olyver; heavily expanded chant in I
Agnus dei			
141	→	1 1 3 3 (separate parts)	Leonel; chant as in Table 5, no. 133 at pitch; chant in IV, rhythmicized with expansions in quasi-motet fashion, though not rhythmically patterned in that wise
142	VI⁸	1 3 5	Olyver; chant in I
Votive antiphon			
50	Nesciens mater	1 3 4	Byttering; chant in I, II, III at the following intervals: +9 (I), +1 (III, II, III), −4 (III), +1 (II, III), at pitch (III)

Leonel dealt only (but with great thoroughness) with the quatreble and treble sights; discanting for singers using the sights of mean countertenor and counter (the latter in a pitch-range below the plainsong) was treated in other handbooks. Neither logically nor in historical terms, therefore, may 'English discant' be used of three-part composition; it may suitably be replaced by the modern term 'homorhythmic'. With a plainsong or plainsong-derived voice as the middle one of three, the usage of the treatises suggests treble, plainsong or tenor, and counter. Outside the special context of church music the everyday terms for three-part music were treble, mean, and tenor (or burden).

The important topic of melodic style comes under the present subject in relation to infilling of rhythmicized plainsong. It is opportune therefore to identify one or two symptoms of change. For convenience, these are styled 'new-style phonemes', on the analogy of units of significant sound in language; two specimens have been indicated by brackets over the extract from Byttering's antiphon *Nesciens mater* (OH 50) in Example 2. These particular musical phonemes occur so rarely in Leonel that their use in two extended Sanctus settings on plainsongs (OH 115, 116) is all the more notable. An anonymous Credo (OH 82) for two, four, and five voices, is a particularly competent example of a fully worked out expansion of the plainsong, placed in a 'cantus secundus', in which new-style phonemes are securely handled in a consummate piece of stylistic transformation. This is the only Ordinary setting in the manuscript in which rhythmicizing of plainsong and telescoping of text were both employed. Naturally, the melodic line of those stretches of text that are not sung by *cantus secundus* cannot derive from the chant. The pieces by Olyver are significant early essays in this craft of plainsong infill and extension as a component of polyphony,[51] termed in some later contexts 'paraphrase'. The procedure has a much earlier prototype in melodic tropes of the kind termed 'meloform', that is, purely musical. Examples are neumae inserted in responds[52] and textless cadential melismata appended to introits.[53]

Compositions for the Ordinary on Freely Composed Tenors

The category of Ordinary compositions, here consisting of Gloria and Credo only, based on a tenor that for convenience may be called *pes*, i.e. a rhythmically patterned voice that is not a plainsong (though this may not always be absolutely certain) comes under scrutiny here on the ground of its use of precise structural proportions. As shown in Table 7, its

[51] A Hosanna by Olyver is quoted in Harrison, *Music in Medieval Britain*, 231–2.

[52] See R. Steiner, 'Melismatic Tropes', *New Grove*, XIX, 183.

[53] See M. Huglo, 'On the Origins of the Troper-Proser', *Journal of the Plainsong & Mediaeval Music Society* 2 (1979), 15–16.

Example 2. Byttering, *Nesciens mater*

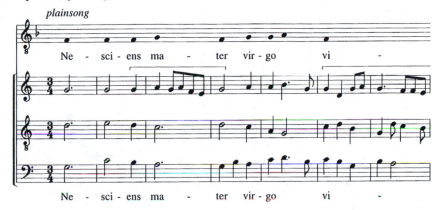

TABLE 7. *Compositions for the Ordinary based on a tenor* pes

Number	Composer	Lines of c-clefs	Isorhythmic data	Overall design
Gloria				
OH 19	J. Tyes	1 1 3	co = 2ta; ta = (2 × 10 black b) + (2 × 12 red b) = 120m + 96m = 216m; thus co = 432m	co is rep in dim by half; length 648m; proportions 2:1
OH 23	Leonel	1 1 3 3	co = 2ta; ta = (9 + 19 imp b with pro ma) + (18 + 10 imp b with pro mi) = 168m + 112m = 280m; thus co = 560m	co is rep in dim by half; length 840m; proportions 2:1
OH 30	Qweldryk (with trope *Spiritus et alme*)	1 (changing to 2) 2 3 4	co = 2ta; ta = (6 + 7 + 5) imp l with temp imp and pro mi = 144m; thus co = 288m	co is rep in dim by half; length 432m; proportions 2:1
LoF 3	Anon.	1 4 5 5	co = 2ta	co is stated 9 times

Credo

OH 85	Bittering (in later hand)	1 1 4 4		18 strains, each equivalent of (6 imp b + 1 b-rest with pro ma) preceded by 2 b-rests, followed by final strain of $3b$ and l extra tempus; length $(12 + 765 + 18)$ $m = 786m$
OH 86	Swynford	1 1 3 3	co = 2ta; ta = $(14 + 21 + 19)$ imp b with pro ma, plus same with pro mi = $324m + 216m = 540m$	co is rep in dim by half; length $810m$; proportions 2:1
OH 88	Qweldryk	1 1 3	co = 2ta; ta = $(16+16)$ imp b with pro ma + $(12 + 14)$ imp b with pro mi = $192m + 104m = 296m$; thus co = $592m$	co is rep in dim by half; length $888m$; proportions 2:1
OH 90 (voices I, IV) + LoF 15 (voices II, III)	Anon.	1 1 3 4	co = 3ta after introitus of 16 imp b with pro ma; ta = $12b = 72m$; thus co = $216m$	co is rep in retrograde, then in original order; the 3 statements are then made in dim by half; length $648m + 324m = 972m$; proportions 2:1

Abbreviations

b	brevis	mi	minor
co	color	pro	prolatio
dim	diminution	rep	repeated
imp	imperfect(um)	s	semibreve
l	long	ST	Solus Tenor
m	minim	ta	talea
ma	maior	temp	tempus

procedures make these pieces almost rank in innovative interest with Ordinary movements based on a plainsong external to that of their own text, next to be considered. Like the latter, they invite interest as pioneer workings of the highly germinative idea of proportionate design applied to the longer texts of the Ordinary. Six of the eight melodies in question (apart from LoF 3, and the Amen of OH 23) are of normal length, and appear pre-designed in the sense of their unit-balance and contour-control. It may seem that a corollary of this is that each of the six may have been a pre-existing, or at least pre-conceived, product, and be entitled to the possibility that it enjoyed some other existence. This, however, is made unlikely by the fact that in five of the six the tenor was made in two or three isorhythmic sections, e.g. that of a Gloria by J. Tyes (OH 19).[54] The exception just referred to, the tenor of Byttering's Credo (OH 85), has eight of its eighteen equal-length units cast in the same rhythm; thus its formal character better corresponds to the term isometric than isorhythmic. The *pes* of an anonymous Gloria in the Fountains leaves (LoF 3) is an abstract one of five notes whose contratenor is its melodic inversion at the fifth below, simultaneously sounded. The tenor of an anonymous Credo (OH 90, the two voices there being completed by the two of LoF 15) has a retrograde statement between two statements as its stands, the whole being repeated in diminution by half.[55]

Compositions for the Ordinary on Other Plainchant Tenors

Nearly half a century after J. Alanus's new-departure motet *Sub Arturo*, the group of compositions in Table 8 is likewise a significant foretaste of the future. Turning from the use of the plainsong of the Ordinary item itself as a basis for its polyphony, the composers of these six pieces took an external plainsong on which to build their settings. The two settings based on chants from the office of Thomas of Canterbury (OH 24, 84) and the two on chants in praise of the Trinity, may be seen as pairs, each with a definite liturgical relevance. Pycard's Gloria with Marian trope (OH 28) may relate both to the priests' festival, the feast day of John the Evangelist (27 December) and to the Nativity of the Virgin. Typp's Credo on *Benedicam te domine* may possibly have had a connection with the new feast of the Name of Jesus, observed, perhaps from the early fifteenth century, in the Sarum rite on 7 August. While these are pioneer anticipations of the structure-type of the complete Ordinary on an extended cantus firmus that was to flourish for two centuries, they probably may not claim absolute

---

[54.] There is a facsimile of the page in W. Apel, *The Notation of Polyphonic Music 900–1600*[4] (Cambridge, Mass., 1949), 365.

[55.] M. Bukofzer, *Studies* 88, 107–8.

priority. At any rate, there is the case of an apparently plainsong cantus firmus in common between a motet in honour of St Louis of Toulouse, bishop and confessor, with texted voices: *Flos inter lilia* and *Celsa cedrus* over the tenor *Quam magnus pontifex* in Ivrea (PMFC v, 7) and a setting of the Gloria in the same manuscript. The tenor, without indication in the Gloria, is cued as [*O*] *quam magnus pontifex* in an incomplete copy of the motet, whose tenor is complete, in Cambrai, Bibliothèque municipale 1328 (1176). Neither tenor text has been found allied to the tune of this tenor.[56] The tenor has exactly the same layout in both compositions. Another case is that of an incomplete Gloria, with its tenor cued as *Descendit angelus domini*, antiphon to the psalms at first vespers of John the Baptist, with the composer's name given as Rentius de Ponte Curvo. This occurs on a flyleaf in Cividale, Museo Archeologico Nazionale LXIII. Rentius is recorded as having been in Cividale in 1407–8,[57] thus within a few years of the writing down of the six mass-movements on an external plainsong in the Old Hall manuscript.

Manfred Bukofzer remarked that in the anonymous (?Leonel) setting of the Gloria (OH 24) based on *Ad Thome memoriam*, the fourth antiphon at lauds on the feast of Thomas of Canterbury, the tenor has a 'vague' repeat, and that in the tenor of Leonel's Credo (OH 84) on *Opem nobis O Thoma*, the antiphon to the canticle Benedictus at lauds on the same day, 'there is no repeat'.[58] Neither comment is valid, nor are the comments on these two items in the more recent edition adequate to their actual structures.[59] It has not been observed that in *Opem nobis* the two statements of the tenor are followed by an extension that can be identified as the neuma of the sixth mode, though the editors of the more recent edition describe the tenor as 'truncated and varied'. It was a normal custom, observed also in the Sarum rite, that at the end of the last antiphon at vespers and lauds and in each nocturn of matins, and of all antiphons to the Magnificat, Benedictus, and Athanasian Creed (*Quicumque vult*), the neuma of the mode was added, except during the three weeks before the Sunday after Easter and in

---

[56] The Gloria is printed in H. Stäblein-Harder (ed.), *Fourteenth-Century Mass Music in France*, Corpus Mensurabilis Musicae 29 (n.p., 1962), 22; see her comment on the identity in Musicological Studies and Documents 7 (1962), 117. The words *O quam magnus pontifex* occur in Franciscan sources as the beginning of the antiphon to the Magnificat in the office of Louis, bishop and confessor, e.g. in the breviary Oxford, Bodleian Library Douce 245, fol. 549; with a tune different from that in the motet in Dublin, Trinity College B. 1. 2 (not foliated). In Analecta Hymnica 26, 273 there is a similar text beginning *O quam clarus pontifex*.

[57] L. Lockwood, 'Cantus firmus', *New Grove*, III, 740; *Répertoire Internationale des Sources Musicales* B/IV/4 (Munich and Duisburg, 1972), 749.

[58] *Studies* 60, 64.

[59] Hughes and Bent, *Old Hall* III 18, 32.

TABLE 8. *Ordinary settings on an external plainsong*

Number	Composer	Cantus firmus	Lines of c-clefs	Isorhythmic data and overall design
Gloria				
OH 24	Anon. (? Leonel)	*Ad Thome*, 4th ♮ at lauds of Thomas of Canterbury, down a 5th with some infill and 11-note extension	$c^3f^3f^3$	$2co = (2 \times ta^A) + (2 \times ta^B)$; $ta^A = 46b$ (each of $6m$), $ta^B = 16b$ (likewise); 2nd co begins $16b$ before end of 2nd statement of ta^A; thus 1st co = $76b$, 2nd co = $48b$; length $124b = 744m$; proportions $23:16$
OH 28	Pycard (with trope *Spiritus et alme*)	*Johannes Jesu care*, last half-strophe of sequence *Johannes Jesu Christo*	1 1 5 5 5 (+ST:5)	co = 2ta; ta = 12 imp b with pro ma = $72m$; thus co = $144m$. It is stated: twice; twice in dim by one quarter; twice in dim by one third; and twice in dim by half; length $288m + 216m + 192m + 144m = 840m$; proportions $12:9:8:6$
LoF 1	Pennard (?)	*Tibi laus, tibi gloria, tibi gratiarum actio*, verse after 1st, 3rd and 5th psalms at lauds on Trinity Sunday	1 2 5 5	co = 3ta; ta = 14 perf b with pro ma = $126m$; thus co = $378m$; this is repeated, and then stated twice in dim to one third; length $378m + 378m + 252m = 1008m$; proportions $3 : (3) : 1 : (1)$

Credo				
OH 84	Leonel	*Opem nobis*, A to Benedictus at lauds of Thomas of Canterbury, down a 5th with some infill, ending with neuma of mode 6	3 5 5	co (i.e. A + neuma) = 3ta; ta = (13 + 13 + 15 + 13) imp b with pro ma = 324m; thus co = 972m; this is stated once
OH 87	Typp	*Benedicam te domine*, 3rd A at lauds on Sundays (or ? on feast of Name of Jesus)	1 3 4	co = 4ta; ta = 16 imp b with pro ma; thus co = 64b = 384m; co is rep with pro mi, i.e. dim by one third = 256m; it is stated again with pro ma in dim to one quarter = 96m; length 736m; proportions 12 : 8 : 3
OH 89	Pennard	*Te iure laudant*, 5th A at lauds on Trinity Sunday; also A to Athanasian Creed on certain feasts and Sundays; ending with neuma of mode 5	1 1 3 3 (+ST:4)	co = 7ta (antiphon) + 3ta (neuma); ta = 8 imp b with pro ma = 48m; thus co = 480m; it is stated again unchanged; length 960m; proportions 1 : 1

For abbreviations see Table 7.

services for the dead.[60] Leonel therefore used the neuma in his cantus firmus as it would have been sung in the antiphon's liturgical place. He deployed the complete antiphon in one statement in three isorhythmic *taleae*, approximating the *taleae* rhythm to some degree, however, to the expansion-mode of treatment by a small amount of infill, mostly in shorter notes. The infilling notes and the addition of the neuma may be observed in a complete transcription of the cantus firmus in parallel with the chant in Example 3.

This procedure of layout and manner of infill are followed in general in the tenor *Ad Thome memoriam*; it seems very likely therefore that this Gloria setting was also composed by Leonel. In addition, these are the only two plainsongs used in the main layer of the manuscript whose pitch was transposed downwards for their polyphonic use, in both cases by a fifth. The *color*, again a complete antiphon, is given two statements, which are offset to two *taleae*, each repeated. Following the end of the second *color* there is a short extension, placed similarly to the neuma at the end of *Opem nobis*. It seems, however, not to have a liturgical function; it has the probably intended effect of bringing the cantus firmus to an end on G, not the final F of the plainsong, and the setting on the final C. In Example 4 the two repeated *taleae* are indicated as I and II, and 1 and 2, respectively.

In these two compositions the effect of the tenor's mode of treatment is to put the movement relation between the three voices closer to that of a non-cantus-firmus setting than to that characteristic of an isorhythmic motet with long-note tenor. It was an original concept to integrate the cantus firmus in this way, and to compose the settings in the manner of many non cantus-firmus settings, as a seamless continuum. The purpose of integration was furthered by the underlaying of text in the tenor (see Example 3) at some points where the treble is momentarily silent.

In his commentary on an anonymous Gloria on an unidentified cantus firmus in the Fountains leaves (LoF 1), Bukofzer made a good case for attributing it to Pennard of Old Hall.[61] Its tenor, which Bukofzer identified as *Tibi laus, tibi gloria, tibi gratiarum actio*, a verse sung after the first, third, and fifth psalms at lauds on Trinity Sunday, is used complete, is repeated, and is then stated twice more in diminution to one third. The Credo by Pennard (OH 89) which inspired Bukofzer's discovery of that cantus firmus, was based on *Te iure laudant, te adorant, te glorificant omnes creature tue, O beata trinitas*, the antiphon to the Athanasian Creed on certain feasts and Sundays.[62] This was sung complete as the tenor, and then repeated. The commentary in the more recent edition notes: 'in the Tenor the last

---

[60.] F. Procter and C. Wordsworth (eds.), *Breviarium ad usum insignis ecclesiae Sarum* I (Cambridge, 1882), dccxiii; II (1889), 475; Harrison, *Music in Medieval Britain* 59.

[61.] *Studies*, 107 and pl. 1.

[62.] *Breviarium* II, 48–9.

Example 3. Tenor of OH 84 (*Credo*, Leonel); plainsong from LBL Lansdowne 493, fol. 19r

Example 3—*cont.*

Example 4. Tenor of OH 24 (*Gloria*, Leonel); plainsong from LBL Lansdowne 493, fol. 19r

Example 4—*cont.*

third appears to repeat and vary the second third'. The case seems at first
to correspond to that in Leonel's Credo on *Opem nobis*. The tenor's
addendum, however, while having a length and contour appropriate to a
neuma, is not identical with any mode five specimen that has been
inspected. These short modally-determined tunes, ceremonial in a liturgy
and normative in a tonary, varied moderately in time and place.

The commentary of the edition also observes: 'Each statement [of the
tenor] has eight rhythmic sections which are mostly identical with each
other.' In fact, however, the total is ten isorhythmic *taleae*, seven for the
antiphon and three for the addendum. Their isorhythm is not com-
promised by the first note of the fifth *talea* being written in Old Hall as a
breve instead of two semibreves (as it is indeed written in the incomplete
concordance on a leaf now in Princeton: Princeton, University Library
Medieval and Renaissance mss 103), nor by two successive identical-pitch
breves being twice written as a long, in *taleae* eight and nine. There is a

divergence, however, in the sixth *talea*.[63] Bukofzer also commented that in both of the settings just considered the composer carried out 'the strange idea of distributing an isorhythmic pattern alternately over two voices'.[64]

With W. Typp's Credo (OH 87) on *Benedicam te domine* and Pycard's Gloria (OH 28) on *Johannes Jesu care*, we come into the sphere of more sophisticated proportions in overall structure. Typp disposed his cantus firmus in a four-times stated pattern of: longa/longa/longa-rest/longa-rest/ maxima/longa/longa. For the first repeat of this he reduced the tenor longa by one third and changed the texted voices to minor prolation from major. For the second repeat he returned the upper voices' prolation to major, and reduced the tenor's longa to one quarter of its first value. The resulting structural proportions are 12 : 8 : 3.

Pycard's disposition of the six-note plainsong excerpt *Johannes Jesu care* presents the very rare case of a structure proportionate in four terms, in this case 12 : 9 : 8 : 6. The changing rhythmic relation to the upper voices is a major point of interest. The beginning of the second *color* involves in the tenor a diminution by one third, but not a change to minor prolation from major, which is also maintained by the tenor's two satellite voices. Nevertheless, Pycard chose to give the two texted upper voices a decided leaning to minor prolation, without interposing a mensuration-signature in that sense. For the third *color*, when the tenor's values were reduced by one third, the composer clearly created this relation in reverse. At the beginning of the fourth *color*, rhythmic equivalence of the upper and lower voices was restored, a mensuration-signature, for perfect time and minor prolation, now being interposed. Diminution of the semibreve must be assumed, in order to continue the proportional process.

Isorhythmic Motets

Of the four isorhythmic motets on identified plainsongs in Old Hall (see Table 9), three belong to the additions entered after the original layer was completed. A notable factor in Byttering's deployment of the complete verse *Sponsus amat sponsam* of the sixth respond *Virgo flagellatur* at matins of Katharine of Alexandria, in his *En Katerine solennia/Virginalis concio* (OH 145) entered in the last section of the original layer, is his using red *figurae* to switch mode and time from perfect to imperfect. The first two statements, in the proportion 2 : 1, both accommodate the tenor's switch and the upper voices' change from minor to major prolation. The third

---

[63.] The text is set in a regular alternation between Cantus I and Cantus II, corresponding exactly to the layout of the tenor. This is but one of a number of different text-plans used in Credo settings in the manuscript.

[64.] *Studies*, 107.

TABLE 9. *Isorhythmic Motets in Old Hall*

Number	Composer	Cantus firmus	Lines of c-clefs	Isorhythmic data and overall design
OH 145	Bittering	*Sponsus amat spon-sam*, verse of 6th R *Virgo flagellatur* at matins of Katharine of Alexandria	1 2 3	co = 2ta; ta = 9 perf l (as 7 black l + 3 red l) = 27 perf b with pro mi = 162m; thus co = 324m; it is rep in dim by half = 162m, and stated again in dim to one third = 108m; length 594m; proportions 6 : 3 : 2
LoF 17	Anon	*Deo gratias*, response to *Ite missa est*	1 1 4 4 (+ST:4)	co = 2ta; ta = 16 imp b with pro ma (which includes 3 imp b with pro mi); thus co = 32 imp b = 192m; co is rep in mensural dim, so that it = 72m; length 264m; proportions 8 : 3

OH 112	Cook	Ab inimicis nostris defende nos Christe, Litany invocation in time of war	1 3 4	co = 2ta; ta = 9 perf l = 27 imp b with pro ma = 162m; thus co = 324m; it is rep in dim by one third = 216m; and stated again in further dim by one third = 144m; length 684m; proportions 9 : 6 : 4
OH 111	Damett	Benedictus Marie filius qui ve, excerpt from Sanctus III with trope Marie filius	1 3 4	co = 2ta; ta = 12 perf l (as 10 black l + 3 red l) = 36 perf b = 216m; thus co = 432m; it is rep in dim by one third (for relation of this to the MS prescription see text) = 288m; it is then stated again in dim to one half = 216m, and finally in dim to one sixth = 72m; length 1008m; proportions 6 : 4 : 3 : 1
OH 113	Sturgeon	[ven]it in nomine Domini, excerpt from Sanctus III with trope Marie filius	2 4 4	co = 2ta; ta = 10 perf l (as 4 black l + 4 red l + rests) = 30 perf b with pro mi = 180m; thus co = 360m; it is rep in dim by one third = 240m, and stated again in dim to one third = 120m; length 720m; proportions 3 : 2 : 1

For abbreviations, see Table 7.

statement, however, with the upper voices reverting to minor prolation, has at the corresponding point a conjunction of duple and triple rhythm. The design as a whole shows a clear articulation of the beginnings of the second and third sections, with a mensuration-signature interposed in each of the upper voices. The anticipation by diminution of the cantus firmus by the cantus (at *Que precabatur*) should be noted.

The Fountains leaves have a motet (LoF 17) with the texts *Humane lingue organis* and *Supplicum voces* on the *Deo gratias* response to one of the *Ite missa est* tunes sung by the deacon at the end of mass (PMFC xv, 36). The tenor's rhythm has a unit of the value of three imperfect breves in minor prolation enclosed within its *talea* of sixteen imperfect breves in major prolation. The mensural prescription in this case is shown at the beginning of a 'Solus Tenor' part, and prescribes a mensural diminution that causes the major prolation notes to be reduced to one third, the minor prolation notes to one half (see Example 5). The resulting proportions are 96 : 36, i.e. 8 : 3. The general flow of the texture is not interrupted at the tenor's change of measure, though there is a small incidence of hocket with its second statement.

On the other hand, Byttering's co-ordination of music design, articulating clearly the tenor's proportionate repeats, coinciding with signalled or implied mensuration changes in all voices, and making these agree with the main text-changes, was a significant trait in three motets entered subsequent to the original layer. Probably symptomatic of that trend to structural and aural clarification is the fact that Cook, in his motet *Alma proles/Christi miles* on the (complete) Litany invocation *Ab inimicis nostris defende nos Christe* (OH 112), and Nicholas Sturgeon in his *Salve mater domini/Salve templum gratie* on the acephalic excerpt *[ven]it in nomine domini* (OH 113), both had three mensuration-signatures written at the end of the tenor's notation, to be applied to three statements of the tenor. Apart from the linkage of its cantus firmus with that of Damett's motet (to be considered next), Sturgeon's tenor has possibly the most leisurely motion in all of its three stages of any motet in the medieval history of the genre. The disposition of the two *taleae* may be thus indicated, where bracketed values are rests; following the tenor's cue is written 'de modo perfecto', indicating that the long is basically equal to three breves:

G A   C G

Talea 1: (dotted-s + s + b) b l (s + s + red-b) red b l
Talea 2: ditto, the sounded notes being F G and G E.

The proportions are an uncomplicated 3 : 2 : 1; the tenor notes remain unusually long, even in the third stage of diminution.

Example 5. Tenor scheme of LoF 17: *Humane lingue organis/Supplicum voces percipe*

The last composition to be considered here, Thomas Damett's *Salvatoris mater/O Georgi deo* on the tenor *Benedictus Marie Filius* (of which Sturgeon's tenor was the continuation) is another rare case of four-stage deployment of a cantus firmus (OH 111). Its notation includes red notes, and the prescription for its statements uses the language of both mensuration and proportion. It reads:

P⁰ sicut iacet de modo perfecto temporis inperfecti
2⁰ per dimidietatem
3⁰ per tertiam partem
4⁰ per 6ᵃᵐ partem.

Mensuration-signatures appear only by interposition in the notation of the voices; a circle-signature in red, an unusual appearance, is placed in the upper voices at the point where the tenor's third statement will begin. Damett's expertise in, or perhaps experimentation with, mensural symbols shows too in his placing a reversed semicircle sign in the upper voices at the beginning of the tenor's second statement. At that point, however, the fall of the voices with the tenor and the prescription 'per dimidietatem' seem not to be in complete agreement, for the relation of the tenor's original (and only) notation to its movement here is in the proportion 6 : 4. Similarly, the fall of the voices with the tenor in the third statement gives it the proportion 2 : 1 to its original writing. Thus while the manuscript's prescription specifies the proportions 6 : 3 : 2 : 1, the proportions in notated sound appear to be 6 : 4 : 3 : 1. This conclusion, however, rests on the assumption, which does not appear impractical, of a constant tempo throughout in terms of the semibreve of the upper voices. The editors of the more recent edition, while noting that the manuscript's prescription is 'misleading', conclude thus their subsequent explanation of its notational practice: 'The theoretical requirements of the canon are thus met, and certain temporal relationships expressed by the canon may have to be remembered in performance.'[65] The markings in their notation, however, advise nothing more precise than 'faster' for the second and third sections and 'slower' for the fourth. The matter verges on the sadly under-researched subject of tempo, a crucial one in any project for the realization in present-day performance of the many modern editions of medieval music now available.

Proportion in Architecture and Music

This essay has been concerned, in its later sections particularly, with adumbrating a grammar and to a small extent identifying a vocabulary of the style of English music at a significant time in its history. The expression 'The Grammar of a Style' stands at the head of the second chapter of John Harvey's book *The Perpendicular Style 1330–1485*.[66] There should be no question here of facile analogy between these two crafts, but some elements, notably that of proportion, in English music and architecture between *circa* 1330 and *circa* 1420 may suggest parallel movements of thought. In noting the relation of these dates to the kingly succession, John Harvey has written:[67]

There is more than mere accidental convenience in the linking of the style to the dynasty: the starting point can be taken as the accession of Edward III in 1327 after the effective interregnum at the end of his father's reign. . . . the adoption of Perpendicular details in royal work within only a few years from their invention provided the means to success. The accepted or Court style was swiftly revolutionised and henceforth became—we might say was promulgated as—the official standard of taste for all buildings of quality.

And later:[68]

Perpendicular . . . was a banner, an aesthetic symbol of the same royal aspirations which led Edward III to declare himself king of France; to take the vow to the Round Table fulfilled in the founding of the Order of the Garter; to promote the national cult of our patron St. George.

Throughout his exposition of Perpendicular, which is lavishly illustrated with photographs and drawings, Harvey repeatedly stressed the 'close personal interest' of Edward III in architectural works in a number of places, from early in his reign. In 1360 he appointed Henry Yeveley, who

---

[65] Corpus Mensurabilis Musicae 46 (*supra*, n. 2), III, 37.
[66] (London, 1978), 56.
[67] Ibid. 14.
[68] Ibid. 19.

had previously been in the service of the Black Prince (b. 1330), as disposer of the king's works of masonry in the Palace of Westminster and Tower of London. The early works at Windsor (Vestry, 1350–1; Chapter House, 1350–3; Dean's Cloister, 1353–6) were carried out under John Spoonlee and William Wynford. One purpose of the great gathering of 1358 was apparently to mark the opening of the Round Tower to house the Round Table. Of Edington Priory Church in Wiltshire, which came under the patronage of the Black Prince in 1351, Harvey noted:[69] 'This royal intervention not merely links the building with the Court style but specifically with the architectural programme at Windsor'; and 'there can be no doubt that architectural advice and probably drawings were coming from John Spoonlee'. J. Alanus (d. 1373) may have been a member of the St George's Chapel community throughout these years of buildings being planned and designed in a rapidly developing new style. He became a canon of Windsor in 1362, and was given a prebend in St Paul's in the following year.[70] Unlike B. de Cluni ('mittens energia artis practice cum theoria') and J. de Porta ('carmineus'), earlier makers of musicians' motets, Alanus ranged himself not among the singers he celebrated, but as a modest successor to a historical line of theorists. It is perhaps not too surprising then that his speculative mind, in an atmosphere where proportion was being applied with new effect both to the overall design of buildings and to the geometrical complexities of their structural details, should have focused on proportional design in his motet, even to the extent of having this sung out in his text. The principle he applied, which was later used, as we have seen, among others by Byttering, Pennard, Tyes, Cook, Damett, and Sturgeon, was further exploited by Dunstable,[71] Dufay, and their successors.

A Note on Chronology and Provenance

Some questions of chronology and provenance concerning the period *circa* 1270 to *circa* 1390 have been touched upon in the course of this essay. Just upon thirty years ago the present writer interpreted the two main kinds of evidence, archival and stylistic, as supporting a conclusion that the first layer of the Old Hall manuscript originated in the reign of Henry IV (1399–1413), and that most of the subsequent additions, including further

[69] Ibid. 85.
[70] M. F. Bond, *The Inventories of St. George's Chapel Windsor Castle 1384–1667* (Windsor, 1945), 34 n. 4.
[71] For a study of this subject see B. Trowell, 'Proportion in the Music of Dunstable', *Proceedings of the Royal Musical Association* 105 (1979), 100–41, with an Appendix of 'Isorhythmic works in the Old Hall Manuscript'.

pieces by Cook and Power, and music by Burell, Damett, and Sturgeon, who were not previously represented, were made in the reign of Henry V (1413–22).[72] Partly as a corollary to this dating of the original layer, it was suggested, also on stylistic grounds, that the date of LoF was 'close to 1400'.[73] Though in 1950 Bukofzer experienced difficulty in assigning an early fifteenth-century date to LoF, on account of its 'white' notation, he inclined to accepting such a date because of the use of that notation for the songs in Cambridge, University Library Add. 5943, whose 'idiom', he wrote, 'can hardly be later than the early fifteenth century'. He decided, however, on *circa* 1425 as a date for these songs and for secular items, with one concordance, in the Bodleian Library, in Douce 381.[74] Eric Dobson demonstrated that the musical part of the Cambridge manuscript is a collection made in and for Winchester College, either in 1395–8 or 1400–1,[75] years when Thomas Turk, first owner of the manuscript, was a fellow of the college (to which Nicholas Sturgeon was elected a scholar in 1399, when he would have been eight to twelve years old).[76] This disposes of any objection, on notational grounds, to dating LoF in the first decade of the fifteenth century, and tends to support, on grounds of seven concordances with the original layer of Old Hall out of its eighteen surviving items, a similar dating for the origins of Old Hall.

The further and inevitably related subject of composers' identities and attachments concerns itself here primarily with the case of 'Roy Henry' whose name is attached to two compositions at the head of the Gloria and Sanctus series respectively.[77] The evidence of John Strecche, canon of the Augustinian Priory of Kenilworth,[78] dismissed by Margaret Bent as written 'in the context of a long laudatory catalogue' and as being 'no more than conventional praise',[79] cannot be so lightly passed off. Strecche was a chronicler, not a courtier. As such, he was engaged in a serious and extended enterprise, as may be judged from the heading of the five books

[72] Harrison, *Music in Medieval Britain*, 220–1.

[73] Ibid. 227 n. 6.

[74] *Studies* 92–5.

[75] E. J. Dobson and F. Ll. Harrison, *Medieval English Songs* (London and Boston, 1979), 22–6. [See also R. Bowers in *Cambridge Music Manuscripts 900–1600*, ed. I. Fenlon (Cambridge, 1982), 84–7.]

[76] Harrison, *Music in Medieval Britain*, 463.

[77] Facsimile of the Sanctus in *Die Musik in Geschichte und Gegenwart* 6 (1957), plate 3 (after col. 64).

[78] Contained in London, British Library Add. 35295.

[79] *New Grove*, XVI, 284, 'Roy Henry'. Professor Bent earlier gave an equivalent verdict, quoting the passage of the chronicle, in her paper 'Sources of the Old Hall Music', *Proceedings of the Royal Musical Association* 94 (1968), 33. There the passage was described as a 'coronation paean', and as 'at best, conventional flattery'. In this view, Bent echoed Brian Trowell's comment at the end of his article 'Heinrich IV' in *Die Musik in Geschichte und Gegenwart* 6 (1957), col. 63. Trowell attributed no music to the subject of this entry.

of his History of the Kings of England, written certainly with some general relevance to Kenilworth Priory:

Incipit historia Regum omnium Anglorum ante monarchiam et post, expulsis Britonibus usque ad tempus Henrici post Conquestum sexti.

Strecche's manuscript, which he compiled, also contains the eight books of Geoffrey of Monmouth's *Historia Regum Britanniae*. His own history of the kings ends with a description of the death of Henry V, clearly written close to the event, and has a poem of sixteen lines entirely concerned with that king's prowess in war.[80] He gave praise also, out of first-hand knowledge, to Henry IV's knightly and warlike qualities:[81]

miles strenuus, in armis acer . . . in bello semper fortunatus . . . et victor ubique gloriosus . . .

but significantly attributed to him peaceful accomplishments also:

in musica micans, et admirabilis litterature et maxime in morali.

There is no reason to consider this as mere flattery; Strecche's evidence must be considered a strong factor in deciding the question of Roy Henry's identity.[82]

Archive research by Roger Bowers has greatly increased our knowledge of Leonel Power's attachments before his already known residence as *generosus* at Canterbury Cathedral Priory from 1441 and his death there in June, 1445.[83] Bowers showed that Power was a member of the household chapel of Thomas Duke of Clarence during the period covered by Clarence's household accounts from Michaelmas 1418 to his death in August 1421. Leonel was among a complement of eight chaplains, sixteen clerks, and four choristers, serving both as clerk and as instructor of the choristers. It seems possible that he had been a member of Clarence's chapel from its beginnings, which according to Bowers may have been at the time of Thomas's marriage in 1411, at that of his elevation to dukedom in 1412, or at Henry IV's death in 1413. Information is still lacking about the previous decade in Power's life; in 1400 on Bowers's estimate he could

---

[80.] The chapter on Henry V has been printed, with an Introduction, in F. Taylor, *The Chronicle of John Strecche for the Reign of Henry V (1414–23)* (Manchester, 1932).

[81.] London 35295, fol. 262r.

[82.] The writing of the name 'Henri[ci] quinti' alongside a four-voice Alleluia with parallel text '*Yma summis*' on a parchment sheet now in the Worcestershire Record Office, referred to in *The New Grove Dictionary*, XVI, 285, s.v. 'Roy Henry', is related to the date of material on the back of the sheet; it has no reference to the authorship of the music.

[83.] R. Bowers, 'Some Observations on the Life and Career of Lionel Power', *Proceedings of the Royal Musical Association* 102 (1976), 103–27, and Harrison, *Music in Medieval Britain*, 42.

have been twenty to twenty-five years old, an age at which a promising
musician could have started on a professional path. It was a time of
increasing demand, when a career as church musician was becoming open
to laymen as well as to those who had taken orders. While Power in his later
life (in 1438 he became a resident of Canterbury and may have thenceforth
been master of the Priory's Lady Chapel choir)[84] was described as *generosus*
or *armiger* (i.e. esquire), Nicholas Sturgeon and Thomas Damett both took
orders and accumulated benefices. Sturgeon had been elected scholar of
Winchester College in 1399, then aged between eight and twelve, so was
there when the songbook, with its French as well as English elements, was
in existence.[85] It appears that Damett was a commoner at the same college
for several years before 1406–7, when he would have been about seventeen.
Both were thus probably in their early twenties in 1413, the first year of
Henry V, when the accounts of the chapel of the royal household show
them as members, which they do again in 1421, the year before Henry's
death. This is true also of John Burell, with two compositions in Old Hall,
neither in the original layer.

On the question of provenance, Roger Bowers ventured in his essay on
Power the suggestions that the 'original destination' of the Old Hall
manuscript was the household chapel of Thomas Duke of Clarence, that
Thomas's death in battle in March 1421 was the reason for the original
scribe's purported 'abrupt and premature abandonment of his original
compilation', and that the manuscript then went to Henry V's chapel.[86]
This would put the date of the manuscript's writing as 1411 at the earliest,
and would presumably leave the identity of Roy Henry undecided. On the
matter of Old Hall's provenance(s) there are assuredly other possibilities
than that of Henry IV's household chapel from around 1402, when a
chaplain was engaged to teach grammar to the chapel boys, to around 1408,
when the king's health began seriously to decline. Those possibilities
cannot be pursued here.

In the meantime the evidences as to chronology, the identities and
associations of composers, and the most likely provenance of Old Hall
point most directly to a date for the original layer of the manuscript as *circa*
1402–8, for the subsequent writing of compositions by Sturgeon, Damett,
Burell, and some anonymi (but not the works by Dunstable and Forest) as
between 1413 and 1422, and for the provenance of the manuscript as the
household chapel of Henry IV (this last subject to further review). The

---

[84.] Bowers, 'Some Observations' 112.

[85.] The term 'Contratenor' appears in the Winchester Songbook, with the notation of a
song with English text and two songs with French text; see the facs. *A Fifteenth-century
Song Book, with an introduction by Richard Rastall* (Leeds, 1973), fols. 162v, 164r, 165v.
The English-language songs are printed in *Medieval English Songs* (see n. 75), 275, 280–91.

[86.] Bowers, 'Some Observations', 109.

most reliable guide to the evidence on all three factors (apart from Bowers's published work) is still Andrew Hughes's exposition of 1967, which is both thoroughly researched and adequately documented.[87]

Editors' Note

Footnotes in square brackets have been added by the editors, who wish to thank Dr Roger Bowers for his help in preparing this study for publication. Since Professor Harrison drafted it, the following publications have appeared, containing material germane to his subject which he was unable to take into account. The character and structure of the *tenor* is among the many aspects of its subject considered in great detail in P. M. Lefferts, *The Motet in England in the Fourteenth Century* (Ann Arbor, 1986). The interaction between French and English composition around the middle of the fourteenth century, and with special regard to the circumstances giving rise to J. Alanus's motet *Sub arturo*, is discussed in Andrew Wathey, 'The Peace of 1360–1369 and Anglo-French Musical Relations', *Early Music History* 9 (1989), 129–74. In 'Fixed Points in the Chronology of English Fourteenth-Century Polyphony', *Music and Letters* 71 (1990), 313–35, Roger Bowers has suggested datings of *circa* 1369–75 for the execution of the manuscript Pierpont Morgan Library 978, of *circa* 1405–7 for the execution of the 'Fountains Fragment' (London, British Library Add. 40011B), and of *circa* 1370–3 for the composition of the motet by J. Alanus, *Sub arturo*. A facsimile edition of London 40011B has been published in *The Fountains Fragments* (Clarabricken, 1987), and an edition of its musical contents in E. Kershaw, *The Fountains Fragments* (Lustleigh, 1989). Finally, on the dating of Old Hall, discussed by Professor Harrison at the end of his study, see also Margaret Bent, 'The Progeny of Old Hall: More Leaves from a Royal English Choirbook', *Gordon Athol Anderson. In Memoriam*, Musicological Studies 49 (Institute of Medieval Music, Henryville, Ottawa, Binningen, 1984), i–xx.

[87.] Andrew Hughes and M. Bent, 'The Old Hall Manuscript: a Re-appraisal and Inventory', *Musica Disciplina* 21 (1967), 97–129.

The Manuscript London, British Library Harley 1709

NICK SANDON

(University College, Cork)

Students of medieval and Renaissance polyphony have all too few complete sources at their disposal. The many incomplete sources are of two main types: fragmentary and partial. Fragmentary sources originally recorded either in score or in some kind of *cantus collateralis* layout the entire texture of the music which they contained, but have subsequently suffered decay, mutilation, or reuse; in consequence the compositions which they contained may now have whole portions missing, while the passages that remain are preserved more or less in their entirety. Among the many examples of English fragmentary sources are the Worcester fragments,[1] the Fountains fragments,[2] the Old Hall manuscript,[3] and the Eton choirbook.[4] Partial sources originally recorded less than the complete texture, usually only a single voice or an instrumental part, of the music; even if they have survived intact their contents are necessarily incomplete. Among numerous examples from England are the Henrician partbooks belonging to Peterhouse, Cambridge (from which the tenor partbook is missing),[5] the

---

[1] Worcester, Chapter Library Add. 68; Oxford, Bodleian Library Lat. lit. d. 20; London, British Library Add. 25031.

[2] London, British Library Add. 40011B.

[3] London, British Library Add. 57950.

[4] Eton College 178.

[5] Cambridge, University Library Peterhouse 471–4. N. J. Sandon, 'The Henrician Partbooks belonging to Peterhouse, Cambridge (Cambridge, University Library, Peterhouse Manuscripts 471–474): A Study, with Restorations of the Incomplete Compositions contained in them', Ph.D. diss. (University of Exeter, 1983). See also N. Sandon, 'The Henrician Partbooks at Peterhouse, Cambridge', *Proceedings of the Royal Musical Association* 103 (1976–7), 106–40.

contratenor and bass partbooks known as *UJ*,[6] and the bass partbook Tenbury 1464.[7] Partial sources can, of course, be fragmentary as well; for example, the treble partbook from the Peterhouse set mentioned above lacks leaves at the beginning and end, and the bass partbook London, British Library Add. 34191 has lost an indeterminate number of leaves.[8] Fragmentary sources have traditionally received a great deal of attention, presumably because a sufficiently high proportion of their contents can be recovered in a state complete enough to persuade scholars that their labours are worth while. Partial sources, on the other hand, have tended to be rather neglected. Yet the latter, too, can be very rewarding objects of study, with much to tell us. The manuscript London, British Library Harley 1709 is one of many such sources.[9] The following remarks about this manuscript do not aim to be exhaustive; they merely draw attention to and speculate on some topics of especial interest. In particular, they consider evidence offered by the manuscript concerning the functions and usage of devotional polyphony in early Tudor England.

Harley 1709 is a paper manuscript, of unknown date and provenance, containing single voices from votive antiphons by composers active during the reigns of Henry VII and Henry VIII. Now in a nineteenth-century binding, it appears to be complete and to have its leaves still in their pristine order; it is also remarkably free of the later scribbles and extraneous material that sully so many comparable sources, for instance London 34191. The pages are approximately 26.5 cm. high by 19 cm. wide; apart from the usual laid-lines and chain-lines (the latter running horizontally about 3 cm. apart), there is no watermark. In rebinding, the original front flyleaf has been preserved in its proper place, and on to it is now pasted a parchment label reading 'Medius', presumably cut from the original cover. On this same flyleaf is the comment, apparently in the hand of the music copyist, 'Medius xxiij antemns in these bok*es*', a comment copied exactly a little lower on the same leaf in what looks like another sixteenth-century hand. Concordances confirm that this is indeed a medius or mean partbook, and (in that all of them are for five voices) indicate that it must have belonged to a set of five partbooks.

   [6] Cambridge, St John's College 234, and Cambridge, University Library Dd. xiij. 27. M. R. James, *A Descriptive Catalogue of the Manuscripts in the Library of St John's College, Cambridge* (Cambridge, 1913), 273–4; and *A Catalogue of the Manuscripts Preserved in the Library of the University of Cambridge* I (Cambridge, 1856), 515.
   [7] See *Tudor Church Music, Appendix* (London, 1948), 8.
   [8] Augustus Hughes-Hughes, *Catalogue of Manuscript Music in the British Museum* I (London, 1906–9), 212 and 261.
   [9] Ibid., 266.

At first sight Harley 1709 is an unusually consistent manuscript, homogeneous in repertory and uniform in physical appearance. It is the only English source of its period to contain nothing but devotional polyphony; some of the compositions in it do, it is true, set texts which also had a liturgical function, but in early Tudor England these texts do not seem to have been set in polyphony when in their liturgical environment. Nevertheless, the repertory of Harley 1709 may be more diverse than it initially appears; I shall return to this point later. Everything about Harley 1709 suggests that it was compiled over a short period of time. It is neatly and carefully copied in a consistent format by a single hand, with elegant and mainly accurate musical notation, carefully spaced text, and competently executed strapwork initials. Most of the copying is in brown or grey-brown ink, but *Gaude virgo mater Christi* (fols. 44v–46v) and *Salve intemerata* (fols. 46v–49r), and *O bone Jesu* (fols. 53v–55r) and *Lauda vivi alpha et o* (fols. 55r–57v), are in a much blacker ink. Throughout the book the copyist seems to have ruled the pages for one composition at a time, always indenting the first two staves of a piece to accommodate an enlarged ornamental initial. The only two works not supplied with a strapwork initial are *Gloria sanctorum decus angelorum* (fols. 37r–39r) and *Te matrem dei laudamus* (fols. 39r–42v). Some pieces have been checked and corrected by the original scribe, or perhaps by an assistant. The end of Tallis's *Salve intemerata* is actually annotated 'ffinis corrigitur'; it is not clear whether the comment applies only to *Salve intemerata* or to the whole book up to this point. Only nine of the twenty-six compositions in the collection carry an ascription, and in at least one case the ascription is probably incorrect; the composers of at least another eight works can be identified from concordances. The setting of *Te matrem dei laudamus* attributed to Thomas Ashwell in Harley 1709 is almost certainly by Hugh Aston. It is attributed to Aston in the Sadler partbooks[10] and in *UJ*, and it forms a pair with the Mass *Te deum* or *Te matrem* ascribed to Aston in the Forrest–Heyther partbooks,[11] *UJ*, and the Henrician Peterhouse partbooks.[12]

The inventory of the contents of Harley 1709 given as Table 1 raises several interesting points. First, there is the discrepancy between the number of works mentioned in the flyleaf inscription, twenty-three, and

[10] Oxford, Bodleian Library, Mus. e. 1–5. See D. G. Mateer, 'John Sadler and Oxford, Bodleian Library, MSS Mus. e. 1–5, *Music and Letters* 60 (1979), 281–95.

[11] Oxford, Bodleian Library Mus. Sch. e. 376–81. See J. Bergsagel, 'The Date and Provenance of the Forrest–Heyther Collection of Tudor Masses', *Music and Letters* 44 (1963), 240–8.

[12] N. J. Sandon, 'Paired and Grouped Works for the Latin Rite by Tudor Composers', *The Music Review* 44 (1983), 8–12.

TABLE I. *Inventory of London British Library Harley 1709*

1.	1r–3v	Gaude plurimum	[Taverner]
2.	3v–5r	Ave dei patris filia	Anonymous
3.	5r–7r	Adoro te domine Jhesu Criste	Anonymous
4.	7r–9r	Stabat mater dolorosa	asshwell
5.	9r–11v	Salve regina pudica mater	ludford
6.	11v–13r	Ave Maria ancilla trinitatis	Anonymous
7.	13v–15v	Sancta Maria mater dei	Anonymous
8.	15v–18r	Salve regina mater misericordie	Anonymous
9.	18r–19v	Salve regina mater misericordie	Anonymous
10.	20r–21v	Stabat mater dolorosa	[Davy]
11.	22r–24v	O domine celi et terre	[Davy]
12.	24v–26r	Tota pulcra es	m thomas hyllary
13.	26r–28v	Salve regina mater misericordie	pygott
14.	29r–30v	O regina celestis glorie	Anonymous
15.	31r–33r	Salve Jhesu mater vera	[Davy]
16.	33r–35r	Ave dei patris filia	[Fayrfax]
17.	35r–37r	Virgo templum trinitatis	R davy
18.	37r–39r	Gloria sanctorum decus angelorum	Anonymous
19.	39v–42v	Te matrem dei laudamus	asshwell [Aston]
20.	42v–44r	Ave cuius concepcio	Anonymous
21.	44v–46v	Gaude virgo mater Cristi	[Aston]
22.	46v–49r	Salve intemerata	[Tallis]
23.	49v–51v	Salve regina mater misericordie	ludford
24.	51v–53r	Salve regina mater misericordie	W Cornyssh
25.	53v–55r	O bone Jhesu	[Fayrfax]
26.	55r–57v	Lauda vivi alpha et o	ffairfax

the number actually in the book, twenty-six. Assuming that the scribe did not simply miscount, it looks as if he thought initially that his task had ended with the copying of Ludford's *Salve regina mater misericordiae*, and decided subsequently to add the last three compositions. If this is what happened, the additions seem to have been made very soon afterwards, for there is no obvious break in the manuscript at this point. If the copyist considered the anonymous *Ave cuius conceptio* to be two pieces rather than one (it is actually a setting of two different texts, as we shall see later, and there is no *custos* at the end of the last stave of the first text), this would make Tallis's *Salve intemerata* the twenty-third and originally last piece, in which case the 'corrigitur' comment at its end could with greater confidence be taken to apply to the entire collection so far.

One intriguing issue concerns the dating of the collection. The chronological range of the music is wide, extending from the earlier 1490s[13] to well into the 1520s and including three generations of composers: Cornysh, Davy, and Fayrfax; Aston, Ludford, Pygott, and Taverner; and Tallis. This is not unprecedented (for instance, the music in the Old Hall manuscript may span a period of some thirty years between the 1390s and the 1420s, and the Eton choirbook originally contained music by composers as far apart in date as Dunstable and Fayrfax); but in no other surviving source do we find Tallis's music in company with works having concordances in Eton.[14] Were it not for the presence of Tallis's *Salve intemerata*, one would be happy to date Harley 1709 in the mid-1520s; none of the other compositions in it needs to be later than about 1525. *Salve intemerata*, however, complicates the picture considerably, mainly because we have no other music by Tallis in a source dating from before about 1540.[15] Although not one of Tallis's best planned and most characterful pieces, this antiphon is plainly the work of a competent composer old enough to have mastered his craft. We do not know Tallis's precise birth-date, but it is difficult to believe that the generally accepted estimate of 1505 can be pushed back much earlier. The problem is not so much that an earlier birth-date would make Tallis impossibly old when he died in 1585 (if he could complete eighty years, there seems no compelling reason why he should not have been good for eighty-five or ninety), but that it would make it even harder to account for the absence of his music from all the other known sources dating from the late 1520s and 1530s.[16] Yet, if we advance the dating of Harley 1709 into the 1530s, its contents take on a decidedly old-fashioned aspect: at least five concordances with the Eton choirbook; none of Ludford's stylistically most advanced antiphons such as *Ave cuius conceptio* and *Domine Jesu Christe*; no copy of Fayrfax's arguably most modern antiphon, *Maria plena virtute*; no music by other young composers of the period, such as Thomas Appleby,

[13.] In the Eton choirbook Richard Davy's *O domine caeli terraeque creator* is annotated 'hanc antiphonam composuit Ricardus Davy uno die collegio magdalene Oxoniis'. Davy was employed by the college in a variety of capacities (including those of clerk, joint organist, and Instructor of the Choristers) during the earlier 1490s; but by 1497 he was a vicar-choral at Exeter Cathedral. See Roger Bowers, 'Choral Establishments within the English Church: their Constitution and Development, 1340–1542', Ph.D. diss. (University of East Anglia, 1976), 6077–8.

[14.] With the exception of Fayrfax's magnificat *Regale*, an Eton piece which remained in the general repertory for considerably longer than anything else in that source; it and three of Tallis's works are in the Henrician Peterhouse partbooks.

[15.] Not, perhaps, so weighty a point as it might seem, because we do not actually have any sources which can be dated securely in the later 1530s.

[16.] Chronologically the next earliest source for any music by Tallis seems to be the Henrician Peterhouse partbooks, dating from 1540–1, which contain his antiphon and mass *Salve intemerata* and his antiphon *Ave rosa sine spinis*.

Thomas Knyght, John Merbecke, Christopher Tye, and William Whytbroke; and only one work known to be by Taverner (his apparently early *Gaude plurimum*, here unascribed). It would be unwise to rely heavily on negative evidence of this kind, but even if we ignore such suggestive omissions as these we are still left with a collection whose overall character is much more redolent of the early 1520s than it is of the 1530s.

The best available compromise between these conflicting considerations is probably to date Harley 1709 in the latter half of the 1520s. As it happens, there is one piece of positive evidence to support such a dating. The first known occurrence of the *Salve intemerata* text is in a book of hours printed by Prévost of Paris for the London bookseller Francis Byrckman and dated 18 July 1527.[17] If this was Tallis's source for the text, and if Tallis obtained it fairly soon after publication, his setting could have been available for copying late in 1527 or early in 1528. If one knew where Tallis was working at this time one might be in a better position to suggest a provenance for Harley 1709. It is well known that often more light is thrown on the provenance of a musical source by the minor composers that it contains than by the major ones; and it is hard to imagine that at so early a stage in his career Tallis's music can have been circulating far afield from his base. Was Tallis perhaps already at Dover Priory,[18] where the earliest known reference locates him as organist in 1532? Unfortunately, the only other composer in Harley 1709 who might have helped us to trace its provenance, Master Thomas Hyllary, appears to be totally unknown.

The anonymous setting of *Sancta Maria mater dei* in Harley 1709 has musical connections with several other early Tudor compositions. Its text, which is printed here with modernized spelling and punctuation, consists of five short petitions to Our Lady followed by a long prose prayer to her.[19] The petitions form a brief litany, and in this section of the piece the composer incorporated the melodic formula to which litanies were chanted. It seems likely that this motive was also quoted intermittently by the other voices in the composition.

Sancta Maria, mater dei: ora pro nobis.
Sancta Maria, regina caeli: ora pro nobis.
Sancta Maria, domina angelorum: ora pro nobis.

[17.] W. G. Hoskins, *Horae beatae Mariae virginis* (London, 1901), 134 (source no. 79), where *Salve intemerata* is entitled *Precatio ad divam virginem Mariam*.

[18.] Tallis's musical appointment at Dover is itself something of a mystery. A cell of the cathedral priory at Canterbury, Dover Priory was small and impecunious; in the early 1530s it had a prior and 12 monks, and a yearly income of about £170: see D. Knowles and R. N. Hadcock, *Medieval Religious Houses: England and Wales* (London, 1971). It is difficult to see how it can have maintained a significant musical establishment.

[19.] The text was first printed in a book of hours in 1502; see Hoskins, *Horae*, 120 (source no. 25).

Sancta Maria, laus omnium sanctorum: ora pro nobis.
Sancta Maria, refugium miserorum: ora pro nobis.

O clemens, O benigna domina, sancta et incomparabilis virgo Maria, pulchra ut luna, electa ut sol, demonibus terribilis, hominibus amabilis, porta paradisi, mater Jesu Christi: te, domina, invocamus, peccatores ne nos despicias, quae soles omnium misereri. Tu es enim gratia plena, dulcis, clemens, virgo fecunda et inter mulieres semper benedicta, quae thronum regalem ideo conscendisti ut sis advocata peccantibus. Rogamus te, veneranda rerum omnium imperatrix et potens regina, per illa beata ubera quae lactaverunt puerum Jesum, per tuum quoque gaudium ineffabile quae creaturis omnibus praelata esse meruisti: ne nos derelinquas sine adjutorio, sed nunc et in hora mortis nostrae sicut scis et vis nos miseros consolare, ut te sequentes regnum filii tui participemus. Amen.

One other English polyphonic setting of *Sancta Maria mater dei* is known to survive.[20] This exists in two sources: the Henrician Peterhouse partbooks, in which it is credited to William Pashe, and London 34191, in which it is ascribed to Thomas Ashwell. Pashe's or Ashwell's setting also quotes the litany formula from time to time in one voice or another, and it has as its cantus firmus a five-note ostinato figure known from several other early Tudor compositions.[21] A third composition to make use of this litany motive is Ashwell's now fragmentary Mass *Sancte Cuthberte*, in which it is used as a long note cantus firmus in the tenor.[22] Litanies, of course, are normally chanted when penitence and intercession are particularly appropriate, for instance in Lent and on rogation days, and in times of trouble; one wonders whether this may be a clue to the original function of polyphonic compositions incorporating this motive. Example 1 presents (*a*) the Salisbury litany formula[23] and quotations from (*b*) the mean voice of the *Sancta Maria mater dei* setting in Harley 1709, (*c*) the setting by Pashe or Ashwell, and (*d*) Ashwell's Mass *Sancte Cuthberte*.

On examination, the texts of the devotional compositions in Harley 1709 turn out to be rather less homogeneous than they at first appear. They are, in fact, an interesting blend of the familiar and the unfamiliar, the old and the new, and some of them especially stimulate curiosity about their

[20]. Edited and completed in Sandon, 'Henrician Partbooks', II, 691–706.

[21]. I have discussed this ostinato, and these conflicting attributions to Pashe and Ashwell, in 'F G A Bflat A: Thoughts on a Tudor Motive', *Early Music* 12 (1984), 56–63.

[22]. London, British Library Add. 30520; fol. 1 has portions of the Sanctus and Agnus of Ludford's Mass *Le roy*, and fol. 2 has portions of the Gloria and Credo of Ashwell's Mass *Sancte Cuthberte*. See Hughes-Hughes, *Manuscript Music*, I, 213.

[23]. Quoted from the Salisbury Processional printed by Richard Pynson in 1502 (facs. edn., Clarabricken, 1980), fol. 31r.: the beginning of the litany in the procession on Wednesdays and Fridays in Lent.

Example 1 (*a*) 1502 Salisbury Processional, fol. 31r

San - cta Ma - ri - a o - ra pro no - bis.

Example 1 (*b*) *Sancta Maria mater dei* (Anon.) (LBL Harley 1709, fol. 13v)

Example 1 (*c*) William Pashe/Thomas Ashwell, *Sancta Maria mater dei* (CUL Peterhouse 471–4, no. 45)

Example 1 (c)—cont.

Example 1 (*d*) Ashwell, Mass *Sancte Cuthberte*, Credo (LBL Add. 30520, fol. 2v)

precise function. The large number of *Salve regina* settings (five, plus Ludford's setting of the closely related text *Salve regina pudica mater*) is particularly striking; no other source later than the Eton choirbook has so high a proportion, and in most sources roughly contemporary with Harley 1709 the proportion is appreciably lower.[24] *Salve regina* was, of course, a votive antiphon of considerable antiquity and prestige, which had also acquired limited liturgical credentials as a processional antiphon.[25] Its presence in a book of hours can almost be taken for granted, and it had been set in polyphony by English composers as early as the mid-fourteenth century;[26] but its long career in English polyphonic settings does seem to have been in decline by the early 1500s. Other established votive and processional antiphons, such as *Ave regina caelorum*, *Alma redemptoris mater*, *Regina caeli laetare*,[27] and *Quam pulchra es*, together with some liturgical antiphons which had come to assume additional votive functions, such as *Tota pulchra es* and *Descendi in ortum meum*,[28] had also been popular

[24.] There are, for example, only two settings among the 41 antiphons in the Henrician Peterhouse partbooks.

[25.] In the Salisbury processional it is among the chants to be sung in special processions (see Pynson's 1502 edn., fols. 167r–168v); but it is not in the Salisbury breviary.

[26.] N. Sandon, 'Mary, Meditations, Monks and Music', *Early Music* 10 (1982), 43–55.

[27.] Like *Salve regina*, *Regina caeli laetare* is not in the Salisbury breviary.

[28.] Respectively the 1st and 5th antiphons at first vespers of the Assumption of our Lady: see F. Procter and C. Wordsworth, *Breviarium ad usum insignis ecclesiae Sarum* III (Cambridge, 1886), 685–8.

with English composers in the early and mid-fifteenth century. By the later fifteenth century, however, they seem largely to have been superseded for musical purposes by a new range of devotional texts, many of which were commonly included in manuscript and printed books of hours of the period. A few of these supplanters were not in themselves new, but were actually of considerable antiquity; *Gaude flore virginali*, for example, was attributed to St Thomas of Canterbury. Many of the devotional texts set by early Tudor composers seem, however, to have been recent productions, and some at least of them found their way into books of hours at about the time when they began to be set in polyphony.

Developments in devotional and literary taste and custom must have been far more gradual and complex than this description implies. It would surely be unrealistic to envisage later fifteenth-century English composers suddenly making a sweeping rejection of devotional texts which had hitherto been frequently set, in order to replace them with texts that had never or hardly ever been set before. There were probably several phases of change, so that, for example, *Gaude flore virginali* grew in popularity with composers between about 1450 and 1500, but was slowly overtaken thereafter by (among others) *Ave dei patris filia* and *Ave cuius conceptio*. Certain items, such as *Salve regina* itself, apparently held their ground better than others. We are, of course, dependent on the accidents of survival in making such assessments as these. There are isolated early sixteenth-century settings of items which seem otherwise to have ceased to be set decades previously.[29] Some texts which had been favoured by composers of Power's and Dunstable's generation but apparently neglected subsequently, have a disconcerting habit of turning up in settings by minor or anonymous composers of the early sixteenth century, in manuscript fragments which are often of a rather scruffy or homespun character.[30] Perhaps such texts retained their popularity in modest or provincial musical establishments long after they were supplanted in institutions which were more fashion-conscious or more aware of literary and intellectual developments. Having made these provisos, however, it remains true that major changes in literary taste are evident in devotional polyphony written in England during the hundred years preceding the Reformation. These changes, their connection with changing attitudes and values, and their musical and wider implications, deserve more systematic and detailed study than they have yet received.

---

[29] The *Ave regina caelorum* ascribed to 'matres (or mens?) maris' in Cambridge, University Library Nn. 6. 46 is a case in point.

[30] e.g. the fragmentary settings of *Beata mater* and *Sancta Maria* discovered several years ago by Andrew Wathey.

As I mentioned above, Harley 1709 is unusual among sources of its period in containing so many settings of *Salve regina*. It is also unusual in including compositions of *Tota pulchra es* and *Gloria sanctorum*, which had been set by English composers in the mid-fifteenth century but had apparently fallen out of favour thereafter.[31] Most of the texts in Harley 1709, however, had no very lengthy history of polyphonic composition behind them. They belong to the new range of devotional items which seems to have become popular with composers around 1500. Judging by surviving examples, some of these items, such as *Ave dei patris filia*, *Stabat mater dolorosa*, *Ave Maria ancilla trinitatis*, *Ave cuius conceptio*, *Gaude virgo mater Christi*, and *O bone Jesu*, were frequently composed in the early sixteenth century, the frequency presumably reflecting the esteem in which they were held. Other widely circulated devotional texts, for example *Adoro te domine Jesu Christe*, seem on the other hand to have been far less attractive to composers or their patrons.

A number of the texts in Harley 1709 and similar sources do not figure in books of hours, and were apparently not part of the common repertory of devotional material at all. Most of these are known in only a single musical setting, and it may be that some at least of them were associated with particular institutions or composers; for instance, no other compositions of the texts set by John Browne in *O Maria salvatoris*, *Stabat virgo mater Christi*, *O regina mundi clara*, and *O mater venerabilis* are known, and the standard catalogues list only these musical settings as sources for them.[32] Were they written by Browne's colleagues, or by Browne himself? Some texts may have been written and set to music for specific occasions. Fayrfax's *Lauda vivi alpha et o*,[33] for instance, concludes unusually with a prayer for the king, which might indicate that it was originally intended for a state ceremony.[34] The rarity of a text may sometimes suggest an attribution for an anonymous setting; for example, *O regina celestis glorie* is otherwise known only from two Eton choirbook settings by Walter Lambe,

---

[31.] There are English settings of *Tota pulchra es* by John Forest and John Plummer, and one of *Gloria sanctorum* by John Dunstable. The *Gloria sanctorum* in Harley 1709, and that of which a single voice is preserved in London, British Library Royal Appendix 58, fol. 58v (see Hughes-Hughes, *Manuscript Music*, 1, 258), are not the same composition.

[32.] These four compositions are printed in *The Eton Choirbook*, ed. F. Ll. Harrison (Musica Britannica 10–12, London, 1956–61), 1, 1–14, 54–63, 72–80, and III, 14–23, respectively.

[33.] In the Henrician Peterhouse partbooks, and edited and completed in Sandon, 'Henrician Partbooks', II, 869–98.

[34.] This may be even more likely in the case of an antiphon by Fayrfax not in Harley 1709, his *Aeterne laudis lilium*, whose text yields the acrostic 'Elisabeth regina anglie ccqa'; see *Robert Fayrfax: Music from the Lambeth Choirbook*, ed. M. Lyon (Madison, Wis., 1985), 70–83.

a fragmentary one in six parts[35] and a lost one in five; this encourages the speculation that the anonymous setting in Harley 1709 may actually be the five-part composition by Lambe now missing from Eton.

Two of the works in Harley 1709 deserve particular attention on account of their texts: the anonymous *Adoro te domine Jesu Christe* and *Ave cuius conceptio*. No other English setting is known of *Adoro te domine Jesu Christe*, which often occurs in books of hours under the title 'Septem orationes Beati Gregorii'. The text is printed in full below, together with the introductory material and the following items, as they appear in a printed book of hours closely contemporary with Harley 1709.[36] The words which do not occur in Harley 1709 are enclosed within square brackets. Abbreviations, contractions, and omissions have been tacitly expanded and supplied, and spelling and punctuation have been modernized.

Quicumque in statu gratiae existens dixerit devote septem orationes sequentes cum septem *Pater noster* et septem *Ave* ante imaginem pietatis merebitur quinquaginta septem milia annorum indulgentiarum, quae a tribus summis pontificibus datae fuerunt: videlicet primo a beato Gregorio, xiiij milia annorum. Secundo a papa Nicolao quinto, xiiij milia annorum, anno domini mccccxlix. Tertio a papa Sixto quarto qui composuit quartam et quintam oratiunculas sequentium suffragiorum has indulgentias duplicavit, anno domini mcccclxxviij.

[Adoro te, domine Jesu Christe, in cruce pendentem et coronam spineam in capite portantem: deprecor te, domine Jesu Christe, ut tua crux liberet me ab angelo percutiente. Amen. Pater noster. Ave.]

Adoro te, domine Jesu Christe, in cruce vulneratum, felle et aceto potatum: deprecor te, domine Jesu Christe, [ut vulnera tua sint remedium animae meae. Amen. Pater noster. Ave.]

Adoro te, domine Jesu Christe, [in sepulchro positum,] myrrha et aromatibus [conditum]: deprecor te, domine Jesu Christe, ut mors tua sit vita mea. [Amen. Pater noster. Ave.]

Adoro te, domine Jesu Christe, descendentem ad inferos, liberantemque captivos: deprecor te ne permittas me illuc introire. [Amen. Pater noster. Ave Maria.]

Adoro te, domine Jesu Christe, resurgentem [a mortuis], ascendentem[37] ad caelos, sedentemque ad dexteram patris: deprecor te miserere mei. [Pater noster. Ave Maria.]

---

[35] *The Eton Choirbook*, III, 161: incipit only.

[36] *Enchiridion preclare ecclesie Sarum* (Paris, 1530), fols. 60v–61r; Hoskins, *Horae* (source no. 91).

[37] Harley 1709 inserts *est* here.

[O domine Jesu Christe, pastor bone, justos conserva: peccatores justifica, et omnibus peccatoribus miserere, et propitius esto mihi peccatori. Pater noster. Ave Maria.]

O domine Jesu Christe, rogo te propter illam maximam amaritudinem passionis tuae [quam sustinuisti] pro[38] me in cruce, [et] maxime quando anima tua[39] nobilissima egressa est de corpore tuo sanctissimo, miserere ergo animae meae in egressu suo. Amen.

[Pater noster. Ave Maria. Credo in deum.

V. Adoramus te Christe et benedicimus tibi.

R. Quia per sanctam crucem tuam redemisti mundum.

Domine exaudi orationem meam.

Et clamor meus ad te veniat.

Oratio. Benignissime domine Jesu Christe, respice super me miserum peccatorem oculis misericordiae tuae, quibus respexisti Petrum in atrio, Mariam Magdalenam in convivio, et latronem in crucis patibulo: concede mihi ut cum beato Petro peccata mea digne deflectam, et cum Maria Magdalena perfecte te diligam, et cum latrone in caelesti paradiso eternaliter te videam. Qui cum patre et filio et spiritu sancto vivis et regnas deus, per omnia saecula saeculorum. Amen.]

The structure of this devotion is plainly based upon that of a memorial: an antiphon without a psalm, a versicle and response, and a prayer, all performed before a religious image, in this case one of Our Lord.[40] Here the opening sevenfold invocation of Our Lord takes the place of the antiphon, and the fact that in Harley 1709 it is set to music as if it really were an antiphon makes the resemblance even more clear. The anonymous composer seems to have supplied music for each invocation; long passages of rest indicate that the mean voice was silent during the first and fourth invocations. He did not, however, set the interpolations of *Pater noster* and *Ave Maria*. The end of every invocation except the fourth coincides with the end of a major musical section, so in every case but the fourth it would have been possible, if desired, to pause for a *Pater* and an *Ave* before resuming. Although one cannot prove it, it is at least possible that this composition was intended to be sung as the first item in a performance of the entire devotion: that is, as a constituent in a conventionally constructed and widely observed memorial. By an unusual stroke of good fortune most of the treble voice of this work has survived in a musical fragment among miscellaneous papers on loan to the British Library.[41] The extract given in

---

[38.] Harley 1709 has *propter*.

[39.] Harley 1709 has *mea*.

[40.] For examples of memorials, see Procter and Wordsworth, *Breviarium* I, pp. viij–xi.

[41.] London, British Library Loan 29/333, opening 25: the top half of a parchment leaf of unknown provenance and date, probably from, or intended for, a choirbook, and apparently used later as a book cover. The preserved portion is 24 cm. high by 34.5 cm. wide; the width

Example 2 leaves no doubt that these voices are from the same piece (see also Figures 1, 2, and 3).

Example 2. *Adoro te domine Jesu Christe* (Anon.) (Treble from LBL Loan 29/333, opening 25; Mean from LBL Harley 1709, fol. 5r)

of the area occupied by the copying is 28 cm. The end of the treble voice has been lost with the bottom of the leaf; the reverse contains no music. I am as nearly certain as it is possible to be that this fragment is in the same hand as that of Harley 1709 itself: a unique coincidence in English music of this period. The fragment is reproduced in Figure 1, with an opening of Harley 1709 in Figure 2 for comparison.

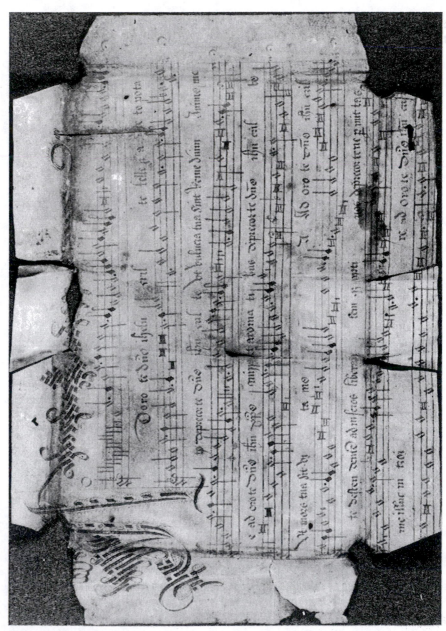

Figure 1. London, British Library Loan 29/333

The anonymous setting of *Ave cuius conceptio* in Harley 1709 offers more definite information about the context and manner in which it was meant to be used. The texts of the antiphon and its associated material are printed in the first column below as they appear in the *Enchiridion* of 1530,[42] where they are entitled *De festivitatibus beate Marie*; the text in Harley 1709 is given in its original spelling in the second column.

Ave cuius conceptio	Ave cuius concepcio
solemni plena gaudio	solempni plena gaudio
celestia terrestria	[*long rests*]
nova replet letitia.	
Ave cuius nativitas	Ave [*long rests*]
nostra fuit solemnitas:	
ut lucifer lux oriens	
verum solem preveniens.	
Ave pia humilitas	Ave pia humilitas
sine viro fecunditas:	sine viro fecunditas
cuius annunciatio	[*words missing*]
nostra fuit redemptio.	nostra fuit redempcio.
Ave vera virginitas	Ave vera virginitas
immaculata castitas:	in macula castitas
cuius purificatio	cuius purificacio
nostra fuit purgatio.	nostra fuit purgacio.
Ave plena in omnibus	Ave [*followed by stroke*
angelicis virtutibus:	*through stave, then by*
cuius fuit assumptio	*long rests ending with*
nostra glorificatio.	*cadence sign* ':']
V. Ora pro nobis sanctissima	[*short rests*]
dei genitrix.	Sancta[43] dei genitrix
R. Ut digni efficiamur	ut digni efficiamur
promissionibus Christi.	promissionibus Cristi.
	Sequitur oremus cum oracione.
	[*at end of stave, not set to music*]

[42] fol. 157.   [43] *Sic.*

Figure 2. London, British Library Harley 1709, fol. 43v

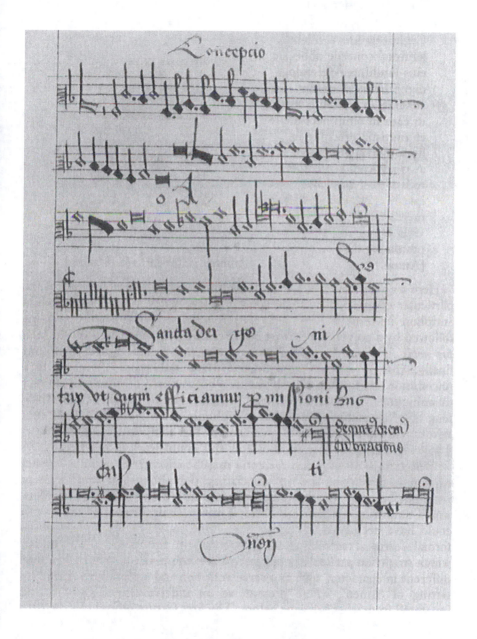

Figure 3. London, British Library Harley 1709, fol. 44r

Oratio. Deus qui nos concep-
   tionis nativitatis annuncia-
   tionis: purificationis et
   assumptionis beate Marie
   virginis gaudia recolendo
   letificas: concede nobis sic
   eius laudibus referendo
   digne insistere et eam
   venerari et amare in terris:
   ut eam in omni necessitate
   et angustia precipue in
   hora mortis presentem et
   auxiliatricem sentiamus et
   tecum post mortem per
   ipsam et cum ipsa gaudere
   mereamur in celis. Qui
   vivis et regnas deus. Per
   omnia secula seculorum.
   [Amen.]   Amen. [*under stave with music*]

Here we are given a very clear indication of how the performance of this particular composition was designed to serve a devotional function. The antiphon itself (*Ave cuius conceptio*) was sung in its entirety and was followed by a polyphonic setting of the ensuing versicle and response (*Ora pro nobis . . . Ut digni efficiamur . . .*); the prayer was then recited; and, finally, the prayer was concluded with a polyphonic 'Amen'. It is uncommon to find in a polyphonic composition of this period such unambiguous evidence concerning its function and usage. Scholars have long believed and suggested that polyphonic votive antiphons were sung devotionally in the context of memorials;[44] this composition offers what is, I believe, a unique illustration of how this could work in practice.

This setting of *Ave cuius conceptio* may be exceptional in offering such explicit information, and in associating polyphony not only with an antiphon but also with other constituents in a memorial. It is, however, worth enquiring whether any other English compositions of this period could have been used in similar ways. One could, for example, look for formal features resembling those revealed in this piece. Two features which might be particularly suggestive are: the juxtaposition of two texts different in character, such as a verse antiphon and a prose prayer; and the setting of 'Amen', where present, as an independent musical section separated from what has gone before. The first feature reproduces the basic

---

[44] See e.g. Harrison, *Music in Medieval Britain*[2] (London, 1963), 295–344.

division of a memorial into an antiphon and a prayer, while omitting the versicle and response which conventionally separate them; if there were a break between the two texts it would allow a chanted versicle and response to be interpolated between the polyphonic antiphon and prayer. The second feature would permit the possibility that a chanted prayer was inserted before the polyphonic 'Amen'. A brief and incomplete survey has so far revealed only a small number of other compositions having characteristics comparable with those of *Ave cuius conceptio*, and it has to be admitted that none of them closely resembles it in structure. These compositions are listed in Table 2. The listed settings of *Ave Maria ancilla trinitatis* should not, it may be argued, have been included in this table, because the juxtaposition of poetic and prose sections is a feature of the devotional item itself, at least in the form in which it usually appears in printed books of hours.[45] On the other hand, the prose portion was not always set; Sturton's *Ave Maria ancilla trinitatis* in the Lambeth choir-book[46] includes only the rhymed acclamations. In the current absence of more compelling evidence it is probably safest to regard the compositions in this table, and others like them, not as attempts to provide polyphony to be sung at various stages during the entire course of a memorial, but as pieces intended to be performed as the first item in a devotion or memorial in the normal way, whose texts reproduce more or less closely the antiphon-versicle-prayer structure of the memorial itself.

The texts of most of the polyphonic items which we loosely call 'votive antiphons' do not have this dual character. Most of them are either antiphons or sequences extracted from their liturgical environment for use in a devotional context, or verse or (more rarely) prose effusions expatiating on the merits and intercessory virtue of a saint. *Tota pulchra es* is an example of the first type; *Stabat mater dolorosa* and *Gloria sanctorum*[47] are examples of the second; *Salve Jesu mater vera* is an example of the third; and *Gaude plurimum* is an example of the fourth. It is not difficult to envisage any of these being sung as the first item in a memorial or a devotion modelled on a memorial, and being followed by a chanted versicle, response, and prayer. Some apparently devotional settings by early Tudor composers do not, however, fit readily into this scheme, because their texts take the form of prayers; they constitute a fifth category

---

[45.] For instance, in the *Enchiridion*, fol. 169.

[46.] London, Lambeth Palace 1; see M. R. James and C. Jenkins, *A Descriptive Catalogue of the Manuscripts in the Library of Lambeth Palace* (Cambridge, 1930–2), 1. The piece is edited in P. Fugler, 'The Unpublished Antiphons in the Lambeth Choirbook', MA diss. (University of Exeter, 1978).

[47.] *Gloria sanctorum* does not seem to have been in any of the secular uses of late medieval England.

TABLE 2. *Compositions having features in common with the anonymous* Ave cuius conceptio *in Harley 1709*

Anonymous (*1709*)	*Ave Maria ancilla trinitatis*	Rhymed acclamations followed by prose prayer
Aston	*Ave Maria ancilla trinitatis*[a]	Rhymed acclamations followed by prose prayer, with break between the two sections
Ludford	*Ave Maria ancilla trinitatis*[b]	Rhymed acclamations followed by prose prayer
Taverner	*Gaude plurimum*	Prose acclamations followed by prose prayer
Aston	*Gaude virgo mater Christi*[c]	Verse antiphon followed by prose prayer
Bramston	*Mariae virginis*[d]	Verse antiphon followed by prose prayer
Anonymous (*1709*)	*Sancta Maria mater dei*	Litany-type invocations followed by prose prayer, with break between the two sections
Pashe	*Sancta Maria mater dei*	Litany-type invocations followed by prose prayer, with break between the two sections
Taverner	*Sancte deus*[e]	'Amen' as separate section
Whytbroke	*Sancte deus*[f]	'Amen' as separate section

[a] In the Henrician Peterhouse partbooks, and edited and completed in Sandon, 'Henrician Partbooks', II, 1135–57.

[b] In the Henrician Peterhouse partbooks, and edited and completed in Sandon, 'Henrician Partbooks', II, 915–35.

[c] *Tudor Church Music* 10 (1929), 85–98.

[d] In the Henrician Peterhouse partbooks, and edited and completed in Sandon, 'Henrician Partbooks', II, 195–208.

[e] In the Henrician Peterhouse partbooks; edited and completed by Hugh Benham in *John Taverner: Votive Antiphons*, Early English Church Music 25 (London, 1981), 131–6, and in Sandon, 'Henrician Partbooks', II, 11–15.

[f] In the Henrician Peterhouse partbooks, and edited and completed in Sandon, 'Henrician Partbooks', II, 384–91.

to be added to the four mentioned above. Harley 1709 does not contain any of these prayer texts, so my examples are taken from other sources.

The text of Ludford's *Domine Jesu Christe*[48] is a lengthy prayer to Our Lord; it closely resembles the longer prayers in books of hours, which are

[48] In the Henrician Peterhouse partbooks, and edited and completed in Sandon, 'Henrician Partbooks', II, 808–22.

themselves modelled on the more extended prayers of the missal and breviary. It is printed as the first text below, together with prayers selected from the *Enchiridion* and the Salisbury missal; spelling and punctuation have been modernized in order to facilitate comparison. The resemblances between these items are plain to see. Ludford's text must surely have been based on and expanded from the second and third prayers, or from prayers like them. A progressive expansion is also evident; the further we move from a liturgical context, from the missal through the book of hours to the musical composition, the longer and more ornate, the less concise and pointed, the prayers become.

Domine Jesu Christe, splendor et imago patris, salus nostra ac vita aeterna, cui cum omnipotente patre et spiritu sanctissimo aequalis est honor, gloria eadem, sempiterna majestas, ac demum substantia una: te invocamus, te adoramus. Tibi magnas gratias agimus pro immensa tua in humanum genus pietate ac clementia, obsecrantes ut ignominiosae crucis tuae passionem quam nostra causa ultro pertulisti amarissimam, interponas tremendo judicio tuo, et animabus nostris (non solummodo dum hostis ille noster antiquus nobis undique insidiatur, quaerens quos devoret, sed potissimum tunc cum mortis institerit hora, ne peccatorum pondere obruti in Gehennae ignem nunquam extinguendum praecipitemur) impartiri quae digneris ecclesiae tuae sanctae: dei pacem quae omnem exuberat sensum, concordiam mutuam, peccatorum omnium veniam, et tuae deitatis suavissimam fruitionem gloriamque sempiternam. Amen.

Domine Jesu Christe, fili dei vivi, qui es verus et omnipotens deus, splendor et imago patris, et vita aeterna, cui est una cum aeterno patre et spiritu sancto aequalis honor, eadem gloria, coaeterna majestas, una substantia: tibi gratias ago, te adoro, te laudo, te benedico, teque glorifico. Ne me, quaeso, perire patiaris, sed salva et adiuva me gratuito munere tuo quem dignatus es redimere pretioso sanguine tuo. Qui cum patre et spiritu sancto vivis et regnas deus, per omnia saecula saeculorum. Amen.[49]

Domine Jesu Christe, fili dei vivi: pone passionem, crucem, et mortem tuam inter judicium tuum et animas nostras nunc et in hora mortis nostrae, et largiri digneris vivis misericordiam et gratiam, defunctis requiem et veniam, ecclesiae tuae pacem et concordiam, et nobis peccatoribus vitam et gloriam sempiternam. Qui cum patre et spiritu sancto vivis et regnas deus, per omnia saecula saeculorum. Amen.[50]

---

[49] *Enchiridion*, fol. 151v.: among the *Suffragia*.
[50] *Enchiridion*, fol. 52v.: the prayer at the Hours of the Holy Cross.

Domine Jesu Christe, qui manus tuas et pedes tuos et totum corpus tuum pro nobis peccatoribus in ligno crucis posuisti, et coronam spinarum a Judaeis in despectu tui sacratissimi corporis super caput tuum impositam sustinuisti, et quinque vulnera pro nobis peccatoribus in crucis patibulo passus fuisti, et nos de sacro sanguine tuo redemisti: da nobis, quaesumus, domine, hodie et quotidie usum penitentiae, abstinentiae, et patientiae, humilitatis, castitatis, lumen, sensum, et intellectum, veram scientiam usque in finem. Per te, Jesu Christe, salvator mundi, rex gloriae. Qui cum patre et spiritu sancto vivis et regnas deus, per omnia saecula saeculorum. Amen.[51]

One can find echoes between other compositions of this type and prayers in devotional or service-books. Here, for example, are the concluding words of Lambe's *O Maria plena gratia*[52] and Mason's *Vae nobis miseris*,[53] together with the Collect from the Mass of the Five Wounds of our Lord. The complete quotation from Matthew 25. 34 was also the Introit of mass on the Wednesday after Easter[54] and the antiphon at lauds in the first week of Lent;[55] neither plainchant seems to have been utilized by Lambe or Mason.

. . . Ora pro nobis, sancta Maria, ut digni efficiamur de numero quibus dicetur in extremo judicio: 'Venite, benedicti patris mei, percipite regnum quod vobis paratum est ab origine mundi.' Amen. (Lambe)

. . . Ut in futura resurrectione delicatam tuam invocationem gaudenter cum electis tuis audiamus te dicente: 'Venite, benedicti patris mei, percipite regnum meum quod vobis paratum est ab origine mundi.' Amen. (Mason)

Domine Jesu Christe, fili dei vivi, qui de caelo ad terram de sinu patris descendisti, et in ligno crucis quinque plagas sustinuisti, et sanguinem tuum pretiosum in remissionem peccatorum nostrorum effudisti: te humiliter deprecamur, ut in die judicii ad dexteram tuam statuti, a te audire mereamur illam vocem dulcissimam: 'Venite, benedicti, in regnum patris mei.' Qui cum eodem patre in unitate spiritus sancti vivis et regnas deus, per omnia saecula saeculorum. Amen.[56]

What should we call such compositions as *Domine Jesu Christe* and *Vae nobis miseris*? The term 'votive antiphon' does not adequately describe their

[51.] F. H. Dickinson, *Missale ad usum insignis et praeclarae ecclesiae Sarum* (Burntisland, 1861–83), 891*–892*.

[52.] *The Eton Choirbook*, II, 31–42.

[53.] In the Henrician Peterhouse partbooks, and edited and completed in Sandon, 'Henrician Partbooks', II, 280–98.

[54.] Dickinson, *Missale*, 370.

[55.] Procter and Wordsworth, *Breviarium*, I, dlxxxviij.

[56.] Dickinson, *Missale*, 751.

character, and may also give a misleading impression of their purpose and usage. It seems at least possible that they were designed not as the first item in a devotion, but as the last, replacing the customary chanted prayer. Perhaps we could call them 'prayer motets'. There is, no doubt, a great deal more to be discovered about their origins, sources, and functions, as indeed there must be about those of the whole repertory of devotional polyphony. This should, I think, be regarded as a major priority. Our understanding of the functional context of early Tudor sacred music as a whole remains limited, patchy, and heavily reliant on assumptions. I do not mean at all to belittle the very valuable research that has been carried out, particularly on archival material; but we need now to complement this by investigating thoroughly the devotional, liturgical, and other religious and literary documents available to us in almost disconcerting abundance.

Index of Sources

Aberystwyth, National Library of Wales
    20145 E: 258
Alnwick, missal of Duke of
    Northumberland: 165
Amiens, printed missal
    of 1487: 158–60, 169
    of 1529: 169
    Bibliothèque municipale
    115: 189, 194–5, 198
    155: 49
Angers, Bibliothèque municipale
    91: 151
    93: 165
    96: 153
    97: 165
Arras, printed missal of 1508: 169
    Bibliothèque municipale 812: 222
Auch, printed missal of 1555: 158, 160
Avranches, printed missal of 1505: 165

Bamberg, Staatsbibliothek
    lit. 5: 27
    23: 55–6, 192
    25: 192
    30: 34
Bangor Antiphoner: 222
Bayeux, Bibliothèque municipale 121: 167
Beauvais, printed missal of 1538: 167
Benevento, Archivio Capitolare
    V. 21: 232
    VI. 29: 157
    VI. 33: 157
    VI. 34: 157
    VI. 35: 155, 157
    VI. 38: 157
Bern, Burgerbibliothek 49: 79
Bologna, Civico Museo Bibliografico
    Musicale Q 15: 316
Boulogne, Bibliothèque municipale 637:
    222
Brussels, Bibliothèque Royale
    II. 3824: 151

lat. 10127–10144: 149–50

Cambrai, printed missal of 1507: 169
    Bibliothèque municipale
    60: 169
    61 (62): 165
    75: 169
    1328 (1176): 313, 335
Cambridge, Corpus Christi College
    111: 223
    140: 223
    183: 257
    473: 4, 11, 34, 44, 47–8, 52–7, 61–99
      passim, 116, 128
    Emmanuel College 248: 249
    Fitzwilliam Museum 369: 176, 198,
      202–4
    Magdalene College F. 4. 10: 206, 264,
      268, 271, 275
    Pepys 1236: 291
    St John's College
    234, see UJ
    D. 21: 216
    D. 27: 165
    E. 8: 291
    Trinity College
    O. 3. 55: 257
    O. 7. 31: 209
    University Library
    Add. 710 (Dublin Troper): 289, 290
    Add. 5943: 350, 352
    Dd. xiii. 27, see UJ
    Ii. 4. 20: 211, 237, 257
    Kk. 2. 6: 165
    Kk. iv. 20: 274
    Mm. 2. 9: 192, 206
    Nn. 6. 46: 365
    Peterhouse 471–4 (Henrician
      Peterhouse partbooks): 355–7,
      359, 361–2, 364, 366, 376, 378
Canterbury, Cathedral Library Add. 6:
    209

Carcassonne, Bibliothèque de la
    Séminaire, missal: 158, 160
Bibliothèque municipale Mb 130: 158,
    160
Chantilly, Musée Condé 564 *olim* 1047:
    315–17, 323
Chartres, Bibliothèque de la Ville, *see*
    Chartres, Bibliothèque
    municipale
Chartres, Bibliothèque municipale
    4: 102, 103 (facs.), 107, 110–19,
        133–4, 137
    47: 56, 111–12, 146
    109: 107, 119, 127, 129–30
    130: 103–4, 105–6 (facs.), 105, 107,
        110–11, 118–34
    520: 111–12, 114, 118–20, 126, 155–6
Cividale, Museo Archeologico Nazionale
    LXIII: 335
Cluny, printed missal of 1493: 152, 167
Cologne, Historisches Archiv 28: 281
Compiègne Antiphoner, *see* Paris,
    Bibliothèque Nationale lat. 17436
Copenhagen, Det Kongelige Bibliotek
    1588: 260
Coutances, printed missal of 1557: 154,
    167

Douai, Bibliothèque municipale
    90: 169
    114: 169
Dublin, Trinity College
    77 (B. I. 2): 335
    78 (B. I. 3): 255–6
    79 (B. I. 4): 273
    80 (B. I. 5): 273
Durham, Chapter Library
    B. III. 11: 55–6, 183
    C. I. 20: 309, 311–13, 316
    University Library, Cosin v. v. 6: 169

Edinburgh, National Library
    18. 2. 13A: 257
    18. 2. 13B: 266
    University Library 211. iv: 256
Engelberg, Stiftsbibliothek 314: 108
Eton College, 178 (Eton Choirbook): 355,
    359, 364, 366–7, 378
Exeter, Cathedral Library 3515: 165

Forrest–Heyther partbooks (Oxford,
    Bodleian Library, Mus. Sch. e.
    376–81): 357
Fountains fragments or leaves, *see*
    London, British Library, Add.
    40011B
Fribourg, Bibliothèque Cantonale et
    Universitaire 260: 309

Gloucester, Record Office, fragment 14:
    278

Hereford, printed missal of 1502: 65
    Cathedral Library, P. 9 VII (Hereford
    breviary): 263
Hyde Abbey, breviary of, *see* Oxford,
    Bodleian Library, Rawl. liturg.
    e 1*

Ivrea, Biblioteca Capitolare
    106: 56
    Ars Nova ms. without shelfmark:
        313, 315–16, 335

Langres, Bibliothèque municipale 312:
    158, 160
Laon, Bibliothèque municipale 238: 48
Le Havre, Bibliothèque municipale 330:
    48
Le Mans, Bibliothèque municipale
    154: 158–60
    188: 237
Leofric Missal: 223
Limoges, Bibliothèque municipale 2: 151
Lisieux, printed missals of 1504 (?), 1517
    and 1547: 167
London, British Library
    Add. 5284A: 216
        5665: 286–7, 291
        15419: 167
        16964: 275
        17006: 158, 160
        18496: 232
        23935: 165
        24198: 288
        25031, *see* Worcester Fragments
        26655: 165
        27630: 108
        28550 (Robertsbridge Codex): 322
        28598: 277
        30520: 361, 364

30850: 53–6, 189, 232
34191: 356, 361
34388: 255
34662: 158, 160, 165
35285: 160, 216
35295: 350–1
39675: 161
40011B (Fountains fragments or
    leaves): 323, 325–6, 329, 332–4,
    338, 344, 346–7, 350, 353, 355
43405–6: 209
57950, *see* Old Hall Manuscript
Arundel 248: 291
Cotton Caligula A. XIV: 11–45 *passim*,
    47
Egerton 2615: 108, 134
    3307: 286, 287
    3511: 157
Harley 622: 165
    978: 304
    1117: 214–15, 234–5, 257
    1709: 355–79 *passim*, 372–3 (facs.)
    3908: 268
    4664: 209, 254
    4951: 155, 158
    5289: 153
Lansdowne 493: 339, 341
Loan 29/333: 368–9, 370 (facs.)
missal of Sherborne: 165
Royal 12. C. xxiii: 214
    12. E. i: 291
Royal Appendix 58: 366
Stowe 12: 262
Lambeth Palace 1: 375
Victoria and Albert Museum
    1346–1891: 49
    L. 404: 158, 160
Westminster Abbey 'Lytlington Missal':
    145, 222
Lyon, Bibliothèque municipale 555: 216

Madrid, Biblioteca Nacional
    288: 148, 153–5
    289: 148
    19421: 148
    Vitrina 20–4: 148, 155
Manchester, John Rylands Library 186:
    218
Mont-Renaud, Antiphoner of: 49, 53–4
Montpellier, Faculté de Médecine H. 159:
    151, 159, 162, 201

Munich, Bayerische Staatsbibliothek, Cod.
    gall. 16: 207

Narbonne, printed missal of 1528: 158,
    160
New York, Pierpont Morgan Library
    736: 260
    926: 252, 254
    M.978: 306, 353
Nidaros Antiphoner: 210
Nîmes, printed missal of 1511: 158, 160

Odense, Breviary of: 210
Old Hall Manuscript (London, British
    Library, Add. 57950): 303, 313,
    323–53 *passim*, 355, 359
Orléans, Bibliothèque municipale 129: 165
Oxford, Bodleian Library
    Barlow 41: 206, 234
    Bodley 547: 219
        579: 158, 160
        775: 4, 11, 34, 44, 47–8, 63, 98
    Can. lit. 344: 155–6
    Digby 90: 312
        109: 260
    Douce 245: 335
    e. Mus. 2: 278
        7: 313
    Gough liturg. 1: 264, 279
    Lat. liturg. b 14: 253
        d 20, *see* Worcester Fragments
        36: 205–38 *passim*
        39: 237
    Laud misc. 299: 250, 277, 280
    Mus. Sch. e. 1–5, *see* Sadler
        partbooks
        e. 376–81, *see* Forrest–Heyther
        partbooks
    New College, 362: 288
    Rawl. A 416: 249
        C. 892: 159–60, 165
        C. 489: 237
        liturg. b 1: 160
        liturg. e 1* + Gough liturg. 8
        (Hyde Breviary): 205–6, 219,
        234
    Selden B 26: 286, 288, 290–1, 297
    Tanner 169: 291
Corpus Christi College 134: 272
Jesus College 10: 216
University College 101: 215, 234, 249

Palermo, Archivio Storico e Diocesano
 8: 155–6
 11: 155–6
Biblioteca Comunale 2. Qq. G. 31:
  166–7
Biblioteca Nazionale xiv. F. 16: 165
Paris, printed missal of 1501: 167
Bibliothèque de l'Arsenal 135: 261, 326
 274: 200
Bibliothèque Mazarine 384: 49, 112
Bibliothèque Nationale
 lat. 776: 155, 158
 780: 158, 160
 864: 152
 875: 155
 903: 112, 155, 158–60
 909: 151
 1084: 155
 1087: 112
 1101: 169
 1105: 153–4
 1107: 49
 1120: 107
 1132: 169
 1135: 155
 1136: 151
 1137: 152
 1139: 107, 129
 1218: 211
 1234: 158, 160
 3549: 107
 8882: 262
 9438: 152
 9439: 151
 10505: 49
 10511: 158–60
 11522: 49
 11631: 105, 134, 137, 140
 12036: 210–13, 215, 217–18, 234,
  237, 256, 276
 12044: 134, 136, 167, 180–5, 197–8
 12584: 53–7, 105–6, 134–6, 167,
  180–2, 187, 197–8, 232
 12596: 106, 134, 136
 12601: 177–83, 188–9, 193–4, 196
  (facs.), 197–8, 201
 13239: 217, 237
 13252: 34, 47
 13254: 165
 14446: 167
 14447: 158, 160

 16304: 210, 234
 17296: 53–7, 116, 134, 232, 237,
  265
 17310: 104, 111, 118
 17436: 210, 232
 18010: 49
 nouv. acq. lat. 1235: 152
 Bibliothèque Sainte-Geneviève 111: 49
Passau, printed antiphoner of 1519: 209
Princeton, University Library, Medieval
  and Renaissance Manuscripts
 103: 342
Provins, Bibliothèque municipale 12: 104,
  111–12, 114, 118–20, 126, 155–6
Queen Isabella Psalter: 207

Ranworth Antiphonal: 265
Rome, Biblioteca Alessandrina
  (Universitaria) 120: 262, 274
 Biblioteca Angelica 477: 165
 Biblioteca Apostolica Vaticana,
  Ottob. lat. 313: 49
  Reg. lat. 586: 106–7, 110, 137–40
   592: 104, 110
  Vat. lat. 5319: 148–9
   6082: 157
 Biblioteca Casanatense
  54: 180–3, 189, 198
  603: 49
Rouen, printed missal of 1497: 158, 160–1,
  163–7
 Bibliothèque municipale
  211 (A. 145): 217
  243 (A. 164): 182, 198–9
  244 (A. 261): 201, 217
  273 (A. 287): 147
  291 (A. 329): 165
  1396 (U. 135): 218

Sadler partbooks (Oxford, Bodleian
  Library, Mus. Sch. e. 1–5): 357
St Albans, printed breviary of 1530: 272
St Gall, Stiftsbibliothek
 339: 147
 390–1 (Hartker's Antiphoner): 55, 66,
  68, 232
Saint-Omer, Bibliothèque municipale
 252: 169
 354: 216
St Petersburg, M. E. Saltykov-Shchedrin
  State Public Library O. v. 1. 6:
  153–4

Saint-Victor-sur-Rhins, noted breviary:
    186–7, 189–94, 198, 200, 202
Salisbury, printed breviary of 1494: 256,
    364
    printed processional of 1502: 292, 361,
        364
        of 1554: 6
    Cathedral Library 152: 244 (facs.), 250,
        270–1
Schlettstadt, *see* Sélestat
Séez, printed missal of 1488: 167
Sélestat, Bibliothèque et Archives de la
    Ville 17 (1153): 95
Shrewsbury, Shrewsbury School, xxx:
    164–5
Solesmes, Rés. 334: 187, 193–4, 198, 200
Stockholm, Riksarkiv, fragment: 255
Stowe Missal: 222

Tenbury College 1464: 356
Troyes, Bibliothèque municipale
    109: 194–5, 197–9
    894: 104, 111–12, 114, 118

UJ (Cambridge, St John's College, 234
    and Cambridge, University
    Library, Dd. xiii. 27): 356–7

Valenciennes, Bibliothèque municipale
    116 (109): 234

117: 169
121: 169
Vallbona, Monastery Library 21: 262
Verona, Biblioteca Capitolare 98: 55–6,
    192
Vienne, printed missal of 1534: 151

Wollaton Antiphonal: 266
Worcester, Chapter Library F.160
    (Worcester Antiphoner): 53–6,
    64, 68, 78–9, 86, 110, 116, 209,
    216, 219, 234–5, 257, 264–5,
    271, 279
    Add. 68, *see* Worcester Fragments
Worcestershire Record Office,
    parchment sheet: 351
Worcester Fragments (Worcester, Chapter
    Library Add. 68; Oxford,
    Bodleian Library, Lat. lit. d. 20;
    London, British Library, Add.
    25031): 355

York, printed breviary of 1533: 237
    Minster Library xvi. N. 3: 313

Zürich, Zentralbibliothek
    Rheinau 28: 189, 232
    30: 149–50

Index of Incipits and Titles

... *ancta quoque/Dei potens* (rhymed office)   256
... *celebret specialius/Dominator domine Birinus* (rhymed office)   254
... *stod ho ere neh*   291

A laudanda ... Ave mater veritatis (polyphonic Alleluia tropes)   305
A sanctarum oraculo (antiphon)   268
A sanctarum oraculo/Auctor virginitatis/Laborantibus (rhymed office)   268
Ab indignatione (offertory trope)   23
Ab inimicis nostris defende nos (litany)   345–6
Ab ipso pueritie (antiphon)   229
Absalon fili mi (motet)   310
Absorbetur (responsory)   277
Accedunt laudes/Surgens Maria/Sacra dedit (rhymed office)   250
Accinxit beata Maria Magdalena (responsory)   236
Ad laudandum celi regem (antiphon)   262
Ad suum igitur (responsory)   236
Ad te levavi (introit)   14
Ad Thome memoriam (antiphon)   335–6, 338, 341
Adest alma dies (introit trope)   30–1
Adest alma virgo (introit trope)   31
Adest preclara (antiphon)   216
Adest Thome (antiphon)   277
Adest Thome/Absorbetur/Granum qui (rhymed office)   277
Adest Thome/Volens deus/Summa cum letitie (rhymed office)   277
Admirabile est nomen tuum (motet tenor)   314–15
Adoremus Christum regem (invitatory)   229
Adoro te domine Jesu Christe   358, 366–7, 369
Advenit ignis (responsory)   55
Aeterne laudis lilium (votive antiphon)   366
Aeterno genitus genitore (introit trope)   27
Aeterno populos (introit trope)   24
Agmina (motet tenor)   310
Agmina sacra (responsory)   56, 88
Agmine credendum/credentium (offertory trope)   15
Agnus dei (polyphonic settings)   306–7, 325, 327, 329
Albanus roseo rutilat (isorhythmic motet)   253
Alleluia ... Iam nunc intonant preconia (sequence 'Pretiosa')   102, 103 (facs.)
Alleluia. Adorabo   51, 149–50, 172
Alleluia. Attendite popule meus 51, 146, 151–2, 154, 156–7, 160, 162, 164, 166, 168, 171–2
Alleluia. Ave dei genitrix   305
Alleluia. Ave Maria   305
Alleluia. Beati quorum remisse   159, 160, 171–2
Alleluia. Beatus vir qui non abiit   150, 171–2

Alleluia. Beatus vir qui timet   149
Alleluia. Cantate domino (Ps. 95)   149, 164, 168, 171–2
Alleluia. Cantate domino (Ps. 97)   149–50, 161, 166, 171–2
Alleluia. Celi enarrant   160, 171–2
Alleluia. Christus resurgens   131
Alleluia. Confiteantur   150, 172
Alleluia. Confitebor tibi   149–50, 152, 154, 156, 162, 164, 166, 168, 172
Alleluia. Confitebuntur celi   149
Alleluia. Confitemini domino   50, 150–2, 154, 161–2, 164, 166, 168, 172
Alleluia. De profundis clamavi   51, 151–2, 154, 156–7, 161–2, 164–6, 168, 172
Alleluia. Deus iudex iustus 48, 51, 146, 151–2, 154, 156–7, 160, 162, 164, 166, 168, 171–2
Alleluia. Dextera dei/domini   51, 150–2, 154, 161–2, 164–6, 168, 172
Alleluia. Dies sanctificatus   104, 105 (facs.), 118, 127–30, 304
Alleluia. Diffusa est gratia   149
Alleluia. Dilexi quoniam   157, 162, 164, 166, 173
Alleluia. Diligam te domine   50–1, 151–2, 154, 156, 160, 162, 164, 166, 168, 171, 173
Alleluia. Disposui testamentum   149–50
Alleluia. Dixit dominus   161, 172–3
Alleluia. Domine deus meus   48, 146, 151, 154, 155–7, 162, 164–6, 171, 173
Alleluia. Domine deus noster   160, 162, 164, 166, 171, 173
Alleluia. Domine deus salutis me   51, 151–2, 154, 156–7, 160–2, 164, 166, 168, 171, 173
Alleluia. Domine exaudi orationem   154, 157, 164, 166, 168, 172–3
Alleluia. Domine in virtute tua   151–2, 154, 156–7, 160, 162, 164, 166, 168, 171, 173
Alleluia. Domine refugium   50, 151–2, 154, 156–7, 160, 162, 164, 166, 168–9, 171, 173
Alleluia. Dominus regit me   156, 167, 171, 173
Alleluia. Dominus regnavit decorem   51, 147, 149–50, 152, 166, 171, 173
Alleluia. Dominus regnavit exultet   150, 152, 157, 164, 166, 168, 171, 173
Alleluia. Elegit te   150
Alleluia. Eripe me   51, 154, 156–7, 160, 162, 164, 166, 168, 171, 173
Alleluia. Exaudi dominus orationem   157, 160, 171, 173
Alleluia. Exultabunt sancti   149–50
Alleluia. Exultate deo   50, 151–2, 154, 156–7, 160, 162, 164, 166, 168, 171, 173
Alleluia. Facta est   173
Alleluia. Gaudete iusti   149
Alleluia. Hic est vere martir   308
Alleluia. In conspectu angelorum   118
Alleluia. In exitu Israel   152, 157, 161, 164, 172–3
Alleluia. In te domine speravi   48, 50, 150–4, 156–7, 160, 162, 164, 166, 168, 171, 173
Alleluia. Iubilate deo   50–1, 149–50, 152, 157, 166, 172–3
Alleluia. Iudica domine   149, 171, 173
Alleluia. Iustus non conturbabitur   149
Alleluia. Lauda anima mea dominum   149–52, 154, 156, 161–2, 164, 166, 168–9, 172–3
Alleluia. Lauda Ierusalem   51, 149–50, 152, 154–5, 157, 161–2, 168, 172–3
Alleluia. Laudate dominum in sanctis   150, 172–3
Alleluia. Laudate dominum omnes angeli   164, 169, 172–3
Alleluia. Laudate dominum omnes gentes
  51, 149, 151–2, 154, 156–7, 161–2, 164, 166, 168, 172–3
Alleluia. Laudate dominum quoniam bonus   149–50, 172–3
Alleluia. Laudate pueri   149–50, 152, 164, 172–3
Alleluia. Letatus sum   50, 149–50, 152, 164, 166, 168, 172–3
Alleluia. Levavi oculos   157, 172–3

Alleluia. Magnus dominus et laudabilis   154, 156, 160, 162, 164, 166, 171, 173

Alleluia. Memento domine David   149–50, 172–3

Alleluia. Misericordias domini   160, 171, 173

Alleluia. Mittat tibi   150

Alleluia. Multifarie olim   104, 105 (facs.), 119, 125–7

Alleluia. Nativitas gloriose virginis Marie   304

Alleluia. Nimis honorati   149

Alleluia. Non vos me elegistis   104–5

Alleluia. Notum fecit   173

Alleluia. Omnes gentes   50, 146, 151–2, 154, 156, 160, 162, 164, 166, 168–9, 171, 173

Alleluia. Ostende nobis   150, 171, 173

Alleluia. Paratum cor meum   50, 149, 151–2, 154, 156–7, 161–2, 164, 166, 168, 172–3

Alleluia. Pascha nostrum. Epulemur in azymis   104, 106 (facs.)

Alleluia. Preoccupemus   146, 149, 154–6, 171, 173

Alleluia. Propitius esto   155, 157, 164, 168, 171, 173

Alleluia. Qui confidunt in domino

    51, 149–50, 152, 154, 156–7, 161–2, 164, 166, 168, 172–3

Alleluia. Qui posuit fines tuos

    51, 149–50, 152, 154–5, 157, 159, 161–2, 164–6, 168–9, 172–3

Alleluia. Qui sanat contritos   50, 149–52, 154–7, 161–2, 164, 166, 168, 172–3

Alleluia. Qui timent dominum   50, 151–2, 154, 156–7, 161–2, 164, 166, 168, 172–3

Alleluia. Quoniam confirmata est   149, 161, 166, 168, 172, 173

Alleluia. Quoniam deus magnus dominus 50, 149–52, 156–7, 161–2, 164, 166, 168, 171, 173

Alleluia. Redemptionem misit   51, 152, 154–5, 157, 159, 161–2, 168, 172–3

Alleluia. Replebimur   155–6, 174

Alleluia. Sancti tui domine   149

Alleluia. Sit nomen   174

Alleluia. Specie tua   149

Alleluia. Stantes erat pedes   174

Alleluia. Surrexit Christus   132–3

Alleluia. Te decet   51, 149–52, 154–7, 160, 162, 164, 166, 168, 171, 174

Alleluia. Timebunt gentes   151, 161–2, 164–5, 172, 174

Alleluia. Venite adoremus   150, 171, 174

Alleluia. Venite exultemus   50, 146, 149–52, 154–7, 160, 162, 164, 166, 168, 171, 174

Alleluia. Venite filii audiat   157, 171, 174

Alleluia. Verba mea   48, 151, 154–7, 160, 162, 164–6, 168, 171, 173

Alleluia. Verbo domini celi firmati   150–60, 171, 174

Alleluia. Video celos apertos   104, 105 (facs.), 118–22

Alleluia. Virga ferax Aaron   304

Alleluia. Virga Iesse floruit   308

Alma proles/Christi miles (motet)   345–6

Alma redemptoris (motet tenor)   314

Alma redemptoris mater (Marian antiphon)   181, 200, 203, 364

Almifico quondam perflatus (introit trope)   14

Anima mea liquefacta (Marian antiphon)   178–9, 193–5, 196 (facs.), 199, 201–2

Anima nostra (offertory)   22

Animis invigilantes (responsory)   260

Ante sextum vero (responsory)   229

Ante thronum trinitatis (motet tenor)   315

Apollinis eclipsatur/Zodiacum signis/In omnem terram (motet)   309, 315–16

Aqua de montis (antiphon)   229

Arva cuncta (Alleluia prosula)   165, 171–2
Ascendit Christus (antiphon)   251
Assumpta est in altum (Marian antiphon)   181
Athanasian Creed (*Quicumque vult*)   335, 337–8
Auctor virginitatis (responsory)   268
Audiebam sonus (responsory)   57
Aurea post Christum (introit trope)   32
Auxilio domini (offertory trope)   22
Ave cuius conceptio (votive antiphon)   357–9, 365–7, 371, 374–6
Ave dei patris filia (votive antiphon)   358, 365–6
Ave Maria   368
Ave Maria ancilla trinitatis (votive antiphon)   358, 366, 375–6
Ave pater Wulstane/Celebremus diem istud/Benedictus sit (rhymed office)   279
Ave presul gloriose/Cuthbertus puer/Christi fortis (rhymed office)   257
Ave primus Anglorum (antiphon)   263
Ave protomartyr Anglorum (antiphon)   253
Ave regina coelorum (Marian antiphon)   181, 200, 203, 364
Ave regina … ave domina (votive antiphon)   327
Ave rex gentis (antiphon)   253, 260, 263, 272–3
Ave rex gentis Anglorum (motet tenot)   313
Ave rex gentis/Sancte idolis/Quidam maligne (rhymed office)   260
Ave rosa paradisi frondens (Marian antiphon)   181
Ave rosa sine spinis (votive antiphon)   359
Ave speculum Anglorum (antiphon)   262–3
Avete (motet tenor)   314, 316, 321, 323

Beata dei genitrix (Marian antiphon)   181
Beata es virgo Maria (Marian antiphon)   182
Beata mater (votive antiphon)   365
Beata mater et innupta virgo (Marian antiphon)   178, 181–3, 185–6, 188
Beata progenies (votive antiphon)   327
Beatam me dicent (Marian antiphon)   203–4
Beatissime regine (responsory)   265
Beatus Benedictus cum iam (responsory)   229
Beatus Benedictus dum iam (responsory)   229
Beatus Patricius (antiphon)   273
Beatus vir Benedictus plus (antiphon)   229
Beatus vir Benedictus qui (responsory)   229
Benedicam te domine (antiphon)   334, 337, 343
Benedicamus domino. Deo gratias   106, 307, 310
Benedicamus patrem (responsory)   56
Benedicat nos deus (responsory)   56, 88
Benedicta et venerabilis (gradual)   114, 307–8
Benedicta sit sancta trinitas (introit)   27
Benedicta tu in mulieribus (antiphon)   219
Benedictio et claritas (responsory)   56
Benedictus (canticle)   335, 337
Benedictus dei famulus (antiphon)   229
Benedictus dei famulus (responsory)   229
Benedictus dominus (responsory)   56, 93–4
Benedictus Kentigernus (antiphon)   267

Benedictus Mariae filius (motet tenor) 347
Benedictus sit (antiphon) 279
Bis seni proceres (inscription) 36

Cantemus omnes (introit trope) 32
Capillis quoque capitis (antiphon) 236
Celebremus concinentes (responsory) 211
Celebremus diem istud (responsory) 279
Celi enarrant (responsory) 88, 90
Celica celestem (introit trope) 19–20
Celsa cedrus (motet voice) 335
Celse deus precibus (offertory trope) 15
Ceperunt postmodum (responsory) 229
Christi fortis (antiphon) 257
Christi miles (motet voice) 345–6
Christi miles (responsory) 266
Christicola perpes sanctis (introit trope) 24
Christicolas cuneos (communion trope) 16
Christo laus (antiphon) 278
Christus surrexit (offertory trope) 23
Circumdederunt V. Quoniam tribulatio (responsory) 102, 103 (facs.), 116–17
Clarisonas Christo prompsit (introit trope) 14
Claudi recti (antiphon) 279
Clemenciam (Benedicamus) 310
Collaudantes et dignam/Beatissime regine/Congaudendum (rhymed office) 265
Comedi favum cum melle (Marian antiphon) 178–9, 192
Compassus nutrici (antiphon) 229
Completum est (responsory) 236
Concupisco (motet tenor) 313–14
Confessio et pulchritudo (introit) 31
Confessor dei Benedictus (antiphon) 229
Confessorum regem (invitatory) 229
Confirmat hoc mysterium (responsory) 278
Confitebuntur celi (offertory) 38
Confitemini (Psalm 104) 24
Congaudendum (antiphon) 265
Congratulamini (responsory) 236
Contritis placidas (introit trope) 37
Convocatis fratribus (responsory) 229
Cornelius centurio (responsory) 219, 224
Cornelius vite eterne (responsory prosula) 219
Credo in unum deum (polyphonic settings) 307, 326, 329–30, 333–5, 337–9, 342–3
Crucifixum in carne, see *Sedit angelus*
Cui pater excelsus (communion trope) 30
Cuius ergo vel saxeum (responsory) 236
Cultor agri (antiphon) 280
Cum ambularent (responsory) 57
Cum aspicerem animalia (responsory) 57
Cum cognovisset (antiphon) 229
Cum discubuisset (antiphon) 236
Cum esses iunior (invitatory) 105

Cum pia per populos (introit trope)   26
Cum populis pietate (introit trope)   34, 43
Cumque in specu (antiphon)   229
Cumque sanctus Benedictus in cella (responsory)   229
Cumque sibi (antiphon)   229
Cumque vir domini (antiphon)   229
Cunctipotens domine (introit trope)   24
Cuthbertus puer bone (responsory)   210, 257

De flore martirum/Deus tuorum militum/Ave rex gentis Anglorum (motet)   313
De ventre matris mee (introit)   28
Decantemus Cannici (antiphon)   256
Deduis de la Chasse   320
Dei potens (antiphon)   256
Deo gracias   346–7
Deo gracias (polyphonic settings; see also *Ite missa est, Benedicamus*)   323
Descendi in hortum (Marian antiphon)   178–9, 193–4, 201–2, 364
Descendit angelus domini (tenor)   335
Descendit de celis (responsory)   54, 86
Deum time (responsory)   56
Deus placabilis indulgencie auctor (prayer)   221
Deus qui beatum Elfegum post pontificalem (prayer)   221
Deus quo nos beati Guthlaci (prayer)   222
Deus tuorum militum (motet voice)   313
Devota deo Mildretha (responsory)   268
Devotus Egilwinus (antiphon)   260
Dicit Andreas (communion)   34
Dictus est Patricio (antiphon)   258–60
Diem festum/Illustris regis/Innocentum dolo (rhymed office)   263
Digno dato sterilis (antiphon)   274
Dilecte mi apprehendam (Marian antiphon)   178–9, 183, 193–4, 201–2
Diluculo valde (responsory)   236
Discipulis flammas (introit trope)   15
Diuturnis inopia (antiphon)   229
Dixit itaque Martha (antiphon)   236
Dolor meus (motet tenor)   314
Dominator domine Birinus (antiphon)   254
Domine Jesu Christe (prayer motet)   359, 376
Domine ne in ira (responsory)   187
Domine non aspicias (responsory)   229
Domine praevenisti (gradual)   114
Dominus dixit (introit)   15–16
Dominus secus mare (introit)   34
Douce playsence/Garison selon nature/Neuma (motet)   316, 320
Dulcis virgo (motet tenor)   314
Dum beatus Benedictus (responsory)   229
Dum beatus vir oraculo (responsory)   229
Dum in hac terra (antiphon)   229
Dum in heremum (antiphon)   229
Dumque super undas (antiphon)   229

Ecce adest dies praeclara (Marian antiphon) 181
Ecce dies venerandus (introit trope) 31
Ecce oculi (introit) 39
Ecce tu pulchra es (Marian antiphon) 178, 188, 190, 193
Ecce vere Israhelita (responsory) 88, 91
Ecce vir (responsory) 96–7
Ecce vir dei Benedictus (antiphon) 230
Ecclesiae psalmista typo decantet ovanter (introit trope) 31
Effectrix rerum sanctarum (introit trope) 27, 43
Ego autem (introit) 17
Ego vos elegi (communion) 34
Egregius Christi (responsory) 273
Electus a fratribus (antiphon) 230
Elegerunt apostoli (introit) 16
Elisabeth ut virgini (responsory) 280
Emissiones tuae (Marian antiphon) 178–9, 188, 191
En Katerine solennia/Virginalis concio (motet) 343
Enchiridion preclare ecclesie Sarum (Paris, 1530) 367, 371, 377
Eodem verso anno (responsory) 230
Epithalamium Christi (Ps. 44) 40–1
Epulemur in azymis, see *Alleluia. Pascha nostrum*
Erat vir domini Benedictus (antiphon) 230
Erat vultu placido (responsory) 230
Eructavit cor meum (offertory verse) 40
Etenim sederunt (introit) 16
Eterne iocunditatis (antiphon) 236
Eterni patris/Elisabeth ut virgini/Scandit montes (rhymed office) 280
Eternum trinumque (invitatory) 236
Euge beate pater (antiphon) 230
Euntibus animalibus (responsory) 57
Ex Joachim quem habuit (antiphon) 254
Ex ore infantium (introit) 21
Ex semine (clausula, motet tenor) 304–5
Ex summa rerum (responsory) 276, 278
Exaltata est gloriosa (Marian antiphon) 177–8, 181, 183–4, 188, 203
Exemplo domini (offertory trope) 16–17
Expetitus a fratribus (antiphon) 230
Exquirebat Maria quem non (antiphon) 236
Exultet iam angelica turba celorum (Praeconium paschale) 21, 261
Exultet omnium turba (antiphon) 230
Eya laudes (antiphon) 266
Eya mater Sion (versus ante officium) 20

Facies et pennas (responsory) 57
Factum est post obitum (responsory) 230
Factus Aaron (responsory) 274
Favus distillans (Marian antiphon) 178, 188, 190
Felix Anna cella/Felix Anna flos/Omnis sanctorum (rhymed office) 249, 253
Felix Hiberniam (responsory) 255
Felix locus (antiphon) 258
Felix namque (responsory) 200

Felix namque es beata (Marian antiphon)   194, 203
Festivum socci ... laetantur ovanter (introit trope)   31
Fidelis Christi confessor Egidius (responsory)   218
Filie regum (offertory)   40
Firmati vero vegetati (offertory trope)   38, 43
Flagrat virtus (antiphon)   280
Florem mundi (rhymed office)   235
Florem mundi periturum (responsory)   209
Floret (motet tenor)   313
Flos inter lilia/Celsa cedrus/Quam magnus pontifex (motet)   335
Fons citharizancium (motet voice: see *Sub Arturo*)   314, 316–17, 322–3, 334, 353
Fons hortorum (Marian antiphon)   178–9, 188, 191, 193
Fortis ut mors (responsory)   236
Frater Maure (antiphon)   230
Frater Maure (responsory)   230
Frondentibus florentibus/Floret (motet)   313
Fuit vir vite venerabilis (antiphon)   215, 230
Fuit vir vite venerabilis (responsory)   209–12, 215, 229–30
Fulgebat in venerando (responsory)   264–5
Fundator (antiphon)   264

Garison selon nature (motet voice)   316, 320
Gaude flore virginali (votive antiphon)   365
Gaude gloriosa (motet tenor)   310–12, 314
Gaude Maria virgo V. Gabrihelem archangelem (responsory)   54, 105, 137, 140
Gaude Maria virgo cunctas ... quae (Marian antiphon)   181, 203–4
Gaude mater Anna (sequence)   253
Gaude plurimum (votive antiphon)   358, 360, 375–6
Gaude Sion ornata/Primus iaspis lapidum/Ad laudandum celi regem (rhymed office)   262
Gaude virgo mater Christi (votive antiphon)   357–8, 366, 376
Gaude virgo salutata (votive antiphon)   305
Gaudeamus (introit)   32
Gaudeamus universi/Fulgebat in venerando/O admirabile beati (rhymed office)   264–5
Gaudeat cunctus populus ... quia lux hodie (introit trope)   20
Gaudet mundus (responsory)   262
Gens laudum (hymn)   273
Germinis excelsi (introit trope)   24
Glad and blithe   288, 290, 296–7, 298–9
Gloria in excelsis Deo (polyphonic settings)   307, 326, 330, 332, 334–6, 338, 341, 343, 350
Gloria patri geniteque (responsory)   56
Gloria sanctorum decus angelorum (votive antiphon)   357–8, 366, 375
Gloria sit patri et genito (introit trope)   27
Gloriosa diei huius sollempnia (responsory)   216–17, 236
Gloriosa es Maria Magdalena (responsory)   216–17
Gloriosa sanctissimi (rhymed office)   265
Gloriosus confessor domini (antiphon)   230
Gloriosus deus V. Dextera tua (gradual)   106, 138, 140
Gloriosus vir sanctus Swithunus (responsory)   78–85
Go (clausula, motet tenor)   114
Granum cadit copiam (antiphon)   275, 277
Granum qui (antiphon)   277

Granumque in tempore (antiphon)   277
Gratias agamus (introit trope)   26
Gratissima virgo species (motet voice)   310–12

Hac in laude patris ... dicamus ovanter (introit trope)   31
Haec est regina virginum (Marian antiphon)   181–2, 188, 203–4
Haec tibi Laurenti flammas (introit trope)   32
Hanc ergo quam lucas (responsory)   236
Hanc ergo toto corde (antiphon)   236
Hec est via (antiphon)   230
Hec est illa Maria (responsory)   236
Hic itaque iam (antiphon)   230
Hic itaque iam (responsory)   230
Hic Osmundus (antiphon)   270
Hic vir despiciens (antiphon)   230
Hierusalum solio (introit trope)   24–5, 43
Hoc mihi donaverat (introit trope)   17, 42–3
Hodie candidati (versus ante officium)   18–19
Hodie lux vera effulserat (introit trope)   20
Hodie martirum flores (responsory)   54
Hodie quemadmodum (introit trope)   44
Hodie sanctus Benedictus per (antiphon)   230
Honor virtus (responsory)   56
Hora est ... quia lux vera fulget (introit trope)   20
Hortus (est) conclusus (Marian antiphon)   182, 193, 202
Hosti pandit (antiphon)   280
Humane lingue organis/Supplicum voces/Deo gratias (motet)   346–7
Hymnidicis te ... veneremur ovantes (introit trope)   31
Hymnidicis te Christe (introit trope)   15–16, 43

Ibo mihi ad montem myrrhae (Marian antiphon)   181
Ida capillorum/Porcio nature/Ante thronum trinitatis (motet)   315
Igitur beatus Benedictus (responsory)   230
Illustris regis (responsory)   263
Imbribus irriguis (motet voice)   314–15
Immensi regis (antiphon)   230
In celesti gloria/Pater pius/Christo laus (rhymed office)   278
In Guillelmi laudibus/Voluntate trutina/Claudi recti (rhymed office)   279
In medio ecclesiae (introit)   17, 19
In omnem terram (motet tenor)   309, 314–17
In omnem terram (offertory)   34
In pagina (antiphon)   264
In septentrionali/Christi miles/Eya laudes (rhymed office)   266
In templo dei (motet voice)   316, 321, 323
In virtute (introit)   40
In visione dei (responsory)   57, 93
Inclita martyrii/Sacrosanctum venerando/Suscipiens martyr (rhymed office)   252
Initio consilio (antiphon)   230
Initio consilio (responsory)   230
Innocentem dolo (antiphon)   263
Intempesta nocte (antiphon)   230

Intempesta nocte (responsory) 230
Inter amenitatis/Revertenti (motet) 313
Inter densas deserti/Imbribus irriguis/Admirabile est nomen tuum (motet) 314–15
Inter natos (responsory) 56
Inter sidereos/Devota deo Mildretha/Regina a summa opulentia (rhymed office) 268
Inter tot et tales (motet voice) 310
Inter usitata/Inter tot et tales (motet) 310
Intrantem Iesum (antiphon) 236
Intret in conspectu tuo (introit) 37
Introduxit (introit) 24
Intuitu placido (introit trope) 34, 36, 43
Invenit se Augustinus (responsory) 208
Inviolata integra (responsory prose) 304
Ipse perspicuas/perspicuos (introit trope) 15
Ista est speciosa (responsory) 200
Iste pastor (Ave speculum)/Gaudet mundus/Novi solis (rhymed office) 262
Iste sanctus (responsory) 88, 230
Ite missa est (polyphonic settings) 307, 344, 346

Jacet granum (antiphon) 280
Jam redeunt gaudia (Alleluia prosula) 44
Jam venit lux vera (introit trope) 20
Jesu Cristes milde moder 291
Jesu redemptor omnium, perpes corona presulum (hymn) 307–8
Joannis sollemnitas/Quem malignus spiritus/Vexatos a demone (rhymed office) 266
Johannes Iesu care (tenor) 336, 343
Johannes Iesu Christo (sequence) 336
Judaea et Ierusalem (responsory) 54
Judicium magno (offertory trope) 23, 43
Justum deduxit (responsory) 217, 230

Kyrie (polyphonic settings) 306–7

Laborantibus (antiphon) 268
Laetabitur (introit) 40
Laetetur cunctus quadro (offertory trope) 24
Lauda vivi alpha et o (votive antiphon) 357–8, 366
Laudemus dominum (introit trope) 31
Laudemus dominum (responsory) 88, 230
Laudemus dominum in hac (invitatory) 230
Laudibus alternis pueros (versus ante officium) 20
Lavit Maria lachrimis (antiphon) 236
Letabundus decantet (sequence) 289, 294
Letabundus exultet ... Regem regum (sequence) 288–91, 294–6
Letare Ierusalem/Factus Aaron/Digno dato sterilis (rhymed office) 274
Letemur omnes (responsory) 230
Letetur omne seculum (responsory) 216, 236
Liber Tramitis 175, 188–9, 198–201
Liberiori genere (antiphon) 230
Lingua mea calamus scribe (offertory verse) 40
Locus iste (motet tenor) 313–14

Lugens pie defunctum (responsory)   236
Lumen ad revelationem gentium (antiphon)   291
Lux vera Christus (introit trope)   19–20, 42
Lux vera emicat (introit trope)   20

Magdalenam sua crimina (antiphon)   236
Magnificat 'Regale'   359
Magnificat anima mea dominum (canticle)   307–8, 335
Magnificat eum (responsory)   217
Magnificavit eum (responsory)   88
Magnum et immensus ... esuriem (offertory trope)   16
Magnus dominus (responsory)   56
Maria Magdalena at altera Maria (responsory)   236
Maria Magdalena et Maria Iacobi (antiphon)   236
Maria Magdalena que fuerat (responsory)   217, 236
Maria plena virtute (votive antiphon)   359
Maria virgo semper laetare (Marian antiphon)   177–8, 181–4, 188, 203
Mariae virginis (votive antiphon)   376
Marionette douche   310
Marshall's Primer   292
Martha inquit dominus (antiphon)   236
Martir Clemens V. Impetra gaudia (responsory)   106, 136
Martyr Thoma/Sacrat Thomas/O Thoma martyr (rhymed office)   276
Mass *Le roy*   361
Mass *Salve intemerata*   359
Mass *Sancte Cuthberte*   361, 364
Mass *Te deum*   357
Mass *Te matrem*   357
Mater patris et filia (Marian antiphon)   200
Medius cantus. Manere (motet tenor)   309
Mellifluis cum melodiis ... Adest enim festa Martini (introit trope)   31
Merito hec patimur (motet tenor)   309
Merito sanctitatis (responsory)   257
Mihi autem nimis (introit)   34
Milan organum treatise   64
Misereatur vestri (responsory)   230
Missus est Gabriel (responsory)   80
Monachus sub clerico (antiphon)   280
Montpellier organum treatise   64, 122
Monumenta aperta (offertory trope)   23
Mors (clausula, motet tenor)   305
Mulier quedam (antiphon)   230
Multitudo languentium (communion)   39
Munere pro tali (introit trope)   24
Musica enchiriadis   52, 59–61, 64, 78, 104
Musicorum collegio/In templo dei/Avete (motet)   316, 321, 323
Mystica pro meritis (introit trope)   32

Ne valeant querulis (offertory trope)   15
Nec in agnos (antiphon)   280
Nequissimo Iude (responsory)   236

Nesciens mater (votive antiphon) 327, 329–31
Neuma (motet tenor) 316, 320
Noli me tangere (antiphon) 236
Non aspicias (antiphon) 230
Non aspicias (responsory) 230
Nos autem gloriari (introit) 24–6
Nos cruce regnantem (introit trope) 25
Noster cetus psallat letus (Benedicamus) 129
Novi solis (antiphon) 262
Now wel may we merthis make 61
Nunc sancte nobis spiritus (hymn) 273
Nursia provincie (antiphon) 230
Nursia provincie (responsory) 230
Nutrici in auxilium (antiphon) 230

O admirabile beati (antiphon) 264–5
O beata Trinitas (responsory) 56
O beati viri Benedicti (antiphon) 230
O beati viri Benedicti (responsory) 230
O bone dux (motet voice) 316
O bone Jesu (votive antiphon) 357–8, 366
O dee virtutum (offertory trope) 22
O desiderabilis/Tractavit Patricio/Dictus est Patricio (rhymed office) 258–60
O diligens Christum (responsory) 236
O domine celi et (celique) terre (votive antiphon) 358–9
O felix felicis (responsory) 236
O felix verbi (responsory) 236
O Georgi Deo (motet voice) 347
O gloriosa dei genitrix (Marian antiphon) 203
O gloriosa genetrix virgo (Marian antiphon) 181
O Iuda et Ierusalem (responsory) 54
O laudanda sanctus Benedictus (responsory) 230
O Maria gratia plena (votive antiphon) 378
O Maria salvatoris (votive antiphon) 366
O martyr et rex/Rex sacer Oswaldus/Rex Oswaldus (rhymed office) 271
O mater venerabilis (votive antiphon) 366
O pastor apostolice (responsory) 55
O pastor pie/ ... /Decantemus Christi (rhymed office) 256
O Philippe/O bone dux (motet) 316
O purpurea (antiphon) 260, 273
O quam admirabilis (responsory) 90–2
O quam gloriosum (responsory) 88
O quam magnus pontifex (tenor) 335
O quam venerandus (antiphon) 230
O quanta vis amoris (antiphon) 236
O radix Iesse (antiphon) 263
O regina celestis glorie (votive antiphon) 358, 366
O regina mundi clara (votive antiphon) 366
O sapientia (antiphon) 73
O Thoma martyr (antiphon) 276
O vos omnes/Locus iste (motet) 313

Occidentem visitavit (antiphon) — 259
Omnes de Saba V. Surge inluminare (gradual) — 106, 138
Omnibus ecce piis (introit trope) — 24
Omnipotens sempiterne deus qui beato Wlmaro (prayer) — 223
Omnipotens sempiterne deus qui omnes sanctorum tuos cum mensura (prayer) — 222
Omnis sanctorum (antiphon) — 253
Opem nobis (antiphon) — 259, 335, 337–9, 342
Optimam ergo partem (antiphon) — 236
Oramus te (antiphon) — 230
Oravit sanctus Benedictus (antiphon) — 230
Ore coruscanti custodes (offertory trope) — 15

Pacifici psallant (offertory trope) — 16
Paradisi porta per Evam (Marian antiphon) — 181
Parcens conversis (offertory trope) — 41
Parcere pacificis (introit trope) — 41
Pastor cesus (antiphon) — 263
Pastor cesus/Studens livor/Granum cedit (rhymed office) — 275
Pastor ingens (antiphon) — 263
Pastor oves (antiphon) — 256
Pater Columba (antiphon) — 256
Pater insignis (responsory) — 56, 92, 230
Pater noster — 368
Pater pius (responsory) — 278
Pater sanctus dum (antiphon) — 230
Pater sanctus dum (responsory) — 230
Patris adest votiva dies (introit trope) — 31
Per quem valle meum (offertory trope) — 22
Per quidam parvulus (antiphon) — 231
Perfudit virtus (introit trope) — 26
Perspicue crucis (introit trope) — 25
Petram cephas ecclesie/Petrus pastor potissimus/Petre amas me (motet) — 309
Petre amas me (motet tenor) — 309
Petre amas me V. Symon Iohannis diligis me (responsory) — 56, 108, 134–5
Petrus pastor potissimus (motet voice) — 309
Porcio nature (motet voice) — 315
Posui adiutorium (responsory) — 217
Posuisti domine V. Desiderium anime (gradual) — 102, 103 (facs.), 112, 114–16
Praemia pro meritis (offertory trope) — 32
Preciosus confessor (responsory) — 231
Predicta nutrix (antiphon) — 231
Predicta nutrix (responsory) — 231
Prepollens magnifice/Animis invigilantes/Devotus Egilwinus (rhymed office) — 260
Preposito plebi magna (responsory) — 245
Presulis Osmundi (responsory) — 270
Primus iaspis lapidum (responsory) — 262
Princeps et pater (antiphon) — 273
Principium reserans (introit trope) — 15, 20
Pro meritis meritam (introit trope) — 32
Processisse paterno (introit trope) — 16
Promissam dudum gaudentes (introit trope) — 44

Psallite domino (responsory) 92
Puer domini Benedictus (responsory) 231

Quae est ista (responsory) 200
Quam clara (antiphon) 278
Quam magnus pontifex (motet tenor) 335
Quam nos auctorem (introit trope) 25
Quam pulchra es (votive antiphon) 364
Quare fremuerunt (Psalm verse for introit, motet) 309
Quare fremuerunt (Psalm 2) 16
Quattuor animalia (responsory) 57
Quattuor facies uni (responsory) 57
Quatuor principalia 311–12
Quem malignus spiritus (antiphon) 266
Quem mare terra polus (antiphon) 272
Quem verum genui natum (communion trope) 40
Qui celum terramque (offertory trope) 22–3
Qui dum heremum (antiphon) 231
Qui mundum mundique (introit trope) 16
Qui pariter cernunt (introit trope) 39, 43
Qui patris es virtus (offertory trope) 15
Qui quondam Moysi (introit trope) 29
Quicumque vult, see Athanasian Creed
Quidam maligne (antiphon) 260
Quidam rusticus (responsory) 231
Quis deus magnus (responsory) 56
Quod mecum mansit (offertory trope) 16, 40
Quoniam secta latronum (motet voice) 309
Quos mea perpetuo (introit trope) 16

Recessit igitur (antiphon) 231
Recordare virgo mater (offertory) 305
Rediens a monumento (responsory) 236
Regali ex progenie (votive antiphon) 263, 327
Regem confessorem (invitatory) 231
Reges Tharsis et insule (offertory) 22
Regina a summa opulentia (antiphon) 268
Regina caeli laetare (votive antiphon) 327, 364
Regis iram non formidans (responsory) 246–7
Regne de pité (motet) 310
Regnum mundi (responsory) 236, 255
Regularis Concordia 109
Relicta domo (antiphon) 231
Relicta domo rebusque patris (responsory) 209
Relictis retibus (motet tenor) 314
Remittuntur ergo ei (antiphon) 236
Reor nescia (motet voice) 313
Replevit de celo (introit trope) 26
Respondens autem dominus (antiphon) 236
Respondit fortissima puella (responsory) 269
Revertenti (motet voice) 313

Rex autem David (antiphon) 310
Rex Oswaldus (antiphon) 271
Rex quem metrorum/Rex regum (motet) 312
Rex regum (motet tenor) 312, 314
Rex regum dominus (communion trope) 30, 43
Rex sacer Oswaldus (responsory) 271
Rex seculorum (antiphon) 231
Rogabat Iesum quidam (antiphon) 236
Roman de Fauvel 313

Sacra dedit (antiphon) 250
Sacrat Thomas primordia (responsory) 211, 276
Sacrosanctum venerando (responsory) 252
Salvatoris mater/O Georgi Deo/Benedictus Mariae filius (motet) 347
Salve festa dies (hymn) 292
Salve intemerata (votive antiphon) 357–60
Salve Jhesu mater vera (votive antiphon) 358, 375
Salve mater domini/Salve templum gratie (motet) 345–6
Salve regina mater misericordie (Marian antiphon) 193, 200, 203, 307, 358, 364–6
Salve regina pudica mater (votive antiphon) 358, 364
Salve sancta parens (introit) 304
Salve templum gratie (votive antiphon) 345–6
Sancta dei genitrix virgo (Marian antiphon) 182, 203–4
Sancta Maria (votive antiphon) 365
Sancta Maria mater dei (votive antiphon) 358, 360–2, 376
Sancta Maria succurre (Marian antiphon) 181–2, 188
Sancte Benedicte confessor (responsory) 92, 94, 231, 235
Sancte dei pretiose (responsory) 54
Sancte deus (votive antiphon) 376
Sancte indolis (responsory) 260
Sancte ingenite (Sanctus trope) 304
Sancte Petre apostolorum (processional antiphon) 106, 134
Sanctimonialis autem (antiphon) 231
Sanctissime confessor (antiphon) 231
Sanctissime confessor (responsory) 231
Sanctissimum presulem Wilfridum (responsory) 211
Sanctissimus martyris Iusti (responsory) 92
Sancto Dunstano/Signifer Christi/In pagina (rhymed office) 264
Sancto regente (responsory) 255
Sanctorum festis ... repetamus ovantes (introit trope) 31
Sanctorum piissime (antiphon) 256
Sanctus (polyphonic settings) 306–7, 324–6, 329–30, 350
Sanctus ante saecula deus (Sanctus trope) 26
Sanctus Benedictus Christi (responsory) 231
Sanctus Benedictus plus (responsory) 231
Scala celo prominens (antiphon) 254
Sandit montes (antiphon) 280
Scolica enchiriadis 52, 60, 104
Sedens ergo ad (antiphon) 236
Sedenti super solium/Confirmat hoc mysterium/Quam clara (rhymed office) 278
Sedit angelus V. Crucifixum in carne (processional antiphon) 131–2

Sélestat organum treatise	95–6
Semel iuravi (communion)	40
Sensit puerpera (antiphon)	264
Sexto namque (responsory)	231
Sicut discipulus (antiphon)	231
Sicut fenum arui (motet tenor)	314
Sicut fragrant (antiphon)	278
Sicut lilium inter spinas (Marian antiphon)	178, 188, 190
Signifer Christi (responsory)	264
Similitudo aspectus (responsory)	57
Simon Iohannis diligis me (communion)	30
Simulabo eum viro (antiphon)	231
Singularis et insignis (offertory prosula)	305
Sint lumbi vestri precincti (responsory)	56, 65–78, 80–1, 85, 88, 90–1, 94
Sol oriens (antiphon)	271
Solennitatem Magdalene (antiphon)	236
Song of Songs	41, 178–80, 188–9, 192, 200
Soror Marthe (responsory)	217
Sospitati pristine (antiphon)	267
Specialis virgo (antiphon)	219
Species firmamenti (responsory)	57
Speciosa facta es (Marian antiphon)	203
Spiritus domini (introit)	26
Spiritus et alme (Gloria trope)	304–5, 307, 332, 336
Splendidus adventum (introit trope)	24
Splendore sollempni (introit trope)	32
Sponsa rectoris (hymn)	304
Sponsus amat sponsum (responsory verse)	343–4
Stabat iuxta Christi crucem (sequence)	290–1
Stabat mater dolorosa (sequence)	358, 366, 375
Stabat virgo mater Christi (votive antiphon)	366
Stand wel moder under rode	291
Stans autem retro (antiphon)	236
Statura erat (responsory)	57
Stirps regalis Britannorum (antiphon)	267
Studens livor (responsory)	211, 275
Sub Arturo plebs/Fons citharizancium/In omnem terram (motet)	314, 316–17, 322–3, 334, 353
Sub tuam protectionem (Marian antiphon)	177–8, 181, 183, 185–6, 188, 203
Sub tuum praesidium (Marian antiphon)	177–8, 181–3, 185–6, 188, 203
Succurre sancta genitrix (Marian antiphon)	181
Summa cum letitie (antiphon)	277
Summae Trinitati (responsory)	56
Summe deus sancta et indivisa (introit trope)	27
Summula musice	315
Super salutem (responsory)	200
Supplicum voces (motet voice)	346–7
Surge aquilo et veni auster (Marian antiphon)	192
Surgens Maria (responsory)	250
Suscipe cum gaudio/Presulis Osmundi/Hic Osmundus (rhymed office)	270
Suscipiens martyr (antiphon)	252

Sustentans humiles (offertory trope) 40

Talis est dilectus (Marian antiphon) 190, 192, 200–1
Tam (clausula, motet tenor) 114
Tantam gratiam (antiphon) 231
Te deum laudamus 52, 307
Te deum patrem (responsory) 56
Te iure laudant (antiphon) 337–8
Te laudent angeli (responsory) 54
Te matrem dei laudamus (votive antiphon) 357–8
Terra tremuit (offertory) 23–4
Thalamum sponsi (antiphon) 255
Tibi Christo regnante (versus ante officium) 18–19
Tibi laus, tibi gloria (votive antiphon) 336, 338
Timete dominum V. Inquirentes (gradual) 102, 103 (facs.), 112–13
Torentem pertransivit (offertory verse) 22
Tota pulchra es (Marian antiphon) 178, 180, 193–4, 199, 201–2, 251, 358, 364, 366, 375
Tractavit Patricio (responsory) 258–60
Tribum quem non abhorruit/Quoniam secta latronum/Merito hec patimur (motet) 309
Tristis est anima mea (motet tenor) 314
Tu capud ecclesie/Tu es Petrus (motet) 306
Tu es Petrus (motet voice) 306
Tu patris sempiternus (verse of *Te deum*) 59
Tulerunt dominum (responsory) 236
Tunc ad locum (antiphon) 231

Unanimes regem (invitatory) 236
Unde coronatus (trope) 32
Undique huc fratres ... reboemus ovantes (introit trope) 31
Unus est dominus (responsory) 56
Ut decus est palmae/plane (offertory trope) 15
Ut tuo propitiatus (responsory verse) 54

Vae nobis miseris (prayer motet) 378
Vatum firma fides (introit trope) 28, 43
Veneranda imminentis/Egregius Christi/Beatus Patricius (rhymed office) 273–4
Veni creator spiritus (hymn) 304
Veni in hortum meum (Marian antiphon) 178–9, 188, 191
Veniat/Venit dilectus meus (Marian antiphon) 178–9, 188, 191–3
Veritatem (motet tenor) 306
Vexatos a demone (antiphon) 266
Via recta orientis (responsory) 231
Victime paschali laudes (sequence) 307
Videns ergo flentem (responsory) 236
Videns hoc Phariseus (antiphon) 236
Viderunt omnes V. Notum fecit (gradual) 106, 137, 139–40
Vir dei mundum (responsory) 231
Vir domini (responsory) 257
Vir domini Benedictus omnium (antiphon) 231
Vir enim domini (responsory) 231
Vir inclitus Dionisius (responsory) 57

Virginalis concio (motet voice) 313, 343
Virgo Christo amabilis (Marian antiphon) 181
Virgo dei genitrix (V. of gradual *Benedicta et venerabilis*) 308, 323
Virgo flagellatur (responsory) 343–4
Virgo mater et filia (motet) 310
Virgo prudentissima (Marian antiphon) 194
Virgo sancta Brigida/Felix Hiberniam/Thalamum sponsi (rhymed office) 255
Virgo templum trinitatis (votive antiphon) 358
Virtutum humilitatis (antiphon) 266
Vix obtinui (antiphon) 231
Volens deus (responsory) 277
Voluntate trutina (responsory) 279
Vos qui admiramini/Gratissima virgo species/Gaude gloriosa (motet) 310–12
Vultum tuum (introit) 32

Worldes blisce have god day 310

Zelo tui langueo/Reor nescia (motet) 313
Zodiacum signis (motet voice) 309, 315–16

Index of Names

Abdon, St 227
Aberdeen 250, 268
Abingdon 150
Achad-Bó (Kilkenny) 256
Adam 25
Ælfege, *see* Alphege
Ælfric 12
Ælsige, Abbot of Bath 223
Æthelwold 24, 47, 49, 53, 58, 98, 169, 264
Agatha, St 226
Agnes, St 226
Alanus, Johannes 309, 314, 316–17, 321–3,
    334, 349, 353
Alban, St 227, 252–3, 260, 282
Alcuin 36
Aldhelm, St 36, 208
Alexander, St 227
Alphege (Ælfege), St 221, 223, 227
Ambrose, St 226
Amiens 168–9
Anchin 169
Andrew, St, Apostle 17, 28, 33–4, 36,
    41–4, 206, 226
Andrew of Fleury 105
Angers 151, 153, 161, 163–5, 167
    Saint-Pierre 105
Anglici, J. 321
Anne, St 32, 249, 253–4, 283
Anonymous 4 107
Anselm of Bec, Archbishop of Canterbury
    153, 281
Anthony, St 175
Apel, W. 146–7, 334
Apollinaris, St 227
Appleby, Thomas 359
Arbroath 212
Arles 155
Arlt, W. 52–3, 64, 108, 131, 136, 141, 289
Arnoul de Grantpoint 319
Arras 167–9
    monastery of Saint-Vaast 169, 209, 222
Arthur, King of Britain 316

Ashwell, Thomas 357–8, 361–2, 364
Aston, Hugh 357–9, 376
Athelstan, King of England 257
Auda, A. 55
Augustine of Canterbury, St 227, 254, 283
Augustine of Hippo, St 29, 107, 207–8,
    213, 228, 308
Aurillac 155
Ausbertus, St 224
Avignon 312
Avranches 163–5, 167
Avril, F. 211

Babb, W. 60
Babolenus, St 106
Backhouse, J. M. 3
Bailey, T. 5
Baldwin of Boulogne, King of Jerusalem
    315
Baldwin of Chartres, Abbot of Bury 58
Bamberg 55–6, 192
Bannister, H. M. 15, 104, 106–7, 131, 137,
    209
Barbatre 319
Barking 164–6, 221
Barnwell 206
Barré, H. 183
Bartholomew, St 228
Bath 219, 222–3, 225
Battle 209
Baudement 319
Bautier, R.-H. 105
Bayeux 166–7, 216–17, 237
Bazas 158, 160
Beauvais 58, 134, 136, 166–7, 211, 218,
    276
Bec 148, 153–4, 159–60, 167, 169
Bede 58, 79
Beleth, Johannes 53
Benedict, St 5, 14, 28, 55–6, 208–11,
    214–15, 217–18, 220, 224, 226–7
Benedict, Abbot of Peterborough 275
Benevento 17, 25, 155

Benham, H. 376
Benoît-Castelli, G. 151
Bent, M. 266, 303, 335, 350, 353
Bergsagel, J. D. 252–3, 255, 357
Bernard of Cluny 188–9, 193, 198
Bernard M. 55
Berry, M. 7
Bertin, St 208, 228
Beyssac, G. 145–6
Birinus, St 254, 282
Bishop, T. A. M. 214
Bittering, *see* Byttering
Björkvall, G. 15, 47, 305
Blaanus, St, Bishop of Kingarth 255
Black Prince 318, 349
Blaise, St 226
Blaise, A. 21
Blanchard, P. 187
Blume, C. 15, 105, 209, 211
Boethius 316
Bond, M. F. 349
Boniface IX, Pope 250
Borren, C. van den 5
Botulf (Botulph) St 208, 255
Boulogne, Saint-Wlmar 315
Bowers, R. 306, 316, 322–3, 350–3, 359
Bradshaw, H. 62
Braga 276
Bramston 376
Bremen 232
Breowa, St 255
Bridget (Brigid) of Kildare, St 211–12,
    255–6, 273, 276, 282
Bridlington 266
Briggs, H. B. 3
Brou, L. 209
Brown, C. 285, 291
Brown, L. E. G. 209
Brown, R. A. 58
Browne, John 366
Bukofzer, M. 260–1, 287, 327–8, 334–5,
    338, 343, 350
Bulst, N. 206
Burell, John 350, 352
Burgate, R. de 305
Burstyn, S. 183
Bury St Edmunds 48, 50, 58, 151, 250,
    284, 313
Byrckman, Francis 360
Byttering 313, 327–8, 330–1, 333–4,
    343–4, 346, 349

Calais 318
Caletot 319
Cambrai 22, 167–9, 211, 276
Cambridge 212
Campbell, Niall, Earl of Dysart and Duke
    of Argyll 2
Cannicus (Kenneth), St 255–6
Canterbury 14, 209, 215, 260, 275, 291,
    318, 326, 352
    cathedral priory of Christ Church 153,
        169, 214, 351, 360
    monastery of St Augustine 153, 221,
        268–9
Canute, *see* Kanutus
Carcassonne 158, 160
Cardine, E. 2, 63
Carley, J. P. 214
Castor (Northants.) 267
Cedda, *see* Chad
Chad (Cedda), St 208, 221, 256, 282
Chadd, D. 324
Charles, Count of Anjou and King of
    Sicily 312
Chartier, M. 187
Chartres 58, 64, 104, 107, 118, 141, 154–5,
    167, 218
    Saint-Père-en-Vallée 111, 118
Chaufecire 319
Chelles 160, 163–5
Chertsey 237–8
Chester-le-Street 257
Chevalier, U. 167, 237
Chezal-Benoît 158–60
Chickweed, C. 241
Chirbury, R. 326
Christine, St 208
Christopher, St 227
Cirencester 216, 219
Cîteaux 194
Cividale 335
Claire, J. 39, 187
Claudius, St, Bishop of Bescançon 262
Clement, St 106
Clement, Simon 322
Clerval, Abbé 218
Climent 319, 322
Clonard (Meath) 264
Cluni, B. de 309, 315, 349
Cluny 5, 52, 112, 151, 167–9, 175–204
    passim, 213, 215
Coldingham 209, 254, 260

Colgrave, B. L. 214, 222
Colhoun, C. K. 3
Colles, H. C. 1
Collins, H. B. 303
Cologne 268
Columba (Colum Cille), St 255–6, 273, 282
Compiègne, abbey of Saint-Corneille 151
Conant, K. 200
Constantine, Emperor 265
Constantine, C. 5, 177
Cook 345–6, 349–50
Corbie 49–50, 52–3, 57–8, 151–3, 159–60, 169, 189, 192, 194–5, 198
Cornelius, St 228
Cornysh, William 358–9
Cotton, Robert 12
Coussemaker, C.-E.-H. de 312
Cranmer, Thomas 292
Crocker, R. L. 179, 193
Cross, Holy 149, 265
  Invention (Finding) 24–8, 41–4, 227
  Exaltation (Raising) 228
Cuthbert, St 79, 210–11, 214, 221, 226, 248, 252, 257, 282
Cyprian 20

Dalton, J. N. 327
Damett 345–7, 349–50, 352
Damian, Peter 175
David, King of Israel and psalmist 14
David of Wales, St 258–60, 275–6, 278, 282–3
Davril, A. 52, 79, 165, 186, 209
Davy, Richard 358–9
De Geer, I. 268
Deerhurst 58
Delaporte, Y. 102
Delisle, L. 177
Denisot 319
Denys de Callors 318–19
Deshusses, J. 212
Dickens, C. 241
Dickinson, F. H. 378
Dijk, S. van 207
Dijon, monastery of Saint-Bénigne 150–1, 154, 159–60, 200–1
Dobson, E. J. 350
Doe, P. 6
Dominic, St 253–4
Dominican Use 161, 164–5

Dömling, W. 108
Dorchester 254–5
Douteuil, H. 53
Dover Priory 360
Downpatrick 160, 162, 164–6
Dreves, G. M. 15, 62, 105, 209, 240
Dronke, P. 310
Droste, D. 284
Duchat (Duthac) 281
Dufay, Guillaume 348
Dunkeld 212
Dunstable, John 253, 349, 352, 359, 365–6
Dunstan, St 98, 169, 221, 223–4, 227, 281
Dunster 223
Durandus of Liège 55
Durham 153, 209, 216, 257, 311, 323
Duthac (Duchat) 281

Easton, Adam 250
Ebba, Abbess of Coldingham 260, 282
Echternach 47
Edington 349
Edmund, St, King of East Anglia and martyr 221, 253, 260–1, 273, 281–2, 313
Edmund Rich, St, Archbishop of Canterbury 260, 262–3, 274, 276, 283
Edward, King and Confessor 14–15, 58, 281
Edward III, King of England 306, 316, 318, 348
Edward, O. T. 258
Egbert, D. D. 207
Eggebrecht, H. H. 61, 120
Egidius de Morino (Murino) 315
Ely 211–13, 217, 219, 237, 257, 277, 279, 284
Erkenwald, Bishop of London 281
Étaix, R. 186, 200
Ethelbert of East Anglia (Hereford), St 260, 263, 281
Ethelbert, King of Kent 263, 281
Etheldreda, St 211–12, 227, 281
Ethelwold *see* Æthelwold
Eufemia, St 223
Eugene, St 56
Eusebius, St 228
Eustace of Boulogne 315
Eve 25
Everist, M. 5
Evesham 205–6, 219, 221–2, 234

Evreux 153, 160–1, 163–5, 167, 170
Excetre, J. 326
Exeter 165, 327, 359

Fabian and Sebastian, SS 226
Fassler, M. E. 188
Fayrfax, Robert 253, 358–9, 366
Fécamp 145, 150, 201, 217
Felix, St 226
Felix and Adauctus, SS 228
Felix and Simplicius, etc., SS 227
Felix, author of *vita* of St Guthlac 222
Felix of Dunwich, St 221
Fernández de la Cuesta, I. 53, 189
Finian, St 264, 283
Fischer, P. 104
Fitzjoscelin, Reginald, Bishop of Bath 223
Flahiff, G. B. 250
Fleury, monastery of
     Saint-Benoît-sur-Loire 52, 58, 64, 79,
     104, 105–6, 154, 160–1, 164–5, 209
Folcwin 224
Fontevrault 151
Fonteyns 327
Forest, John 352, 366
Francis, St 250, 278, 280
Franco of Cologne 316
Freising 209
Frere, Walter Howard, Bishop of Truro v,
     2–5, 11, 13–14, 18, 48, 62–4, 66, 80,
     145, 183, 192–3, 206, 209, 218, 288
Froger, J. 170
Fugler, P. 375
Fulbert, Bishop of Chartres 200
Fuller, S. 60, 102, 107, 120, 128, 141
Fuller-Maitland, J. A. 3

Gabriel, archangel 29
Gace de la Buigne 319, 321
Gaillac 155
Galilee 34, 36
Gallo, F. A. 61
Ganz, P. 58
Gaston Fébus, Count of Foix and Béarn
     314
Gautier, L. 62
Gauzelin, Abbot of Fleury 104
Geoffrey of Monmouth 265, 351
George, St 227, 318, 322, 348
Georgiades, T. 328
Gerald of Wales (Giraldus Cambrensis)
     259–60, 282

Gerard of Brogne 224
Gervasius, St 227
Ghent, monastery of St Peter 224
Gilbert of Sempryngham, St 264, 282
Giles, St 218, 228
Giraldus Cambrensis, *see* Gerald of Wales
Gjerløw, L. 209–11, 216
Glasgow 266
Glastonbury 148, 214, 215, 222
Gloucester 250
     St Peter's 216–17
Gneuss, H. 11
Godfrey of Bouillon, King of Jerusalem
     315
Göllner, T. 108
Gopillet 319
Gordianus, St 227
Gordon, C. A. 146
Gorgonius, St 228
Goscelin 269
Grandisson, John, Bishop of Exeter 327
Gransden, A. 58
Grasse 158, 160
Greene, R. L. 287, 291
Gregory, St 55, 79, 226, 264–5, 316
Grierson, P. 222
Guido of Arezzo 60–1, 64, 70–8, 83, 95–7,
     316
Guillemin Dorge 319
Guisborough Priory 160, 162, 166–7, 216,
     219
Gundreda, wife of William de Varenne,
     Count of Surrey 175
Gushee, M. 102–4, 105–7, 133, 136–7
Guthlac, St 214, 221–3, 226
Gy, P.-M. 16

Haas, M. 61, 141
Hadcock, R. N. 360
Hadrian, St 228
Hallinger, K. 180
Handschin, J. 63, 99, 102, 104, 111, 131
Hanley Castle 165
Hansen, F. 201
Harbor, C. M. 3
Harrison, F. L. v, 3, 287, 303, 308–9, 323,
     330, 350–1, 366, 374
Hartker of St Gall 55, 96
Hartzell, K. D. 169, 252–5, 269, 282
Harvey, J. 6, 348–9
Haughmond 161, 163–5

Hawte, Sir William, *miles* 291
Helen, Empress 265
Helene, Henricus 315
Henderson, W. 161, 165, 285
Henry of Lancaster 318
Henry II, Emperor 199
Henry II, King of England 260
Henry IV, King of England 349–52
Henry V, King of England 350–2
Henry VII, King of England 356
Henry VIII, King of England 275, 356
Heorstan 223
Hereford 159–62, 164–5, 208, 216, 219,
    284
Hermes, St 228
Herrgott, M. 188
Hertford 318–22
Hesbert, R.-J. 34, 53, 66, 112, 146–7, 149,
    170, 176, 179–80, 183, 189, 210, 218,
    232, 240, 289
Heslop, T. A. 215
Hiley, D. 3, 101, 111, 148, 150, 153, 262
Hippolytus, St 228
Hofmann, J. B. 41
Hofmann-Brandt, H. 219
Hohler, C. 79, 205, 211, 214, 217, 248,
    257, 263
Holder, S. 175–6, 202
Holder-Egger, O. 224
Holschneider, A. 52, 54, 64, 71, 85, 94,
    98, 101–2, 104, 106–9, 116, 128, 137,
    139
Horneby, John 250, 280
Hosken, K. P. 3, 6
Hoskins, W. G. 360, 367
Hourlier, J. 57, 177
Howells, H. 2
Hugh, Abbot of Cluny 175–6
Hugh, St, Bishop of Lincoln 281
Hughes, Andrew 211, 239, 242, 251,
    275–6, 286, 303, 335, 353
Hughes, Anselm 2–7, 63, 148, 303
Hughes, D. G. 136
Hughes-Hughes, A. 356, 361, 366
Huglo, M. 47–9, 53, 55–8, 105–6, 111,
    134, 136, 145, 148, 151, 180, 186,
    219, 330
Hugo 321
Hugutio 311
Hunt, J. E. 292
Hunt, R. 275

Hunt, W. 223
Huntingdon 212
Husmann, H. 11, 145–7, 275
Hyllary, Thomas 358

Ida of Lorraine, St 316
Innocents, Holy 20, 22, 41–3
Iona 256
Isidore 311
Israel 37
Iversen, G. 15–16, 26, 34
Ivrea 56

Jacobsson, R. (= Jonsson, R.) 47
James, St 227, 249
James, M. R. 356, 375
James, R. 6
Jammers, E. 64
Januarius, St 227
Jehan de Danville 318
Jehan Roussel 319
Jenkins, C. 375
Jerome 105
Jerusalem 25, 165, 315
Joachim 32
Johannes (choirman) 321
Johannes de Muris 315
Johansson, A.-K. 32
John II, King of France 316–23
John XXII, Pope 312
John ('Johannes Afflighemensis') 96, 193
John and Paul, SS 227
John de Beverlaco 311
John of Beverley, St, Archbishop of York
    221, 281
John of Bridlington, St 266, 283
John of Reading 318
John of Tewkesbury 311–12
John the Baptist, St 18, 28–30, 41, 43, 56,
    227–8, 335
John the Evangelist, St 14, 17–20, 34,
    41–3, 146, 227, 249, 322, 334
Jones, H. L. 3
Jonsson, R. (*see also* Jacobsson) 15–16, 47,
    55, 96
Jumièges 145, 150, 217–18
Just, St 17

Kanutus Lavard (Knut, Canute), St 252
Katherine of Alexandria, St 309–10, 343–4
Kenilworth 208, 350–1

Kenneth, *see* Cannicus
Kentigern, St 266–7
Ker, N. R. 12, 165, 223, 312
Kershaw, E. 353
Kiddell, S. G. A. 3
Kildare 211, 255
Kilkenny 256
King, P. 212
Kingarth 255
Knowles, D. 360
Knut, *see* Kanutus
Knyght, Thomas 360
Kyneburga, St 267
Kyneswitha, St 267

La Couture 237
Labory, G. 105
Lambe, Walter 326, 366–7, 378
Lamothe, D. 5, 177
Lanfranc of Bec, Archbishop of
    Canterbury 153, 176
Lanzo, prior of Lewes 176
Lapidge, M. 11, 24, 98
Laurence, St 14, 28, 30–2, 41–3, 228
Lawley, S. 208, 237
Le Roux, R. 201, 206
Le Huray, P. 292
Leaver, R. A. 292
Leech-Wilkinson, D. 47
Lefferts, P. M. 274, 303, 313, 353
Legg, J. W. 145, 165, 222
Leo, St 227
Leofric, Abbot of St Albans 253
Leonardi, C. 26
Leonel, *see* Power
Leonin 107
Leroquais, V. 146, 169, 175, 177, 189,
    202, 210–11, 216
Lesnes 158, 160
Leufred, St 227
Lewes, Cluniac priory 175–6, 198, 202–4
Lichfield 221, 256
Liège 55, 183
Lille, Abbey of Saint-Pierre 160, 164–5
Limoges 153
    cathedral of St Stephen 151–2
    monastery of Saint-Martial 107, 151–2,
        155, 169, 285
Lincoln 212, 250, 284
Lisieux 166–7
Lockwood, L. 335

London 318–19, 322, 326
    St Paul's Cathedral 349
    Tower of London 349
Louis, St, Bishop of Toulouse 312, 335
Louis, R. 52
Louis IX, St, King of France 312
Lucy, St 218, 226
Ludford 358–9, 361, 376–7
Lund 212
Lütolf, M. 240
Lyon, M. 366

Maas, C. 104
Machabey, A. 48
Macharius, St 268
Machaut, Guillaume de 315, 324
McLachlan, Dame Laurentia (= Abbess
    of Stanbrook) 165
McPeek, G. S. 286
Magnus, St, Count of Orkney 268, 282
Maguelone 158, 160
Mainz 16
Marcellus, St 226
Marchiennes 169
Margaret, St 223, 227
Marguerite, 'la custuriere' 319
Maribo 212
Marix, J. 322
Mark, St 227
Marmoutier 182, 194, 198–9
Martin, St 12, 28, 56, 227
Mary, Blessed Virgin 14, 19, 23, 32–3, 41,
    175–204 *passim*, 226, 228, 249, 251,
    280, 282–3, 334
Mary Magdalene, St 215–18, 221, 224,
    227, 236
Mas, J. 158
Mason, John 378
Mateer, D. 357
Mathelin 319, 321
Matthew, St 228
Matthias, St 226
Maur, St 199, 226
Maurice, St 207, 228
Meaux Abbey 287
Menesto, E. 26
Merbecke, John 360
Merlet, R. 218
Metz 48
Michael, St 14, 28, 149
Michel Girart 319

Migne, J.-P. 188
Mildred (Mildretha), St, Abbess of
    Minster-in-Thanet 12, 268–70, 281
Millar, E. G. 11
Misset, E. 62
Mocquereau, A. 63
Mohlberg, L. C. 21
Molesme 194
Mont-Saint-Michel 145, 150
Montecassino 155
Montier-la-Celle 194–5, 197–9
Montolieu 158, 160
Moses 29–30
Muchelney 209, 218

Nantes 276
Narbonne 158
Nereus, St 227
Nevers 151–3
Nichasius 321
Nicholas, St 226
Nicholson, E. W. B. 57
Nidaros 209, 216
Niger, Radulfus 250
Ninian, St 270
Nivelles 149
Noble, Jeremy 4, 6, 146, 158, 167, 169
Nonantola 179, 198
Norberg, D. 41, 240
Norman, Normans, Normandy 148,
    150–1, 153–4, 160, 167, 201, 257, 281
Norwich 216, 284
Notre-Dame, *see* Paris

Odense 211–12
Odo de Lagery, prior of Cluny 175
Oesch, H. 60
Olmütz 217
Olyver 329–30
Orléans, H. D' (Duc d'Aumale) 318, 320
Osbert de Clare 281
Osith, St 281
Osmund, St 242, 245, 249–50, 270, 283
Oswald, Bishop of Worcester 98
Oswald, St, King of Northumbria 56,
    78–9, 208, 221, 271
Oswin, St, King of Northumbria 260,
    271–3, 282
Ormar, St 96
Ouen, St 221, 228
Oxford 311

Magdalen College 359
Oxford Movement 3

Packe, Thomas 291
Page, C. 287
Palermo, Cathedral 155–6
Palisca, C. 60, 193
Pallart, J. 321
Pantin, W. A. 323
Paris 53, 55, 58, 167–8
    Notre-Dame 107, 285, 304, 308
Parker, Archbishop 62
Parkes, M. B. 12
Pashe, William 361–2, 376
Passau 209
Patay, A. 187
Patrick, St 255–6, 273, 282, 289
Paul, St 14, 26, 149, 175, 219, 226–7
Peacock, P. 6
Peckham, John, Archbishop of Canterbury
    278
Pellegrin, E. 106
Pennard 336–8, 349
Perotinus 304–5
Peter, St 5, 28, 30, 36, 41–3, 105–6, 149,
    175, 219, 224, 226–7
Peterborough 205–6, 209, 216, 264, 267,
    271, 275, 284
Philip VI, King of France 316, 319
Philip and James, SS 227
Phillips, C. S. 62
Phillips, N. C. 52
Piper, A. 311
Planchart, A. E. 11–40 *passim*, 47, 55,
    57–8, 60, 98, 109
Plummer, John 366
Pontefract 215, 234, 249
Pontigny 262
Porta, J. de 349
Potenciana, St 227
Power, Leonel 326–30, 332, 335–9, 341–2,
    350–2, 365
Powers, H. 193
Prague 217
Praxedis, St 227
Prévost 360
Prisca, St 226
Priscus, St 228
Processus, St 227
Procter, F. 208, 338, 364, 368, 378
Protus, St 228

Prüm 47
Pycard 326, 334, 337, 343
Pygott 358–9
Pynson, Richard 361, 364
Pythagoras 316

Qweldryk 332–3

Ramsbotham, A. 303
Rankin, S. 53, 58, 98–9, 101, 109, 113, 257, 269
Ranton 165
Ranworth 284
Raphael, archangel 274, 283
Rastall, R. 352
Rathier, monk of Lobbes 55
Reading 249, 305
Reckow, F. 59–60, 85, 131, 141
Regensburg 44
Reginald of Durham 260
Reichenau 27
Reims 34, 151, 319
Renaudin, A. 167, 180–1, 197
Rennes 151
Rentius de Ponte Curvo 335
Richard of Chichester, St 262, 274, 281, 283
Richard of Hampole 274, 283
Robert, Abbot of Corbie 53, 189
Robert of Anjou, King of Naples and Sicily 312
Robert of Gloucester, canon of Hereford 278
Robertson, A. 2
Robertus de Hoyo 321
Robson, R. B. 311
Roesner, E. H. 310, 322
Rome 41, 175
Ronton 165
Rouen, Cathedral 153
Rouen, monastery of Saint-Ouen 153, 154
Rufinus, brother of St Chad 208
Rufus, St 228
Rule, M. 221
Runciman, S. 315
Ryman, J. 285

Sabine, St 228
Sachs, K.-J. 61
Sadie, S. 6
Sahlin, M. 287

St Albans 153, 253, 255, 272, 284
Saint-Amand 169
St Andrews 211–14, 256, 276
Saint-Bénigne, *see* Dijon
Saint-Benoît-sur-Loire, *see* Fleury
Saint-Bertin 216, 222, 224
Saint-Corneille, *see* Compiègne
St Davids 260
Saint-Denis 49–50, 52–3, 56–8, 112, 116, 151–3, 159–60, 193, 200, 217, 237, 265
Saint-Étienne (Loire) 218
Saint-Evroult 145, 147, 150
St Gall 44, 66, 95
Saint-Germain-des-Prés 47, 201, 217, 237
Saint-Laurent de Longré 158
Saint-Magloire 22, 34, 47
Saint-Martial, *see* Limoges
Saint-Maur-des-Fossés 49, 53, 56, 58, 64, 105–6, 134, 167–8, 180–2, 187–8, 197–8, 219
Saint-Omer 168–9
Saint-Pierre-des-Fossés, *see* Saint-Maur-des-Fossés
Saint-Quentin 166–7
Saint-Vaast, *see* Arras
Saint-Valéry 160–1, 163–6
Saint-Wandrille 153, 160, 163–7
Saint-Yrieix 112, 155, 159
Salisbury (*see also* Sarum) 192, 249, 270
Salzburg 209
Samson, St 208
Sanders, E. 287, 291, 303–5
Sandler, L. F. 207
Sandon, N. 306–7, 311, 355, 357, 361–2, 376
Sandwich 318
Sankey, P. E. 3
Sarum Use (= Use of Salisbury; *see also* Salisbury) 161, 163–5, 170, 206, 208, 210, 219, 249–50, 253, 256, 258, 264–5, 283, 292, 306, 324, 334, 377
Saxer, V. 215–17, 236–8
Schlager, K. 111, 118, 146, 209, 280
Schmid, H. 52
Scholastica, St 5
Schrade, L. 311–12, 320
Scott, C. K. 288
Séez 166–7
Seiwold, Abbot of Bath 222
Sens 151–3, 315

Seven Sleepers, SS 227
Sharpe, R. 269
Sheppard, John 324
Sherborne 164–5, 214
Sherr, R. 63
Sicily 148, 151, 153–5, 161, 163–5, 167
Silos, Santo Domingo de 53, 56, 189, 218–19
Simon and Jude, SS 34
Simon de Montfort 274, 283
Sixtus, St 227
Smits van Waesberghe, J. 60, 73, 75, 104
Smoldon, W. L. 5
Solesmes 3, 62, 63, 169
Sparks, E. H. 327
Spoonlee, John 349
Stäblein, B. 111
Stäblein-Harder, H. 335
Stainer, Sir J. 2
Stanbrook, Abbess of, *see* Dame Laurentia McLachlan
Stauffacher, M. 108
Stavelot, St Remacle 275
Steiner, R. 197, 305, 330
Stephanus (choirman) 321
Stephen, St 15–17, 118, 140, 146, 227, 287
Stephen of Liège 55, 56
Stevens, D. 3, 275
Stevens, J. 285–7, 289, 291
Stirnemann, P. D. 211
Stone (Staffs.) 207–8, 225
Strecche, John 350–1
Stubbs, Thomas 253
Stubbs, W. 224
Sturgeon, Nicholas 345–6, 349–50, 352
Sturton 375
Swithun, St 53, 55, 66, 78–9, 96, 208, 227, 274, 282
Swynford 333
Symon, boucher de Londres 319
Szantyr, A. 41

Tait, J. 318
Tallis, Thomas 357–60
Taverner, John 358–60, 376
Taylor, F. 351
Temple, E. 11
Teviotdale, E. 14
Thierry of Amorbach 52
Thomas, St, Apostle 12, 226
Thomas, Duke of Clarence 351–2

Thomas of Canterbury (Thomas Becket), St 207, 211–12, 258–60, 262–3, 272, 275–8, 280, 282, 285, 334–5, 337, 365
Thomas Cantilupe, St, Bishop of Hereford 278, 283
Thomas of Lancaster 281
Thompson, P. 259
Thomson, R. M. 260–1, 263
Thurstan of Caen 148
Tiburtius, St 226
Timothy, St 228
Tite, G. C. 12
Toledo 276
Tolhurst, J. B. 165, 206, 216, 221, 234
Toulouse 155
Tours 57, 64, 106, 151, 268
Townsend, D. 214
Treitler, L. 96–7
Troarn 166–7
Trowell, B. 5–6, 278, 318, 322, 349–50
Tubal Cain 316
Tunstede, Simon 312
Turk, Thomas 350
Turner, B. 6
Turner, D. H. 3, 48, 148
Tybba, St 267
Tye, Christopher 360
Tyes, J. 326, 332, 334, 349
Tynemouth Priory 272
Typp, W. 324, 326–7, 334, 337, 343

Ulrich (Udalric) of Zell (Cluny) 188–9, 198
Urban, St 227
Urban II, pope 175
Uzès 158, 160

Vaast (Vedast), St 56
Valous, G. de 167
Vaudreuil, Normandy 319
Verdun 48
Vernon 165
Verona 55–6, 190
Vézelay 216
Vezin, J. 58
Villehardouin, Geoffroi, de 315
Vincent, St 221, 223, 226
Virgil 36
Vitalis, St 227
Vitry, Philippe de 309–10, 312–13, 315–16, 320, 322–3

Waddell, C. 182–3, 194, 200–1
Waeltner, E. L. 59–60, 71, 73–4, 95
Wagner, P. 4, 66, 68, 180, 278
Walker, J. H. 207
Walters [Robertson], A. E. 49, 200
Wandrille, St 217, 224
Warner, Abbot of Rebais 260, 273
Warner, G. F. 222
Warrell, E. H. 3
Warren, F. E. 222
Washington, H. 2, 6
Wast 315
Wathey, A. 278, 353, 365
Watson, A. G. 12
Weale, W. H. J. 62
Wer[e]burga, St 221, 279
Wessex 254
Wessington, John 311
Westacre 216, 219
Westminster Abbey 145, 150
Westminster Palace 349
Whitby Abbey 160, 162
Whytbroke, William 360, 376
Wilfred, St 221
William, St, Archbishop of York 248, 279, 282–3
William de Varenne, Count of Surrey 175–6
William of Dijon (= William of Volpiano) 150, 200–1, 206
William of Malmesbury 224, 269
William the Conqueror 175
Williams, R. V. 2
Wilmart, A. 177
Winchcombe 234
Winchester 11–45 *passim*, 47–58 *passim*, 59–99 *passim*, 101–2, 109–10, 113–14, 116–17, 127–9, 134, 141, 151, 169, 217, 219, 254, 264, 274, 284
New Minster 48–50, 148, 154
Old Minster (St Swithun's) 49–50, 237
Winchester College 350, 352
Windsor 318, 321, 349
St George's Chapel 306, 349
Winterbottom, M. 98
Withern 270
Woods, I. 256
Woolley, R. M. 264
Worcester 56, 153, 284, 304
Wordsworth, C. 208, 338, 364, 368, 378
Wordsworth, John, Bishop of Salisbury 2, 62
Wormald, F. 11, 223
Wulfhad, St 207–8
Wulfhere, father of St Chad 208
Wulfstan, cantor, Old Minster, Winchester 47, 98
Wulfwine of Bath 223
Wulmar, St 221, 223–4, 227
Wulstan, St, Bishop of Worcester 246–7, 279, 282
Wulstan, D. 5
Wycombe, W. de 304
Wynford, William 349

Yeveley, Henry 48
York 164–6, 208, 216–19, 250, 256, 264–5, 279, 284
Abbey of St Mary 161, 164–6

Zachariah 29
Zaminer, F. 120